Ethnic Diasporas and the Canada-United States Security Community

Ethnic Diasporas and the Canada-United States Security Community

From the Civil War to Today

David G. Haglund

ROWMAN & LITTLEFIELD
Lanham • Boulder • New York • London

Published by Rowman & Littlefield
A wholly owned subsidiary of The Rowman & Littlefield Publishing Group, Inc.
4501 Forbes Boulevard, Suite 200, Lanham, Maryland 20706
www.rowman.com

Unit A, Whitacre Mews, 26-34 Stannary Street, London SE11 4AB

British Library Cataloguing in Publication Information Available

Library of Congress Cataloging-in-Publication Data Available

ISBN 978-1-4422-4269-2 (cloth : alk. paper) -- ISBN 978-1-4422-4270-8 (electronic)

♾™ The paper used in this publication meets the minimum requirements of American National Standard for Information Sciences Permanence of Paper for Printed Library Materials, ANSI/NISO Z39.48-1992.

Printed in the United States of America

Contents

Preface

In March 2011, New York congressman Peter T. King, chairing the Homeland Security Committee of the House of Representatives, led a group of fellow Republicans in chastising a prominent Muslim organization in the United States, the Council on American-Islamic Relations (CAIR), on the grounds that the advocacy group was assisting the work of terrorist organizations bent on undermining American security, and had therefore, in King's words, "discredited" itself. Particular worry was being expressed regarding the organization's presumed role in radicalizing Muslim youth—a worry that the spirited rebuttal of CAIR's executive director, Nihad Awad, could hardly begin to chase from the minds of the majority Republican membership of the committee. Awad remonstrated with King about turning the hearing into a "political theater" and told committee members that "no one is more concerned about terrorism in the United States than we are."[1]

With recent well-publicized incidents fresh in mind of what was at the time just beginning to be called "homegrown terrorism," it was assuredly not unusual that the King committee would have launched hearings into the phenomenon of radicalization among elements of America's Muslim diaspora. Still, there was a certain irony in the committee's being chaired by the Irish American King, for it had not been all that long ago that similar suspicions were being aroused regarding the political reliability of his own "ethnic" community and its organizational representatives. Sometimes, the venue for airing these suspicions was the very same Congress in which King would later pursue his own investigation. During a heated Senate debate over the ratification of the Versailles treaty in 1919, one Democratic legislator, John S. Williams of Mississippi, smarting from sustained Irish American opposition to the treaty (on the basis that it would ensnare America in a morally dubious League of Nations perpetuating British rule over Ireland), expressed his exasperation over claims that had been getting made with regularity, both during the war and immediately after it, to the effect that English-descended Americans such as Williams were not "real" Americans at all, but rather sellouts to British imperialism and betrayers of the American Revolution. During the recent period of American wartime neutrality, from August 1914 to April 1917, such charges had been aired frequently by members of the country's two largest ethnic minorities, the Irish Americans and the German Americans, and Williams had had enough of them—thus his sardonic observation that "[w]e have reached the point where no man can be a real American unless he is an Irish-American or a German-American." The comment was intended to serve not only as a reminder about who *really* was entitled to speak for America (namely its Anglo majority), but also as a warning to ethnic minorities to watch their step. One of Williams's correspondents expressed this latter, minatory, aspect more dramatically, in a letter written at a time, in late October 1919, when America was already in the throes of the "red scare" of the early postwar period, by posing the question, "Are the Bolsheviks any worse than the Irish?"[2]

In Peter King's case, it was not just ethnic descent that underlay the irony; he himself had at one time been a very vocal enthusiast of the Irish Republican Army during the "troubles" in Northern Ireland in the 1980s, prior to becoming a supporter of the peace process in that violence-wracked British province a decade later and eventually denouncing the IRA, after 9/11, for what he took to be its anti-American response to the attacks by al Qaeda. As one British journalist noted at the time of King's committee hearings, Ireland had "made" King, in the sense of his being able to tap into the local Irish American electorate's nationalist sensibilities during the 1980s and 1990s, in a way that enabled him to vault from a lowly position as comptroller of New York's Nassau County to a seat in the House of Representatives in Washington, a leap greatly facilitated, according to this reporter, by King's public and strong support of the IRA. "The Congressman most closely associated with a terrorist organisation is now one of the most hawkish antiterrorist members of Congress. If there's an irony there it's one that Congressman King does not spend much time dwelling upon."[3] To America's important British ally, King looked, for years, every bit a security nuisance as he himself was arguing America's Muslims were—a nuisance whose origins could be, indeed *had* to be, traced back to "ethnic" identification.[4]

If one wanted a means of personalizing the broader questions with which this book on ethnicity and security in North America is concerned, it would be very difficult to improve on this example. What Voltaire wrote about God might be aptly paraphrased here: if Peter T. King did not exist, it would be necessary to invent him. For in a very real way, the story I tell in these pages, about the manner in which ethnic diasporas could be argued to have had an impact upon the quality of security relations between the United States and Canada, starts with King's fellow Irish and carries through to the recent objects of his concern, Muslims living in North America. In between these two cases, a third ethnic diaspora, the Germans whose presence in America dates from the late seventeenth century, will make an important appearance of their own. In all three instances, as I will show, there have been interesting and significant complications for North American regional security associated with diasporic activism.

The tale that unfolds in these pages concerns political phenomena that are hardly novel staples of inquiry. Terrorism, which forms part of my analysis but by no means the major part, is of course an age-old security challenge, even if, like so many other political challenges, it did not acquire its label until fairly recently (at least as historical problems go), finding its first application in connection with the deliberate use of violence by a *state*, Jacobin France.[5] Mostly, though, it is construed as a violent vehicle for eliciting change desired by *non-state* actors, and it will be in this second sense that I use it in this book.[6] The same comment about novelty applies, mutatis mutandis, to diasporas, as well as to their efforts at attaining political influence through the kind of practices that in this book I construe, broadly, as "lobbying."[7] What *is* new in this book is my application of comparative historical analysis as a means of shining important empirical and theoretical light on the regional security arrangement known as the North American security community (sometimes, "zone of peace").

Even in respect of this fairly recent manifestation of bilateral security cooperation, there is a chronologically lengthy saga to unfold, since much of the narrative and analysis in this book precedes the creation of the security community, and indeed speaks to that which did so much, in the years between the Civil War and the First World War, to frustrate regional security cooperation in North America, namely the phenomenon of diasporic activism. The narrative has its origins a century and a half ago, in California, hence the punning allusion in my introductory chapter's title (perhaps only comprehensible to aging baby boomers like myself) to a once-popular song celebrating an event taking place during the "summer of love" of 1967. Nothing captured so well the spirit of that season's pilgrimage of thousands of young people to San Francisco's Haight-Ashbury district as Scott McKenzie's ballad "San Francisco," one stanza of which tunefully celebrated the significance of those "people in motion."[8] Those sojourners would come to be remembered in popular lore as "hippies," or "flower children," and though possessed of vastly different demographic profiles from those of the people in motion about whom I write in this book, there is one element the cohorts have in common: San Francisco.

It is to that city, during the first year of the American Civil War, that we can trace the origins of the phenomenon of ethnic-diasporic activism that I will argue was to prove so significant for the evolution of security arrangements on the North American continent over the course of ensuing decades. What Terence Bellew McManus, a veteran of a failed Irish rising against British rule in 1848, could not achieve in life nevertheless became an endeavor to which his body (though not his soul) was more successfully applied in death. For following McManus's untimely demise in San Francisco in mid-January 1861, his corpse was to become skillfully, if somewhat astonishingly, exploited by Irish republican members of a new group starting to become known generically as the "Fenians"—a group that creatively employed the deceased McManus, on both sides of the Atlantic, as a valuable symbol of the cause of Irish freedom.

Never having been a member of the recently formed Irish Republican Brotherhood while alive, McManus certainly became a potent token of Fenianism in the ten months following his death. His road to nationalist glory began in August 1861, when he was exhumed by local partisans from his initial burial place in San Francisco's Lone Mountain cemetery. Thence he commenced an extraordinary maritime journey, first to New York City, where on 16 September obsequies were performed for a second time, in St. Patrick's Cathedral no less, and with the blessing of the local Catholic hierarchy. After a month's interment in a vault at the city's Calvary cemetery, his corpse got underway once more on 18 October, when it was placed aboard the transatlantic steamer *City of Washington,* bound for Cork. From this southwestern Irish seaport, McManus made his final terrestrial journey, this time by train to Dublin, where on 10 November he was laid to rest in Glasnevin cemetery. It had been a most unusual trip, one that by the time it neared its end had snowballed into a major political happening, just as his exhumers had hoped. Indeed, to some observers of Irish political history, McManus's dead body served to breathe new life into a political movement, Fenianism, which until that point had been nearly as defunct as he was.[9]

As noted by one chronicler of this saga, the Dublin reburial served as the occasion for the city's (and the country's) first widespread expression of nationalist sentiment since the funeral, more than fourteen years earlier, of "the Emancipator," Daniel O'Connell. And it would take another thirty years after the "earth finally enclosed upon McManus's much be-speeched remains" for yet another funeral, this time of Charles Stewart Parnell, to eclipse McManus's own in political signification. Such had been the symbolism of his long voyage to the "Pantheon of Irish martyr-dom by virtue of the grandfather of Irish wakes."[10]

In the end, more than a half century would elapse before Fenianism, often referred to as "physical-force nationalism," managed, improbably, to forge the passage of Ireland from British rule into self-determination and, eventually, republican independence. But in North America, it would hardly require that many years for Fenianism, and more generally Irish American nationalism, to begin complicating regional security arrangements, in what has to be considered the fullest and, to date, most consequential, aspect of ethnic-diasporic "politicking" ever experienced in North America. However, if it was the most consequential case of diasporic activism with important implications for North American security, it was far from being the only one. Two other times, during the past century and a half, the quality of Canada-United States security relations found itself being affected by political activism associated with diasporas that had become established in North America. Those three cases (the Irish Americans, the German Americans, and the Muslim North Americans) constitute the substance of this monograph's Part Two.

In learning and writing about these cases, I have incurred many debts, which it is my pleasure to acknowledge here. Funding for this project was provided by a grant awarded me in 2008 by the Social Sciences and Humanities Research Council of Canada, to whom I express my deep gratitude. Support from this source was mainly used for hiring four Queen's students to serve as research assistants; three were graduate students at the time (Tudor Onea, Tyson McNeil-Hay, and Dru Lauzon), and the fourth an undergrad (Omer Aziz). Warmly I thank them all. Also at Queen's, I am deeply indebted to the Faculty of Arts and Science, for providing sabbatical funding in 2009–2010, and again in the first half of 2014, enabling me to conduct the research and complete the writing of this book.

I embarked on the research that resulted in this book during that first sabbatical, somewhat ironically perhaps, since I was spending the bulk of the 2009–2010 academic year in Paris, where I held the Chaire d'Études Canadiennes, which was housed in the Institut du Monde Anglophone, of the Sorbonne Nouvelle. It was in Paris that I began systematically to develop the ideas and themes that emerge in these pages. I am inordinately grateful to the director of the Institut, Professor Jean-Michel Lacroix, for his constant support and friendship during that sabbatical. Also in Paris I discovered a remarkable and invaluable source of materials on Ireland, in the library of the Irish Cultural Center, around the corner from the Pantheon. The tail end of the sabbatical had me deepening my study of things Irish, thanks to the kindness of Professor Liam Kennedy, director of University College Dublin's Clinton Institute for American Studies, who provided me with an office and library access for two months in the spring of 2010.

I continued the research over subsequent years, and when time and teaching duties permitted, I availed myself of visits to the New York City Public Library, a repository for materials on that city's large Irish and German communities. Also in New York I benefitted from access to materials in the collection of the American Irish Historical Society. Most of all, I am indebted to the librarians of my own university, Queen's, who made sure that if something I needed was not available locally, it would speedily get headed my way via interlibrary loan. By the time I commenced my recent (half) sabbatical, I was ready to start writing up my results, and found myself able to do this in the very pleasant surroundings of Hanover, New Hampshire, where I was fortunate enough to spend the winter quarter of 2014 as a Visiting Scholar attached to Dartmouth College's John Sloan Dickey Center for International Understanding. I warmly thank the Center's director, Daniel Benjamin, for the generous support and collegiality extended. Plans for my research stay in Hanover had been put in motion prior to Dan's arrival at Dartmouth, and it is to the Center's former associate director, Christianne Hardy Wohlforth, whom I am ultimately indebted for this wonderful opportunity. Enthusiastically I thank her, as well as the two anonymous reviewers of the manuscript for Rowman & Littlefield. I cannot say enough about the enthusiasm shown for this project by Marie-Claire Antoine, senior acquisitions editor at the press, without whose consistent support the project would have been a much more arduous undertaking to bring to fruition.

Finally, and most of all, my wife, best friend, and life's companion, Susan Murphy, is responsible for whatever might be good about this book, as well as for anything else of use that I have managed to accomplish over the past four-plus decades. All that is not so good, in these pages as elsewhere, remains, as usual, my own doing. To Susan, I dedicate this book, with much love.

NOTES

1. Quoted in Scott Shane, "Hearing Puts Muslim Group in Hot Seat," *New York Times*, 11 March 2011, online ed.

2. Quoted in Edward Cuddy, "'Are the Bolsheviks Any Worse than the Irish?' Ethno-Religious Conflict in America during the 1920s," *Éire-Ireland* 11 (Autumn 1976): 13–32, quotes at pp. 16 and 32.

3. Alex Massie, "Peter King: The Congressman behind the Radical Islam Public Inquiry," *Telegraph* (London), 9 March 2011, online ed.

4. As will be explained in greater detail in the following chapters, I am using "ethnicity" in a broad sense in this book, so as at times to stand as a near-surrogate for religion. For this reason, we can still speak properly of a Muslim diaspora, as for instance does Behrooz Ghamari-Tabrizi, "Loving America and Longing for Home: Isma'il al-Faruqi and the Emergence of the Muslim Diaspora in North America," *International Migration* 42 (June 2004): 61–86.

5. See Bruce Hoffman, *Inside Terrorism*, rev. and exp. ed. (New York: Columbia University Press, 2006), pp. 3–4.

6. See Alex P. Schmid, "Frameworks for Conceptualizing Terrorism," *Terrorism and Political Violence* 16 (Summer 2004): 197–221.

7. By "broadly," I group together two sorts of influence attempts frequently placed under the "lobbying" umbrella, the first being efforts to petition the U.S. government (almost always Congress) in order to affect the formulation of legislation and the second being attempts to sway the course of elections by appeals to "bloc voting."

8. McKenzie, whose birth name was Philip Wallach Blondheim, is best remembered for that one song. He died in late August 2012.

9. Leon Ó Broin, *Fenian Fever: An Anglo-American Dilemma* (New York: New York University Press, 1971), p. 3, writes that the "MacManus [sic] funeral was a turning point in Irish history; from it the Government recognised that the IRB was a formidable force." But Richard Vincent Comerford, *The Fenians in Context: Irish Politics and Society, 1848–82* (Dublin: Wolfhound Press, 1985), pp. 78–79, cautions "[i]t is wise not to overstate the *political* significance of the episode, . . . Almost the only incontrovertible interpretation that can be put on the affair is that large numbers of people were in a mood for a public spectacle in Dublin on 10 November 1861." Not only is the political meaning of McManus's protracted funeral ambiguous, so too is the spelling of his last name, with many writers adding an "a" to its prefix.

10. Louis R. Bisceglia, "The Fenian Funeral of Terence Bellew McManus," *Éire-Ireland* 14 (Fall 1979): 45–64, quotes at pp. 60–62. Glasnevin has also been likened to another, more famous, memorial to honored dead: London's Westminster Abbey; see Owen McGee, "'God Save Ireland': Manchester-Martyr Demonstrations in Dublin, 1867–1916," *Éire-Ireland* 36 (Fall/Winter 2001): 39–66, citing from p. 57.

Introduction

People in Motion:
Demography and Security in North America

For many years, scholarship in the area of international security relations has regularly included analysts who have riveted their attention upon "demography," a rubric taken to refer to the systematic analysis of populations—their size, their distinctive characteristics, and their propensity to move around, both within the boundaries of territorial units and, importantly, beyond those boundaries.[1] So it is more than a bit unusual to find it announced, as we periodically do, that "demography is back"[2]—for the good and obvious reason that it never really went anywhere. Nevertheless, it cannot be denied that, of late, there has been a renewal of emphasis upon the relationship between certain demographic variables and international security. This book is consistent with that trend, focusing as it does upon one particular demographic category and its implications for regional security in one particular part of the world. The category bears the name *diasporas*, or to be more precise, "ethnic" diasporas. The region is North America, by which I really mean the northern portion of the continent, comprising both the United States and Canada, upon which this study concentrates.[3]

Much of the work done on demography over the years has betrayed a clear *quantitative* orientation, in the sense that population size, and the implications associated therewith, have constituted the primary concern of researchers. This has been so not only among demographers themselves, but also on the part of international relations (IR) specialists investigating the linkages between population size and security. Realist (and other) theoreticians have not been inattentive to the important contribution that population size can make to a state's relative capability, or its "power." One analyst, during the latter stages of the Cold War, even developed a (more or less) quantitative means of measuring this capability, in which the size of a country's population constituted a central aspect of its "critical mass," with this latter being symbolized by C in the following formula: $Pp = (C+E+M) \times (S+W)$.[4] Equations such as these might no longer be in fashion among specialists in international security, but the demographic variable (critical mass) so prominent in this formula of Ray S. Cline is very much on people's minds these days, especially

1

when thoughts turn to the implications for the international system of China's much-commented "rise." It takes nothing away from the impressive annual growth rates registered by that country's economy over the past 30 years to observe that few would be spending much time pondering the systemic portents of those growth rates if China did not also happen to be the world's most populous place, with some 1.25 billion inhabitants giving its power rankings an obvious boost.

Others who have plowed quantitative research furrows in their bid to understand demography's challenges have put their emphasis upon "carrying capacity," that of the planet, and their speculations incline them to wonder whether Mother Earth simply has too many children to support in a proper manner, either due to resource shortages or to environmental constraints, or to a combination of the two. For those inclined to dwell upon the shortages and the constraints, it is not too difficult to spin theoretical forecasts of impending resource conflict, even "resource war," between states, with China once more figuring centrally in the forecasts.[5] Again, the line of inquiry is not a novel one, and one thinks of the pessimistic projections made a generation or so ago by a school of "Malthusian" interpreters of demographic trends, all convinced that the world had far too many inhabitants to remain a sustainable habitat.[6]

Recently, however, some demographers and IR specialists have been shifting their focus more toward what we might deem *qualitative* aspects of demography, inquiring into the composition rather than the overall size of a population, with emphasis upon such phenomena as "age pyramids," fertility rates, and gender-distribution ratios.[7] It is with the *qualitative* demographic aspect that this book is concerned, although clearly there is a profound sense in which quantitative demography puts its impress upon North American security, given the distribution pattern of population north of the Rio Grande, with the United States boasting of a population nearly ten times that of Canada—a distribution pattern that, for some analysts of a "structural realist" bent, virtually decrees certain security policy orientations on the part of the lesser and the dominant members of this dyad.[8] However, rather than upon population *size* in North America, my attention is going to be concentrated upon population *flows*—that is, upon the sort of population flows that are subsumed under the label of diasporas, referring to groups whose membership demonstrates particular ethnic provenance and characteristics.

Diasporas have lately, and not for the first time, been attracting scholarly and media attention. Debates about them have been known to touch off heated disputes, certainly in discussions of American foreign policy, where diasporas are fairly regularly linked to the phenomenon of "ethnic lobbying." One thinks, in this regard, of the controversy sparked more than half a dozen years ago by John Mearsheimer and Stephen Walt over whether an Israel "lobby" in the United States was distorting the country's foreign policy in the Middle East and frustrating its pursuit of the "national interest."[9] The often polemical tone of that debate over an Israel lobby has been reprised more recently, with the publication in early 2014 of a book on U.S. policy toward the creation of Israel, written by John B. Judis, whose thesis is that although President Harry S Truman had misgivings about recognizing the new Jewish state in the spring of 1948, his ultimate decision to do so was driven partly by pressure from pro-Israeli lobbyists in the United States, and partly out of fear of losing support from America's Jewish voters in the upcoming presidential election.[10]

The melodramatic tone of these recent debates aside, the reality is that ethnic diasporas have been associated with discussions of American foreign policy for at least a century and a half, and it is far from obvious that the controversies surrounding not just the so-called Israel lobby but also organizations and initiatives championed by numerous other ethnic groups in the United States could ever approximate the level of intensity generated by earlier polemics about "ethnic politicking."[11] At times, ethnic-diasporic involvement in foreign policy has spilled over into the broader North American context, with implications for security relations between the United States and its neighbor to the north, Canada. It is those implications that I seek to detail in this book.

Nor has it simply been in North America that attention has been directed at the real or apprehended security implications of diasporas. Western Europeans, even more than North Americans, have been immersed in their own profound, sometimes almost existential, discussions regarding the ultimate meaning of diasporas (in their case, usually Muslim ones) for their divers national and regional identities—discussions that were taking on an ever more alarmist tone until the European Union's ongoing sovereign debt crisis exploded in 2010, followed four years later by the turmoil in Ukraine, both of which displaced the diaspora issue from the Europeans' front burner, if only temporarily.[12]

When one contemplates North America's lengthy experience with population flows, it is easy to see why demographic change has played such an interesting part in the respective countries' histories, stretching from the seventeenth century to more recent times. After all, both the United States and Canada have widely been regarded as "immigrant societies," and more than that, they have each been said sometimes to have commenced on their respective paths to national development very much as "settler societies," with the onset of British and French colonization efforts in the New World. In short, both the United States and Canada have been nothing if not the product of demographic fluxes that started four centuries ago. Demography, however, is a vast and fertile concept, as is the subsidiary issue of ethnic diasporas. So in a bid to delimit my scope of inquiry, I select for detailed analysis one feature of the two North American countries' security relationship. That feature is the Canada-United States "security community." In the scholarly works on international relations, security communities are said to possess particular significance. They do so because they hold out the prospect that armed conflict between sovereign states can be effectively abolished, and this even though, as we shall see in chapter 2, specialists continue to disagree about what exactly has relegated such conflict to the outer margins of plausibility. As to the significance of security communities, by contrast, there is little disagreement. As commonly understood, these entities represent a pattern of relations between political units about which it can be said that force, or even the threat to use force, has simply been taken off the list of options available to policy makers when they are engaged in dispute-resolution processes with other members of the community.[13]

Thus my research puzzle concerns the impact that ethnic diasporas might be argued to have had upon the origins and evolution of the North American security community, with all that this would imply for a related security dispensation on the continent, the Canada-United States alliance. Canada-United States relations have often been held up as representing the world's first security community, as well as its most robust one; similarly, the Canadian-American collective defense arrangement (the alliance) has been said to constitute the most "special" of either country's particular set of "special relationships." Often, their bilateral security relations have been considered a beacon to the more benighted regions of the world—a beacon whose radiance has at times been captured in the invocation of a, or to be more accurate, *the* "North American Idea."[14] As we will see, there is some reason to doubt the former claim, about North America's constituting the world's oldest security community; but the latter claim, appertaining to the "specialness" of their security links, does possess more substance.

Indeed, as this is written the two North American countries, with differing degrees of emphasis and relish, are continuing to mark the bicentennial of the last armed conflict between them, the War of 1812.[15] Precisely because it has been such a long time since the two have been engaged in the unpleasant business of fighting against each other, there sometimes is a tendency to imagine that the years since 1814 have been characterized by relatively amicable, and sustained, bilateral security relations, so much so that some even believe the North American security community can be dated back two whole centuries. Such, of course, is far from the case; and to a nontrivial degree, the reason why the North American security community took so long to be born has had more than a little to do with the political activism of certain ethnic diasporas on the continent. This was definitely so over the six decades spanning the period between the American Civil War and the First World War, and some have argued that during the last two decades, diasporas have reemerged as a perturbing factor in North American security affairs, with a few scholars even hinting darkly at the potential of diaspora-related challenges to the security community itself.[16]

Over the past 150 years, three diasporas have garnered particular attention because of the suspicion that they could or did have a pernicious impact upon the quality of security relations between Canada and the United States. In the first two of these cases, the diasporas were mainly situated in the United States; in the most recent one, it has been a diaspora based in both North American countries that has served to stimulate security concerns on the part of policy makers. I refer to the Irish Americans, the German Americans, and, most recently, the Muslim North Americans. It is upon these three groups, respectively, that the case studies in this book will concentrate. These diasporas, or so it has been maintained, have made their mark upon North American security relations in two ways.

First, they (in widely varying degrees) have been implicated in "filibustering," in the oldest sense of that word, as connoting violence inflicted by irregular armed combatants based in one state upon targets in a nearby state,[17] the kind of decidedly unneighborly conduct that today might be subsumed under the broader, generic, label of "terrorism," as well as the more specific one of "jihadism"[18]—representing the sort of activity that if it were not kept in check could easily have dire implications for security cooperation. Less emotively, we might adopt a contemporary name for those engaging in this kind of cross-border violence, and call its practitioners either "non-state armed actors" (NSAAs) or "clandestine transnational actors" (CTAs).[19] However we choose to label them, the consequences of their activity can be problematical for security communities, as we are going to see in the case studies in this monograph's Part Two, especially the first and third of them.

Second, and in many ways much more important than the activities of the NSAAs/CTAs, have been the security implications that are said to attend the completely legal practice of "ethnic lobbying," whereby ethnic interest groups seek to exploit the "politics of pressure" in a bid to gain influence over foreign policy decisions; in this context, for reasons that will be explained in some detail in chapter three, it is the United States that serves as the primary locus of such interest-group politicking, rather than Canada. Thus much of the discussion in this chapter will focus upon the debate over the extent to which ethnic (and other) interest groups have been able to gain a role in shaping the American "national interest." My task in this book, then, is a complicated one, of exploring how diasporas, either through their filibustering or their lobbying, or both, have been argued to have sought and even exerted "influence" over the evolving pattern of security relations between the United States and Canada for a period of some 150 years.

In trying to come to grips with the task, I engage in two somewhat different sorts of scholarly analysis. First, and this is the purpose of the first three chapters, I need to contextualize (or "theorize") the question before us. There is little point in trying to elaborate so-called truth claims

regarding the impact of diasporas upon North American security cooperation, and especially the North American security community, without
delving into two areas. To this end, the subject matter I choose to cover in
chapters one and two is the evolution of North America from a "zone of
war" to a "zone of peace" (i.e., a security community), starting with a
discussion of the debate over the nature and meaning, symbolic or otherwise, of the Canada-United States border. In so many ways, the border
regime deserves to be comprehended metonymically, as representing
something much more significant than the mere management structure
for a line of territorial demarcation, with some arguing (as we shall see)
that it is so pregnant with import for the very future of the North
American security community as to make the prospects of the latter in-
separable from those of the former. Whether this is so or not, it still
remains that any discussion of the Canada-United States security community that fails to incorporate border realities, past and present, is a
woefully incomplete discussion, and much of chapter one is dedicated to
analyzing how the Canada-United States border has been variously conceived as somehow emblematic of the quality of the bilateral relationship
more generally.

Chapter two carries forward the analysis begun in the previous chapter, and completes the story of the passage of North America from the
"zone" (or "dominion") of war that it had for so long been[20] to something
altogether different, a security community (or "zone of peace"). Of particular note in this regard is chapter two's discussion of security relations
between the two large English-speaking lands, the United States and the
United Kingdom. In this latter respect, it is important to remember that
until the interwar decades, the quality of Canada-United States relations
would be determined in considerable measure by the quality of Anglo-
American relations, such that it became impossible to take the measure of
the former without invoking the record of the latter; as John Bartlet Brebner expressed it so pithily apropos Canada-United States bilateral ties,
"for satisfactory intelligibility the relationship must include Great Britain."[21]

The first two chapters, partly historical, partly theoretical, set the stage
for chapter three's assessment of the mooted role of ethnic diasporas in
North American security, with an emphasis upon how and why diasporas have been of such significance, periodically, in debates about
American foreign policy. Accordingly, the major focus of this chapter is
the recurring interrogation within the United States as to whether ethnic
interest groups have been gaining influence over the shaping of the country's foreign policy, and if so how they have achieved this, and with what
consequences for the national interest. There is, to be sure, an echo of this
debate that gets heard in Canada, too,[22] especially given the understandable practice of federal political parties, when trying either to gain or
cling to power, of catering to blocs of ethnic voters.[23] Sometimes analysts

are moved to pronounce that Canadian policy, for instance toward Israel, is largely if not entirely a function of this desire to reap an ethnic electoral harvest, such that in the judgment of two critics of the Harper government, "Canada now outrivals the United States in its total commitment to whatever Israel does."[24] However, because of the marked structural differences both in the two countries' domestic political systems and in their relative capability in the international system, the impact of the *lobbying* activities of Canada-based ethnic pressure groups has been mostly inconsequential for North American security relations, and thus for the continental security community. This has decidedly not been so for some of the *U.S.*-based ethnic lobbies.

The next three chapters consist in the three case studies that constitute its empirical core. The first two case studies are mainly historical; the third is very contemporary. Chapter four examines what is in many ways the most interesting diaspora ever to have become established in North America, or anywhere else, for that matter—interesting not least for its assumed impact upon the quality of security relations between the United States and the UK, and therefore between the former and Canada: the Irish Americans. Chapter five looks at an even larger diaspora, again one possessed of a fairly ambitious, if late-emerging, political agenda—an agenda that by the start of twentieth century would be directed largely at attempting to frustrate Anglo-American entente and eventual alliance, with related implications for Canada-United States security cooperation: the German Americans. The final case, explored in chapter six, concentrates on the debates and controversies that have swirled around the North American Muslim diaspora during the past two decades, a period of time when policy attention was increasingly being brought to bear upon a region, the "greater Middle East," that in many ways constituted the "kin community" of a politically active, North America-based, diaspora of Muslims.

In chapter seven I try to draw together the various theoretical, conceptual, and historical skeins into a synthesis that seeks, among other things, to provide insight into contemporary policy problems, and to do so by extrapolating from past events knowledge that may offer guidance for contemporary thinking about what is, after all, but the latest instance of a fairly old phenomenon in international relations: the impact of ethnic diasporas upon interstate security relations. Although the three cases are interesting in and of themselves, the political scientist in me wants me to do more than just tell a story about them. Accordingly, it is my hope that I might, by this "case study" approach to a contemporary policy conundrum in North American (and indeed, in international) security, make a contribution to what Alexander George once called "generic knowledge" of contemporary policy problems.[25]

It is sometimes remarked of those who specialize in international relations from the disciplinary standpoint of political science—the discipline that ever since the Second World War has held IR in a tight embrace—that they have used (or abused) history primarily out of a desire to "ransack" the past for useful data points, and little else.[26] It is probably, and regrettably, true that for an earlier generation of IR scholars steeped in a political science epistemology patterned too closely upon some "hard" sciences like physics and not enough upon other sciences like geology,[27] ransacking did figure as a principal modus operandi. But times have changed, and increasingly scholars of international security have been turning to history for different philosophical, epistemological, and methodological purposes.[28] This is especially true for security analysts whose focus is upon foreign policy and who are increasingly said to be working from a perspective dubbed "neoclassical realism."[29]

Whether or not this book warrants being placed under that currently voguish rubric I cannot say, and only partly because it is not exactly apparent to me what "neoclassical realism" is supposed to mean, or how it might differ from the "classical realism" that I confess to finding of some epistemological appeal.[30] But this assuredly is a book that takes history seriously. I share the view that the importance of history, and historical case studies, to political scientists inheres largely in its and their ability to help us "contextualize" current policy dilemmas, although I realize that in so saying I may well expose myself to the objection from some historians (and others) of being a devotee of "presentism" or, perhaps even worse, of "whiggishness."[31]

No one has framed the matter of contextualizing better than Paul Pierson, whose insistence upon the need for social scientists to "put politics in time" is well worth quoting here: "Placing social analysis in time implies recognizing that any particular moment is situated in some sort of temporal context—it is part of an unfolding social process. Now 'context' has become, for many in the social sciences, a bad word—a synonym for thick description, and an obstacle to social-scientific analysis." Pierson goes on to note that over the past few decades political science and other social sciences have succumbed to what he terms a "decontextual revolution" championed by enthusiasts of regression analysis and rational-choice theorizing. To these epistemological revolutionaries, "historically oriented analysis in the social sciences has often been criticized as a particularly egregious example of backward thinking." The revolutionaries may have a point if by context they simply mean clutter; but the more important sense of context, and the one missed by the revolutionaries, holds it to be essential for both explanation and understanding. Failure to take seriously this more profound sense of context translates, as far as Pierson is concerned, into nothing short of a "scientific disaster," because it strips researchers of what they are most in need of, namely the situational awareness that can only be acquired from their possession of "defining locational information."[32]

It is in this spirit of providing such locational information that I offer the case studies, which although mostly (but not totally) independent of each other empirically, contain enough conceptual and theoretical points of similarity to sustain the claim that together, the trio of cases does contribute to generic knowledge in scholarly, and perhaps even policy, domains. As we are to see in what follows, there really is not much that is completely new under the sun, particularly when that orb illuminates the relationship between demographic flows in North America and the origin and evolution of the Canada-United States security community.

NOTES

1. See Neil Howe and Richard Jackson, "Demography and Geopolitics: Understanding Today's Debate in Its Historical and Intellectual Context," in *Political Demography: How Population Changes Are Reshaping International Security and National Politics*, ed. Jack Goldstone, Eric Kaufmann, and Monica Duffy Toft (New York: Oxford University Press, 2012), pp. 31–48.

2. See, for example, "A New Science of Population," *Economist*, 19–25 May 2012, pp. 91–92.

3. Geographically, of course, North America extends from the Canadian Arctic archipelago to the Panama Canal.

4. The other expressions stood for "perceived power" (Pp), "economic capability" (E), "military capability" (M), "strategic vision" (S), and "will to implement the strategic vision" (W); see Ray S. Cline, *World Power Assessment 1977: A Calculus of Strategic Drift* (Boulder, Colo.: Westview Press, 1977).

5. See Michael Klare, *Resource Wars: The New Landscape of Global Conflict* (New York: Holt, 2002); Robert Kaplan, *The Revenge of Geography: What the Map Tells Us about Coming Conflicts and the Battle against Fate* (New York: Random House, 2012); Aaron Friedberg, *A Contest for Supremacy: China, America, and the Struggle for Mastery in Asia* (New York: W. W. Norton, 2011); Kent Calder, *The New Continentalism: Energy and Twenty-First-Century Eurasian Geopolitics* (New Haven, Conn.: Yale University Press, 2012); Dambisa Moyo, *Winner Take All: China's Race for Resources and What It Means for the World* (New York: Basic Books, 2012); and Stephen Burgess and Janet Beilstein, "This Means War? China's Scramble for Minerals and Resource Nationalism in Southern Africa," *Contemporary Security Policy* 34 (April 2013): 120–43.

6. See, inter alios, Paul R. Ehrlich, *The Population Bomb* (New York: Ballantine Books, 1968); Robert L. Heilbroner, *An Inquiry into the Human Prospect* (New York: W. W. Norton, 1975); Lincoln H. Day and Alice Taylor Day, *Too Many Americans* (New York: Dell, 1964); and above all, Donella H. Meadows et al., *The Limits to Growth* (New York: Universe Books, 1972). For critical assessments of that era's Malthusians, see David G. Haglund, "The New Geopolitics of Minerals: An Inquiry into the Changing International Significance of Strategic Minerals," *Political Geography Quarterly* 5 (July 1986): 221–40; and Jock A. Finlayson and Haglund, "Whatever Happened to the Resource War?" *Survival* 29 (September/October 1987): 403–15.

7. See John May, *World Population Policies: Their Origin, Evolution, and Impact* (New York: Springer, 2012); and Derek S. Hoff, "The False Alarm over U.S. Fertility," *New York Times*, 17 April 2013, p. A23.

8. For instance, Patrick Lennox, *At Home and Abroad: The Canada-US Relationship and Canada's Place in the World* (Vancouver: UBC Press, 2009).

9. John Mearsheimer and Stephen Walt, "The Israel Lobby," *London Review of Books* 28 (23 March 2006); and Mearsheimer and Walt, *The Israel Lobby and U.S. Foreign Policy* (New York: Penguin, 2007). For a particularly heated rebuttal, see Abraham H. Fox-

man, *The Deadliest Lies: The Israel Lobby and the Myth of Jewish Control* (New York: Palgrave Macmillan, 2007).

10. John B. Judis, *Genesis: Truman, American Jews, and the Origins of the Arab/Israeli Conflict* (New York: Farrar, Straus and Giroux, 2014).

11. For a good overview, see Tony Smith, *Foreign Attachments: The Power of Ethnic Groups in the Making of American Foreign Policy* (Cambridge: Harvard University Press, 2000). Also see David M. Paul and Rachel Anderson Paul, *Ethnic Lobbies and US Foreign Policy* (Boulder, Colo.: Lynne Rienner, 2009).

12. For examples of that alarmist mood, see Sylvain Besson, *La Conquête de l'occident: Le projet secret des islamistes* (Paris: Ed. du Seuil, 2005); Henryk M. Broder, *Hurra, wir kapitulieren!: Von der Lust am Einknicken* (Berlin: Wolf Jobst Sieder, 2006); Bruce Bawer, *While Europe Slept: How Radical Islam Is Destroying the West from Within* (New York: Doubleday, 2006); Lorenzo Vidino, "The Danger of Homegrown Terrorism to Scandinavia," *Terrorism Monitor* (October 2006); Walter Laqueur, *The Last Days of Europe* (New York: Thomas Dunne Books, 2007); Leslie S. Lebl, "Radical Islam in Europe," *Orbis* 54 (January 2010): 46–60; and Thilo Sarrazin, *Deutschland schafft sich ab: Wie Wir unser Land aufs Spiel setzen* (München: Deutsche Verlags Anstalt, 2010).

13. See Emanuel Adler and Michael Barnett, "Security Communities in Theoretical Perspective," in *Security Communities*, ed. Adler and Barnett (Cambridge: Cambridge University Press, 1998), pp. 3–28; and Vincent Pouliot, "The Logic of Practicality: A Theory of Practice of Security Communities," *International Organization* 62 (Spring 2008): 257–88.

14. James A. Macdonald, *The North American Idea* (Toronto: McClelland, Goodchild and Stewart, 1917). Also see Norman Hillmer, "O. D. Skelton and the North American Mind," *International Journal* 60 (Winter 2004–2005): 93–110.

15. For reasons having a lot to do with "identity," it has primarily been Canada that has been placing such emphasis upon this conflict, as is argued in Claire Turenne Sjolander, "Through the Looking Glass: Canadian Identity and the War of 1812," *International Journal* 69 (June 2014): 152–67.

16. See, for instance, Joel J. Sokolsky and Philippe Lagassé, "Suspenders and a Belt: Perimeter and Border Security in Canada-US Relations," *Canadian Foreign Policy Journal* 12 (January 2006): 15–29.

17. Although this kind of U.S.-based activity was commonly directed toward Central America and the Caribbean prior to the Civil War, there were also notable incursions of irregular forces into Canada during that period; see Robert E. May, *Manifest Destiny's Underworld: Filibustering in Antebellum America* (Chapel Hill: University of North Carolina Press, 2002).

18. One analyst, commenting on terminological sensitivities, has found it strange that America's 2010 *National Security Strategy*, in calling for the defeat of "violent extremists," including and especially adherents of al Qaeda, managed to avoid any reference to jihadism or radical Islamism. "The unwillingness to describe accurately the movement and ideology that poses a serious threat to the United States, its interests, and allies, as well as to Muslim communities in which radical Islamism contends for power, represented a striking omission." Robert J. Lieber, *Power and Willpower in the American Future: Why the United States Is Not Destined to Decline* (Cambridge: Cambridge University Press, 2012), p. 24.

19. See, respectively, Diane E. Davis, "Non-State Armed Actors, New Imagined Communities, and Shifting Patterns of Sovereignty and Insecurity in the Modern World," *Contemporary Security Policy* 30 (August 2009): 221–45; and Peter Andreas, "Redrawing the Line: Borders and Security in the Twenty-First Century," *International Security* 28 (Autumn 2003): 78–111.

20. See Fred Anderson and Andrew Cayton, *The Dominion of War: Empire and Liberty in North America, 1500–2000* (New York: Viking, 2005).

21. John Bartlet Brebner, "Canada in North American History," *Mississippi Valley Historical Review* 34 (March 1948): 653–59, quote at p. 656.

22. In particular, see *The World in Canada: Diaspora, Demography, and Domestic Politics*, ed. David Carment and David Bercuson (Montreal and Kingston: McGill-Queen's University Press, 2008).

23. Although the federal Liberals were quite accomplished at wooing the ethnic vote when they were in power, this is sometimes forgotten by analysts who seem to think the Conservatives invented the practice. For an example of such amnesia, see Jeffrey Simpson, "For the Next Two Years, It's All about the 10 Percent," *Globe and Mail* (Toronto), 21 December 2013, p. F2. Also of relevance here is another analyst's comment about the Harper government's insistence on "scoring points with immigrant communities in Canada"; see Kim Richard Nossal, "Old Habits and New Directions Indeed," *International Journal* 69 (June 2014): 253–57, quote at p. 256. A useful corrective is the reminder, by one former diplomat, turned scholar, that "pandering on foreign policy for electoral gain to any segment of Canada's admirably diverse population is fair game for any party smart enough to figure out the winning angles. The Liberals used to excel at this. The Conservatives have captured the ball with great skill." See David M. Malone, "Top Dog at External," *Literary Review of Canada* 22 (June 2014): 26–27, quote at p. 27. For evidence that the Liberals are elbowing themselves back into this particular game, see Craig Offman, "Liberals Cultivate Growing Power of Mandarin Vote," *Globe and Mail*, 19 August 2014, pp. A1, A13.

24. Ian McKay and Jamie Swift, *Warrior Nation: Rebranding Canada in an Age of Anxiety* (Toronto: Between the Lines, 2012), p. 226.

25. See Alexander L. George, "Knowledge for Statecraft: The Challenge for Political Science and History." *International Security* 22 (Summer 1997): 44–52, quote at pp. 47–48.

26. See Paul Gordon Lauren, "Diplomacy, Theory, and Policy," in *Diplomacy: New Approaches in History, Theory, and Policy*, ed. Lauren (New York: Free Press, 1979), pp. 3–18, quote at p. 5.

27. For this criticism, see John Lewis Gaddis, "History, Theory, and Common Ground," *International Security* 22 (Summer 1997): 75–85, citing from pp. 78–79.

28. Relevant here is the special thematic section published in *International Security* in 1997, under the guest editorship of Colin Elman and Miriam Fendius Elman, from which two articles cited above (n. 25 and n. 27) have been drawn. See their "Diplomatic History and International Relations Theory: Respecting Difference and Crossing Boundaries," *International Security* 22 (Summer 1997): 5–21.

29. See Steven Lobell, Norrin Ripsman, and Jeffrey Taliaferro, eds., *Neoclassical Realism, the State, and Foreign Policy* (Cambridge: Cambridge University Press, 2009).

30. Some scholars regard the terms to be virtually synonymous, for instance Colin Elman and Miriam Fendius Elman, when they observe that there are two contemporary streams of IR theorizing that testify to a rapprochement between certain political scientists and diplomatic historians, with the IR pair consisting of "constructivism and classical or neoclassical realism." See their "Introduction: Negotiating International History and Politics," in *Bridges and Boundaries: Historians, Political Scientists, and the Study of International Relations*, ed. Elman and Elman (Cambridge, Mass.: MIT Press, 2001), pp. 1–36, citing at p. 33. Others, however, root neoclassical realism firmly in structural-realist soil. See, in particular, Fareed Zakaria, *From Wealth to Power: The Unusual Origins of America's World Role* (Princeton, N.J.: Princeton University Press, 1998); and Brian Rathbun, "A Rose by Any Other Name: Neoclassical Realism as the Logical and Necessary Extension of Structural Realism," *Security Studies* 17 (May 2008): 294–321. For an especially thoughtful analysis of the varieties of neoclassical realism, see Tudor Onea, "Putting the 'Classical' in Neoclassical Realism: Neoclassical Realist Theories and US Expansion in the Post-Cold War," *International Relations* 26 (June 2012): 139–64.

31. But for a vigorous defense of employing the present to better understand the past (and vice versa), see Ernst Mayr, "When Is Historiography Whiggish?" *Journal of the History of Ideas* 51 (April–June 1990): 301–9.

32. Paul Pierson, *Politics in Time: History, Institutions, and Social Analysis* (Princeton, N.J.: Princeton University Press, 2004), pp. 168–69.

ONE

"Geopolitical" Borders and North America's Hobbesian Past

Mythologizing the 49th Parallel

WHAT "VANISHING" BORDER?

Difficult as it may be to believe today, there was a time, fifteen or so years ago, when the publishers of the highly respected annual compendium on Canadian foreign relations, *Canada among Nations*, could in all earnestness bring out a volume focusing on Canada-United States relations bearing the title *Vanishing Borders*. In their introductory chapter to this addition to the series for the year 2000, coeditors Maureen Appel Molot and Fen Osler Hampson asked whether there remained any real significance to the Canadian-American border, in light of the galloping integration that had been characterizing North American economic affairs over the previous decade. Their choice of title, they explained, was intended to reflect "not only the growing depth of the relationship since implementation of [the] Canada-United States Free Trade Agreement (FTA) in 1989, but also the larger impact of globalization, which, in commercial and financial terms, has further reduced the significance of borders." Still, they did sound a cautionary note, observing that globalization was also bringing in its train some "more nefarious items" —namely, drugs, guns, and illegal migrants—with implications for cross-border transit. Thus emerged a paradox: "[b]orders may be vanishing in some respects, but in others they are being erected."[1]

Surprisingly, on their list of "nefarious" categories there was a very conspicuous omission, one whose absence would very shortly come to appear nothing other than shocking. That missing item was terrorism.

13

And it would be terrorism—specifically terrorism associated with radical Islamists, or "jihadism"[2]—that would for a time emerge as the single most problematical aspect, by many orders of magnitude, beclouding the future of what had widely, and not completely illogically, been regarded as that most exceptional of all international frontiers, the much bally-hooed "longest undefended border" on the planet: the storied, if misla-belled, "49th Parallel."[3] More than any other single aspect of contempo-rary international relations, the challenge of jihadism has been respon-sible for what has been termed the "rebordering" of North America,[4] with the United States growing so much more attentive to security impli-cations associated with its northern border with Canada that it became possible for some scholars to begin speaking of the "Mexicanization" of the Canada-United States border.[5]

In truth, it might make even more sense to reverse the imagery and advert to the "Canadianization" of the United States-Mexico border, for what has primarily whetted American interest (and continues so to do) in respect of the country's southern border is the prospect of large-scale immigration fuelled by the desire for economic opportunity and a better life, and this even though recent data reveal that over the past few years, just as many Americans have been migrating to Mexico as have Mexicans to the United States (legally that is, for when *illegal* migration gets added to the mix, statistics become less reliable, for good reason).[6] Whatever the real size of current demographic flows from Mexico to the United States turns out to be, those flows had been getting largely propelled by the same urge that once led huge numbers of Canadians southward into the United States, from the mid-nineteenth century until the first half of the twentieth century: the quest for economic improvement.[7] So massive had been that earlier movement of people that one student of Canada-United States relations could accurately report in 1907 that "of all the living persons of Canadian birth in 1900, more than one-fifth were settled in the United States," such that five of the top ten North American sub-federal (i.e., provincial or state) jurisdictions in which Canadians happened to be living at the dawn of the twentieth century were located in the United States.[8]

Today, we are far removed from that earlier era of Canadian-American demographic integration, not just temporally but also tempera-mentally. For what the rise of the jihadist specter did was trigger a de-cline in the degree of mutual trust evinced by political elites, though perhaps not publics, on either side of the Canada-United States border.[9] Emblematic of this mood shift is a book coauthored in 2007 by a former American diplomat and a former Canadian federal politician, which ap-peared at a particularly low point in the bilateral relationship—a low point that had to no small degree been a consequence of the jihadist challenge and the respective American and Canadian responses thereto, including and especially the Iraq war of 2003. Commenting on what had been practically a love-in between American and Canadian leaders during most of the 1980s, when Ronald Reagan and Brian Mulroney presided, respectively, over American and Canadian political fortunes, authors David Jones (the diplomat) and David Kilgour (the politician) lamented the recent depressing tone of bilateral relations, characterized by a "move from best friends to 'best friends like it or not' (with the 'not' portion of the cycle in ascendance). Each side is acting as an 'injustice collector' more interested in nurturing grievances and totting up 'points' than in devising creative solutions."[10]

From the Canadian perspective, anxiety focused largely on the impact border "hardening" could have on the country's economic prospects, given the sizeable (though of late, dwindling) share of the Canadian GDP dependent upon exports to the United States.[11] From the American perspective, the decline in trust related to a worry that Canadians were not living up to their side of a bargain that was struck in the late summer of 1938, a bargain elsewhere dubbed the "Kingston dispensation," in reference to a reciprocal security understanding reached by both countries' leaders, Franklin D. Roosevelt and William Lyon Mackenzie King, just prior to the outbreak of the Second World War. It was an understanding according to which each country would show itself to be almost as concerned for the legitimate physical security interests of the other as it was for its own. This "dispensation," or ordering principle, owes its name to the Ontario city where President Roosevelt, during the dramatic days in August 1938 when the fate of Europe's, and the world's, peace teetered in the balance, offered his assurances to Canadians that in the event worse came to worst and a war broke out pitting Britain, and therefore Canada, against Germany, the United States would "not stand idly by" should a foreign aggressor seek to bring the combat to Canadian territory. Roosevelt made this pledge at Queen's University, and while he did not mention Germany in particular, he hardly needed to: everyone knew the target of his words. Prime Minister King, for his part, committed Canada to do all in its power to assure that no action of its own would compromise American security interests, issuing this response a few days later, in a different Ontario setting, the town of Woodbridge. For more than three-quarters of a century, the Kingston dispensation has remained the normative core of the bilateral security relationship.[12]

THE *60 MINUTES* VERSION

Beginning in the second half of the 1990s, American security officials acquired the habit of casting nervous glances northward, suspecting that Canadian refugee and immigration policies and procedures were allowing the slipping into the country of individuals bent not so much on improving the quality of their own lives as on diminishing that of

Americans'.[13] Canada, they were starting to think, was, however unwittingly, rolling out a welcome mat for terrorists intent on using its territory as a "safe haven" from which to mount operations against the United States. And since by this time the contemporary manifestation of what really was an old and recurring phenomenon in international security, namely terrorism, was becoming increasingly associated with the Islamic world, it followed that American officials should become worried about the security implications possibly associated with Canada's expanding Muslim diaspora. As we will see in chapter six, the recent rise of "home-grown" terrorism has, ironically, somewhat deflected American security worries from Canada's to the United States' own Muslim diaspora, with one result being that over the past few years American officials have begun to revisit the logic of so-called border hardening in favor of a reconceptualization reliant upon a different metaphor, the security "perimeter."[14] This reconceptualization, ongoing as I write these words, is an enterprise in which American security planners have been joined by their Canadian counterparts, in a wide-ranging initiative bearing the omnibus title "Beyond the Border."[15]

However much the mood (and the metaphors) appertaining to the relationship between the border and homeland security may be changing of late, there can be no gainsaying that in the immediate aftermath of 9/11 and for the following several years, it did look to more than a few observers in the United States as if the border with Canada was turning into a security liability. Some even held it to be the weakest link in the country's chain of "homeland" defenses. There were indeed reasons for Americans to think this way, even if a great deal of alarmist fiction managed to work its way into discussions of the problems that Canada-based jihadists might be causing for the Canada-United States security relationship. To take one example among many fictive renditions, on Christmas Eve 2002, New York's junior senator, Hillary Clinton, sounded the tocsin that five (or more) jihadists were making their way southward from Canada—a scare that turned out, like so many similar ones, to be false, and led Canada's immigration minister, Denis Coderre, to ask her to apologize for fearmongering. This Clinton refused to do, responding that it was precisely because Americans had grown so anxious about border security that even false alarms were becoming "all too believable," and adding that "I take very seriously my responsibility to speak out about the U.S. government's responsibility to allocate increased resources to the protection of our northern border, and I will continue to do so."[16]

Nor was it only American observers who were thinking this way; some Canadians were themselves noticing a similar trend, one that had Canada developing an undesirable as well as *undesired* reputation during the closing decades of the twentieth century as being a territorial base from which terrorist groups, Sikh and Tamil extremists prominent among these, could mount operations against their distant foes. In the words of one analyst specializing in the study of North American borders, by the end of the twentieth century, "virtually every known terrorist organization in the world had some presence in Canada," just as they had, he added, in the neighboring United States itself.[17] Canada had even served as the staging area for what was, prior to 9/11, the "worst terrorist attack in modern history,"[18] the destruction in late June 1985 of an Air India flight from Montreal to London, blown out of the sky over the Irish coast by an onboard bomb planted by Canada-based Sikh extremists. All 329 people aboard the Boeing 747 perished. But because the target of the terrorists was India and not the United States, and possibly also because nearly all of the Canadian citizens among the dead had been relatively recent immigrants from India, the repercussions of this outrage for Canadian, and American, security were minimal, almost to the point of being undetectable. This relative insouciance in the face of terror vanished as a result of 9/11, to be replaced by a new and troubling perspective, one that would see the Canada-United States border becoming endowed with more "geopolitical" relevance than it had known for many decades.

Those Americans, and Canadians, who were convinced that Canada had allowed itself to become a safe haven for terrorism did not have their worries dispelled by a late April 2002 broadcast of the popular CBS documentary show *60 Minutes*, featuring interviews with two retired Canadian officials whose professional responsibilities had recently lain in the spheres of intelligence and immigration policy. As portrayed by the two, David Harris and James Bissett, Ottawa was running a refugee and immigration system that was, to put it mildly, so loosely supervised that even the dimmest terrorist would find it child's play to set up shop in the country, and by so doing establish a foothold on the continent.[19] Truth to relate, in Canada the perception for some time had been rather general that the country's refugee policy *could* stand reform, indicating a fair degree of dismay with a status quo that, in the words of one Canadian expert, had become "racked by dysfunction, waste, and corruption."[20]

Obviously, it did not take this television show alone to set American officials wondering about border security. Many in the United States seem to have believed, and some apparently still do believe, that at least a few of the 9/11 terrorists entered their country via Canada. In the immediate aftermath of the attacks, one former American intelligence analyst, Vince Cannistraro, made it known that as many as five of the terrorists might have slipped into the United States from Canada, some travelling by ferry from Nova Scotia to Maine before continuing on to Boston's Logan airport.[21] A member of Congress, James Traficant (D-Ohio), soon to become a disgraced *former* member because of chronic wrongdoing, asserted in front of his House colleagues two weeks after the September attacks that "the two planes that struck the World Trade Center, those individuals came through Canada."[22] In reality, not only did none of the hijackers enter the United States from Canada, but all nineteen of them had originally been issued valid U.S. visas by the State Department, eleven of them by the same consular officer stationed in Jeddah, Saudi Arabia.[23]

Try as they might to dispel the notion (and try they *did*), Canadian officials could not convince Americans that the border was secure in the weeks and months following the attacks. Although many in Canada chose to interpret the flurry of incorrect, often incoherent, statements emanating from American sources as a part of a "blame Canada narrative,"[24] the reality was otherwise, given that opinion surveys taken at the time revealed, just as subsequent ones would continue to reveal down to the present, that the overwhelming majority of Americans actually held and continue to hold extremely positive views of Canada, a country they almost always rank as their favorite foreign land.[25] So why would this country full of Canada fans at the same time be so eager to affix "blame" upon that over which they had grown so accustomed to fawning?

The problem lay elsewhere, and in large measure Americans' inability to take solace from Canadian assurances was owing to their realization of how incapable their *own* border authorities had been of preventing terrorists from entering the United States *directly from overseas*, with the logical inference being that if the sprawling U.S. Immigration and Naturalization Service (INS), coupled with the vaunted and well-funded American intelligence services, could not have prevented the establishment of al Qaeda sleeper cells in America, then it was at least as likely, and probably much more likely, that relatively "laid-back" Canada, with its propensity chronically to underspend on defense as well as to minimize the gravity of threats, would be a place terrorists would find to their liking—perhaps not as a target, but certainly as a staging area and support base for operations directed against American targets. Added to this assumption was an empirical reality discussed in chapter six: during the late 1990s there *had* been two well-publicized attempts by jihadists based in Canada to infiltrate the United States, with the intent of detonating explosives targeted at American transit facilities, respectively the New York subway system and the Los Angeles airport.

So, whatever else the border had become on and after 11 September 2001, it was symbolically and substantively a different kind of place, far from being the "permeable" membrane it was once widely regarded as having been.[26] Because the Canada-United States border had, for such a lengthy period, been held to be almost utterly bereft of "strategic" import, it was easy for post-9/11 observers to imagine that everything relating to it had now changed, and that henceforth the two countries would be entering uncharted terrain on matters involving their common frontier; such was the legacy of the "longest-undefended border" mythologizing. As Peter Andreas reminds us in respect not just of that Canada-United States line but of interstate boundaries generally, the international system seems to be heading, albeit with *one* major difference, "back to the future." It is a future in which security worries are once again becoming focused upon interstate borders, for reasons related in no small measure to demographic flux. The major difference is that while borders today may be locales where "[g]eopolitics is alive and well, [. . . it] is increasingly based on policing matters," instead of, as so often used to be the case, the passage of armies across those selfsame borders. "Consequently," Andreas continues, "geopolitics is transformed, not transcended. . . . Thus, far from being viewed as passé, borders should be brought back as a centerpiece in the analysis of world politics."[27]

GET REAL? THE "RETURN" OF GEOPOLITICS TO THE CANADA-UNITED STATES BORDER

The Canada-United States border was certainly becoming just such a centerpiece in the analysis of security relations in North America by the first decade of the twenty-first century.[28] Toward the end of that decade, Barack Obama's newly appointed secretary of the Department of Homeland Security, Janet Napolitano, surprised and upset many Canadians when, in a speech delivered at the Brookings Institution in Washington, DC, on 25 March 2009, she called for a "real" border to be constructed between the United States and its two continental neighbors, Canada and Mexico. She went on to urge her audience to "get used to" the idea that the Canada-United States border was going to have to become more like the United States-Mexico one, although it is not clear why she thought such a harmonization in what had been two very different border-management regimes was required. To be sure, like some others in official (and unofficial) American circles, Napolitano was also initially confused about whether the 9/11 terrorists had relied, in part, on a Canadian base of operations. But it almost appeared to this one-time governor of Arizona that political correctness rather than strategic necessity was primarily shaping the desire to endow America's two borders with a basic similitude. As she put it, "one of the things that we need to be sensitive to is the very real feelings among southern border states and in Mexico that if things are being done on the Mexican border, they should also be done on the Canadian border."[29]

What better evidence that geopolitics was indeed "alive and well" at a spot from which it had been believed absent for so long? For several decades, it had been easy to forget that there ever was a time when the Canada-United States border *had been* fairly "real," if by that adjective we mean to suggest that it was possessed of strategic (or geopolitical) significance not unlike that associated with international boundaries elsewhere. As we will see later in this chapter, the Canada-United States border was once a line of uncertain demarcation in what was a North America characterized more by war than by peace; and even after the establishment of the Canada-United States "security community," the border remained a place from which geopolitics had never *completely* been expunged—not during the last half of the twentieth century, and certainly not even during the heyday of Canada-United States border panegyrics, the interwar years, as well as the short interval between Canada's and America's respective entries into the Second World War, September 1939 to December 1941. Let us take a closer look at that halcyon era, which contains interesting implications for the current discussion of the security (or lack thereof) of the border.

In a relative sense, the Canada-United States border assuredly did look a lot different back in that earlier period. On a planet constantly menaced by the threat and reality of the violent breaching of frontiers, it never loomed more as an exception to a dismal rule than it did in those years bracketing the end of the First World War and America's entry into the Second. Following that latter contest, the Canada-United States border, while remaining a site of peaceful interchange, would lose some of its earlier distinctiveness, if only because interstate frontiers elsewhere, nowhere more so than in Western Europe, were themselves beginning to emerge as untroubled bits of real estate. But prior to that second global cataclysm, and in stark contrast with what was still very much a war-prone Western Europe between the two world wars, the vast reaches of North America occupied by Canada and the United States did give every evidence of constituting a gigantic, and blessed, oasis, a happy place from which the god Mars had been forever banished, and whose condition of innate peacefulness could find its most symbolic signification in the nature of their shared border. Far from being a barrier dividing Canadians and Americans, it was conceptualized as the place of their most fruitful interactions, serving, in the words of F. R. Scott, as the two peoples' "friendly meeting ground," a connecting tissue rather than a demarcation line. And, to the extent the border possessed *any* relevance whatsoever, it was commercial not geopolitical, which is what one would expect from its resembling nothing so much as a "mere tariff."[30]

Nor did the coming of war, even into the irenic fastness of northern North America, fundamentally alter the narrative. Quite to the contrary, Canada's entry into the Second World War in September 1939 only served further to differentiate North American boundaries from those blood-soaked frontiers in the Old World. When it came to bestowing praise upon this sociopolitical institution, absolutely nothing could top the tribute to the Canada-United States border's pacific qualities than the rhapsodizing it received in an Oscar-winning war film appearing in the summer of 1941, billed on Canadian and British marquees as *The 49th Parallel*, but more familiar to American audiences under the title *The Invaders*. Canadian diplomat Vincent Massey narrated the stirring prologue to the movie, which began with a panorama of long stretches of the border, filmed from a low-flying plane. It is worth quoting here, in its entirety.

I see a long, straight line athwart a continent.
No chain of forts, or deep flowing river, or mountain range,
but a line drawn by men upon a map, nearly a century ago,
accepted with a handshake, and kept ever since.
A boundary which divides two nations, yet marks their friendly meeting ground.
The 49th parallel: the only undefended frontier in the world.[31]

Certainly, there was much truth in the film's depiction of the exceptionalism of the Canada-United States border during such a troublous moment in global politics. But there was also a great deal of cant in it. It was not simply the clichéd latitudinal reference of the Canadian and British title: after all, as I noted above, most of Canada's population back then lived, just as it does today, *south* of the fabled 49th—to say nothing of those three-quarters of a million Americans who live north of it, in Alaska. Much more than this, though, was wrong with the picture being presented to theatergoers. The plotline of the film suggested that the hopes of survivors of a Nazi U-boat sunk in Hudson Bay by a Canadian warplane—to wit, that they might slip into the United States, which, being at the time still neutral in the global conflagration, would accord them an opportunity to get back to the Fatherland and back into the fray—were misplaced hopes. This was because, or so the film's conclusion leads the viewer to believe, there existed seamless security cooperation between officials on either side of the line (in this case the Niagara River separating Ontario and New York State, and not the storied parallel), such that the last member of the crew still at large could be cleverly, though not totally legally, turned back to Canada, where life in a prisoner-of-war (POW) camp awaited. On both sides of the line, according to this script, officials knew what the threat was, as well as how to cooperate in parrying it—and this, at a time when America was still neutral.

The reality was different, however. The point is that even back in its salad days as a "friendly meeting ground," the Canada-United States border, pace Frank Scott and Vincent Massey, did possess ongoing geopolitical relevance. This was so because both countries would come to adopt, during the interwar period, policies toward the European balance of power that were bound to have implications for the border. After a period of years during which the North American neighbors temporarily shared a mind-set that led each to regard itself as a "producer" of security for "consumption" by ingrates elsewhere (especially European ingrates)—a mind-set associated with a grand strategy of "isolationism" properly conceived, as connoting a refusal to become involved in the European balance of power[32]—there occurred, late in the 1930s, a parting of the ways between Canadian and American strategic preferences. By the time of the Sudetenland crisis in the late summer of 1938, which had served as the backdrop of Roosevelt's Kingston declaration, it was apparent that should Britain once more become involved in a war against Germany, so too would Canada be involved.

Thus was presented a potential dilemma to American security planners, who until the late summer of 1940 remained hopeful that the United States could stay out of the fighting in Europe. It was a dilemma that received some short-lived notoriety among specialists in Canada-United States relations in the wake of the Germans' stunning offensive against France in the spring of 1940. A couple of weeks before the French agreed to armistice terms with their conquerors, there appeared a book carrying the evocative (some held, provocative) title, *Canada: America's Problem*. It was written by the Canada correspondent of the *New York Times*, John MacCormac, and its thesis was a simple one: at the current, highly worrisome, juncture of world politics, no country anywhere on earth was as important as Canada had become for America's "homeland security" (not a term, obviously, MacCormac could use, as it was decades away from being coined).[33] MacCormac had begun researching his project well before the German lightning offensive in the west and had started drafting the chapters during the closing months of what was dubbed the "Phony War," that half-year stretch of virtual noncombat that came to characterize almost all of the European theater (the Winter War pitting Finland against the Soviet Union being a notable exception) between the invasion and subjugation of Poland in September 1939 and the Nazi conquest of Denmark and Norway the following April. He put the finishing touches on his proofs shortly before the Germans were putting their own finishing touches on the French army, that is, in the first half of May 1940, by which time the Nazi western offensive against France and the Low Countries was in full force. The book was published on 7 June, less than three weeks before France surrendered. In short, the global horizon had darkened menacingly between the project's beginning and its end, and the author's mood changed accordingly, growing ever more alarmist.

So, what *was* America's "Canada Problem," as glimpsed at such a parlous time in transatlantic security relations? For starters, the two North American countries happened to possess differing perspectives on the European balance of power, as well as the utility of employing military force as a means of securing political objectives. Canadians during the second half of the twentieth century and into our current one would become so used to believing that America really *was* from Mars, and Canada from Venus,[34] that they developed historical amnesia regarding the country's own martial past.[35] Lost to the collective consciousness of a "peaceable kingdom" is the recollection of occasions, specifically during the onset stages of the First and Second World Wars, when it was stay-at-home American presidents who sought to remain above the European fray, while Canadian prime ministers, with varying degrees of enthusiasm, marched their people off to war.

And therein lay the problem. Canada, or so MacCormac argued, compromised America's grand strategy, at a moment when that strategy was very much oriented toward keeping the United States out of the European war that had begun the previous September. With hindsight, it is easy for us to forget that this ever was or could have been a grand strategic aspiration of America's, so aware are we now of what did transpire, namely that the United States was soon going to enter the war, and in so doing would end up becoming a staunch ally of Canada's and Britain's. But things looked quite otherwise to observers in 1939 and into the first half of 1940; it would not be until the late summer of 1940 that President Roosevelt took the fateful decision that made American involvement in the war well-nigh inevitable. This he did when he breached international law, rather blatantly but to widespread applause in Canada and the UK nonetheless, and transferred a part of neutral America's forces-in-being—those fifty so-called over-aged destroyers—to the Royal Navy in exchange for long-term leases on British bases in the Western hemisphere (the famous "destroyers-for-bases" deal).[36] However, this historic decision was still a few months in the future when MacCormac was writing, and he himself was of the view that American abstention from the conflict was much more likely than American participation in it.

Nor was he alone in thinking America would remain aloof from the combat. As John Herd Thompson and Stephen J. Randall remind us, "[i]n historical retrospect, U.S. entry into World War II had taken on an air of the inevitable. . . . The difficulty . . . is that . . . Americans' distaste for Nazi Germany did not translate directly into support for Britain" at the time France was being knocked out of the war by the German juggernaut.[37] The previous autumn, shortly after Canada had declared war on Germany, the most important figure in the isolationist "America First" movement, Col. Charles A. Lindbergh, had aimed some menacing shafts at Canadians, telling them in effect that they had no right to drag America into a war merely because they preferred having a king to a president. The celebrity aviator's outburst may have been, as MacCormac wrote, "tactless," but it was not illogical, because as the *Times* correspondent saw things, Canadian belligerency "makes isolation impossible for the United States."[38] It presented America with a geopolitical Hobson's choice: either it would have to go to war to save Canada in the event things turned out poorly in Europe and Hitler sought his revenge against Canada in North America itself; or it would have to abandon the pretense that the Monroe Doctrine constituted a security guarantee for the entire Western Hemisphere, and leave Canada to its fate. Something had to give, and because of this strategic conundrum, "Canada, for the United States, has become the most important foreign country in the world."[39]

Was this really so? As one of only two land neighbors of America, Canada was always going to be fairly strategic terrain as far the United States was concerned. But propinquity alone could not and did not generate the kind of policy significance MacCormac claimed to detect. There was, additionally, a very significant criterion that had to be fulfilled in order for Washington to deem any particular country to be its fundamental problem, and that criterion was the perception of such country's being vulnerable to being either enticed or coerced into accommodating the preferences of America's likely adversaries, thereby jeopardizing American interests, including and especially physical security interests. Starting in the second half of the 1930s and continuing into 1940, the feeling was growing in Washington that should Germany succeed in winning to its side some or most of the Latin American republics, then it would be only a matter of time before it established military bases in the Western Hemisphere—rendering nugatory what is sometimes referred to, these days, as the "stopping power of water."[40] In the immediate aftermath of the French defeat, American strategists became convinced that within a year, a Germany victorious in Europe, abetted by its Axis partners, would commence a military penetration of the American hemisphere via the "soft underbelly" of Latin America, effectively depriving the United States of the oceanic barrier protecting the New World from the depredations of the Old. *This* really was the problem, as far as American strategic planners were concerned, during the late spring and summer of 1940.[41]

THE REAL BORDER AND THE "FRANZ VON WERRA PROBLEM"

MacCormac may have fundamentally misstated the gravity of America's "Canada problem," but his stress upon differing strategic preferences as between the two North American countries, prior to America's entry into the Second World War, was well-placed. It can even provide some guidance for how we might think about the nature of the contemporary Canada-United States border, and not just during that period discussed in the previous section of this chapter, when "undefended border" fetishism was at its peak. Let us get back to both that period and the film *The 49th Parallel*. What turned out to be so wrong with the story line of the movie was its implicit assumption that the border really *had* become totally devoid of geopolitical substance. It was one thing for moviemakers, diplomats, and sundry other panegyrists to eulogize the comparative placidity of the border, for as noted earlier, when contrasted with other international frontiers, it assuredly did bask in a positive glow. But it was quite another thing to pretend that the border had *no* strategic significance whatsoever. And that is why the happy ending of the movie, which sees justice being done and a Nazi submariner getting returned to Canada by cooperative American border authorities, did misrepresent matters.

Therein lies an important reminder regarding the contemporary security significance of the Canada-United States border. It is true that the twentieth century inaugurated a new and more optimism-inducing era in Canada-United States security relations, one that was bound to have an impact upon the meaning of their common border, stripping away much of its former lugubrious geopolitical significance, legacy of a time when the frontier had been a locus of actual or apprehended combat, a "killing ground" to be discussed in the next section of this chapter. But the border never did, even at the height of its eulogization, become a totally "geo-politics-free" region, nor could it have done so. To illustrate the point I have chosen an obscure figure from the Canada-United States historical record to stand, eponymously, for a "problem" of a different nature than that of MacCormac's imaginings, but one that, withal, has come back to complicate Canada-United States security relations in recent years. Ge-nerically, it is the problem adverted to in the introduction, of what Peter Andreas called CTAs (for clandestine transnational actors).[42] It is, in oth-er words, the problem associated with the "non-innocent" transit of indi-viduals from one country to the other, even and especially at a time when official relations between the two countries are so good that neither government would or should have any reason to wish such transit to take place. In part, the problem of such harmful transit is a question of inad-vertence; but at its roots are sometimes found policy differences some-how attributable to the realm of what is termed "high politics," usually taken to imply developments credibly linked with matters of war and peace. It is in the nature of things, and derivative of both countries' "sovereign" status, that neither the United States nor Canada can or will see global challenges in exactly the same manner. That they adopt some-what different policy responses to such challenges follows as a matter of logic. As a result, even the most placid international frontier will become capable of generating friction between neighbors, even though neither intends this to happen.

This is what makes the "Franz von Werra problem" so interesting for a study such as this, which explores demography's impact upon Canada-United States security relations. Although the German diaspora in the United States possessed, as we shall discover in chapter five, consider-able significance for the evolving nature of those security relations a cen-tury or so ago, I do not invoke von Werra here to make any claim about that particular diaspora. Indeed, to the extent his case reveals anything useful at all, it is rather more applicable to the contemporary dilemmas associated with the last of my three in-depth studies, the one probing the relevance of the North American Muslim diaspora. Somewhat improb-ably, perhaps, the tale of this long-forgotten German aviator speaks, in however sotto voce a fashion, to the same kind of problem that has more loudly troubled Canada-United States relations in recent years. It is a problem exemplified by the border-security alarmism addressed earlier in this chapter, one that initially found its roots in differentiated threat perceptions as between the North American countries, and the policy responses consequent thereupon.

Von Werra's case also exposes the Panglossian fallacy inherent in *The 49th Parallel*, and shows why geopolitics proved so difficult to extirpate even during the fabled golden age of the storied frontier.[43] This harmful-transit challenge is not a new complication in bilateral relations, but it did return with a vengeance after 9/11, leading many observers to imagine that it had never really existed previously. As such, they argued, it represented something both novel and highly disturbing to security relations within North America. Canada, many were now prepared to argue, had finally, if for radically different reasons, become the kind of "problem" John MacCormac had so long ago imagined it to be, the country of greatest importance to American security, which, they said, was being jeopardized by a stubborn and perplexing refusal to safeguard against jihadists crossing the border to attempt attacks on American lives and property. A few observers were even moved to claim that failure to address this "new" [sic] problem could have such serious implications for the Canada-United States "security community" as to put its very future into question.[44]

Specifically, the problem under examination in this section takes its name from the story of a real-world Luftwaffe pilot, Oberleutnant Franz von Werra, whose ME-109 fighter plane had been downed over Kent, England, during the late summer of 1940. He was originally interned in two British prisoner-of-war camps in England, escaping from the first and, after being apprehended, briefly fleeing the second as well, only to be recaptured yet again. Following several more months in captivity in England, he was placed on board a Halifax-bound ship with fellow POWs early in January 1941, the ultimate destination of the group being Camp W, an internment facility built by the Canadian government in Neys, Ontario, on the north shore of Lake Superior.

Von Werra would never reach Camp W. On 23 January, he jumped off his train as it slowed to traverse the eastern Ontario town of Smiths Falls. He was accompanied by a fellow POW, who was soon caught. Not so von Werra, who incredibly managed in the dead of winter to make his way southward by foot and thumb to the St. Lawrence River, which ice-clogged body he even more incredibly succeeded in crossing, reaching shore in the small upstate New York community of Ogdensburg. He hitchhiked into town from the riverside (ironically enough, bumming this ride from a Canadian working in Ogdensburg), where the local police picked him up on a vagrancy charge the night of 24 January. After a few days in jail, von Werra was brought before Judge John H. Wells, to whom he pleaded guilty to vagrancy, receiving for this offense a suspended sentence.

Von Werra had sensed, quite accurately, that if he could somehow get out of Canada and into the still-neutral United States, it would be possible for him to be returned to Germany and to combat. Indeed, this is what did transpire, but not before some international diplomatic intrigue, beginning with both Canada and Britain imploring the United States to hand over to them this challenger of their security interests. Instead, von Werra was turned over to local U.S. immigration authorities, who remained undecided what to do with him. While they were pondering the matter, Berlin dispatched the German consul in New York City, Hans Borchers, northward to Ogdensburg, where a $5,000 bond was posted to secure the flyer's release, pending the resolution of a new case against him, of having entered the United States illegally. Von Werra accompanied Borchers to New York City, where he resided for nearly two months, until warned by German authorities about a looming possibility of his being sent back to Canada. On this warning, he departed New York, bound for El Paso, Texas, from which city he crossed into Mexico dressed as a migrant worker. Subsequently, he made his way southward, on a circuitous journey that took him through Panama, Peru, and Bolivia, before finally arriving in the Brazilian capital, Rio de Janeiro, in the middle of April 1941. From there, he flew back to Europe, on board a plane bound for Rome operated by the Italian airline, Lati, the last remaining commercial airline linking the New World to Axis-occupied Europe.[45]

In the end, von Werra's saga demonstrates the wisdom in the apothegm about being careful what one wishes for, as he did in fact make it back into combat, and is thought to have been the only POW in Canada ever to have done so. He lost his life in action off the Dutch coast later in the war. He was twenty-seven. Had he never escaped custody, he might have lived to a ripe old age, quite possibly settling down in postwar Canada, as did so many former German prisoners of war.[46] But von Werra's tale demonstrates something else, with bearing on the thesis of this book. Although it does not warrant overemphasizing the matter, it is obvious that in facilitating, however unintentionally, von Werra's return to combat, the United States did take a step that was unfavorable to Canadian (and British) physical security interests. It clearly did not do so out of any desire to harm those interests, and the disservice done to Canada in this instance was not particularly great; to the contrary, as far as anyone knows, it was so slight as to be well-nigh undetectable. Instead, America's "sin" in Canadian eyes at the time of its neutrality was not so much one of commission (as in releasing one of the country's sworn enemies and so opening up the prospect of his attacking Canadian military personnel somewhere and sometime in the future) as it was one of *omission*—omitting, precisely, to join the war effort against Nazi Germany.

I relate the events surrounding von Werra mainly to provide some useful historical background to the homeland-security "dilemmas" that have cropped up since 9/11—dilemmas that if taken out of context can seem to be both new and potentially intractable.[47] But in fact they are neither, and placing things in perspective is not only helpful, it is essential if we are to fully understand how the phenomenon of "people in motion" in North America can be said to possess conceptual, analytical, and policy relevance appertaining to the rise and evolution of the North American security community. Let us therefore begin our inquiry specifically into what is meant when North America is described as a "zone of peace," asking in the chapter that follows this one how, why, and when this felicific condition was reached, and what, if anything, might disturb it in the future. To commence this investigation, a bit of analysis a contrario is in order, for to comprehend that North American zone of peace, we need to know something about the security order that it supplanted, namely the very lengthy period of time when North America was, unmistakably, a zone of war.

NORTH AMERICA'S HOBBESIAN PAST

To say again: real, or geopolitical, borders are hardly a new phenomenon in the northern half of North America. Taken in the long sweep of the continent's history, they have been the rule, rather than the exception to the rule, and this is because during that long sweep from the seventeenth century down to the present time, relations between the North American neighbors were more often characterized by warfare and hostility than by peace and amicability. It is important to recognize this lengthy martial experience, because an obstinate habit of many who think about North American security is to regard the region as somehow constituting an historic aberration—so much so that it has been possible for scholars and policy advocates to wax enthusiastically about a, or better, *the*, "North American Idea" as representing a welcome departure from the otherwise depressing consequences of life in an international system characterized by anarchy.[48]

But if the North Americans somehow managed to find the secret of living blissfully together, it has only been a fairly recent discovery. For as between today's Canada and the United States, a geopolitical, if often indeterminate, border had existed that was nearly as old as the Europeans' presence on the continent itself. Yet because it is so often thought that "history" for both the United States and Canada only began fairly recently as these matters go—1776 for the Americans, when independence from Britain was declared, and 1867 for Canada, when today's federation was established, albeit within the British empire—it is easy to forget that the Old World was very much present in the New, such that the rivalries of the former were necessarily projected into the territory of the latter.[49] If Europe lived in a "Hobbesian" world, then so, too, did the developing polities of the New World. Because of this, the portion of eastern North America settled by French and English was, if anywhere on earth could be said to have been, a zone of war, the kind of setting where life could be counted upon to be "nasty, brutish, and short."[50] In the well-chosen words of one historian of the colonial era, "[w]ar was a fundamental part of life in early America. A man or woman who lived to adulthood in colonial times by definition lived through war."[51] Much the same has to be said of life in early Canada, to whose inhabitants the rifle was figuratively, and sometimes literally, attached to the plow, so ubiquitous was the warfare that stamped their collective psyche with a profoundly militaristic impress.[52] Throughout that formative era, the Kantian alternative to this zone of war, the Canada-United States security community (or zone of peace), lay far in the future.

Few remember them today, but four great-power wars pockmarked the face of North America between 1689 and 1763, all occurring prior to the political "birth" of America and Canada but certainly wars that, in retrospect, have to be regarded as conflicts between Americans and Canadians. These were the intercolonial wars pitting English against French, with each side backed by its aboriginal allies. They were the War of the League of Augsburg (1689–1697), brought to a close with the Treaty of Ryswick, and known in North America as King William's War; the War of the Spanish Succession (1702–1713), ending with the Treaty of Utrecht, called in North America Queen Anne's War; the War of the Austrian Succession (1744–1748), ending with the Treaty of Aix-la-Chapelle, known in North America as King George's War; and the Seven Years' War (1756–1763), better remembered in North America as the French and Indian War, and terminated with the Treaty of Paris, ceding Canada to England.[53]

It would not be much of an analytical stretch to describe these conflicts as representing what post-Cold War scholarship has labelled "ethnic conflict," controversial though this category admittedly is.[54] Apropos of that long, depressing, and bloody period stretching from 1689 to 1763, Crane Brinton has written, persuasively, that not until the emergence of the Soviet nuclear threat would America's homeland security ever again become so profoundly menaced by foreigners as it had been during those earlier years.[55] There was a major difference between the two eras, though. During the Cold War, the Soviet threat remained mainly latent, even if unspeakably appalling in its potential for death and destruction. For Americans of the earlier period, the threat from the north was real, often horrifically so, just as for Canadians of that time the threat from the south was likewise. For more than three-quarters of a century, Americans and Canadians engaged in warfare against each other, not all the time, but often enough so as to give every appearance that, on the frontier separating their respective heartlands, ethnic cleansing was both the means and the end of policy, and though none at the time could have stylized what they were waging as ethnic conflict, what else should we, today, term it to have been?

Consider what might be taken as the two defining qualities of such conflict: 1) that it feature violence directed at civilian populations of a differing ethnicity, who are regarded as being not only legitimate but choice targets of brutal attack, a principal aim thereof being to sow terror; and 2) that it have as a major objective the purging of specified ethnic communities from geographically defined territories—that is, that it constitute the "cleansing" of such communities from these regions. On both counts, it is apparent that if we are to use the disputed category of ethnic conflict anywhere and at any time, then the frontier separating French and English holdings on the North American continent during the seventeenth and eighteenth centuries more than fills the bill as a locale of such contestation. And for good measure, if what IR realist theorists conceptualize as the "security dilemma" can be injected into the discussion, then it is also obvious that the frequency with which the offensive military capabilities along the frontier dominated over defensive ones only rendered more acute the problem of ethnic conflict. This was so because the very nature of a security dilemma inheres in the uncertainty and anxiety that must attend one's own thinking about one's neighbors' level of military preparations, when the latter take shape under conditions of international anarchy, especially when an existing empire decays or when two empires first come into conflict over a disputed "sphere of influence," as was the case in North America during the era of the colonial wars.[56]

Therefore, of conflict between Canadians and Americans during the formative decades of their not-so-peaceful coexistence, we can make three observations: 1) it was frequent; 2) it was bloody, maybe not so much in terms of the absolute numbers of casualties as in the brutal manner in which the slayings occurred; and 3) it did result in territorial cleansing of ethnic groups, either via their mass transfer from territories in which they had already settled or because of their having been prevented from settling in the first place. In respect of the first item, the frequency of strife between Americans and their northern neighbors, it has to be said that hardly had their respective mother countries, Britain and France, begun to establish a toehold on the North American continent than they began to fight each other, as for instance in 1613, when Captain Samuel Argall attacked Acadia; or, in 1629, when the French Huguenot David Kirke took Quebec for England and held it for three years, until it was handed back in the Treaty of Saint-Germain-en-Laye; or in 1654, when Oliver Cromwell ordered Robert Sedgwick of Boston to take Port Royal and other settlements on the Bay of Fundy, only to have these returned to France in 1667 with the Treaty of Breda, ending the Second Anglo-Dutch War.[57]

Nevertheless, these early military operations do not warrant being branded instances of ethnic conflict; they featured small-scale and fairly mild applications of force, according to traditional "European" norms of warfare, and as a result had little in common with what was soon to come in North America. Besides, territories seized in these initial skirmishes, far from being "cleansed" of their possessors, were routinely handed back to them. It would not be until the onset of the first of the colonial wars, King William's War, that the era of ethnic conflict would begin between the Canadians and the Americans. I am going to concentrate mainly on this war, partly because space does not permit an equal discussion of all four wars, but mostly because it suffices to illustrate the claim regarding ethnic conflict better than the other three.

There had already, it is true, been instances of ethnic conflict in North America prior to 1689, but these did not directly pit Canadians (i.e., French) against Americans (i.e., English). To the extent the European settlers were involved in them at all, these earlier episodes featured sanguinary struggles in which both French and English fought, separately, against their respective indigenous adversaries on their own side of the geopolitical frontier. For the French, this meant the Iroquois, with whom a long conflict commenced in 1609 and reached its crescendo of brutality with the raid on Lachine eighty years later, in August 1689, costing more than one hundred French settlers their lives.[58] For those Americans who were the most significant neighbors of the French on the continent, that is to say primarily the New Englanders, the fighting commenced with the short war of 1637 against the Pequots, only to reignite in the vastly more deadly King Philip's War, of 1675–1676.

This latter war, which pitted the New England colonies—Plymouth, Massachusetts Bay, Rhode Island, and Connecticut—against an Algonquian coalition led by Philip (also known as Metacom, sometimes Metacomet) and his Wampanoags,[59] was noteworthy not only in foreshadowing the ethnic conflict that would lie ahead for the region, but also for the brutality and high cost of the struggle, which for both sides could and did appear to be a fight to the finish, nothing short of a "war of extermination,"[60] whose outcome was to determine who would preside over, or even get to live in, the disputed territory.[61] On a per capita basis (i.e., rate of casualties suffered by the total population, combatant as well as noncombatant), this short war is generally remembered, when it is remembered at all, as having been the bloodiest in American history, not excluding even the Civil War. More than half of the English settlements (fifty-two out of a total of ninety) were attacked during the year of fighting, with thirteen being destroyed, while some 10 percent of the combat-eligible English males ended up as casualties. High though the rate of casualties may have been among the English, it paled in comparison with the losses sustained by their Indian adversaries (both combatant and noncombatant). At the start of the war, Philip's army counted 2,900 combatants, out of a total indigenous population of 11,000; within a year, some 2,430 combatants and noncombatants had been killed or captured, and most of the Algonquian survivors had fled the region.[62] The question as

to who would dominate the region—English or Algonquian—looked, finally, to have been settled.

Those appearances might well have translated into reality had not a
new existential challenge, for a while greater even than that pitting settler
against original inhabitant, appeared in the aftermath of King Philip's
War—a challenge posed to the English by none other than the world's
most powerful state, France, which had established a foothold in regions
to the north and, increasingly as time went by, to the west of the frontiers
of English settlement. Already by the time of King Philip's War there had
been some in New England who were convinced (wrongly) that a French
hand had been orchestrating the Algonquian military campaign; shortly
after the war's ending, however, it was becoming understood, correctly
this time, that France, and through it Canada, would be an ever-growing
menace to American interests, so much so that at times the specter of
English settlement being pushed into the sea loomed large. It was not a
specter that sober calculation of "objective" power balances on the North
American continent should have nourished, given that at the time of
King Philip's War English settlers on the continent outnumbered French
settlers by a margin of more than twenty to one (200,000 compared with
slightly more than 10,000) and that the gap never would close during the
ensuing century (standing at 1.25 million to 60,000 by the time the final
colonial war started, in 1754).[63]

Still, the English (or, Americans) were characterized by nothing so
much as their disunity, making their real military capability much, much
less than the sum of their fractious parts. As well, only half of the English
(around 100,000) lived in the provinces most at risk when the colonial
contests began—New England and New York. In theory, France would
be able to upgrade vastly its own military presence on the continent,
being at the time indisputably the world's ranking military power, with a
homeland population that stood at twenty million, nearly six times that
of its British enemy.[64] For good measure, France could also tap into a
network of effective Indian alliances, something New England could
hardly do after the carnage of 1675–1676, which all but depopulated the
region of its original inhabitants. While New York may have been able to
seek support from the Iroquois, the latter were careful to pick the wars in
which they would join, meaning that there were considerable stretches
after the "great peace" of 1701 with the French during which they opted
for neutrality, rather than alliance with the English.[65] So to the latter, the
threat seemed real enough in their northernmost zones of settlement on
the continent, where in the decades following 1676 "French influence
among the more remote tribes was increasing, giving a dark hint as to the
nature of coming wars."[66]

It has often been remarked of the first three of those colonial wars that
they constituted something of a sideshow for both France and its European great-power rival, Britain, with only the fourth and last of them

turning into a decisive struggle with profound implications for international "systemic change."[67] This is not how the earlier wars looked to Americans and Canadians caught up in the fighting; for them, the first two wars in particular furnished a harrowing, and über-Hobbesian, perspective on life in the continental zone of war.[68] King William's War, the initial one, testifies to this better than anything else.

The brunt of fighting that ensued subsequent to the Lachine raid was borne by settlers on the New York frontier, as well as settlers in northern New England. The major raids of that war took place early against civilian targets in frontier communities—in February 1690 in New York's Mohawk Valley, against Schenectady; the following month in New Hampshire, against Salmon Falls; and then in May in Maine, against Casco—left some hundred settlers dead, and more importantly contributed to sowing terror along the frontier and thus deterring further English settlement.

In all, during that first war, it is likely that 650 Americans (mostly New Englanders) were either killed in raids or died in captivity, while the Canadians suffered about 300 dead, with their Indian allies losing a further 100. The Iroquois bore the heaviest relative burden of all, with perhaps 650 lost, a toll that contributed directly to their deciding to abstain from the next two colonial wars.[69] To put the American and Canadian losses in perspective, around one in every 230 settlers perished, or some .0043 percent of the European population in the English and French parts of North America. Projected onto current population levels in North America, this would be equivalent to Canada losing 129,000 in war, or the United States 1.29 million. Compared with battlefield deaths in Europe during the same period, the total numbers lost to ethnic conflict in North America may not have been large, but the relative numbers were high, and the psychic trauma associated therewith was considerable.

I have tarried somewhat on the colonial wars, especially on the first of them, to make the simple and obvious point that there really was, for a considerable length of time, nothing particularly "exceptional" about the North American political landscape, or the most symbolic expression thereof, the Canada-United States border, a consummately geopolitical construct if ever there was such a thing. And while Canadians, for the most part, sat out the American independence war with England that broke out shortly after the last of the intercolonial wars ended, it did not take long for Americans and Canadians once more to be duking it out with each other, this time most memorably in the War of 1812, the bicentenary of which is being marked, with more enthusiasm on the Canadian than on the American side, as I write these words.[70] Partly that war is being celebrated for reasons linked to national egoism, but there is also a more positive normative spin given to the commemoration, as it is often remarked, on both sides of the border, that since this was the last time

Canadians and Americans ever engaged in armed conflict against each other, the War of 1812—or at least, its ending in 1814—can be taken as the starting date for the North American "long peace," thus it constitutes an appropriate means of symbolizing the "North American Idea."

Nothing could be further from the truth, however. For by the time the Treaty of Ghent brought that war to a close in late December 1814, the construction of the North American regional security community (the Canada-United States zone of peace) still lay many decades in the future. Following 1814, fear of war, as well as the occasional sporadic employment of force in Canada-United States relations, continued to be, if not the norm, then at least an ever-present consequence, either of cross-border tensions of a distinctly North American provenance, or of strategic rivalry between the United States and the UK, with Canada necessarily becoming caught up in this rivalry. During the late 1830s and early 1840s, Canadian territory was targeted by the nineteenth-century version of what some political scientists today call "non-state armed actors,"[71] groups who in that earlier era bore the label "filibusterers." Sometimes claimed to be a distinctly American innovation in matters appertaining to international security,[72] filibustering actually testifies to an old practice of "freebooting" by which non-state actors sought to use territorial sanctuaries in one country as springboards for offensive operations against another, usually neighboring, country.

The practice may have been old, but it was an American writer who gave it its English name, when in late 1851 George Templeton Strong exulted, on learning that the Cuban freebooter and slavery enthusiast Narciso López had just been executed by the Spanish authorities after being captured on a second attempt at raising insurrection on the island, that "[i]f this little band of militant philanthropists and self-consecrated missionaries of Republican scum has been exterminated, it will be long before filibusterism recovers from the shock." Strong's gleeful optimism was misplaced; within half a decade so widespread would use of the term become that *Harper's New Monthly Magazine* could be moved to prophesy in 1855 that filibustering was going to "occupy an important place in our vocabulary."[73] And while filibustering is usually considered to have been an activity largely focussed upon America's southern neighborhood, non-state armed actors bent on exploiting American territory to launch operations against Canada continued to feature prominently in North American security relations, notwithstanding that the 1842 Webster-Ashburton Treaty between the United States and the UK yielded an American agreement to crack down more forcibly than heretofore upon the practice, frowned upon as it was by both international law and America's own laws of neutrality.[74]

Filibustering's flamboyant reentry into North American security affairs following the Civil War would continue to provide graphic evidence of why the continent's "long peace" should never be dated from 1814.

Between 1866 and 1870, "Fenianism" would constitute an objective and immediate challenge to the physical security interests of British North America, so much so that this threat from U.S.-based Irish nationalists is considered to have been a principal stimulus for the creation of Canada's federation in 1867, leading British North Americans to seek safety in unity, and their fellow citizens in Great Britain to shift more of the burden for the defense of North American interests to Canadians and other British North Americans.[75] But filibustering, or Fenianism, or terrorism— however one wishes to depict the visage of non-state armed actors in North America—was not the only reason for drawing back from any premature pronouncement regarding the onset of the North American zone of peace; as time went on, a second, quite legal, source of American-Canadian tension would appear, in the guise of "ethnic lobbying" efforts mounted by two large U.S.-based diasporas whose growing worries regarding Anglo-American rapprochement would have profound implications for Canadian-American security, as will be discussed in chapters three and four.

For the moment though, let us return to the business of puzzling out the historic transformation in regional security affairs associated with the transit of North America from its Hobbesian age to its Kantian one. In particular, let us try to answer a couple of questions. The first is, what is supposed to be meant by a Kantian "zone of peace"? And the second is, when, and why, did the North American security picture brighten so considerably that henceforth the continent's lengthy Hobbesian experience could become virtually expunged from collective memory, on either side of the Canada-United States border?

NOTES

1. Fen Osler Hampson and Maureen Appel Molot, "Does the 49th Parallel Matter Anymore?" in *Vanishing Borders: Canada among Nations 2000*, ed. Molot and Hampson (Don Mills, ON: Oxford University Press, 2000), pp. 1–23, quote at p. 2.

2. See Farwaz A. Gerges, *Journey of the Jihadist: Inside Muslim Militancy* (Orlando, Fla.: Harcourt, 2007).

3. I say mislabelled, because of course most of Canada's population lives *south* of the fabled 49th, so that whatever else this parallel of latitude is supposed to conjure up, it should never be taken to represent the most accurate line of *demographic* demarcation between Canadians and their southern neighbors. For a useful corrective to the mythic depiction of the border as some sort of liminal nirvana, see Richard A. Preston, *The Defence of the Undefended Border: Planning for War in North America, 1867–1939* (Montreal and Kingston: McGill-Queen's University Press, 1977).

4. Peter Andreas and Thomas J. Biersteker, eds., *The Rebordering of North America: Integration and Exclusion in a New Security Context* (New York: Routledge, 2003). Also see Daniel Drache, *Borders Matter: Homeland Security and the Search for North America* (Halifax, NS: Fernwood, 2004).

5. For this imagery, see Peter Andreas, "The Mexicanization of the US-Canada Border," *International Journal* 60 (Spring 2005): 449–62.

6. Notwithstanding the ambiguity, as well as controversy, surrounding the numbers of *illegal* immigrants, most contemporary researchers believe that the days are past when Mexicans flocked to the United States in search of enhancing their economic prospects. See Damien Cave, "For Migrants, New Land of Opportunity Is Mexico," *New York Times*, 22 September 2013, pp. 1, 9; Douglas S. Massey, "Battlefield: El Paso," *National Interest*, no. 102 (July–August 2009), pp. 44–51; and Carl Meacham and Michael Graybeal, *Diminishing Mexican Immigration to the United States* (Washington, D.C.: Center for Strategic and International Studies, July 2013). But for the ongoing difficulties facing U.S. authorities trying to halt illegal immigration, most recently by vast numbers of unaccompanied children from Central American lands, compare Ross Douthat, "Immigration Reform's Open Invitation," *New York Times*, 22 June 2014, "Sunday Review," p. 11.

7. See David G. Haglund, "A Security Community—'If You Can Keep It': Demographic Change and the North American Zone of Peace," *Norteamérica* 2 (January–June 2007): 77–100.

8. Those top ten "Canadian" jurisdictions were Ontario (with 1,858,787), Quebec (1,560,190), Massachusetts (516,379), Nova Scotia (435,172), Michigan (407,999), New Brunswick (313,178), New York (226,506), Manitoba (180,859), Maine (133,885), and Minnesota (114,547). See Samuel E. Moffett, *The Americanization of Canada* (Toronto: University of Toronto Press, 1972; orig. pub. 1907), pp. 10–11. Also see Marcus Lee Hansen, *The Mingling of the Canadian and American Peoples* (New Haven, Conn.: Yale University Press, and Toronto: Ryerson Press, 1940).

9. In fact, there has been for some time a cyclical pattern in the degree to which mutual trust characterizes the bilateral relationship, as argued in Charles F. Doran, *Forgotten Partnership: U.S.-Canada Relations Today* (Baltimore: Johns Hopkins University Press, 1984).

10. David T. Jones and David Kilgour, *Uneasy Neighbo(u)rs: Canada, the USA and the Dynamics of State, Industry and Culture* (Mississauga, ON: John Wiley and Sons, 2007), pp. xiii–xiv.

11. Exports account for roughly a quarter of the country's GDP, with almost three-quarters of these going to the American market; see Alexandre Gauthier and Katie Meredith, *Canada's Merchandise Trade with the World: 2011*, Publication no. 2012-41-E (Ottawa: Library of Parliament, 13 July 2012), p. 2. Reflective of the economic logic of Canada's approach to border management is Monica Gattinger and Geoffrey Hale, eds., *Borders and Bridges: Canada's Policy Relations in North America* (Don Mills, ON: Oxford University Press, 2010).

12. David G. Haglund, "North American Cooperation in an Era of Homeland Security," *Orbis* 47 (Autumn 2003): 675–91.

13. See Stephen E. Flynn, "Beyond Border Control," *Foreign Affairs* 79 (November–December 2000): 57–68.

14. Jason Ackleson, "From 'Thin' to 'Thick' (and Back Again?): The Politics and Policies of the Contemporary US-Canada Border," *American Review of Canadian Studies* 39 (December 2009): 336–51; Colin Robertson, "Beyond the Border and Regulatory Reform," *Policy Options* 33 (December 2011–January 2012): 56–60; and Brian Bow, "'Security Perimeter': From Horrifying to Ho-Hum in Ten Years?" CDFAI *Dispatch* 12 (Spring 2014): 17–18.

15. This multidimensional bilateral initiative was launched by President Barack Obama and Prime Minister Stephen Harper at a meeting in Washington on 4 February 2011, under the ambitious title, "Beyond the Border: A Shared Vision for Perimeter Security and Economic Competitiveness." The intent is to deepen bilateral cooperation not only in respect of security, but also of trade, law enforcement, and critical infrastructure (including cybersecurity). See Government of Canada, *What Canadians Told Us: A Report on Consultations on Perimeter Security and Economic Competitiveness between Canada and the United States* (Ottawa: Department of Foreign Affairs and International Trade, 2011), available at www.borderactionplan.gc.ca. A useful source of information on the ongoing development of this initiative is the "Beyond the Border" blog avail-

able through the website of the Canada Institute of the Wilson Center in Washington, accessible at www.wilsoncenter.org/program/canada-institute.

16. Quoted in "Coderre Calls for Apology from Hillary Clinton," *Globe and Mail* (Toronto), 9 January 2003, p. A1. Coderre is now the mayor of Montreal.

17. Edward Alden, *The Closing of the American Border: Terrorism, Immigration, and Security since 9/11* (New York: HarperCollins, 2008), p. 129.

18. Stewart Bell, *Cold Terror: How Canada Nurtures and Exports Terrorism around the World*, rev. ed. (Toronto: John Wiley and Sons, 2007), p. 38.

19. Colin Freeze, "Canada Tarred Again as Haven for Terrorists," *Globe and Mail*, 26 April 2002, pp. A1, A14. The segment was broadcast on Sunday, 28 April.

20. Stephen Gallagher, "Canada's Dysfunctional Refugee Policy: A Realist Case for Reform," *Behind the Headlines* 58 (Summer 2001): 1. Also see Colin Freeze, "Paris Embassy Official Bribed for Visas," *Globe and Mail*, 5 September 2002, online ed.; and "Corrupt Immigration Consultants Denounced," *Globe and Mail*, 6 September 2002. As well, see Howard Adelman, "Canadian Borders and Immigration Post 9/11," *International Migration Review* 36 (Spring 2002): 15–28.

21. See Jeff Sallot, Andrew Mitrovica, and Tu Thanh Ha, "Canadian Connection Suspected in Hijackings," *Globe and Mail*, 13 September 2001, pp. A1, A13.

22. Quoted in John Ibbitson, "U.S. Points the Finger Due North," *Globe and Mail*, 27 September 2001, pp. A1, A11.

23. Alden, *Closing of the American Border*, pp. 148–50, 182–85. Incredibly, two of the hijackers, Mohammed Atta and Marwan al Shehhi, even received Immigration and Naturalization Service approval of their student visa applications to take flying lessons, some six months *after* their fiery deaths on 11 September.

24. For an intriguing study of American media criticism of Canada during this period, see Laura McGee, "When 'Bomb Canada' Is Really Just a Metaphor: Using the American Jeremiad to Reinterpret Anti-Canadianism in the American Press," *American Review of Canadian Studies* 42 (March 2012): 51–66.

25. Illustratively, Gallup reported in early March 2008 that "Canada and Great Britain have topped Gallup's country rankings each of the 12 times since 1989 that both countries have been measured, although in most cases Canada has led Great Britain by a few percentage points. The only other country to approach 90% favorability over the years has been Australia"; see "Americans' Most and Least Favored Nations: Canada and Great Britain Remain the Most Popular Allies," available at http://www.gallup.com/poll/104734/americans-most-least-favored-nations.aspx.

26. See John J. Bukowczyk et al., *Permeable Border: The Great Lakes Basin as a Transnational Region, 1650–1990* (Pittsburgh, Penn.: University of Pittsburgh Press, and Calgary: University of Calgary Press, 2005).

27. Peter Andreas, "Redrawing the Line: Borders and Security in the Twenty-First Century," *International Security* 28 (Autumn 2003): 78–111, quotes at pp. 82, 109.

28. Bryan Mabee, "Re-imagining the Borders of US Security after 9/11: Securitisation, Risk, and the Creation of the Department of Homeland Security," *Globalizations* 4 (September 2007): 385–97.

29. Quoted in John Ibbitson, "Obama's Message: Glory Days of Open Border Are Gone," *Globe and Mail*, 26 March 2009, pp. A1, A15. Also see Allan Gotlieb, "We Need Borders without Boundaries," *Globe and Mail*, 2 April 2009, p. A15. Napolitano is said to have remarked that when she was governor she worked more closely with her counterpart in Sonora, Mexico, than she did with neighboring New Mexico's governor. See Robert A. Pastor, *The North American Idea: A Vision of a Continental Future* (New York: Oxford University Press, 2011), p. 109.

30. F. R. Scott, "The Permanent Bases of Canadian Foreign Policy," *Foreign Affairs* 10 (July 1932): 617–31, quote at p. 618.

31. Massey was then serving as Canada's high commissioner to the UK. His actor brother, Raymond, had an important part in the movie, whose top billing, nevertheless, was shared by Laurence Olivier, Leslie Howard, and Eric Portman. The film, based on a screenplay written by Emeric Pressburger, was directed by Michael Powell.

32. See David G. Haglund, "Le Canada dans l'entre-deux-guerres," *Études inter-nationales* 31 (December 2000): 727–43.

33. John MacCormac, *Canada: America's Problem* (New York: Viking, 1940).

34. To employ planetary imagery popularized a decade or so ago, at a time when the Western alliance was split by intense disputes over the wisdom of war with Iraq; see Robert Kagan, *Of Paradise and Power: America and the New World Order* (New York: Alfred A. Knopf, 2003).

35. Reflective of this yearning for a return to Venusian strategic mores is Ian McKay and Jamie Swift, *Warrior Nation: Rebranding Canada in an Age of Anxiety* (Toronto: Between the Lines, 2012). But for a more celebratory assessment of Martian ways, see Patrick James, *Canada and Conflict* (Don Mills, ON: Oxford University Press, 2012).

36. The Hague Convention of 1907, although allowing neutrals to trade legally with belligerents and still maintain their neutrality, specifically prohibited any transfer of forces-in-being to belligerents, which of course was the whole point of the swap. As for the vintage of these destroyers, in official Washington much emphasis was put on their being somewhat ancient, when in fact they had mostly been built over the past quarter century—not such a long period when one considers that the USAF continues to operate with success B-52 bombers dating from the early Cold War or that the RCAF's "top-of-the-line" CF-18 fighter-bombers, in action over Libyan skies just a few years ago, are today as "ancient" as were those American destroyers transferred to Britain in late 1940. On the destroyers-bases exchange, see James R. Leutze, *Bargaining for Supremacy: Anglo-American Naval Collaboration, 1937–1941* (Chapel Hill: University of North Carolina Press, 1977), 72–93, 114–27; and Philip Goodhart, *Fifty Ships That Saved the World: The Foundation of the Anglo-American Alliance* (Garden City, N.Y.: Doubleday, 1965).

37. John Herd Thompson and Stephen J. Randall, *Canada and the United States: Ambivalent Allies*, 3rd ed. (Athens: University of Georgia Press, 2002), pp. 151–52.

38. MacCormac, *Canada: America's Problem*, p. 13.

39. MacCormac, *Canada*, p. 13.

40. For this aquatic imagery, see John J. Mearsheimer, *The Tragedy of Great Power Politics* (New York: W. W. Norton, 2001), p. 127.

41. I have elaborated on this in my *Latin America and the Transformation of U.S. Strategic Thought, 1936–1940* (Albuquerque: University of New Mexico Press, 1984).

42. Andreas, "Redrawing the Line."

43. During that golden era, border tranquillity was disturbed by criminal and related activity stemming from *domestic* policy differences in respect of alcohol, with Prohibition in the United States serving as an enticement to the illegal transport of liquor from Canada to a thirsty American marketplace. But these frictions were matters of policing rather than of strategy, and can be excluded from discussions implicating militarized "geopolitics" with the border-management regime.

44. See, for one instance, Patrick Lennox, "From Golden Straitjacket to Kevlar Vest: Canada's Transformation to a Security State," *Canadian Journal of Political Science* 40 (December 2007): 1017–38.

45. The airline's South American operations would soon be closed down by Brazilian authorities, in December 1941, thanks to some interesting skullduggery orchestrated by the British security coordinator in the United States, a Canadian named William Stephenson, whose code name was "Intrepid." Details of Lati's closing can be found in Michel Fortmann and David G. Haglund, "Public Diplomacy and Dirty Tricks: Two Faces of United States 'Informal Penetration' of Latin America on the Eve of World War II," *Diplomacy & Statecraft* 6 (July 1995): 536–77, citing from pp. 562–63. Also see Leslie B. Rout Jr. and John Bratzel, *The Shadow War: German Espionage and United States Counterespionage in Latin America during World War II* (Frederick, Md.: University Publications of America, 1986), pp. 110–14.

46. This episode is recounted in John Melady, *Escape from Canada! The Untold Story of German POWs in Canada, 1939–1945* (Toronto: Macmillan, 1981), pp. 83–98.

47. The case for their intractability is made by Frank P. Harvey, "The Homeland Security Dilemma: Imagination, Failure and the Escalating Costs of Perfecting Security," *Canadian Journal of Political Science* 40 (June 2007): 283–316.

48. At one time it was very much the hope of a few policy advocates that North America's "exceptionalism" might somehow serve as an example to more benighted regions of the planet, helping cure them of their chronic war-proneness. See James A. Macdonald, *The North American Idea* (Toronto: McClelland, Goodchild & Stewart, 1917). For a critique of this eupeptic perspective, see Norman Hillmer, "O. D. Skelton and the North American Mind," *International Journal* 60 (Winter 2004–2005): 93–110.

49. See Fred Anderson and Andrew Cayton, *The Dominion of War: Empire and Liberty in North America, 1500–2000* (New York: Viking, 2005); and Eliot A. Cohen, *Conquered into Liberty: Two Centuries of Battles along the Great Warpath That Made the American Way of War* (New York: Free Press, 2011).

50. To cite this familiar passage, from Hobbes's 1651 masterpiece, *Leviathan*.

51. Richard I. Melvoin, *New England Outpost: War and Society in Colonial Deerfield* (New York: W. W. Norton, 1989), p. 12.

52. Jean-Yves Gravel, *Le Québec et la guerre* (Montréal: Boréal Express, 1974), p. 5. Also see William J. Eccles, *France in America* (Markham, ON: Fitzhenry and Whiteside, 1990; orig. pub. 1972).

53. See Howard H. Peckham, *The Colonial Wars, 1689–1762* (Chicago: University of Chicago Press, 1964); and Ian Kenneth Steele, *Guerillas and Grenadiers: The Struggle for Canada, 1689–1760* (Toronto: Ryerson Press, 1969). The final war's European name is a slight misnomer, as the fighting actually began in 1754 not 1756, and did so in North America, not Europe.

54. Some scholars even deny that such conflict exists. For the tenor of this debate, see Hugh Donald Forbes, "Toward a Science of Ethnic Conflict?" *Journal of Democracy* 14 (October 2003): 172–77; Marc Howard Ross, "The Role of Evolution in Ethnocentric Conflict and Its Management," *Journal of Social Issues* 47, 3 (1991): 167–85; and Vernon Reynolds, Vincent Falger, and Ian Vine, eds., *The Sociobiology of Ethnocentrism: Evolutionary Dimensions of Xenophobia, Discrimination, Racism, and Nationalism* (London: Croom Helm, 1987).

55. Crane Brinton, *The Americans and the French* (Cambridge, Mass.: Harvard University Press, 1968), pp. 51–52.

56. Although he was writing about the former Yugoslavia and ex-USSR in the 1990s, what Barry Posen had to say about the link between security dilemmas and ethnic conflict equally applies to North America during the colonial era; see Barry R. Posen, "The Security Dilemma and Ethnic Conflict," *Survival* 35 (Spring 1993): 27–47.

57. Jean Pellerin, *La Nouvelle-France démaquillée* (Montréal: Éd. Varia, 2001), pp. 66–67; Reuben Gold Thwaites, *France in America, 1497–1763* (New York: Harper and Bros., 1905), pp. 25–28; Richard W. Van Alstyne, *The Rising American Empire* (New York: Oxford University Press, 1960), pp. 9–11.

58. George T. Hunt, *The Wars of the Iroquois: A Study in Intertribal Trade Relations*, 2nd ed. (Madison: University of Wisconsin Press, 1960).

59. In addition to the Wampanoags, the anti-English coalition included such other Algonquian peoples as the Nipmucks, Pocumtucks, Narragansetts, and Abenakis; on the English side were the Pequots and Mohegans, and to the west of the embattled region were to be found the Mohawks, members of the Iroquois confederation and longtime foes of the Algonquians. See Jill Lepore, *The Name of War: King Philip's War and the Origins of American Identity* (New York: Knopf, 1998), pp. xi–xiii.

60. Douglas Leach, *Flintlock and Tomahawk: New England in King Philip's War* (New York: Macmillan, 1958), p. 243. Also see James D. Drake, *King Philip's War: Civil War in New England, 1675–1676* (Amherst: University of Massachusetts Press, 1999).

61. In the words of one historian, not since the early (or "beachhead") years of settlement on the continent had the English come closer to being driven from North America than they did in 1676; see Stephen Saunders Webb, *1676: The End of American Independence* (New York: Alfred A. Knopf, 1984), pp. xxv–xxvi.

62. James A. Morone, *Hellfire Nation: The Politics of Sin in American History* (New Haven: Yale University Press, 2003), pp. 80–81; Melvoin, *New England Outpost*, pp. 93–96.

63. This fourth intercolonial conflict was the only one that began in North America; see Fred Anderson, *Crucible of War: The Seven Years' War and the Fate of Empire in British North America, 1754–1766* (New York: Alfred A. Knopf, 2000).

64. Stella H. Sutherland, *Population Distribution in Colonial America* (New York: Columbia University Press, 1936); Evarts B. Greene and Virginia D. Harrington, *American Population before the Federal Census of 1790* (New York: Columbia University Press, 1931); Pierre Goubert, *Louis XIV and Twenty Million Frenchmen*, trans. Anne Carter (New York: Pantheon Books, 1970).

65. Gilles Havard, *The Great Peace of Montreal of 1701: French-Native Diplomacy in the Seventeenth Century*, trans. Phyllis Arnoff and Howard Scott (Montreal and Kingston: McGill-Queen's University Press, 2001).

66. Leach, *Flintlock and Tomahawk*, p. 250.

67. There is a difference between "systemic" and "systems" change internationally. The former entails changes in the way power is distributed, while the latter suggests a major alteration in the very organizing principle of the system, as for instance when the modern states system supplanted the medieval European system. See Robert Gilpin, *War and Change in World Politics* (Cambridge: Cambridge University Press, 1981), pp. 41–43.

68. On these first two conflicts, see Samuel A. Drake, *The Border Wars of New England: Commonly Called King William's and Queen Anne's Wars* (New York: Charles Scribner's Sons, 1897).

69. Peckham, *Colonial Wars*, pp. 54–55.

70. In Canada this war is often construed as a major step toward the solidification of the "national identity" because it was seen as a victory over the *Americans*; in the United States it is also taken as generative of national identity, because it has been regarded as an opportunity to salvage national honor by holding to a draw the *British*. See, respectively, Stephen Marche, "That Time We Beat the Americans: A Citizen's Guide to the War of 1812," *The Walrus*, March 2012, pp. 24–31; and Steven Watts, *The Republic Reborn: War and the Making of Liberal America, 1790–1820* (Baltimore: Johns Hopkins University Press, 1987). The best recent study of this conflict is Alan Taylor, *The Civil War of 1812: American Citizens, British Subjects, Irish Rebels, and Indian Allies* (New York: Knopf, 2010).

71. See Diane E. Davis, "Non-State Armed Actors, New Imagined Communities, and Shifting Patterns of Sovereignty and Insecurity in the Modern World," *Contemporary Security Policy* 30 (August 2009): 221–45. On the transborder events of those years, see Albert B. Corey, *The Crisis of 1830–1842 in Canadian-American Relations* (New Haven, Conn.: Yale University Press, and Toronto: Ryerson Press, 1941).

72. For this claim, see Walter A. McDougall, *Promised Land, Crusader State: The American Encounter with the World Since 1776* (Boston: Houghton Mifflin, 1997), p. 235; and William H. Goetzmann, *When the Eagle Screamed: The Romantic Horizon in American Diplomacy, 1800–1860* (New York: Wiley, 1966), p. xvi.

73. Both quotes from Robert E. May, *Manifest Destiny's Underworld: Filibustering in Antebellum America* (Chapel Hill: University of North Carolina Press, 2002), pp. 1–4.

74. See Wilbur Devereux Jones, *The American Problem in British Diplomacy, 1841–1861* (London: Macmillan, 1974); and Wilbur Devereux Jones, *To the Webster-Ashburton Treaty: A Study in Anglo-American Relations, 1783–1843* (Chapel Hill: University of North Carolina Press, 1977).

75. See Charles P. Stacey, "Britain's Withdrawal from North America, 1864–1871," *Canadian Historical Review* 36 (September 1955): 185–98. On the regional and transatlantic geopolitical fallout of the Fenian phenomenon, see Brian Jenkins, *Fenians and Anglo-American Relations during Reconstruction* (Ithaca, N.Y.: Cornell University Press, 1969); and Jonathan Gantt, *Irish Terrorism in the Atlantic Community, 1865–1922* (Houndmills, UK: Palgrave Macmillan, 2010).

TWO

From Zone of War to Zone of Peace

Origins and Evolution of the Canada-United States Security Community

THE KANTIAN TRANSFORMATION

Over the past century or so, one fundamental aspect of North American regional security has stood out among all others: Canada and the United States managed to develop a habit of relating to each other that has truly been light-years, and not merely one hundred years, removed from their previous existence as cohabitants of the Hobbesian jungle described in chapter one. As a result, they might for many decades be said to have resided in a Kantian paradise (if any place on earth can be so stylized).[1] Such a radical reversal of behavioral patterns begets an equally radical reversal in the words and symbols employed to capture the "essence" of that altered security relationship, with "zone of peace" having emerged as the replacement trope for that other semantic construct, the previous chapter's "zone of war."

Nor is there anything spurious about that replacement metaphor. Notwithstanding the numerous frictions that do and must crop up between the two sovereign neighbors, and quite irrespective of whether their common border still contains vestiges of "geopolitical" provenance such as those discussed in the previous chapter, hardly anyone seriously argues that force, or even the threat to employ force, constitutes a means of dispute resolution in the North American countries' bilateral relations. If for no other reason than this, it has to be said that there truly *is* something remarkable about the North American "security community." It certainly is not the world's only such regional grouping of sovereign

41

states, and as we will see later in this chapter, even claims that it was the world's *first* such grouping need always to be taken with a grain of salt. Nevertheless, there is a quality to the bilateral security relationship that, if not unique in any affective sense, is nevertheless singular in a behavioral and empirical one. In a nutshell, the Canada-United States security community is often said to be "idiot proof," in that it is extremely hard for most observers to imagine how it might possibly unravel.

My objective in this chapter is to delve into this manifestly robust security community, asking what it signifies, when it began, and how it has developed over time. I do this to set the backdrop for subsequent chapters' inquiry into the manner in which ethnic diasporas might be reckoned conditioning elements in its rise and evolution. Accordingly, the place to start this chapter's investigation of the North American Kantian order is with the eponym itself; for if Thomas Hobbes could personify the "old" bilateral security relationship, then surely the new can best be encapsulated by reference to Immanuel Kant, often deemed to have been the progenitor of what we today know to be "democratic peace theory,"[2] itself seen by some as constituting the necessary and sufficient ideational underpinning of the North American zone of peace. So let us turn to this eighteenth-century German philosopher, and ask how, and why, he looms as an appropriate symbol of that which so distinguishes recent and contemporary North American security, the Canada-United States security community.

Everyone remembers Kant as the author of a famous treatise on "perpetual peace," even if few recall the inspiration for the title he chose, to wit, a sign on a Dutch inn bearing that name, depicting, of all things, a graveyard—presumably to entice those in search of a genuinely solid night's sleep.[3] Although often regarded as a wooly minded idealist by critics, Kant not only had a sense of humor but also possessed a well-honed sense of perspective. He knew just how difficult a job it would be for lasting peace to be effected between sovereign states. Indeed, long before the concept became a staple of some IR theorists, Kant was quite familiar with the notion that was later given the name "security dilemma," which posits the unintended impact that one state's *defensive* preparations can have on its neighbors, who discern in those same preparations *offensive* intent.[4] But just because a thing is difficult to achieve, he argued, is not a reason to give up the attempt, and he believed that it was the duty of conscientious leaders to continue striving for peace.

For many analysts of international security, the surprise ending of the Cold War seemed a fitting occasion for recollecting that Kant's aspiration might finally become a reality.[5] With this sudden outbreak of enthusiasm for lasting peace came something else, a wave of scholarly writing establishing the theoretical and conceptual bona fides of zones of peace cropping up in various, perhaps soon to be interlinked, parts of the planet. Not surprisingly, Europe drew the lion's share of this attention, as the

Cold War's termination opened the prospect of the extension of Western liberal-democratic values throughout the heretofore divided, and often war-torn, continent that had been the cynosure of so much killing and misery during the previous century. Words penned nearly a quarter century ago by Richard H. Ullman testified to this hope: "[n]o longer is there a serious likelihood of war among Europe's major states. . . . There is every chance, therefore, that coming generations will look upon Europe as a zone of peace."[6] They would do so, it was asserted, because liberal democracy was going to become the predominant aspect of the *internal* polities making up the European state system, with even *Russia* included among the membership of the liberal-democratic family.[7]

Not everyone, of course, bought into the uplifting notion that somehow peace in Europe and elsewhere could be best kept between states as a result of developments *within* them—this latter reflecting the primacy of a level of analysis popularized by Kenneth Waltz as the "second image," one that Waltz himself did not find most helpful for explaining why or how wars might be prevented.[8] Instead, some scholarly analysis was predicated on the thought that what had most kept Europe's regional peace since 1945 had, ironically, been the bifurcation of the continent into competing blocs led by superpowers who, between them, "sat on" the normally disputatious Europeans, rendering it impossible for them any longer to tear each other apart.[9] This is what was implied so clearly in the metaphor one German researcher highlighted, during the Cold War, as the principal source of the (Western) European peace after 1945: the American "pacifier."[10] This structuralist explanation of Europe's long peace found its strongest expression in a pair of ominously titled articles authored by the University of Chicago's John Mearsheimer, advancing the thesis that the Cold War's passing might not be something to celebrate, given some likely, and bleak, alternatives to the erstwhile bipolar rivalry.[11]

Mearsheimer and other scholars of a structuralist bent aside, the tide of opinion was running in a more optimistic direction,[12] both within Europe and in North America, and if the latter continent remained relatively "understudied" from the point of regional integration, it was for good reason: it had been such a long time, after all, since life in North America had paid the kind of homage to Hobbesian ways that had been so recently and regularly on display in Europe, that few saw much cause to theorize, and even less to rhapsodize, the wonder-working properties of regional integration on the western side of the Atlantic—save perhaps as an object lesson for less fortunate peoples in places far from North America's shores. If regional integration was the solution to the problem of great-power war, North America had no need for tutelage. In its case, unlike that of Europe, it was definitely not an instance of *la nécessité oblige.*

Still, there was a way in which theoretical trends appertaining to European security began to find an echo among scholars of North American security, in a manner that would have certainly surprised, and possibly even befuddled, proponents of the "North American Idea" of the early twentieth century. Even if North Americans did not need any guidance as to how best to keep the regional peace, it still remained that they might learn a thing or two from theoretical discussions of the emergence of the European security community.[13] And it was those discussions that helped bring Kant into the North American picture in the post-Cold War period, adding an innovative dimension to the scholarly debate about the origins and evolution of the continental security community.

THE (NORTH) AMERICANIZATION OF IMMANUEL?

No one has done more to draw attention to the North Americanization of Kantian analysis than Stéphane Roussel, whose study on the continent's "long peace" remains an indispensable starting point for discussions of the Canada-United States security community.[14] This is hardly to suggest that prior to the post-Cold War fascination with Kantian zones of peace there was little discussion of the happy state of affairs in North America; it is simply to suggest that there was no reason for deeply theorizing how and why the North American neighbors had become so peacefully disposed toward each other. It was as if the irenic quality of their relations needed no explanation at all, so strongly was it assumed that it represented the behavioral norm in a special part of the planet—a norm, it could almost be thought, that somehow resided in the geopolitical DNA of exceptional people living on an exceptional continent.[15]

Thus it was that exponents of the "North American Idea" during the early decades of the twentieth century could chalk up the regional peace to sheer good neighborliness of both Canadians and Americans. No one expressed the thought better than Canada's leading foreign-policy intellectual during the interwar period, Oscar Douglas Skelton, who abandoned an academic career at Queen's University to become the principal foreign-affairs advisor to Canadian prime ministers, and especially to the long-serving William Lyon Mackenzie King. Was Canada, because of its historic ties to Britain, primarily a "European" land, wondered Skelton, or should it more properly be construed as a "North American" one? During the early decades of the twentieth century, this question packed a powerful normative and epistemological punch in Canada, and not for nothing did one of the country's leading historians reflect, as recently as the mid-1990s, that "there was a time, not so many years ago, when to speak of Canada as a North American nation was viewed, at least in some quarters, as heresy."[16]

As far as Skelton was concerned, Canada unquestionably *was* a North American country.[17] As early as the mid-1920s, during the debate over whether Canada should assume any obligations in connection with Britain's signing of the Locarno treaties intended to guarantee key interstate borders in Europe—treaties raising in his mind the possibility of Canada's being sucked into another war on that continent—Skelton ventured to ask, "Do we owe anything to Europe?" He did not just mean continental Europe, either, for his views on Canada's obligations to Great Britain and imperial defense were marked by a conviction that the time was long past when Canada needed to stake out a posture of greater independence from what had only recently ceased to be regularly referred to as the British Empire, and had begun to be called the British Commonwealth. Such a nationalist stance might have carried risks in an earlier period, but security matters had evolved so dramatically on the North American continent that Skelton could answer, with confidence, his own question:

> Canada lies side by side for three thousand miles with a neighbour fifteen times as powerful . . . She knows that not a country on the Continent of Europe would lift its little finger to help if the United States were to attack her. Her security lies in her own reasonableness, the decency of her neighbour, and the steady development of friendly intercourse, common standards of conduct, and common points of view. Why not let Europe do likewise? [18]

Skelton could not have applied the social science term "security community" to his assessment of Canada's regional security position, as that expression was still many years away from being coined. But if he lacked its label, he appreciated well enough the contents of the security package whose virtues he extolled. It would take another few decades for Karl Deutsch and his team of research collaborators to provide the label, when during the late 1950s they presented a compelling case for thinking that the increase in societal transactions across international boundaries in what we today know of as the West might hold the key to the fostering of political integration, and with that of attaining lasting peace even in an international system that continued to feature numerous sovereign states (i.e., in an international systemic structure characterized by "anarchy" properly considered). [19]

Deutsch and his colleagues distinguished between two kinds of security communities: "amalgamated" ones, where there was an effective central government to maintain the peace between constituent units (e.g., the United States, *or* Canada); and "pluralistic" ones that were made up of discrete sovereign states, but that nevertheless lacked the normal behavioral traits of separate political entities cohabiting in the "international anarchy," most significant of which being their propensity to warfare. Although both kinds of security communities are important, the analysis in this book is mostly concerned with the second kind, pluralistic security communities. Among these latter, Canada *and* the United States (the conjunction here is critical) figure centrally in the scholarly debate about security communities.

And what exactly *are* such communities? They are security dispensations, or arrangements, in which the use of force by one member of the community against another member for purposes of settling intragroup disputes has simply become inconceivable; they neither go to war against one another nor even *consider* doing so. Instead, whatever problems that inevitably arise between them, they undertake to resolve peacefully. With neither organized armed conflict nor the *threat* of such conflict playing a part in the resolution of intragroup problems, policy makers and other policy elites are able to entertain "dependable expectations" that peaceful change will be the only kind of change that occurs. [20]

If one takes them seriously, if it can be accepted that these entities not only exist but also are durable, then their spread holds out the promise of resolving the problem of war in international relations—not just in certain fortunate regions such as North America, but in the wider world beyond. They become, in short, the contemporary institutional manifestation of the long-standing aspiration toward perpetual peace. He was not the first thinker to dream of lasting peace, but Immanuel Kant certainly did provide a memorable label for the mechanism by which such peace was to be obtained, which is one of the reasons for considering him such a pioneer among security-community theorists. Kant imagined the rise of a *foedus pacificum* ("pacific federation"), by which he did *not* imply a world government. Far from it, he had in mind a community of sovereign states each of which would be constrained by domestic institutions from resorting to violence against its fellows. [21]

Often, theorists used to imagine (some still do) that international peace could never break out unless something were done about the problem of international anarchy—meaning the territorial division of the planet into sovereign political entities. [22] Kant himself never believed that world government was the solution to world conflict; his remedy rested upon changes in the ideological structure of sovereign government, not in its elimination, and in particular the substitution of apparently war-prone monarchical rule by "republicanism," a concept that would subsequently become conflated with liberalism. [23] For some time now, thinkers have seized upon the ideological dimension to establish a link between liberal democracy and peace, but rather than emphasize as Kant had done the institutional constraints imposed by the people upon a ruler's ability to take them to war, they have stressed instead the ability of liberal-democratic norms to keep war at bay, as these norms become "externalized" via (or so it is said) an "inter-subjective" process of "collective-identity" formation, which leads opinion shapers in cognate societies to imagine that the resolution of conflict can only take place *between* liberal democracies in the same manner as it occurs *within* them (i.e., without any of the disputants resorting to force or the threat thereof).

This is why the "(North) Americanization of Immanuel" is slightly misleading, for though the suggestion conveyed by the rubric may certainly direct our thoughts to visions of perpetual peace, the mechanisms by which those who, like Stéphane Roussel, envision warfare has been made to disappear from the northern half of North America owe much more to the norms and values than they do to the institutional constraints Kant perceived, and emphasized, in "republican" forms of government. Thus emphasis is placed upon an aspect of collective identity predicated largely if not exclusively on the shared *political* practices of two countries that, because of the fundamental isomorphism of their liberal-democratic systems, generate reliable expectations that problems between them will always be resolved precisely as problems within each get resolved: peacefully, if sometimes noisily so. As Roussel explains,

> the chief characteristic of the North American international order de- rives not from something unique to the Canadian-American relation- ship, but rather from a quality equally on display in Western Europe in the postwar era, something broadly known as an international "liberal order." The particular North American aspect of this order has often been overlooked because, unlike various European international sys- tems created after major conflicts, its elements are defined more by practices than by formal enunciations. . . . This order has, however, well and truly existed; it is apparent in the patterns of cooperation between the two states and comes most into focus when these patterns are viewed through the prism of their shared liberal values.[24]

There can be no question but that both North American polities are well-established liberal democracies, and have been for some time. Nor does anyone dispute that they constitute a pluralistic security commu- nity. This being said, there are some alternative explanations for why they can be regarded as constituting such a community. These explana- tions fall into three major categories. The first, let us call it the "structural- ist" category, holds that there really is nothing surprising about the North American peace, and thus nothing requiring explanation, at least not in any sophisticated theoretical fashion. Neither the United States nor Canada senses in the other the kind of "threat" that would lead to the contemplation or use of force. Realistically, this is due to the vast dispar- ities in the two countries' relative capability (or, "power"). As such, the structuralist category primarily boils down to an assessment of U.S. threat perception and intent, for while one might hypothesize that Cana- da could perceive a threat to its physical security emanating from the United States, it is hardly likely that any sentient Canadian policy maker would imagine that the country possessed some military means of rebuff- ing such a threat, in which case pondering a forceful defense of the coun- try against an America that had turned hostile to it would be the equiva- lent of pondering a life without taxes or old age—in short, an exercise in utopianism. In the case of the United States, so long as no one in a posi- tion of authority in Washington could see the need to contemplate using force against Canada to resolve a dispute with it, then it would be point-less to threaten and to plan for such an eventuality. Why waste precious bureaucratic resources worrying about something that will never come to pass?

A second explanation, more often encountered explicitly than the above-discussed structuralist version of the North American peace (which is typically bruited sotto voce if at all), focuses on the sorts of transactions that so captured the attention of Deutsch and his colleagues. Here, the nub of the argument is that interdependence renders not just illogical but effectively impossible any drastic deterioration in relations between the two countries, because any clash of arms on their part would be counterproductive, and even if it hurt one side (Canada) more than the other, it would still impose significant hardship on the stronger country, the United States. Thus with both countries having so much to lose, and so little to be gained that could not better be obtained through peaceful intercourse, "transactionalists" have no difficulty accounting for the North American zone of peace.[25] It simply makes such good sense that any alternative to it can readily be dismissed as irrational.

A third explanation uses the same emphasis upon norms and values favored by the democratic peace theorists to arrive at the same end point, of peaceful relations. What differs in respect of this camp's emphasis upon values is that instead of their making liberal democracy and all its accoutrements the pillar of the security community, they emphasize oth-er bases of the collective identity they hold to be a characteristic of the two North American societies. Rather than seeing in the externalization of liberal-democratic norms and practices the seedbed of peaceable rela-tions between the two countries, they argue that different elements of commonality—cultural ones inhering in a common language and civil-izational heritage—supply the shared identity that keeps the peace. We might, with some trepidation, label this third explanatory category the "Anglosphere" variant,[26] and while it possesses some obvious flaws (not the least being Canada's "French fact"), it at least suggests a necessary, even if not sufficient, condition for the flowering of the North American community in the first place, namely the rapprochement between the two great English-speaking countries, the United Kingdom and the United States. I return to this extremely important consideration in a subsequent section of this chapter, but we need to tarry just a bit longer upon the "(North)-Americanization-of-Immanuel" theme, in a bid to probe more closely the contention that it was, first and foremost, their liberal-demo-cratic *political* values that ushered in the two countries' pluralistic secur-ity community.

If that in fact were the case, and if we could presume that liberal democracy in North America had become reasonably solidified during the second half of the 1860s, for reasons related both to the ending of the American Civil War in 1865 and the formation of the modern Canadian federation two years subsequently, then it would follow that their secur-ity community, mutatis mutandis, should have become established rea-sonably soon after, possibly even simultaneously with, the founding of the Canadian state. Thus the puzzle of timing, which I try to unravel in the next section of this chapter, should be easily resoluble: the North American security community should have taken shape in the second half of the nineteenth century, and because of this it could equally be considered to have marked the first such appearance of a pluralistic se-curity community anywhere in the modern era. To so assess chronology, however, is fundamentally wrong, not least because it overlooks entirely the important part that ethnicity, and in particular ethnic diasporas, would come to play in the origins and the evolution of security coopera-tion in North America. As we will discover later, diaspora-rooted politi-cal activism was an important factor, among other factors, delaying the establishment of the continental security community, such that even though both North American countries might have been characterized, after 1867, as liberal democracies, it would still take some decades for the security community to form.

So let us therefore turn to this intriguing issue of timing. In the follow-ing two sections of this chapter, we are going to discover not only why it is so inaccurate to date the onset of the North American "long peace" from the early years of the nineteenth century (with the Treaty of Ghent in 1814, ending the War of 1812), but also why it is no less inaccurate to imagine that the North American security community took shape in that century's second half. Not until the twentieth century would there arise a security community in North America; of this there can be little dispute. More important are two other questions. When in the twentieth century did it appear? And how would we know that it had "arrived"?

THE VEXING QUESTION OF CHRONOLOGY

To determine when the North American security community might be said to have become established is not an easy matter, for it requires us to be able more or less to pinpoint that moment after which it could be authoritatively assumed that "dependable expectations of peaceful change" were henceforth going to be the only assumptions worth enter-taining in matters appertaining to continental security. Firstly, we would need to know whose dependable expectations were most important—the public's? The policy makers'? Both? We would also want to have some means of assessing the quality of those expectations. Should we rely on positive attestations regarding the need for peace, as revealed, say, by survey data, or the musings of editorialists, preachers, and political lead-ers? Or would it be preferable to infer from the *absence* of evidence of harmful intent the likelihood of peaceful change having established itself as the only kind of change that could henceforth be anticipated? And if the latter, what would constitute the best "evidence" of such absence of intent? These matters are as vexing as they are important, and perhaps the best way to resolve their inherent ambiguities would be to come at things from a pragmatic, empirical angle, and simply ask this question: When was the first time that the two countries ever felt so sanguine about the future of bilateral relations that they were willing to abandon any further military planning for potential warfare against each other? For sure, this is hardly the only pragmatic test one might apply, but it would seem to be the most definitive one, given what we think we know about the constant propensity of states to track, assess, and plan to respond to "threats," no matter whence they arise. Moreover, we can also know with some confidence the date(s) by which such war planning had become a thing of the past. Accordingly, this will be the test I apply in seeking to establish the moment of the security community's establishment. That moment happens to be closer to our own time than is customarily thought.

Alternatively, one could of course simply let theory determine the chronology. If, for instance, the most important assertion of democratic peace theory is that war between liberal democracies is an effective impossibility—the closest thing we have to an "empirical law" in international relations, to cite an oft-repeated observation of one scholar[27]—then it would seem to follow that once liberal democracy has become sufficiently entrenched in both (or all) members of the community, violence or threats of same could be decreed, axiomatically, to have become a thing of the past. Thus we would establish the origins of the security community concurrently with the solidification of the members' liberal-democratic norms and practices, assuming that we could detect when such solidification took place.

There are two problems with this hypothetico-deductive approach, however. The first and most important of these, at least insofar as the argument in this book is concerned, is that sometimes it has been the very workings of liberal democracy that so contributed to the fostering of neighborly ill will, rather than to the inculcation of the kind of "we-feeling" in North America held to be generative of lasting peace. As noted in this book's introduction, the phenomenon of ethnic politicking has at times taken on a particular kind of influence-seeking behavior known as "lobbying," an activity that is so much a part of America's *liberal-democratic* political heritage as to have earned for itself, not entirely facetiously, the sobriquet of the "fourth branch" of American government—the other three branches being the executive, legislative, and judiciary. Lobbying is embedded in America's very constitution, the first amendment to which guarantees citizens the right to petition government, which must mean that it also invites them to attempt to influence legislation, including legislation touching upon matters of security and defense.[28] So if liberal democracy, often said to be synonymous with "liberal pluralism" in the American context, presupposes the necessity (or at least the unavoidable presence) of lobbying, it must follow that pressure groups whose primary motivation includes the advancement of self-proclaimed "ethnic" interests can, and sometimes do, pose as complicating elements in the shaping of the American "national" interest, with what have been, at times, non-negligible implications for the North American security dispensation. In chapter three, I return to this very important aspect of American liberal democracy, which will feature so powerfully in the first two of our case studies.

The second reason why it is misleading to allow theoretical deductions to serve as a proxy in the attempt to date the onset of the Canada-United States security community can be glimpsed in an early twentieth-century controversy that flared up between the two countries—a controversy moreover that certainly did feature a "key" policy maker (in the event, the president of the United States) threatening to employ force against Canada as a means of resolving a bilateral territorial dispute in a manner comporting with his own reading of the legal principles and stakes involved. That controversy, over the shape of the Alaskan "Panhandle," might not, at first glance, appear to have much to do either with democratic peace theory or the origins of the North American security community, but the facts argue otherwise.

Obviously, not all IR scholars subscribe to democratic peace theory (DPT).[29] Neither, in fairness, do all of DPT's adherents claim that there has *never* been a war between liberal democracies, much less do they deny that sometimes threats to employ force in conflict resolution have been issued by one liberal democracy against another. There is more than a little wisdom in Michael Doyle's observation that the theory's critics do have a point: "If the liberal [DPT] thesis is anything like normal social science, we will discover exceptions—interliberal wars or interliberal crises—with some of the latter resolved by (from the liberal view) luck rather than by principled respect, institutional restraint, and commercial interest."[30] Depending on how one chooses to brand (or, in IR jargon, to "code") certain wars and crises, it is even possible to argue that dustups between liberal democracies have been so frequent as to constitute not the exceptions that make the rule, but rather the observable regularities that disconfirm it.

In introducing the Alaska dispute here, my purpose is not to weigh in on these larger claims about the tenability of DPT, a theory that I personally hold to be reasonably plausible, if not completely watertight. Rather, I bring in Alaska as a means of helping us to date the onset of the North American security community. I also suggest an interesting irony about Alaska, to wit, that in this case liberal-democratic norms and values, rather than inhibiting violent conflict resolution, might actually have had the perverse effect of making such conflict resolution more rather than less likely.

There is a basal normative asymmetry in the way in which this long-ago controversy gets imagined in the two North American countries. Americans, if they recall it at all, interpret it within the larger context of the Anglo-American "rapprochement," a tale that had the happy ending I will discuss below, in this chapter's next section. But for Canadians, the episode has a different meaning, one whose dénouement conveyed a much more sinister message derived from realpolitik. They interpret the manner in which the Alaskan boundary was settled in 1903 as nothing less than a craven betrayal by Great Britain of a loyal Canada that perforce, even as recently as the start of the twentieth century, always slept with one eye open, in fear that its aggressive neighbor to the south might, when the moment became ripe, pounce upon it.[31] Canadians, then and now, have subscribed to the view that the United States "shafted" them on the Panhandle issue, and that—even worse—the British were complicit in the crime, effectively "sacrificing" Canadian interests and territory to the cause of closer Anglo-American understanding. In Canadian political mythology, which habitually casts the country in the role of survivor (if not of victim), Alaska provides that most poignant of moments, the time when noble little Canada was done in by *two* bullies.

There is another way to conceptualize things. In IR terminology, as opposed to national mythologizing, the controversy is sometimes less emotionally contextualized as representing just another instance of an age-old dilemma within alliances, whereby the smaller state (in our case, Canada) fears being abandoned by its larger protector (Britain), because that protector worries about becoming entrapped in a war as a result of its obligation to safeguard its ally. Nearly four decades ago, one British analyst explicitly likened what had occurred in respect of Alaska to the troubles then afflicting NATO, as a result of differences over the wisdom of détente with the Soviet Union: "In the hostage country, Canada, there was a running debate—about the credibility of its guarantor, about whether its own interests might be sacrificed in the process of détente that followed the Civil War—analogous in many ways to what we have witnessed in Western Europe in the 1970s."[32]

This analogy may be telling in respect of a structural dilemma inherent in alliances, but it is silent on the merits of this particular dispute, as well as on the perceptions and personalities of the key actors in the drama. On the American side, by far the most important personality was the president, Theodore Roosevelt. On the Canadian side, it was likewise the central political figure in the country, Prime Minister Wilfrid Laurier. What Laurier sought was, on the surface, reasonable enough: an adjustment to the contours of the Panhandle in such a way as to benefit Canadian economic interests. It seemed to make sense, since everyone who knew anything about the boundary in the far northwest of the continent understood that the *exact* line separating Alaska from British Columbia remained a matter of some indeterminacy. And while such territorial ambiguity had been not particularly controversial throughout most of the nineteenth century, things changed dramatically and quickly, subsequent to the August 1896 discovery of gold by the prospector George Washington Carmack on Bonanza Creek, in southwest Yukon's Klondike region.

What Canada wanted was direct access from the Klondike gold fields to the Pacific Ocean. This meant obtaining from the United States some portion of the territory that had come into the latter's possession when it purchased Alaska from Russia in 1867, specifically the northern Panhandle settlements of Dyea, Skagway, and Pyramid Harbor, all at the head of the Lynn Canal. If Canada could accomplish this, it would provide the desired outlet to saltwater. Roosevelt's stance on Alaska is represented by Canadians as having been unreasonable, with a basis in neither international law nor geopolitical need, but rather being impelled by nationalist ideology. In fact, however, the opposite is far closer to the truth, for it was Roosevelt rather than his Canadian counterpart, Laurier, who was operating with the backing of international law. Moreover, and here is the irony, it was Laurier, far more than Roosevelt, whose behavior might be said to have been inspired by ideological commitment—in his case, to the idea that among liberal democracies who find themselves in dispute, all issues can be resolved via peaceful compromise. For Laurier acted as if he truly did believe that force or even the threat to use force had simply become foreclosed as an option available to the United States, something that had been rendered inconceivable, precisely by dint of the two countries' liberal-democratic orders.

How unwise Laurier turned out to be, in drinking the Kool-Aid of DPT. The problem is that Roosevelt saw things in a radically different way, America's liberal democracy to the contrary notwithstanding. What to Ottawa looked to be a fairly trivial, and eminently rational, request being made of a fellow liberal democracy appeared to be anything *but* to the president. Roosevelt understood there to be a large legal principle at stake, and as he put it in a July 1903 letter to the chief justice of the U.S. Supreme Court, Oliver Wendell Holmes, the "claim of the Canadians for access to deep water along any part of the Canadian coast is just exactly as indefensible as if they should now suddenly claim the island of Nantucket." The previous year, he had been even more graphic, complaining to his secretary of state, John Hay, about the Canadians' having submitted a "wholly false claim . . . in a spirit of bumptious truculence." Roosevelt added that "if trouble comes it will be purely because of their own fault; and although it would not be pleasant for us it would be death for them."[33]

It may be true that particular contours of the boundary line were open to dispute, but from Roosevelt's point of view, the overriding principle that so inspired him concerned what he took to be America's legal right to an *unbroken littoral* running from Alaska proper down to the southern tip of the Panhandle. And in this position, he happened to have had rather firm support from international law. For the principle of the uninterrupted littoral had been established and recognized back in 1825, when the British and the Russians drew the line separating their territorial holdings in northwest North America. And it was this territorial settlement that governed the purchase by the United States from Russia in 1867; no one disputed it at the time (though there always was some uncertainty about the exact limits of the boundary landward, as well as in the *Portland* Canal, at the Panhandle's southern tip). Until the gold rush, the unbroken littoral was not a bone of contention.[34] Notwithstanding the established legal status of this principle, Laurier—some say because he was fuelled by his ideological (liberal) conviction that liberal democracies invariably seek and find compromise solutions to diplomatic problems—expected not only that the United States would abandon the unbroken littoral but that the UK, which had been *one of the designers* of the unbroken littoral scheme in the first place, would provide the necessary support to "entice" the Americans into making the compromise Laurier was banking on, and thought Canada deserved.

On both counts, Laurier was to be disappointed. The conclusion of the dispute would contribute greatly to a sharp—albeit temporary—deterioration in Canadian relations not only with the Americans, but with the British as well. Although Roosevelt made it plain to all and sundry that if he had to, he would deploy troops to Alaska to defend America's territorial holdings, he much preferred to find a diplomatic solution. This came in the form of an international commission established to end the dispute, not by arbitration (as some wrongly believed at that time), but instead by negotiations designed to provide a diplomatic climb-down for Canada, with British (and tacit American) support. This is not how the affair was perceived in Canada, though. In Canada, the perception was of an American president clearly intent upon playing the part of scofflaw by making a public mockery of the very process that Canadians regarded as essential to resolving the dispute. There was, on this point of style more so than on that of substance, merit in the Canadian view, for although the six commissioners chosen to "resolve" [sic] the dispute (three from the United States, three from Canada/Britain) were supposed to be "impartial jurists of repute," few of them could fit such a description.

In the case of the American delegation, the gap separating personalities from impartiality was particularly glaring, with two members, ex-senator George Turner of Washington State and Senator Henry Cabot Lodge of Massachusetts, being well known for their hostility either to Canada (Turner) or to Britain (Lodge); both had publicly declared themselves opposed to any compromise even before the talks had begun. The third American member, Secretary of War Elihu Root, was, comparatively, a model of impartiality—and when the only such model from one side happens to be a secretary of *war*, it speaks volumes about the meaning of impartiality.

Nor were matters all that different on the other side. Canada placed two members on the commission who were just as parti pris as the two American senators. They were Sir Louis-Amable Jetté, lieutenant governor of Québec, and a legal expert from Ontario, Allen Bristol Aylesworth, soon to become a Laurier cabinet minister. Each was as committed to the Canadian claim as the Americans were to theirs. The third member of the British/Canadian team, and in retrospect the only one on either side who could possibly be said to have been impartial, was Richard E. Webster, or as he is more well-remembered, Lord Alverstone, the chief justice of England. Alverstone sided with the American contention about the inviolability of the unbroken littoral, but was nevertheless instrumental in Canada's obtaining a favorable adjustment of the border elsewhere in the Panhandle.

This latter has hardly been noticed by Canadians, who at the time and ever since have been convinced Alverstone acted as Judas Iscariot, selling out Canada not for financial but for geopolitical gain, namely the desire to facilitate Britain's rapprochement with the United States. Sometimes Alverstone appears, in the Canadian historical consciousness, to be even more of a cad than Roosevelt. In reality, neither man could objectively be said to have acted in a villainous manner; nor were their stances profoundly detrimental to Canada's interests, unless those interests be construed in such a manner as to equate the frustration of Canadian desire with the flouting of morality and common sense.

In the case of Roosevelt, what hardly anyone in Canada recalls about his administration is that *for the first time in American history* a chief executive would voluntarily preside over his country's territorial shrinkage. Despite having the reputation of a committed imperialist and rabid expansionist, Theodore Roosevelt in early 1909 turned over to his successor, William Howard Taft, an America that was actually smaller than the one he had inherited in September 1901, upon assuming the presidency following the assassination of William McKinley. This was entirely due to his conceding to Canada territory in Alaska that had previously been held by the United States. In Alaska, Roosevelt abandoned a claim to territory larger than the state of Rhode Island, or more than 600 square miles; the territorial cession consisted in two islands in the Portland Canal (Wales and Pearse), plus a bit of the landward fringe of the Panhandle itself. This cession exceeded the square mileage added through the acquisition of the Panama Canal Zone, also during his administration.[35]

But so durable has the sacrifice myth proved, that when the Roosevelt years were over, to be followed by a "slate-cleaning"[36] era associated with the presidency of the likeable Taft, Canadians breathed a sigh of collective relief. Yet even though it cannot be denied that, following the Alaska unpleasantness, Canada-United States relations took a profound turn for the better, it still does not mean that the North American security community had become established, if the best token of its founding is to be, as adumbrated above, the abandonment of war plans. Still, what can be said with some certainty is that by the beginning of the twentieth century, a necessary condition for the establishment of a regional security community in North America looked to have been in place. This condition was the "great rapprochement" between the two large English-speaking powers, the UK and the United States. For so long as it could appear to be possible that the two countries might resolve their differences through forceful means, or even threats thereof, then it would have been extremely difficult for anyone to imagine that as between Canada and the United States dependable expectations of peaceful change had become the norm.

THE "PRIME FACET" OF ANGLO-AMERICAN RAPPROCHEMENT

From the above discussion of the Alaska controversy, it is obvious that even as late as 1903 it would still not have been possible for policy elites in either the United States or Canada to rule out definitively the use of force in conflict resolution—not with the most important North American "policy elite" of them all, America's twenty-sixth president, making it known that he was prepared to rely on the American army to enforce his country's understanding of the boundary regime against the Canadian claim. And though it is certainly the case that the slate-cleaning era ushered in a period of greatly improved bilateral relations, the moment had yet to arrive when either country could feel sufficiently sanguine about regional peace to discontinue further war planning against the other.

Still, that moment was fast approaching, and it had been provided an undeniable fillip by a major development in great-power relations that occurred during the last decade of the nineteenth century: the historic transformation in the quality of bilateral diplomacy between the two English-speaking powers, the United States and the UK. Given the tight and continuing constitutional linkages between the latter and Canada—the foreign policy content of which would only alter substantially starting in the second half of the 1920s, by which time Canada's sovereign status was becoming more and more demanded and conceded—peace between Canada and the United States was necessarily dependent upon the quality of relations between the latter and the UK. So long as the possibility of conflict existed between the two most powerful states in what would soon be dubbed the "North Atlantic triangle,"[37] and until such time as Canada could be deemed fully independent rather than a constitutional appendage of the UK, then it followed that forceful means of conflict resolution between the North American neighbors were going to remain imaginable, at least insofar as concerned sentient policy makers in either land, even if not their respective publics.

The radical improvement in the quality of relations between the large English-speaking powers may not have been a sufficient cause of the "outbreak" of regional peace in North America, for if it had been, the Alaska controversy would never have taken the path it did. But that improvement can certainly be regarded as a necessary step on the road to North America's security community. Let us take a closer look at this historic development, which fully warrants the appellation given it by Bradford Perkins: the "great rapprochement."[38] To grasp the significance of this strategic revolution, it is essential to recall just how troubled relations had been between America and its former mother country, and for how long. The lengthy period spanning the American Revolution and the beginning of the twentieth century had been characterized at the extreme by warfare and the threat of warfare, and more generally simply by recurrent diplomatic wrangling and ennui; in other words, it was an extended string of years in which the Anglo-American relationship, rather than auguring the much-vaunted "special relationship" it would become during the twentieth century, looked like nothing so much as another dreary replication of age-old power balancing in the international anarchy.[39]

Exactly *what* set in motion this new era of policy comity and when precisely it took root remain topics of contention. For instance, some scholars argue the great transformation in Anglo-American diplomacy, from a state of (potential) war to a zone of stable peace, occurred in 1895, in the midst of the most acrimonious dispute the two countries had known since the ending of the American Civil War three decades previously.[40] Others date the transformation to the "hinge year" of 1898.[41] And one reading of Bradford Perkins would have him identifying the turning point in the relationship as 1896, because of the defeat in that year's presidential election of the Democrat William Jennings Bryan, a "silverite" who appealed to the Anglophobic sentimentality so widespread among the country's populists, to whom nothing came so easily as to blame a scheming England for seeking to keep innocent Americans impaled on a "cross of gold" erected by devilish London bankers. Thus, says Perkins, that 1896 election, "so important in American political history, was also important for diplomacy and even for relations with England. It ushered in sixteen years during which British governments, thankful of their narrow escape, did their best to eliminate tension between the two countries."[42]

Perkins, however, is an anomaly in this matter of chronology. Usually, it is only the two other years, 1895 and 1898, which compete for the claim to have ushered in the rapprochement. The selection of 1895 bespeaks a view that the most important development in Anglo-American relations during this entire period occurred with the short-lived threat of war between the two countries over what, on the surface, looked to be a most unlikely bone of contention: a boundary dispute between Venezuela and Britain involving the latter's territorial possession, British Guiana. For a brief but intense moment in December 1895, war between the English-speaking countries loomed as a probability if not a certainty, largely due to Washington's anger at what it took to be Britain's disrespect for the Monroe Doctrine, which America interpreted as giving it the right to intervene in any and all territorial disputes between European powers and Latin American republics.[43] To those choosing 1895 as the starting date for the rapprochement, it took the specter of "fratricidal" war to remind elites in both countries of the need for a saner, and safer, alternative to resolving bilateral disputes than fighting them out. Seen thusly, the Venezuelan crisis turned out to be that rarest of strategic gifts, endowing policy makers on either side of the Atlantic with a precious glimpse into a choice of futures: they could have a catastrophic war, or they could have rapprochement and, who could say, perhaps eventually even alliance or (re)union? It is for this reason that one writer has high-lighted the learning experience provided by this narrow escape as the "prime facet" in the birth of bilateral friendship.[44]

The events of 1895 have captured not only the attention of historians, but also of many IR theorists. Critics of DPT have seized upon the crisis as evidence against the theory's claims regarding the violence-inhibiting features of liberal-democratic norms and practices; to these critics, 1895 serves as a sobering reminder not of liberal democracy's ability to keep war at bay, but rather of the inability even of otherwise similar political entities to inoculate themselves against the vicissitudes of power balancing within an anarchical setting, carrying with it the eternal peril of inter-state warfare. According to them, externalized liberal-democratic norms and values had nothing to do with the two countries' narrow escape from war in 1895. In the words of one such critic, "[t]here is virtually no evidence that supports a democratic peace theory explanation of the Venezuela crisis's outcome."[45] Instead, that outcome is best explained by structural realities, namely, the rise of American power at a time when Britain was growing concerned about an even greater menace to its interests associated with the burgeoning strength, closer to home, of Germany. Thus, it is said, considerations of realism and of relative capability (i.e., power), rather than of liberalism and of normative compatibility, determined the outcome, as Britain had no alternative but to accommodate American interests and power.[46]

Interestingly, some writers seize upon this very matter of British accommodation of a rising America as evidence in favor of DPT, or at least of some other "collective-identity" alternative to the "structural" version of realism, which accords such heavy weight to relative capability as a determinant of state action. Sometimes, structural-realist formulations take the form of "power-transition" theory, about which we are hearing and reading a great deal these days, given the anxiety evinced in so many quarters about the mooted "rise" of China, and especially about whether it can occur without a major war ensuing sometime in the future. Reflecting upon the logic of power-transition theory, one scholar has noted how unexpected the Anglo-American rapprochement really was, after the Venezuela incident. "From the realist standpoint these two countries were natural, almost certain enemies, for they stood at the apex of the international power structure," observes Stephen Rock. America was rising, Britain declining, and therefore the latter state should have sensed and acted upon the challenge presented to it by the former. "Yet this is not what happened. Instead of meeting in battle, Britain and the United States were reconciled, drawn together in part by a common desire to counter other potential adversaries."[47] Not only was there no "hegemonic" clash between the two long-standing competitors in 1895, but something remarkable—nay, unprecedented—transpired: the ranking power accepted the rise of its erstwhile "challenger" to the point of seeking to socialize it via rapprochement into its vision of world order, in the bargain making of it a buttress of its own power. For this reason alone, the 1895 crisis is occasionally held to contain lessons for the twenty-first century, with some writers anticipating that what Britain could manage to arrange with America, the latter might be able to arrange with China.[48]

The other serious contender for the starting point of the rapprochement is 1898, which while not totally lacking resonance with certain realist postulates, nevertheless appeals more to the constructivists, highlighting as it does the emergence of a transatlantic "collective identity" built upon ethnic and even racial presuppositions derivative of "Anglo-Saxonism,"[49] admixed with a dollop of gratitude for services rendered. What made 1898 such a significant year in the ideological quest for Anglo-Saxon harmony if not unification—according to one writer, the "*annus mirabilis* in Anglo-American relations"[50]—was the welcome support shown by British public and elite opinion to the United States at the time of its war with Spain, a war that elsewhere in Europe met with varying degrees of scorn and contempt on the part of both publics and rulers.[51] Not so in Great Britain, however, where alone among the European powers there was widespread approval of American military action against the decaying Spanish empire.[52] This was much appreciated by many Americans, including such figures as the assistant secretary of the navy, Theodore Roosevelt, who just three years earlier had been touting the therapeutic aspects of an American war against Britain![53]

Now the latter country was receiving credit from a grateful America not only for its political support, but also because it was widely (if not accurately) held in the United States that Britain had even made a signal *military* contribution to the American war effort, as a result of Royal Navy captain Edward Chichester's moving his ships between American and German vessels in Manila Bay, thereby preventing, or so it was thought, the latter from impeding the former's preparations for an attack upon the city. Although the Germans were not, in fact, trying to frustrate Admiral Dewey's bombardment of Manila, and Chichester was not interpositioning his vessels, this is not what Americans at the time believed; instead, they recalled, with much appreciation, that Chichester had "saved Dewey from a stab in the back at a critical time. . . . More than any real episode, this imaginary one contributed to the belief that England was the only friend America had during the war with Spain."[54]

When it came time to reciprocate, a short while later during the Boer War, American policy makers demonstrated a similar understanding and support for Britain's predicament, which is why it is incorrect to write, as some continue to do, that "every other great power—France, Germany, the United States—opposed London's actions" in South Africa.[55] To be sure, large non-Anglo ethnic groups in America did tend strongly to oppose British policy—in particular the Irish Americans, about whom we will learn much more in chapter four—but the administration in Washington gave backing to London, as did a sizeable minority of the country's English-descended population, many of whom were beginning to find allure in the Anglo-Saxon racialist vogue (sometimes called "race patriotism") of the century's final years.[56] Exact figures are impossible to come by, but it appears that of the several hundred Americans who went to South Africa to fight in that war, more did so on the British side than on the Boer side, although as one student of this issue has remarked, sometimes the choice was a function of linguistic rather than of *political* solidarity.[57]

With the dramatic improvement in relations between the United States and the UK came thoughts about an impending alliance between the two, a prospect that began to seem as if it were the solution to the problem of war—not simply on the North American continent, but importantly, throughout the entire world, based on the premise that the combined weight of the Anglo-Saxon powers would prevent any successful balancing against them, and thus would suffice to keep the planetary peace. Some analysts descry the contemporary Anglo-American alliance in those events of the turn of the nineteenth century. Charles Kupchan, for instance, writes that the rapprochement of that fin de siècle did not just bring about an historic transformation in the manner in which the two English-speaking powers had been accustomed to relating to each other. Something even more consequential was set in motion, a "strategic partnership that has lasted to this day."[58] Nor is Kupchan alone in detecting an incipient alliance in the years just prior to the turn of the century.

However, it is a chronological fallacy to locate the origins of the U.S. *alliances* with either Britain or Canada in the heady atmosphere of Anglo-American cordiality of the turn of the century. At best—albeit this *was* a very important improvement—one can say that the rapprochement, whatever it suggested for the future of alliances, at least boded very well indeed for the fostering of a security community, especially the one in North America that is our concern here. That continental security community predated the appearance of the North American alliance by a few years, a temporal gap that confirms the need for caution whenever we find ourselves tempted to employ "security community" and "alliance" as synonymous terms, a topic to which I return in the following section of this chapter.

To this point, though, I have been approaching the issue of chronology in a tangential manner. Therefore, let me now directly state *when* I think the Canada-United States security community might be said to have emerged, and how we would know this to have been so. Recall that the measure proposed earlier was a simple empirical one, dependent not upon the two states' doing something, but rather on their *ceasing* to do something. What they ceased doing was to allocate scarce bureaucratic resources to the practice of planning warfare against the other. As noted previously, there do exist other means of trying to establish the onset of a security community, but this one seems to be the most definitive of them all, given the existence of archival sources capable of documenting when, even if not why, the mutual war-planning activities came to an end.

So what do the archives reveal? They tell us that as far as Canada was concerned, the business of plotting warfare against the neighbor to the south actually managed for a few years to outlive not only the slate-cleaning era, but also the First World War, during which Canada and the United States were, after April 1917, de facto allies for a brief period, notwithstanding American insistence upon having entered the global conflict as an "associated power" not an ally. Between 1921 and 1928, Canadian war planning embraced, in a document known as "Defence Scheme No. 1," the possibility that preemptive military strikes might have to be launched against northern U.S. cities, in self-defense.[59] For their part, American war planners continued, even if only in a desultory fashion, to develop the idea that military action against Canada (by dint of its status as a member of the British empire/commonwealth) might remain necessary, in the event of a war pitting the United States against the UK, with the latter possibly in alliance with Japan. These American plans took shape under the rubric of the "color plans" developed in the interwar period, with RED plans drafted for contingencies involving U.S. combat against Britain and the dominions, and RED-ORANGE presupposing an alliance between the British and Japanese empires.[60]

Not until 1937 would American planning horizons shift radically, in a manner comporting with contemporary strategic reality. That was the year when the war and navy departments would officially replace the obsolescent color plans with the new RAINBOW plans directed at Germany, Italy, or Japan, or all three together.[61] We can take, therefore, 1937 as being a definitive marker for the purposes of establishing the chronology of the Canada-United States security community, though common sense might dictate that the beginning of this new security dispensation in North America must have been earlier. By "definitive marker" I mean to suggest the latest moment by which we can date the establishment of the continental security community. Regardless of when, in that first half of the twentieth century, one might choose to set the clock running on the latter, the chronology matters, and takes on comparative significance for the broader story I tell in these pages. Two comparative matters are worth highlighting, insofar as concerns the Canada-United States zone of peace: the first is a temporal one, and the second a much more important qualitative assessment regarding the robustness of the North American zone of peace. Let us now find out why.

THE NORTH AMERICAN SECURITY COMMUNITY IN COMPARATIVE CONTEXT

In respect of the temporal issue, it is sometimes remarked that Canada and the United States managed to achieve the first pluralistic security community in modern times. They were subsequently to find company, when Western Europeans at last learned how to live together in peace (if not harmony). Even though one might dispute the exact timing and cause(s) of the transformation in European security, it is widely conceded that a European security community did emerge after the Second World War.[62] This reading of sequencing would suggest that prior to that global conflagration, there had been only one modern security community, and it was located in North America. Such an assumption, of course, was the central thrust of that intellectual conceit we encountered earlier, the "North American Idea" predicated upon a sharp distinction between the pacific New World and the bellicose Old.

However, the reality turns out to be a bit different. A good case can actually be made that the modern international system's first pluralistic security community arose not in North America at all, but in *Europe*, of all places—specifically in Scandinavia subsequent to the 1905 breakup of the monarchical union between Sweden and Norway, as a result of the latter's desire for full sovereignty from the country with which it had been linked since 1814. And while rumors of war circulated widely in the immediate wake of this breakup, the two neighbors managed, withal, to draw back from the brink, though they came closer to it than is usually thought, especially by those who have invoked the Scandinavian "analogy" for the purposes of promoting territorial revisions elsewhere, including in Canada.[63] Employing the same means of dating the onset of the security community as we applied to the North American one, that is, the abandonment of war-planning activities, we can determine that the Scandinavians managed by a decade or so to beat the North Americans to the starting line, their zone of peace being now thought to have begun in the middle of the 1920s, by which time planners in Oslo and Stockholm ceased to prepare for conflict pitting the one country against the other.[64]

The second comparative issue concerns the robustness of the Canada-United States security community, as measured against the European one. Here things become a bit more complicated, because the temptation exists to invoke at one and the same time two different security arrangements: security communities and alliances. Perhaps it might be permissible to take some guidance here from Oscar Wilde's witticism regarding temptations—that the best way to get rid of one is to yield to it. Though there is the risk of analytical sloppiness in following Wilde's advice, there just might be some benefit in bringing into the discussion the dispensation known as *alliance* in order to shed some comparative light on our major concern here, security community. This is because it is sometimes argued, by adherents of DPT, that alliance can be taken as a necessary *consequence* of a security community erected as between liberal democracies. This is known as the theory of the "democratic alliance," whose chief proponent has been Thomas Risse. I introduce this theory here because it speaks to the issue of security community robustness, our main concern in this section.

In brief, the term "democratic alliance" does not simply mean an alliance of democratic countries; that would be an uninteresting as well as unnecessary, because redundant, construct. As employed here, the term represents an alliance that can a) take shape independently of the existence of threat, and b) manifest a greater robustness than what we might term "garden-variety" alliances, these latter concocted between states who share no liberal-democratic values but are instead motivated to bond together by fear of a common foe. The theory of the democratic alliance turns on its head the traditional realist conception of alliance formation, which holds that states feeling imperilled by a powerful foe will band together in self-protection, perhaps even discovering in the process that they have, outside of the defense and security realm, some interests and even values in common with their new allies.[65] For Thomas Risse, this is to put the cart before the horse: states first feel a sense of kinship with others of their ilk, then they develop a collective identity that undergirds the sense of community, and, in turn, that "sense of community, by delimiting the boundaries of who belonged to 'us,' also defined 'them' . . . In other words, the collective identity led to the threat perception, not the other way around."[66]

Now, in developing the theory of the democratic alliance, Risse had in mind NATO, rather than the Canada-United States alliance (a separate thing, as I explain below). He clearly saw the former as having its roots in shared liberal-democratic values of three principal Western powers, the United States, the UK, and France. Here is what he tells us about NATO's coming into existence:

> One could . . . argue that the North Atlantic Alliance represents an institutionalization of the security community among democracies. While the perceived Soviet threat certainly strengthened the sense of common purpose among the allies, *it did not create the community in the first place*. NATO was preceded by the wartime alliance of the United States, Great Britain, and France, which also closely collaborated to create various postwar regimes in the economic and security areas.[67]

The trio of countries selected to demonstrate the mooted transit from security community to alliance was not a good one, however, and this for several reasons. Not the least important of these was that there *was* no security community involving the three countries, either during or shortly after the war.[68] Still, the thought arises that perhaps elsewhere in the North Atlantic area one might find a trio of states that provides a better fit between the theory and the reality.

Can it be, mindful of what was argued earlier regarding the "prime facet" of Anglo-American rapprochement, that the North Atlantic triangle members—the United States, the UK, and Canada—were able to develop their respective bilateral alliances as a result of their prior elaboration of a security community? If they did, it would give support to the "strong thesis" of the theory, the variant that holds open the possibility of alliances forming independently of threat. But even if the North Atlantic triangle cannot generate support for the strong thesis, perhaps there might still be merit in asking whether the weaker variant of the theory tells us something about the robustness of security communities—in our case, tells us that the North American security community has been strengthened as a result of the two countries also being military allies? Lest it be thought that to raise this possibility is simply to traffic in truisms, it bears stressing that there are signal differences between these two sorts of security dispensation. Firstly, not all allies can be said to be nested within a security community, for if this were true, then Greece and Turkey (both NATO allies) would long ago have ceased to contemplate having to use force against each other—and the Soviet Union would never have invaded its Warsaw Pact allies Hungary (1956) and Czechoslovakia (1968). Secondly, not all security communities lead to alliances, the best example here being that selfsame pluralistic security community that was the world's first, between Sweden and Norway: the former state is neutral, the latter is a member of NATO. They are friends, but they are not allies.

So what, if anything, can invoking the Canada-United States alliance tell us about the robustness of the Canada-United States security community? For starters, it cannot be argued that so doing will lend support to the strong thesis of the theory of the democratic alliance. If it be accepted that the North American security community emerged with the abandonment of planning for war in North America, then we can date, as argued above, its "arrival" concurrently with the elaboration of RAINBOW. This means that since 1937 there has been a pluralistic security community embracing Canada and the United States. But there would not be any alliance between the two countries for another three years. And when that alliance was made, during a period of global crisis in the summer of 1940, it was very much a function of threat that motivated the two countries to undertake, together, the collective defense of North America.

It is sometimes claimed, to this day, that France and America are each other's "oldest allies." The problem with this is twofold. First, France has had far "older" allies than the United States—Sweden for instance during the Thirty Years' War, to say nothing of the "Auld Alliance" with Scotland, dating to the end of the thirteenth century.[69] Even more important is the second difficulty with the "oldest allies" claim: the alliance's brevity. The collective-defense agreement struck by the United States and France in 1778 had effectively become a dead letter with the ending of hostilities following the American Revolution. Some say the alliance's demise was sealed as early as the Paris peace talks of 1782–1783 when, in Walter McDougall's provocative term, American negotiators "double-crossed" the French and negotiated a separate peace with Britain.[70] Others maintain that it was the French, through their indifference to America's request for assistance in getting the British to vacate their forts south of the Great Lakes, who triggered the unravelling of the pact. In this view, France's unwillingness to help rendered the alliance moribund, even if it would require several more years for it finally to receive its "death blow," coming with the Washington administration's proclamation of neutrality in 1793 and its signing of the Jay Treaty the following year.[71]

One thing is certain: sixteen years after Yorktown, the two erstwhile allies were engaged in an undeclared, if real, naval war against each other. In fact, though still its nominal ally, France became the first country *against* which an independent America ever entered into combat.[72] The 1778 alliance was officially put out of existence with the 1800 Treaty of Mortefontaine, and if there would be brief moments, such as between 1812 and 1814, when they found themselves fighting the same (British) enemy as cobelligerents, they were assuredly not allies.[73] It would not be until 1949 that the two old "friends" would once more become continuous allies, with the Washington treaty and the formation of NATO.

It turns out that America's alliance with Canada is actually its oldest ongoing collective-defense arrangement, though this is often overlooked. Partly, the problem is with the nature of the defense bonding between the two states, an event that took place in stages and lacked being institutionalized through the kind of formal treaty that sometimes is held to be a sine qua non for alliance formation. But of course there is nothing about alliances that requires them to be established through treaties, and as Stephen Walt reminds us, alliances can have an informal existence under international law yet still be every bit as meaningful as, often even more meaningful than, formal pacts: the operative notion is that these security arrangements represent effective instances of reciprocated defense collaboration, no matter how they are brought about.[74] In the case of the Canadian-American alliance, the starting point is generally considered to have been an executive agreement instead of a treaty. This was the "Ogdensburg Agreement," reached by President Franklin D. Roosevelt and Prime Minister Mackenzie King in the upstate New York town of that name, in mid-August 1940.[75] This accord led directly to the creation of the first of what would be a long line of binational defense arrangements, the Permanent Joint Board on Defense (PJBD), which set to work planning a series of measures to enhance continental security.[76]

In time, the PJBD would be supplemented with, and to an important extent even eclipsed by, newer institutional means of strengthening North American defense cooperation, among the most relevant of these being the Military Cooperation Committee (MCC) of 1946, the North American Air (now Aerospace) Defense Command (NORAD) of 1958, and more recently the Binational Planning Group (BPG) of 2002–2006.[77] To these must be added a thick network of other accords, committees, and arrangements pertaining to North American defense, whose numbers are no easy matter to keep count of, but which run into the several hundred.[78] Thus, in a manner distinctly different from most of America's transatlantic relations, the United States and Canada were solidly allied (if not always in total agreement on perceiving and responding to threat) well before the formation of NATO, and would almost certainly still be allied had the latter organization never come into existence.

Quite apart from its status as America's "oldest" (continuous) ally, Canada's alliance ties contribute to the robustness of the continent's security community because of the overlap between "homeland security" and the normative core of the security community. Early in chapter one I made reference to the "Kingston dispensation," which I said was the central normative buttress of the two countries' security relationship. It, too, preceded the elaboration of the Canada-United States alliance, but because of its intimate and inextricable connection with homeland security it is just as much an aspect of the North American collective-defense arrangement as it is of the security community. By its very nature, it makes the Canada-United States alliance empirically more "special" than any of the defense and security linkages either North American country might have with other allies, elsewhere. It does so because it establishes the boundary conditions for Canadian participation in American "homeland security."[79] Significantly, the Kingston dispensation implies a level of reciprocal obligation that exceeds those that define either a security community *or* an alliance; for in the case of the former, the obligation is that one does not make or threaten armed conflict against one's neighbor, while in the case of the latter (if NATO's Article 5 is taken as a guide) the obligation extends to treating armed attack upon an ally as tantamount to an armed attack upon oneself (with the response to same, however, being left to the discretion of the allies—which in reality can mean doing a great deal, or doing nothing at all).[80]

In contrast, there is little that is permissive about the Kingston dispensation. It is an arrangement shot through with expectations, on both sides, that the quality of "good neighborliness" in North America entails an indefeasible, and mutual, obligation whereby each state pays utmost heed to the legitimate security interests of the other within the boundaries of North America. To phrase it colloquially, each is said to "have the other's back." Specifically, the United States is expected *never* to shirk the job of protecting Canada against external aggression, while it is expected *always* to refrain from exploiting its vast power to transgress against Canadian territory; Canada, for its part, is expected to prevent any aggression being mounted from within its borders against American territory.[81] Compared with the kind of security guarantees that the United States routinely offered its allies elsewhere during the Cold War, and continues to offer (some of) them even today, there is nothing "extended" about its "deterrence" of potential aggression against Canada; the latter country forms, due to the inescapable nature of contiguity, part of America's "core" deterrence structure. The same applies, mutatis mutandis, in respect of Canada's own commitment to the United States. This is why, during the past two decades, there has been a recurrence of interest in the question whether developments linked somehow to ethnic diasporas might have a negative impact upon the continental security community.

The second half of this book will focus exclusively on just how diasporas based in either, or both, of the two countries might be said to have been implicated in the rise and evolution of the continental security community. But before we get to the three case studies that constitute the empirical core of this study, there is one more theoretical and policy area to explore, concerning the manner in which tenable connections can be drawn between ethnic diasporas and international security, particularly but not exclusively in North America. This is the topic of chapter three.

NOTES

1. The allusion is most often associated with planetary imagery suggested by Robert Kagan more than a decade ago, save that Kagan was referring not to North America but to Western Europe, which he argued was "entering a post-historical paradise of peace and relative prosperity, the realization of Immanuel Kant's 'perpetual peace'. . . . Americans are from Mars and Europeans are from Venus." Robert Kagan, *Of Paradise and Power: America and Europe in the New World Order* (New York: Vintage Books, 2003), p. 3.

2. On Kant as the founding father of this theory, see Michael Doyle, "Liberalism and World Politics," *American Political Science Review* 80 (December 1986): 1151–69; and Michael Doyle, *Ways of War and Peace: Realism. Liberalism, and Socialism* (New York: W. W. Norton, 1997), pp. 252–58.

3. I am grateful to Tudor Onea for bringing this to my attention.

4. The name is credited to John Herz, *Political Realism and Political Idealism* (Chicago: University of Chicago Press, 1951). Another seminal contribution is Robert Jervis, "Cooperation under the Security Dilemma," *World Politics* 30 (January 1978): 167–214.

5. Scholars still debate when the bipolar ideological and strategic contest between the United States and the USSR actually did end, with popular choices usually being either November 1989, with the breaching of the Berlin Wall, or December 1991, with the disappearance of the Soviet Union. I think the best date is 16 July 1990, when German chancellor Helmut Kohl met with Soviet leader Mikhail Gorbachev in the Caucasus region of Russia, to hammer out an agreement that enabled the soon-to-be unified Germany to remain a member of the North Atlantic Treaty Organization. For that historic meeting, see Konrad H. Jarausch, *The Rush to German Unity* (New York: Oxford University Press, 1994), p. 167.

6. Richard U. Ullman, *Securing Europe* (Princeton, N.J.: Princeton University Press, 1991), p. xi.

7. See, for instance, James E. Goodby, *Europe Undivided: The New Logic of Peace in U.S.-Russian Relations* (Washington, DC: United States Institute of Peace Press, 1998).

8. Kenneth N. Waltz, *Man, the State, and War: A Theoretical Analysis* (New York: Columbia University Press, 1954).

9. See Helga Haftendorn, "Foreign Troops in a Changing Europe and Germany: A Structural View," in *Homeward Bound? Allied Forces in the New Germany*, ed. David G. Haglund and Olaf Mager (Boulder, Colo.: Westview Press, 1992), pp. 19–40.

10. Uwe Nerlich, "Western Europe's Relations with the United States," *Daedalus* 108 (Winter 1979): 87–111.

11. See John J. Mearsheimer, "Back to the Future: Instability in Europe after the Cold War," *International Security* 15 (Summer 1990): 5–56; and Mearsheimer, "Why We Will Soon Miss the Cold War," *Atlantic Monthly*, August 1990, pp. 35–50.

12. Even some prominent realists of a non-structuralist bent shared in the optimism; see for instance Michael Mandelbaum, *The Dawn of Peace in Europe* (New York: Twentieth Century Fund Press, 1996).

13. Titles representative of the rediscovery of Kant include Bruce Russett, ed., *Grasping the Democratic Peace: Principles for a Post-Cold War World* (Princeton, N.J.: Princeton University Press, 1993); James Lee Ray, *Democracy and International Politics: An Evaluation of the Democratic Peace Proposition* (Columbia: University of South Carolina Press, 1995); John Owen, "How Liberalism Produces Democratic Peace," *International Security* 19 (Fall 1994): 87–125; Lars Erik Cederman, "Back to Kant: Reinterpreting the Democratic Peace as a Macrohistorical Learning Process," *American Political Science Review* 95 (March 2001): 15–32; Wade Huntley, "Kant's Third Image: Systemic Sources of the Liberal Peace," *International Studies Quarterly* 40 (March 1996): 45–76; and James Bohman and Matthias Lutz-Bachmann, eds., *Perpetual Peace: Essays on Kant's Cosmopolitan Ideal* (Cambridge, Mass.: MIT Press, 1997).

14. Stéphane Roussel, *The North American Democratic Peace: Absence of War and Security Institution-Building in Canada-US Relations, 1867–1958* (Montreal and Kingston: McGill-Queen's University Press, 2004). For an analysis that extends, both chronologically and thematically, the Roussel thesis, see Caroline Patsias and Dany Deschênes, "Unsociable Sociability: The Paradox of Canadian-American Friendship," *International Politics* 48 (January 2011): 92–111.

15. See, for an exploration of this claim, Donald Barry, "The Politics of 'Exceptionalism': Canada and the United States as a Distinctive International Relationship," *Dalhousie Review* 60 (Spring 1980): 114–37.

16. Ramsay Cook, *Canada, Quebec, and the Uses of Nationalism*, 2nd ed. (Toronto: McClelland and Stewart, 1995), pp. 174–75.

17. See Norman Hillmer, "O. D. Skelton and the North American Mind," *International Journal* 60 (Winter 2004–2005): 93–110.

18. Quoted in Norman Hillmer, "The Anglo-Canadian Neurosis: The Case of O. D. Skelton," in *Britain and Canada: Survey of a Changing Relationship*, ed. Peter Lyon (Lon-

don: Frank Cass, 1976), p. 76. Also see Hillmer, ed., *O. D. Skelton: The Work of the World, 1923–1941* (Montreal and Kingston: McGill-Queen's University Press, 2013).

19. Karl Deutsch et al., *Political Community and the North Atlantic Area* (Princeton, N.J.: Princeton University Press, 1957). By anarchy "properly considered" is emphatically not meant *chaos*, but merely the absence of an overarching institution (viz., a world state, or a globe-spanning empire) aspiring to maintain order.

20. Emanuel Adler and Michael N. Barnett, "Governing Anarchy: A Research Agenda for the Study of Security Communities," *Ethics & International Affairs* 10 (1996): 63–98, quote at p. 73.

21. Immanuel Kant, "Perpetual Peace: A Philosophical Sketch," in *Kant: Political Writings*, ed. Hans Reiss (Cambridge: Cambridge University Press, 1991), pp. 93–130.

22. For an excellent discussion of various visions of sustainable peace, see F. H. Hinsley, *Power and the Pursuit of Peace: Theory and Practice in the History of Relations between States* (Cambridge: Cambridge University Press, 1967).

23. Kenneth Waltz, "Kant, Liberalism, and War," *American Political Science Review* 56 (June 1962): 331–40.

24. Roussel, *North American Democratic Peace*, p. 231.

25. For examples of this means of accounting for the Canada-United States security community, see Joseph S. Nye. Jr., "Transnational Relations and Interstate Conflicts: An Empirical Analysis," in *Canada and the United States: Transnational and Transgovernmental Relations*, ed. Annette Baker Fox, Alfred Hero, and Nye (New York: Columbia University Press, 1976), pp. 367–402; as well as Robert O. Keohane and Nye, *Power and Interdependence: World Politics in Transition* (Boston: Little, Brown, 1977). For a robust critique of this perspective, compare Brian J. Bow, *The Politics of Linkage: Power, Interdependence, and Canada-US Relations* (Vancouver: UBC Press, 2009).

26. For a recent study of this postulated community embracing the United States, the UK, Canada, Australia, and New Zealand, see Srdjan Vucetic, *The Anglosphere: A Genealogy of a Racialized Identity in International Relations* (Stanford, Calif.: Stanford University Press, 2011). On its applicability to Canada, see David G. Haglund, "Relating to the Anglosphere: Canada, 'Culture,' and the Question of Military Intervention," *Journal of Transatlantic Studies* 3 (Autumn 2005): 179–98.

27. See Jack S. Levy, "Domestic Politics and War," in *The Origin and Prevention of Major Wars*, ed. Robert I. Rotberg and Theodore K. Rabb (Cambridge: Cambridge University Press, 1989), pp. 79–100, quote at p. 88.

28. James Deakin, *The Lobbyists* (Washington, DC: Public Affairs Press, 1966), pp. 5–6. Also see Charles McCurdy Mathias Jr., "Ethnic Groups and Foreign Policy," *Foreign Affairs* 59 (Summer 1981): 975–98.

29. Skeptics include Errol A. Henderson, *Democracy and War: The End of an Illusion?* (Boulder, Colo.: Lynne Rienner, 2002); Dan Reiter, "Why NATO Enlargement Does Not Spread Democracy," *International Security* 25 (Spring 2001): 41–67; and Thomas Schwartz and Kiron K. Skinner, "The Myth of the Democratic Peace," *Orbis* 46 (Winter 2002): 159–72. An excellent source for the scholarly dispute over DPT is Michael E. Brown, Sean M. Lynn-Jones, and Steven E. Miller, eds., *Debating the Democratic Peace: An* International Security *Reader* (Cambridge, Mass.: MIT Press, 1997).

30. Michael W. Doyle, "Reflections on the Liberal Peace and Its Critics," in *Debating the Democratic Peace*, p. 361.

31. Though an American himself, one writer's assessment of the controversy neatly sums up the standard Canadian historiography; see Thomas A. Bailey, "Theodore Roosevelt and the Alaskan Boundary Settlement," *Canadian Historical Review* 18 (June 1937): 123–30.

32. Alastair Buchan, "Mothers and Daughters (or Greeks and Romans)," *Foreign Affairs* 54 (July 1976): 645–69, quote at p. 648.

33. Quoted in William N. Tilchin, *Theodore Roosevelt and the British Empire: A Study in Presidential Statecraft* (New York: St. Martin's, 1997), pp. 38, 43. Nantucket lies off the southeastern coast of Massachusetts, of which state it forms a part.

34. The best study of the dispute remains Norman Penlington, *The Alaska Boundary Dispute: A Critical Reappraisal* (Toronto: McGraw-Hill Ryerson, 1972). Also see Tony McCulloch, "Theodore Roosevelt and Canada: Alaska, the 'Big Stick' and the North Atlantic Triangle, 1901–1909," in *A Companion to Theodore Roosevelt*, ed. Serge Ricard (Chichester, UK: Wiley-Blackwell, 2011), pp. 293–313.

35. See Frederick W. Marks III, *Velvet on Iron: The Diplomacy of Theodore Roosevelt* (Lincoln: University of Nebraska Press, 1979), p. 34.

36. For this imagery, see J. L. Granatstein and Norman Hillmer, *For Better or for Worse: Canada and the United States to the 1990s* (Toronto: Copp Clark Pitman, 1991), pp. 35–36.

37. For the introduction of this metaphor into scholarly analyses of transatlantic security relations, see John Bartlet Brebner, *North Atlantic Triangle: The Interplay of Canada, the United States and Great Britain* (Toronto: McClelland & Stewart, 1966; orig. pub. 1945).

38. Bradford Perkins, *The Great Rapprochement: England and the United States, 1895–1914* (New York: Atheneum, 1968).

39. On the history of this transatlantic relationship, see Kathleen Burk, *Old World, New World: Great Britain and America from the Beginning* (New York: Grove Press, 2009); Kenneth Bourne, *Britain and the Balance of Power in North America, 1815–1908* (Berkeley: University of California Press, 1967); Harry Cranbrook Allen, *The Anglo-American Relationship since 1783* (London: Black, 1959); Charles S. Campbell Jr., *From Revolution to Rapprochement: The United States and Great Britain, 1783–1900* (New York: John Wiley and Sons, 1974); and Robert Balmain Mowat, *The Diplomatic Relations of Great Britain and the United States* (London: E. Arnold, 1925).

40. As well as Amanda Foreman, *A World on Fire: Britain's Crucial Role in the American Civil War* (New York: Random House, 2010), see Howard Jones, *Union in Peril: The Crisis over British Intervention in the Civil War* (Chapel Hill: University of North Carolina Press, 1992); and Ephraim Douglass Adams, *Great Britain and the American Civil War*, 2 vols. (London: Longman, 1925).

41. So labeled by Christopher Hitchens, *Blood, Class, and Empire: The Enduring Anglo-American Relationship* (New York: Nation Books, 2004), p. 166.

42. Perkins, *Great Rapprochement*, pp. 25–26.

43. Jennie A. Sloan, "Anglo-American Relations and the Venezuelan Boundary Dispute," *Hispanic American Historical Review* 4 (November 1938): 486–506; and Walter LaFeber, "The Background of Cleveland's Venezuelan Policy: A Reinterpretation," *American Historical Review* 66 (July 1961): 947–67.

44. Marshall Bertram, *The Birth of Anglo-American Friendship: The Prime Facet of the Venezuelan Boundary Dispute—A Study of the Interrelation of Diplomacy and Public Opinion* (Lanham, Md.: University Press of America, 1992).

45. Christopher Layne, "Kant or Cant: The Myth of the Democratic Peace," in *Debating the Democratic Peace*, pp. 157–201, quote at p. 178. Sharing this perspective, albeit somewhat less stridently, is William R. Thompson, "Democracy and Peace: Putting the Cart before the Horse?" *International Organization* 50 (Winter 1996): 141–74.

46. For a nicely nuanced critique of this full-bore structuralism, see Aaron L. Friedberg, *The Weary Titan: Britain and the Experience of Relative Decline, 1895–1905* (Princeton, N.J.: Princeton University Press, 1988).

47. Stephen R. Rock, *Why Peace Breaks Out: Great Power Rapprochement in Historical Perspective* (Chapel Hill: University of North Carolina Press, 1989), pp. 40–42.

48. See, for such an optimistic application of historical "lessons," Yongping Feng, "The Peaceful Transition of Power from the UK to the US," *Chinese Journal of International Politics* 1 (Summer 2006): 83–108.

49. On Anglo-Saxonism, see Paul Kramer, "Empires, Exceptions, and Anglo-Saxons: Race and Rule between the British and US Empires, 1880–1910," *Journal of American History* 88 (March 2002): 1315–53; as well as Stuart Anderson, *Race and Rapprochement: Anglo-Saxonism and Anglo-American Relations, 1895–1904* (Rutherford, N.J.: Fairleigh Dickinson University Press, 1981); George Edward Gordon Catlin, *The Anglo-*

Saxon Tradition (London: K. Paul, Trench, Trubner, 1939); and H. Perry Robinson, *The Twentieth Century American: Being a Comparative Study of the Peoples of the Two Great Anglo-Saxon Nations* (Chautauqua, N.Y.: Chautauqua Press, 1911).

50. David H. Burton, "Theodore Roosevelt and His English Correspondents: The Intellectual Roots of the Anglo-American Alliance," *Mid-America* 53 (January 1971): 12–34, quote at p. 33.

51. France was one of the European countries most opposed to America's war with Spain. See Louis Martin Sears, "French Opinion of the Spanish-American War," *Hispanic American Historical Review* 7 (February 1927): 25–44; Octave Noël, *Le Péril américain* (Paris: De Soye et fils, 1899); and Sylvia L. Hilton and Steve J. S. Ickringill, eds., *European Perceptions of the Spanish-American War of 1898* (New York: Peter Lang, 1999).

52. Geoffrey Seed, "British Reactions to American Imperialism Reflected in Journals of Opinion, 1898–1900," *Political Science Quarterly* 73 (June 1958): 254–72.

53. At the time of the Venezuela dispute, Roosevelt was inclined to want the United States to go to war, so as to help restore the country's martial fiber. William James remarked that he was then in his *"Sturm und Drang"* period, one in which any foe, but Britain especially, would do as a means of fortifying what Roosevelt took to be a flagging national spirit. James quoted in William Henry Harbaugh, *Power and Responsibility: The Life and Times of Theodore Roosevelt* (New York: Farrar, Straus and Cudahy, 1961), pp. 97–98.

54. Perkins, *Great Rapprochement*, pp. 46–47. Also see Alfred Vagts, "Hopes and Fears of an American-German War, 1870–1915: I," *Political Science Quarterly* 54 (December 1939): 514–35.

55. Fareed Zakaria, *The Post-American World* (New York: W. W. Norton, 2009), p. 172. For a corrective, see John Henry Ferguson, *American Diplomacy and the Boer War* (Philadelphia: University of Pennsylvania Press, 1939), p. ix: "In spite of the fact that public opinion in the United States came to be overwhelmingly in favor of the Boers, the American government acted throughout the war as if in friendly alliance with England, and by doing so did much to prevent intervention by the European powers, thus assuring the annihilation of the Boer republics."

56. Stuart Anderson, "Racial Anglo-Saxonism and the American Response to the Boer War," *Diplomatic History* 2 (Summer 1978): 219–36; and Reginald Horsman, *Race and Manifest Destiny: The Origins of American Racial Anglo-Saxonism* (Cambridge, Mass.: Harvard University Press, 1981). For an attestation to the conviction that blood *is* thicker than water, see Andrew Carnegie, "Does America Hate England?" *Contemporary Review* 72 (July–December 1897): 660–68.

57. One former Rough Rider who had served in Cuba with Theodore Roosevelt went off to fight alongside the underdog Boers, only to discover that they spoke *Dutch*, so he switched and joined the British forces! See Byron Farwell, "Taking Sides in the Boer War," *American Heritage* 27 (April 1976): 21–25, 92–97.

58. Charles A. Kupchan, *How Enemies Become Friends: The Sources of Stable Peace* (Princeton, N.J.: Princeton University Press, 2010), p. 2.

59. See James Eayrs, *In Defence of Canada: From the Great War to the Great Depression* (Toronto: University of Toronto Press, 1964), pp. 70–78, 323–28. Also see Richard A. Preston, *The Defence of the Undefended Border: Planning for War in North America, 1867–1939* (Montreal and Kingston: McGill-Queen's University Press, 1977).

60. Christopher M. Bell, "Thinking the Unthinkable: British and American Naval Strategies for an Anglo-American War, 1918–1931," *International History Review* 19 (November 1997): 789–808.

61. Louis Morton, "Germany First: The Basic Concept of Allied Strategy in World War II," in *Command Decisions*, ed. Kent Roberts Greenfield (Washington, DC: Office of the Chief of Military History, Department of the Army, 1960), pp. 12–22.

62. But for the claim that there were the two regional security communities originating at more or less the same time in the early twentieth century, one in North America and the other in Scandinavia, see Richard Ned Lebow, "The Long Peace, the

End of the Cold War, and the Failure of Realism," *International Organization* 48 (Spring 1994): 249–77.

63. On the events leading to the rupture of Norway's union with Sweden more than a century ago, see Michael Stolleis, "The Dissolution of the Union between Norway and Sweden in 1905: A Century Later," in *Rett, nasjon, union—Den svensk-norske union-ens rettslige historie 1814–1905*, ed. Ola Mestad and Dag Michalsen (Oslo: Universitetsforlaget, 2005), pp. 35–48. On the romanticizing of the 1905 case, see David G. Haglund and John Erik Fossum, "Is There a 'Norway' in Québec's Future? 1905 and All That," *Québec Studies* 45 (Spring/Summer 2008): 167–89.

64. As argued in Magnus Ericson, "A Realist Stable Peace: Power, Threat, and the Development of a Shared Norwegian-Swedish Democratic Security Identity 1905–1940" (PhD dissertation. Lund University, Sweden, 2000).

65. See Stephen M. Walt, "Why Alliances Endure or Collapse," *Survival* 39 (Spring 1997): 156–79.

66. Thomas Risse-Kappen, *Cooperation among Democracies: The European Influence on U.S. Foreign Policy* (Princeton, N.J.: Princeton University Press, 1995), p. 32.

67. Risse-Kappen, *Cooperation among Democracies*, p. 32.

68. For an elaboration, see David G. Haglund, "The Case of the Missing Democratic Alliance: France, the 'Anglo-Saxons' and NATO's Deep Origins," *Contemporary Security Policy* 25 (August 2004): 225–51.

69. See Pierre Goubert, *The Course of French History*, trans. Maarten Ultee (London: Routledge, 1991), p. 116.

70. Walter A. McDougall, *Promised Land, Crusader State: The American Encounter with the World since 1776* (Boston: Houghton Mifflin, 1997), p. 25.

71. Richard W. Van Alstyne, *The Rising American Empire* (New York: Oxford University Press, 1960), pp. 70–76. Also see Todd Estes, *The Jay Treaty Debate, Public Opinion, and the Evolution of Early American Political Culture* (Amherst: University of Massachusetts Press, 2006); Marvin R. Zahniser, *Uncertain Friendship: American-French Diplomatic Relations through the Cold War* (New York: John Wiley and Sons, 1975), p. 70; and Bradford Perkins, *The First Rapprochement: England and the United States, 1795–1805* (Berkeley: University of California Press, 1967).

72. See Gardner W. Allen, *Our Naval War with France* (Boston: Houghton Mifflin, 1909); and Alexander De Conde, *The Quasi War: The Politics and Diplomacy of the Undeclared War with France, 1797–1801* (New York: Scribner, 1966).

73. On the distinction between cobelligerent and ally during those years, see Lawrence S. Kaplan, "France and Madison's Decision for War, 1812," *Mississippi Valley Historical Review* 50 (March 1964): 652–71.

74. Stephen M. Walt, *The Origins of Alliances* (Ithaca, N.Y.: Cornell University Press, 1987), p. 1: "I define *alliance* as a formal or informal relationship of security cooperation between two or more sovereign states. This definition assumes some level of commitment and an exchange of benefits for both parties."

75. Insight into the changing context of Canada-United States security debates in the half decade preceding the accord can be found in Frederick W. Gibson and Jonathan G. Rossie, eds., *The Road to Ogdensburg: The Queen's/St. Lawrence Conferences on Canadian-American Affairs, 1935–1941* (East Lansing: Michigan State University Press, 1993).

76. See Christopher Conliffe, "The Permanent Joint Board on Defense, 1940–1988," in *The U.S.-Canada Security Relationship: The Politics, Strategy, and Technology of Defense*, ed. David G. Haglund and Joel J. Sokolsky (Boulder, Colo.: Westview Press, 1989), pp. 146–65.

77. See Dwight N. Mason, "The Canadian-American North American Defence Alliance in 2005," *International Journal* 60 (Spring 2005): 385–96.

78. No one knows exactly how many such agreements have been reached. The most recent compilation, made by the BPG, lists at least 851 but mentions that some of these may no longer be operative. Bi-National Planning Group, *The Final Report on Canada*

and the United States (CANUS) Enhanced Military Cooperation, Peterson AFB (CO), 13 March 2006, Appendix G.

79. Or so I have argued in "The US-Canada Relationship: How 'Special' Is America's Oldest Unbroken Alliance?" in *America's 'Special Relationships': Foreign and Domestic Aspects of the Politics of Alliance*, ed. John Dumbrell and Axel R. Schäfer (London: Routledge, 2009), pp. 60–75.

80. The wording of Article 5 is instructive, for it obliges each ally to "assist the Party or Parties so attacked by taking forthwith, individually and in concert with the other Parties, such action as it deems necessary." *The NATO Handbook: Fiftieth Anniversary Edition, 1949–1999* (Brussels: NATO Office of Information and Press, 1998), p. 396.

81. Sometimes this element of reciprocity can be overlooked, even by otherwise knowledgeable students of Canada-United States relations. Consider the case of none other than John Bartlet Brebner, the Canadian-born professor of history at Columbia University who did so much to energize scholarship on the bilateral relationship during the 1940s, through his insistence upon the symbolism of the North Atlantic "triangle." Writing nearly a decade after the King-Roosevelt exchange of commitments, Brebner argued that there had, in fact, been *no* Canadian counterpart to the U.S. president's expression of support at Kingston. "Canada said 'thank you,' but studiously avoided acceptance of the offers lest she mortgage her freedom." Brebner, "Canada in North American History," *Mississippi Valley Historical Review* 34 (March 1948): 653–59, quote at p. 654.

THREE

Diasporas and Their Impact upon Global and Regional Security

The Question of "Ethnic Lobbying"

THE RETURN OF "ETHNICITY" TO GLOBAL AND REGIONAL SECURITY

As noted in the introduction, a spirited, at times even venomous, debate over the mooted role of ethnic diasporas in U.S. foreign policy (and by extension global security) was triggered more than a half-dozen years ago when two well-respected theorists of international relations delivered their judgment on what they took to be the growing and pernicious impact of an "Israel lobby" upon America's foreign policies toward the Middle East.[1] To put it mildly, the two professors, the University of Chicago's John Mearsheimer and Harvard's Stephen Walt, touched a nerve.[2] Some critics came close to tarring Mearsheimer and Walt with the brush of anti-Semitism. One such was Abraham Foxman, the national director of the U.S.-based Anti-Defamation League (ADL), who protested, apropos the initial version of the Mearsheimer-Walt thesis that appeared in the *London Review of Books*, "[p]lease note that I am *not* calling Mearsheimer and Walt 'anti-Semites'"—and then proceeded, notwithstanding this disclaimer, essentially to link them with the latter by asserting that "their article repeats and supports myths and beliefs that anti-Semites have peddled for centuries," as well as to accuse them of "giving aid and comfort to some of the most despicable people in our society." Just in case anyone should miss his point, he went on to note that the two professors wrote with "subtlety and pseudoscholarly style that makes their poison all the more dangerous" than the ideas propagated by avowedly neo-Nazi groups.[3]

Some, less impassioned, opponents of the professors' theory rested their objections upon methodological and epistemological bases.[4] And still others thought that the allegation of undue influence on the part of pro-Israeli interest groups simply missed the point altogether, because it vastly understated the degree to which America's support of the Jewish state needed to be explained by long-standing tendencies in American strategic culture, such that Mearsheimer and Walt were looking in all the wrong places in their bid to find out why America was such a staunch supporter of Israel. Walter Russell Mead, for instance, thought that the large demographic cohort he labelled "gentile Zionists" had far more to do with America's pro-Israel policies than any ethnic pressure groups headquartered on K Street.[5] For his part, Andrew Bacevich remarked that U.S. support for Israel merely represented a continuation of a long-standing impulse to expand America's interests in, and preserve its access to, as much of the rest of the world as possible, an urge that was practically as old as the country itself, betraying a "penchant for expansionism [having] nothing to do with Israel."[6]

Whatever else might be said on either side of this polemic, no one should ever assume that claims of ethnic interest groups' exercising "undue" influence over the shaping of American foreign policy are anything new, or even particularly unusual. Such claims have a lengthy pedigree, both in U.S. foreign policy scholarship and, increasingly, among those whose principal scholarly and policy interests are focused upon global security. Indeed, it is difficult if not impossible to disaggregate claims regarding ethnic diasporas and U.S. foreign policy from those associated with diasporas and security writ large, for reasons I will relate below. Nor is it possible to dissociate this body of scholarship from debates of a more restricted focus, such as the ones I concentrate upon in this book: the postulated impact of diasporic groups upon the rise and evolution of the Canada-United States security community.

Bluntly stated, foreign-policy problems that can be said to display some decidedly "ethnic" coloration have hardly been a novel feature of international or regional security. We have already seen, in chapter one, how "ethnic conflict" (though no one called it that at the time) came to characterize relations between Canadians and Americans along their shared boundary for a considerable period of years during North America's lengthy "Hobbesian" era. And even after the decades of recurring Canadian-American conflict (ethnic or otherwise) had come to an end with the Treaty of Ghent in late 1814, drawing to a close the War of 1812, peace had hardly become the default geostrategic condition in North America. Another century would elapse before Canadians and Americans could truly begin to think and act as if a new, more promise-filled, era had begun, one made manifest not only through the establishment of a North American security community, but also by the development of such an enhanced degree of security and defense interdependence as to make of the two countries each other's most "special" ally in the behaviorally significant fashion detailed at the end of the previous chapter.

Such security and defense interdependence did not come about effortlessly in North America, and among the reasons for the continental neighbors' tardiness in entering this new and more salubrious era was ethnic-diasporic activism in the decades following the American Civil War. So let us in this chapter attempt to take the conceptual and analytical measure of such political activity, as it is recounted and theorized in contemporary scholarship. In particular, we are interested in discovering what diasporas are, why they are said to be of relevance to global and regional security, and how they seek this elusive quality known as "influence" — especially influence over foreign-policy decision making in one country more than any other, the United States. As remarked in the introduction, Canada itself is sometimes argued to be a well-suited arena within which the kind of diasporic activism known as "lobbying" can take place, but if it is such a spot, it pales in comparison with the United States in this regard, for reasons discussed below. Where Canada *has* ranked as a more central element in the debate over ethnic political activism, of course, relates to a different kind of diasporic activity, discussed in subsequent chapters, namely that associated with clandestine transnational actors. Canada has, in this latter regard, been willy-nilly on both the receiving and delivery ends of such actors' exertions, as we shall see in the three case studies that make up three of the final chapters of this book.

Both variants of ethnic-diasporic activism are important, but this chapter will focus only upon the legal and constitutional variant, since it has really been the aspect of diasporic activism synonymous with ethnic lobbying that can be considered to have had the greatest historical impact upon the quality of Canada-United States security relations. This is in no small way because of the degree to which ethnic lobbying (broadly construed) had been conducted with the aim of preventing the construction of an Anglo-American alliance during the early decades of the twentieth century. Moreover, to the extent that a scholarly debate with applicability to North American (as well as global) security has resurfaced of late, it has done so largely on the assumption that the struggle mounted by diasporas intent on improving the lot of their "kinfolk" elsewhere has invariably brought to the forefront the question of how such groups might gain influence over the shaping of *America's* policy toward their real or imagined "homeland."

This is not to say that non-American developments are irrelevant to the contemporary debates about how and why diasporas have recently (re)emerged as important topics for scholars of international and regional security; but it is to highlight why the American-based diasporas are conceded analytical pride of place among the many such ethnic-interest groups scattered throughout the world. Therefore, to answer the question as to why so much attention has been getting accorded over the past two decades to diasporas, we begin by pursuing a pair of analytical paths, each having its roots in the structural transformation in international security that attended the ending of the Cold War a quarter century ago. The first involves the appearance (reappearance, in reality) of a new and troublesome development in global security, "ethnic conflict." The second concerns the debate within U.S. foreign policy circles subsequent to the disappearance of the quondam Soviet adversary—a disappearance that many observers were beginning to think had "deprived" American decision makers of a most useful tool for understanding and defending the country's very national interest: threat from a fellow great power. I pursue each of these paths in the following two sections of this chapter, but it bears reiterating here that the scholarly and policy interest in the linkage between diasporas and security was not *caused* by the ending of the Cold War, although it certainly was *rekindled* by that momentous development.

ETHNIC DIASPORAS, ETHNIC CONFLICT, AND THE ENDING OF THE COLD WAR

There is nothing strange, these days, in anyone's positing a connection between ethnic-diasporic activism and international security, or between the former and American foreign policy. That it might seem to be otherwise, as indicated by the acerbity of the Mearsheimer-Walt controversy (to say nothing of the more recent one surrounding John Judis),[7] has much to do with one particular manner in which the debate triggered by the professors became framed. To those unfamiliar with the long and, at times, consequential record of ethnic-diasporic activism in U.S. foreign policy, it almost appeared as if American Jews represented the archetypal case of diasporic lobbying, if in fact they had not been the very inventors of the practice. From this it could sometimes be made to seem that in their absence, no one would have been much interested in trying to explore whether ethnic diasporas could possibly seek to influence either America's foreign policy, or global and regional security.

Such claims are highly misleading. The first source of confusion is a conceptual matter, stemming from the very meaning of "diaspora" in scholarship in international relations (IR) and comparative politics. This concept has sometimes been so closely associated, in its demotic applications, with world Jewry as to imply the virtual exclusion of almost all other ethnic (including religious) identities from being within the rubric's purview.[8] The second source of confusion owes a great deal to historical amnesia, which clouds the judgment of analysts tempted to believe that those who militate on behalf of Israel are so well-organized and influential as to serve as ethnic-diasporic activism's ne plus ultra, such that even if there might be other diasporic groups around, they cannot be said to match the effectiveness of the Israel lobby, the veritable platinum standard for the practice, because of its assumed ability to achieve influence over American foreign policy toward the Middle East. The upshot is these other groups tend to get downplayed in, sometimes even eliminated from, the discussion, largely because of their ostensive fecklessness.

On both counts, the source of the confusion is apparent. To begin with, it is simply wrong to restrict inquiry into so-called ethnic lobbies as narrowly as appears to have happened with the furor over the Israel lobby thesis. While it is true that Jews have certainly figured among the world's diaspora groups, they have scarcely been the only identity bearers to be associated with the concept. Nor were they even the first. Diaspora is a word that comes to us from the Greek, the etymological components of which being *speiro* (= to sow) and *dia* (= over).[9] It does so most appropriately, because despite its subsequent and frequent connection with Jewish populations, the concept originally referred to the dispersal of ethnic *Greeks* around the Mediterranean basin in the sixth century BCE. As one scholar explains, in this original usage, diaspora had a positive connotation, closely linked with the expansion and consolidation of the power of key Greek city-states, through the colonization of places that had originally been populated by non-Greeks.[10] This understanding is in marked contrast with a different, more somber sense of diaspora in recent times, which has the concept often linked with the tragic history of groups (viz., diasporic Jews) that by and large were, and saw themselves as being, "involuntary exiles."

This more recent denotation fails to do justice to the concept, as it will be employed in this book, even if it is obvious that many members of at least one of the three diasporas that follow this chapter, the Irish Americans, have indeed self-styled as involuntary exiles. But whether one has left one's "ancestral" homeland willingly or otherwise is irrelevant to the meaning of diaspora as a term of *analysis*, though it can be highly relevant in helping give substance to a political agenda (as we are going to discover in chapter four). So how *should* we assess the meaning of diaspora? For guidance on this matter we could do much worse than to turn to the insights of one particularly accomplished conceptual analyst, Rogers Brubaker.

He is no enthusiast, at the best of times, of "conceptual stretching."[11] And he particularly worries about the veritable proliferation of diaspora as a term of art among legions of social scientists ever since the ending of the Cold War. To Brubaker, this widespread use of a contested term poses a set of serious challenges to our ability to comprehend and explain important developments. As he sees matters,

[t]he problem with this latitudinarian, "let-a-thousand-diasporas bloom" approach is that the category becomes stretched to the point of uselessness. . . . If everyone is diasporic, then no one is distinctively so. The term loses its discriminating power—its ability to pick out phenomena, to make distinctions. The universalization of diaspora, paradoxically, means the disappearance of diaspora.[12]

Therefore, in order to preserve its utility, it is essential, he instructs us, to delimit the concept's distinguishing characteristics. For Brubaker, three distinctions are crucial. First, the group in question must have been dispersed from its original homeland. Second, it must retain a strong homeland orientation. And third, there must exist some "boundaries" setting it apart from others in the new host-state(s) in which it has become established. But delimitation is not all that is required, if the concept is going to generate useful scholarly applications. It must also be qualitatively "tamed," by which Brubaker means that we need to be wary of the fallacy of "groupism," which he holds to be a tendency to ascribe to diasporas certain "essentialist" traits, said to differentiate them from others in the host-state, and to do so in such a way as to conflate theories about diasporas with teleological claims about the groups' destinies. To guard against this conflation, Brubaker urges that if we must take diaspora seriously as a concept, we treat it as a category of *practice* more than as one of *analysis*, given that it is far too frequently employed "not so much [to] *describe* the world as [to] seek to *remake* it."[13]

There is much worth pondering in Brubaker's critique. Although it is not exactly clear whether dispersal requires, as some scholars insist it must, the distribution of a diasporic group to *two or more* host-states, it is obvious that without "dispersal" in its most restricted dictionary meaning, that is, of betokening the process by which organisms spread from one place to another, there would be no diaspora, anywhere, needing to be discussed. Thus as I employ the concept in this book, I take the dispersion criterion in that most restrictive sense, even though it can fairly be remarked of all three of my case studies that they more than fill the dispersal bill as it is loosely interpreted, by dint of their having a presence in several host-states. Nevertheless, there exist some ethnic groups that are so exclusively concentrated in only one host-state that it would seem odd in the extreme for them to be excluded a priori from consideration within the diasporic set. One thinks, in this regard, of the Cuban diaspora, which to most intents and purposes is resident exclusively in the United States,[14] and much the same would have to be said of the Mexican and many other Latino diasporas, whose effective "dispersal" had been to the United States and to the United States only.[15]

I introduce the Cuban Americans into the discussion here because their experience speaks, in some important ways, to the second of Brubaker's defining characteristics, namely that diasporas must retain a strong orientation toward the homeland. Usually, this gets expressed positively, reflecting what Woodrow Wilson once referred to, in discussing America's diasporic dilemmas on the eve of the First World War, as the "ancient affections"[16]—affections, I hasten to add, that the president himself considered to be a most worrisome feature of domestic politics at that time. But as we realize in the case of the Cuban diaspora, their homeland orientation has not implied any notable desire to advance the interests of the kin-state's government (until very recently, perhaps, with the gradual emergence of a new generation of Cuban Americans, less animated than their elders have been by hostility toward the post-1958 regime in Havana). Admittedly, the Cuban diaspora is not the only one to have featured a dyspeptic orientation toward the kin-state's government, but usually the affective significance of homeland orientation runs in a direction leading more toward affinity than disgust. The point remains that the members of the diaspora must, one way or the other, care deeply about the fortunes of the land(s) they left behind. In this respect, while the referent object of the diaspora's sentimental attachment must be the homeland, the latter need not be a single, existing, state (though so often it is).

The reason why the object of the diaspora's sentimental attachment need not be a state is because we are interested precisely in *ethnic* diasporas, and ethnicity is a concept that itself connotes, among other things, racial, cultural, linguistic, and even religious markers of identity, and not merely so-called nationalist ones thought to be derivates of those juridical-legal entities we know of as states.[17] So, for quite a few ethnic diasporas, the homeland can indeed be a state, even a powerful one as in the case of the Chinese diaspora. But for others the homeland may consist in a piece of another state or states, as it does for the Kurdish groups residing in Iraq, Turkey, Syria, and even Germany and elsewhere. Or it may have nothing to do with any current state, whether in whole or in part, existing only in historical myth and memory, as it did for the Jewish diaspora for so many centuries. And, though it seems at times as this stretches the concept entirely beyond recognition, we can speak of some diasporas, such as the Muslim one, whose affective referent object cannot be any particular kin-state, given the plethora of countries whence Muslim migrants originate, but must instead be a region whose principal mobilizing allure resides in religious convictions.[18]

Brubaker's third defining stipulation for diasporas, that they maintain "boundaries" between themselves and the dominant demographic/identity group(s) in the host-state, is simply another way of saying that the minority cannot become too assimilated into the host-state's culture so as to lose a sense of itself as being, in a non-negligible fashion, a separate community. A good example of how an ethnic group can cease to be a politically relevant diaspora—an example that will feature centrally in chapter five—is the German Americans. As that chapter will reveal, a great many Americans, when asked in recent decennial censuses to identify the ethnicity with which they associate themselves, answer "German." Yet it would be unwise for us to construe today's German Americans as constituting a diaspora, given how insignificant is the homeland orientation—usually so insignificant as to be non-detectable. Indeed, some scholars will tell you that today's German Americans (and, by extension, German North Americans) no longer even constitute an ethnic group, such is the degree of their fundamental assimilation into American (and Canadian) society.[19] This is a far, far cry from the situation of German Americans a century ago, when they not only unequivocally did form an ethnic diaspora, but could be, and were, said by many observers to loom as a major complicating factor in Anglo-American (and therefore Canadian-American) strategic relations.

An important, though hardly the only, factor contributing to the reawakening of interest in ethnic diasporas over the past quarter century has been the gruesome phenomenon of ethnic conflict. For sure, not all diaspora groups have had their sentimental attachments to homelands awakened and magnified by the specter of gross injustices being visited upon people who are so like themselves in nearly all ways, save one: they are locked in conflict far from the comforting shelter of any host-state, and thus are in need of being supported by their more fortunate kinfolk elsewhere. But more than a few diasporas have, of late, become mobilized precisely because of the reemergence of this old, if only recently labelled, aspect of strife in global affairs that we call ethnic conflict. And it is precisely this reemergence of a very bad business that requires us to handle with a bit of skepticism Brubaker's aforementioned stricture regarding "essentialism."

It is not that Brubaker's caution on this score is necessarily misplaced; it is rather that his dismissal of "groupism" carries some risk of throwing out the baby with the bathwater. At the very least, some scholars who dedicate themselves to the study of ethnic conflict are less certain that essences have such scant *analytical* significance as Brubaker contends they possess. It may well be that most social scientists who study the perplexing phenomenon of ethnicity (and its spawn, ethnic conflict) are prone to assessing their concept(s) as being fundamentally ideational, but if so, there does remain a clear and unambiguous minority of objectors, who insist upon investing ethnicity with exactly the sort of "essential" qualities against whose invocation Brubaker warns. Of this minority, it is charitably said that they fail to realize that reality is "socially constructed." Less charitably, they are chided for being "primordialists," bestowing altogether too much meaning upon such ostensible markers of ethnicity as language or skin color, or both, and not according enough attention to the realm of ideas and ideology. The result, it is maintained, is that the minority fail to recognize the more or less "optional" nature of identity, which can be adopted and shed with surprising ease, as the occasion warrants.[20]

In so many ways the distinction above really is artificial, for is there *anyone* who would dispute that social reality is, and *has* to be, what observers tend to make of it?[21] Nor is the acknowledgment that the distinction is more apparent than real especially recent: as long ago as 1919 the great French historian Lucien Febvre was instructing his students that the "spirit" of history was and had to be idealist, because "all . . . social facts, are facts of belief and opinion. Are not wealth, work and money not 'things' but human ideas, representations and judgments of things?"[22] One could go back even further, well before Febvre's time, for instance to the late seventeenth century, and similarly recall John Locke's observation about meaning being "arbitrary, the result of social convention."[23] From this, however, it does not follow that social actors are immune or otherwise resistant to fashioning their identity largely out of primordialist bricks and mortar; to the contrary, such labor is a fairly regular activity on their construction sites.[24]

All of this is to remark that ethnicity is a contested concept in the human sciences. Now, if ethnicity is a contested concept,[25] much more so is the notion of ethnic conflict, which itself has done so much to reignite interest in diasporas' assumed impact upon global and regional security. As with the parental rubric, so with the offspring: ethnic conflict can itself be interpreted in two major ways, linked to the abovementioned distinction between the constructivists and the primordialists. And while the latter have little difficulty believing that animosities between culturally distinct groups can—and will continue to—spill over into violent clashes precisely because of the cultural differences,[26] many of the former want to put the causal emphasis elsewhere, for instance upon the deliberate manipulation of sentimentality by unscrupulous or even criminal agitators, such that what is so often trumpeted as ethnic conflict, they say, really turns out to be something much different. In the words of one of those who are skeptical that the notion adds very much to our understanding of reality, if "ethnic war" is supposed to connote a kind of Hobbesian struggle of "all against all and neighbor against neighbor, [then] ethnic war essentially does not exist." Instead, what is often mistakenly identified as pent-up communal hatred finally getting uncorked is "something far more banal: the creation of communities of criminal violence and pillage," inspired by nonideological thugs.[27]

There are even some scholars who would have us abandon altogether the category of ethnic conflict, which they dismiss as little more than a conceptual "holding pen for a herd of disparate descriptive events,"[28] if not an outright "myth."[29] No doubt the abolitionists have a point; still, and at the risk of siding with an essentialism that can appear to some as decidedly old-fashioned, and to others as defiantly wrongheaded, I will assume that ethnic conflict *is* a concept worth retaining, and that it can be taken to suggest "a sense of incompatible vital interests [that] generates hostility; and that this hostility, if sufficiently intense, finds expression, under specifiable circumstances . . . in deadly attacks of members of the opposing group."[30] I further confess that I find it very difficult to imagine how, absent the recent focus of so many analysts of global and regional security upon ethnic conflict, diasporas would of late have been receiving anything like the amount of scholarly attention that has come their way.[31] This is *not* to claim that without the uptick in ethnic conflict following the ending of the Cold War no one today would be very much interested in diasporas; rather, it is simply to maintain that ethnic conflict has certainly helped to spur scholarly writing and thinking about the manner in which diasporas can be said to make an impact upon security relations.[32]

There are a variety of ways in which diasporas have been argued to have such an impact.[33] Sometimes, no particular impact at all is intended, yet if the size of demographic flows (for instance, of refugees) is large enough, then security implications associated with diasporas can and do emerge, as happened in the early post-Cold War period when inflows of refugees from the fighting in the former Yugoslavia and elsewhere triggered a surge in nativist agitation and sometimes violence in immigrant-receiving countries in Europe, including and especially Germany.[34] Often, however, diasporas have an *intended* impact upon global and regional security. Some of their politically engaged members might, for instance, purchase arms from some third country, or even their host-state, and ship these to compatriots in a civil war in the homeland (one thinks, in this respect, of the involvement of the Tamil diaspora in the recently ended civil war in Sri Lanka). Or bombs might be planted on board international passenger aircraft. Or raids could be launched against the hated regime in the kin-state from a safe refuge in the host-state. Or, to take a highly contemporary instance of diaspora activism, they might work to effect a "reunion" of the part of the host-state in which they currently live with the country to which their region once belonged, in keeping with the phenomenon known as "irredentism," so visibly on display in the late winter of 2014 with the Russian military incursion into Crimea, sought and warmly welcomed by this Ukrainian region's Russian diaspora, who constitute the majority of its population. But these examples hardly exhaust the inventory of ways in which it might be said that ethnic diasporas make their mark upon regional and even global security. Often much more significant, certainly so for the claims I advance in this book, are the legal, constitutional activities of diasporas as they attempt to acquire influence over states' foreign policy making.

In this latter regard, two sorts of influence attempts stand out. First, there are those initiatives mounted by the diaspora with a view to gaining a voice in the foreign policy decision making of the kin-state. The other, and the topic of the section immediately below, consists in their efforts to acquire a role in the shaping of the host-state's policy toward the latter (the kin-state) and its neighbors. In both cases, the ending of the

Cold War served as a catalyst for ethnic-diasporic activism. In the first instance, of diasporas seeking a voice in the shaping of the kin-state's foreign policy, the effect stemmed from the removal of what had been, during the bipolar era of ideological and strategic rivalry between the United States and the USSR, a kind of "structural overlay" that had resulted in the freezing of tensions between ethnic communities—tensions that had been latent but kept under control by decisions of the superpowers to maintain a lid on regional rivalries. Especially was this so in parts of Europe that had once lain within the Soviet sphere of influence, but that began to find themselves no longer of great relevance to Moscow in light of the diminution of superpower ill will.[35] The process was accelerated when the collapse of the Soviet Union itself in late 1991 meant that there would now be many more foreign policies open to contestation by groups within the diaspora, an example being the efforts of Armenian Americans to gain the upper hand in fashioning the foreign policy of the newly independent government in Yerevan.[36]

In the second instance are the exertions of ethnic diasporas determined to exploit the legal channels available to them in the American political system so as to gain some leverage over the crafting of U.S. foreign policy initiatives intended, directly or indirectly, to affect the interests of the kin-state. Why the U.S. domestic arena should have become such a cynosure of ethnic-diasporic activism is the topic of the next section of this chapter. Following immediately upon that discussion, the subsequent two sections will grapple with the challenging issue of how one might assess or otherwise demonstrate the influence that diasporic pressure politics is intended to attain.

ETHNIC DIASPORAS AND THE CHALLENGE TO AMERICA'S "NATIONAL INTEREST"

Diasporic influence upon state policy constitutes the most important manner through which an impact can be had upon international security, and no state these days is as welcoming an arena for the politics of pressure as America appears to be, given that one obvious consequence of the removal of its quondam Soviet rival was that, henceforth, the world would have only one superpower—and *it* was it. But even before the onset of the era of "unipolarity" as the prominent structural characteristic of the international security system,[37] America, by dint of a constitutional makeup that facilitated pressure-group activities and a demographic makeup that virtually compelled them, had been the most interesting and, in policy terms, significant forum for ethnic diasporas to make their myriad voices heard in the shaping of foreign policy. As Melvin Small reminds us, the United States is hardly the only land with a multiethnic democracy, but it *is* the "only one among them that lacks the ability to suppress the cacophony of voices from electorally powerful ethnic groups."[38] But if it is true, and it is, that the United States has for the past 150 years been consistently a site of influence attempts mounted (whether successfully or not) by ethnic diasporas, it has only been in the last quarter century that the policy "payoff" of ethnic lobbying has been considered by many to be at its most elevated historical level (a claim that needs to be regarded with some skepticism).

How is it said that the Cold War's ending gave new and unusual prominence to the role of diasporas in debates about American foreign policy? A few answers suggest themselves, the first of which we explored in this chapter's preceding section, with its discussion of ethnic conflict. But the ending of the Cold War had other consequences beyond the loosing of hitherto suppressed interethnic tensions. In particular, it endowed American foreign policy with what appeared to be a new, and to many, troubling dynamic, one that had the country's very "national interest" becoming the object of contestation on the part of so-called parochial forces, for it looked as if what a key advisor to Mikhail Gorbachev had once prophesied had now come to pass. During the closing stages of the Cold War, at a moment when it was all but certain that the bipolar ideological contest would soon be but a receding memory, Georgi Arbatov is said, somewhat tongue-in-cheek, to have remarked to an American interlocutor, "we are going to do a terrible thing to you. We are going to deprive you of an enemy."[39] And, to so many, this is precisely what happened during the 1990s, the much-commented "post-Cold War decade." Those were years during which American policy intellectuals could be found busying themselves with a new pastime, the "Kennan sweepstakes," so named because of the search for a replacement master concept in foreign policy that might provide the kind of yeoman service to which George Kennan's notion of "containment" had for so long been put, a vade mecum for referencing America's true national interest.[40]

Thus the second impact of the Cold War's ending on debates over U.S. foreign policy: in eliminating bipolarity itself, and elevating America to the rank of "sole surviving superpower," it apparently gave, as so many argued, enhanced importance to the struggle for influence over the country's foreign policy debates, in the process magnifying the leverage that would accrue to interest groups skillful and fortunate enough to gain sway over decisions taken in Washington. Who could gainsay the enhanced stakes, in a land that had suddenly and indisputably become in *relative* terms what it had been in absolute terms for some decades, the undisputed most powerful actor on the world stage?

Nor was this all. With no overarching national security interest left to structure those foreign policy debates, the field was wide open for those groups promoting less-than-national (or, "parochial") interests to make their running. Although hardly the only analyst to descry and decry this new trend, Samuel Huntington probably gave stronger voice than anyone else to what was coming to be regarded as a negative consequence of the Cold War's ending, the lack of any clear threat that might stand as a powerful vehicle for imparting instruction to American foreign policy making.[41] In a 1997 article in *Foreign Affairs*, Huntington expressed the fear that America's foreign policy risked becoming the plaything of potent interest groups who cared not a whit for the national interest, being exclusively focused on championing the special interests they had been created to foster. Among the class of special interests, two kinds were particularly invidious: commercial interests and ethnic ones. All was not yet lost, for rather than see the country's foreign policy becoming corrupted by either, or both, of those interests, Huntington recommended that America retrench, greatly delimiting the scope of its internationalism. He was convinced that a modest (i.e., significantly downsized) foreign policy offered the best hope for the future, and this because the "*de novo* mobilization of . . . resources from a low base, experience suggests, is likely to be easier than the redirection of resources that have been committed to entrenched particularistic interests."[42]

There was one further development, heralded as being either a consequence or a corollary of the Cold War's demise—an epistemological development that would come to figure centrally in both scholarly and policy discussions involving the national interest/ethnicity nexus. It was the rise of a new "paradigm" in IR and foreign policy theorizing that threatened to unseat "realism" from the dominant position it had occupied in the scholarship on American foreign policy ever since the era of the Second World War. The new paradigm was known as "constructivism" (or "social constructivism"), and its sudden popularity, even and especially in intellectual precincts that had hitherto been *chasses gardées* of the realists, was held to have resulted in no small measure because of shifting geopolitical as well as theoretical sands. The ending of the Cold War, and therefore of bipolarity, obviously made life more complicated for those who had assimilated what Kenneth Waltz had been saying and writing about the basic stability of bipolarity.[43] Not that everyone had been in agreement with Waltz during the Cold War, not even all realists,[44] but at least there was for a time a certain *descriptive* merit in taking as seriously as Waltz did the implications of the bipolar world—implications that ceased to be worth thinking about once their structural precondition disappeared. Many assumed that the (temporary?) derailing of structural realism à la Waltz meant the end of realist predominance in IR theory, hence the emphasis upon the "turn" it and the cognate field of U.S. foreign policy analysis were ostensibly in the process of making, away from realism and toward some other body of theory, constructivism to be precise.

This constructivist turn was argued to be one in which "cultural" variables were going increasingly to make themselves felt in states' decision making, post-bipolarity, nowhere more so than on the campuses and in the think tanks of the sole surviving superpower. And with culture's appearance as a variable to reckon with came another concept that was bound to be important: "identity."[45] This latter concept would be elevated to a prominent position in constructivist accounts of international outcomes, occupying for these theorists a position as central as that long held by "power" for a certain kind of realist theoretician; identity would be the core organizing concept for realism's challenger, endowing shape to cognition and signification to interests.[46] Perceptive observers of the new epistemological challenge sweeping the ranks of IR theory at that time were not slow to pronounce upon what it portended for debates in the narrower realm of U.S. foreign policy. One scholar, John Ruggie, predicted that in the new "threatless" era that had resulted from the disappearance of the Soviet Union, America's ideological identity, what he called its "inorganic nationalism," would henceforth serve to provide guidance to policy making, as a more than adequate replacement for the now-vanished threat.[47]

Ruggie would not lack for company in foreseeing the emergence of identity as the surrogate structuring vehicle for threat, imparting meaning to interests. Nor should it be thought that, because of their stress upon identity, the constructivists had the field entirely to themselves. No less a realist than Huntington hopped on the identity bandwagon, expounding not just in the aforementioned *Foreign Affairs* article, but more comprehensively in the last book he would ever publish prior to his death in 2008, the central place that the concept occupied in the making of America's foreign policy. Unlike Ruggie, who believed that America's ideological identity pointed in the direction of an ongoing foreign policy coherence and international leadership—and this because a key component of the intellectual genetic code of its inorganic nationalism was argued to be a commitment to "multilateralism"—Huntington took a dimmer view of what identity held in store for America and its role in the world.

Thus in *Who Are We? The Challenges to America's National Identity*, Huntington was only too willing to acknowledge the centrality of the constructivists' core concept, revealing himself, in the book's opening pages, to be in thorough accord with their insistence upon identity's structuring impact upon interests: "We have to know who we are before we can know what our interests are."[48] But instead of taking comfort from the power of inorganic nationalism to keep American foreign policy focused upon a coherent national interest, Huntington worried that an increasingly "multicultural" (and Latino) America was going to render nugatory a central ingredient of the country's *organic* nationalism, with the result being incoherence in policy making, or worse. Optimists might take comfort from America's multilateral "ideology," and even be able to convince themselves that their side had won the Kennan sweepstakes by discovering in "engagement and enlargement" (viz., of liberal democracy) the new lodestar of American foreign policy in the post-threat era,[49] but Huntington's own reading of that ideology, or "creed," was decidedly less sanguine. He worried very much that America's "ostensibly secular" political creed (what others might call its inorganic nationalism) was really predicated upon ideational values that privileged *cultural* (i.e., organic) values, the two most important of which being Anglo-Protestantism and the English language, such that Anglo-Protestant culture was the "paramount defining element of American identity."[50]

Hence the dilemma, to Huntington, one triggered in large measure by the rise in significance of diasporas the post-Cold War era. Nowhere outside of America could or did these ethnic interest groups have such prominence, and this only partly because of the country's international primacy. True, being the sole surviving superpower mattered, but even more important was America's historic role of having been, and continuing to be, an immigrant-receiving country. The upshot of the two trends was clear, and to Huntington highly disturbing: "American politics is increasingly an arena in which homeland governments and their diasporas attempt to shape American policy to serve homeland interests. . . . The more power the United States has in world politics, the more it becomes an arena of world politics, the more foreign governments and their diasporas attempt to influence American policy, and the less able the United States is to define and to pursue its own national interests."[51]

Huntington's forebodings were nothing new, for much the same used to be said about the ostensive distorting power exercised by the country's diasporas during an era running from the American Civil War to the First World War, when America was far more "multicultural" than it has become in more recent years, even if that label had not yet come into use. And while today's Kulturkampf in the United States raises important questions regarding the country's relations with Mexico and some of its other Latin American neighbors, there appears to be little in the contemporary American culture wars that bears heavily upon the quality of Canada-United States security relations—certainly not anything remotely approaching the degree to which in an earlier era bilateral security affairs in North America used to be so frequently, and quite often negatively, affected by the activities of certain U.S.-based diasporas. There has been, of course, anxiety evinced in the United States about the security implications of elements in the continent's Muslim diaspora, and for a brief period following the 9/11 attacks attention was being directed at *Canada's* Muslim diaspora as a potential source of trouble in the bilateral security relationship. But more recently, as chapter six will argue, the U.S. debate about possible security challenges associated with Muslims in North America has been focused more upon America's own Muslim diaspora than upon Canada's.

This is simply to acknowledge that what we would now label "multiculturalism" has had a lengthy and eventful history on the North

American continent. Although contemporary Canada might be said to have so woven multiculturalism into the fabric of its national identity as to have effectively "constitutionalized" it (not without significant misgivings, however, among Québec sovereigntists),[52] it is really in the United States that the concept has had its greatest policy resonance,[53] not just for reasons related to identity but also and especially for those appertaining to foreign and security policies. The word only entered demotic usage in July 1941, in an essay that Iris Barry published in the *New York Herald Tribune Books*, reviewing Edward Haskell's *Lance: A Novel about Multicultural Men*. As used both by the novel's author and his reviewer, multiculturalism implied someone who was free of chauvinistic impulses. Gradually, the term came to be employed as a synonym for "multiethnicity," and started to get widespread currency in English Canadian newspapers and journals in the 1960s and 1970s, as a means of describing the demographic makeup of the country's large cities.[54] It would not be long before it found application in the United States and elsewhere.

If the word was a late arrival on American shores, the phenomenon it was intended to express was nearly as old as the country itself. From its very inception as an outpost of European settlement in the seventeenth century until the early decades of the twentieth century, America had been a "country of immigration."[55] With the major exception of involuntary migrants arriving from Africa as slaves, almost everyone else coming to America prior to the middle of the twentieth century did so directly from Europe, or indirectly so (as in the case of immigrants from Canada). Until the 1890s, the majority of European immigrants hailed from lands located in the northwestern part of the continent (the British Isles, Germany, and Scandinavia). In retrospect, this era in U.S. immigration history would become remembered as that of the "old immigration," and while it was not totally free of nativist backlash,[56] it was characterized overall by a continual open-door approach to European immigration. The belief was widespread that as a rising power with the resources and space to accommodate a much larger population, America needed and could easily adjust to the migratory influx. Not until the twentieth century would immigration become a controversial enough issue to effect a fundamental revision of that earlier, liberal, approach, which had been animated not only by the empirical conviction that the "melting pot" was working efficiently, but also by the normative assumption that the country could and should be a refuge for all seeking its shelter. We are going to discover in the two subsequent chapters how large a part foreign policy considerations were to have in the revision of America's immigration policy, given the belief of so many in the years 1914–1917 that the country's multicultural mix endangered national security, even raising the prospect that a tilt toward either group of European belligerents could, in the dramatic words of one historian, "bring [. . .] on a civil war at home."[57]

But the revision also owed a great deal to matters not linked to the European fighting. Changing attitudes toward ethnicity and "race" conspired to feed a growing apprehension about immigration, especially as the most recent waves to arrive from Europe, from the 1890s on, were doing so more and more from the southernmost and easternmost portions of the continent. This period became known as the era of the "new immigration," and increasingly the argument was being made that people from these other European countries were incapable of successfully assimilating into American society.[58] By the 1920s, therefore, a new attitude toward immigration became pronounced in the United States, and until the revisions of 1965, policy generally was restrictive.[59] Since 1965, however, there has been an approximation of that earlier pattern, in that the United States once more has become a significant immigrant-receiving country. However, there was one major difference from that earlier, liberal, era: after 1965, Europe would figure as an inconsequential source of immigrants, while other regions, especially Asia and Latin America, would become the major sources of the country's new arrivals. As a result, there have been renewed and intensified debates about immigration, now that so much of it was stemming from the so-called Third World. Many observers were growing convinced that this latest wave of immigration was bound to have profound implications for both America's identity and its public policies, including its foreign policy.[60]

LOBBYING BROADLY CONSTRUED: PUBLIC OPINION AND THE "ETHNIC VOTE"

In this latest debate about immigration's meaning for America, worried voices were raised not merely about the impact upon the country's foreign policy but upon its very survival as a cohesive political (perhaps even, territorial) entity. Sounding a decidedly Huntingtonian note a decade prior to the publication of *Who Are We?*, historian Arthur Schlesinger Jr. ventured to ask whether America itself was on the verge of fracturing in the post-Cold War era, due to the combination of geopolitical and demographic factors we have been discussing in this chapter. He suspected that it was, because a "cult of ethnicity has arisen both among non-Anglo whites and among nonwhite minorities to denounce the goal of assimilation," with the result being a reversal of the nation-building project ratified in the catchphrase e pluribus unum, the second element of which was now coming to be emphasized, to the detriment of the third. Failure to reestablish the clear dominance of the "one" over the "many" would, Schlesinger was convinced, imperil the "historic idea of a unifying American identity."[61]

Others went even further. Peter Brimelow saw in the 1965 liberalization of immigration policy "Adolf Hitler's posthumous revenge on

America," because the effect of the abandonment of the restrictionist measures imposed back in the 1920s had been to "trigger [. . .] a renewed mass immigration, so huge and so systematically different from anything that had gone before as to transform—and ultimately, perhaps even to destroy—the one unquestioned victor of World War II: the American nation, as it had evolved by the middle of the twentieth century."[62] In the view of Patrick Buchanan, however, the revenge being meted out was less Hitler's than Montezuma's, with America's failure to regain control of its southern border signifying nothing less than its cultural (and perhaps, territorial) dismemberment, as a result of the *reconquista* of part of the country, the Southwest, which looked like it was becoming "a giant Kosovo, a part of the nation separated from the rest by language, ethnicity, history, and culture, . . . reabsorbed in all but name by Mexico."[63]

In this section I am going to take it as given, the alarums about America's disintegration to the contrary notwithstanding,[64] that the only debate worth pondering, at least for my purposes in this book, concerns the one about how ethnic diasporas are held to be capable (or not) of attaining influence over the shaping of American foreign policy. To say again: although in both Canada and the United States it has been remarked that ethnic interest groups have been busily flexing their "lobbying" muscles, it is only in the latter country that one has encountered interesting implications for continental security stemming from ethnic-diasporic activism of a *legal* nature. Canada's direct experience with ethnic-diasporic activism possessed of regional security significance has been more consistently associated with the extralegal initiatives mounted by clandestine transnational actors (CTAs) or non-state armed actors (NSAAs), or both.

Irrespective of whether we are analyzing either the legal or extralegal variants of diasporic activism, we need to be clear on the matter of *agency*. When we talk and write about diasporas and their impact, we are resorting to shorthand to express a more complicated idea. As such, we impute a property to a collectivity of which it cannot reasonably, in its entirety or often even in large part, be said to possess much—the property of agency. The diaspora does not and cannot "act" in any manner suggestive of cohesion, much less unanimity, among its membership. Instead, the "agents" in question will always be groups that are smaller yet more focused than the larger demographic body on whose behalf they claim to be acting. Thus we speak and write metonymically when analyzing "ethnic-diasporic" activism (including this practice we call lobbying), as an economical but also necessary means of making the point that something inherent in ethnicity might possess geopolitical significance.[65] By way of rough analogy, we might theorize ethnic-diasporic activism, mutatis mutandis, the way that Mao Zedong theorized "agrarian socialism," where the peasantry were to constitute the "lake" in which the revolutionary agents "swam"—in other words, the enablers of agency, rather than the agents themselves.

Similarly fluid is the notion of lobbying, which can and often does refer merely to groups' directly petitioning various governmental entities (in the United States' case, typically the Congress).[66] It can also, like so many other concepts in political analysis, be stretched, so as to embrace both the publicity campaigns and the electoral behavior (perceived or real) of diaspora members, which in turn become subsumed in a much broader debate regarding the impact (or lack thereof) of public opinion upon foreign policy in a democracy such as the United States. Therefore when I refer to the influence attempts made by the two large U.S.-based diasporas (the Irish Americans and German Americans), I construe lobbying in its broadest sense, subsuming both the practice of petitioning legislators and the attempts to influence both public opinion and public policy by resorting to the presumably potent "ethnic vote" in federal elections—above all, those presidential elections about which it might be said that important issues of foreign policy were being put before the electorate.

This latter consideration, appertaining to the electoral clout said to be in the possession of certain diasporas, taps into a larger debate regarding the part public opinion does and should play in the making of American foreign policy, given that the most effective forum in which, presumably, the public "speaks" and therefore "influences" the ballot box. There is, of course, no scholarly consensus on whether U.S. foreign policy making does pay much, if any, heed to the often aleatory instruction imparted through public opinion. Much less is there any agreement as to whether it is a good thing or not for governments to pay such heed in the first place. In the case of both aspects of diasporic activism that hew to a legal, constitutional path, namely lobbying narrowly conceived and lobbying more broadly construed so as to include voting, there is similarly more disagreement than agreement among the experts, rendering incredibly complex the task of attempting to demonstrate how, or even *if*, ethnic-diasporic activism can be said to yield influence over the policy process.

Some skeptics can be encountered who dismiss outright the thought that such ethnic diasporas *can* shape U.S. foreign policy, and they insist to the contrary that it is always raison d'état, as interpreted, explained, and promoted by the foreign policy professionals, that prevails in policy making. Sometimes, the skeptics argue, these central decision makers will give the appearance of acting according to the preferences (some say, instructions) of ethnic lobbies, but the cause and effect relationship between state and lobby is precisely that between the dog and its tail: it is the former that wags the latter, not the other way around. Seen in this light, states at times (should the need arise) skillfully exploit the lobbies, so as to get these latter to promote policy choices that they had little part in designing, but from whose design they might nevertheless hope to derive advantage. Interpreted thusly, there really is nothing causally significant about diasporas and their militancy, although it can certainly be interesting to make note of how the state conscripts the diaspora for its own purposes.[67] But on those items that truly matter in foreign policy making, the job of defining and defending the national interest remains the preserve of central decision makers.

Now, the classical realist in me has sympathy with the statist, and skeptical, perspective. There have been clear and frequent instances when the skeptics seem to express the relationship between state and diaspora just about right.[68] Still, it seems more than a bit abrupt to dismiss outright the possibility that ethnic diasporas might indeed have an impact upon the course of U.S. foreign policy, especially for someone such as myself, whose argument in this book depends very much upon some kind of postulated and important connection between diasporic influence and the North American security community. So I am perforce going to proceed as if theories of ethnic influence over U.S. foreign policy do deserve a careful airing. Let us start with the widest set of such theories, which try to link public opinion causally with foreign policy making, and take the best expression of the former to be vox populi as revealed at the ballot box.

A half century ago, diplomatic historian Ernest R. May injected a cautionary note into the gathering debate as to whether foreign policy makers were according suitable attention to the wishes of the public, when designing an agenda intended to enhance the promotion of the national interest. Addressing the two principal ways in which the debate in the United States had been getting framed—to wit, by querying whether in fact the policymakers *did* pay attention to the public, and (quite irrespective of the answer to this) asking whether they *should* pay attention—May lamented that there was in America a widespread "ideology" reflective of the view that in a democracy such as the United States, it only made sense that the public's will should be understood, and its desires accommodated, in matters not only of domestic public policy, but also and especially of foreign policy.

Even realists such as Hans Morgenthau and George Kennan took the argument to be halfway correct: they thought, although they very much regretted, that foreign policy *was* too often being crafted according to expressed public preferences, with the result being that the expertise of the professionals was getting overlooked, with predictably baneful results. May, however, was dubious about assertions that opinion really *did* possess great significance in the design and articulation of policy, and he especially doubted that the public could and did make its preferences known, and accepted, through the ballot box—a view he criticized as reflecting "traditional Enlightenment assumptions about democratic processes," yet a view he found utterly lacking in empirical support. "The fact is," he averred, "that there is almost no evidence to support the proposition that officeholders have to heed public opinion when deciding issues of foreign policy." He called on scholars to examine critically the assumptions regarding popular will as expressed in elections, especially when such assumptions were being made about foreign policy, the issues appertaining to which he called "the extreme cases. Except on rare occasions, as in 1900 and 1920, such issues have not divided parties. Seldom have they gripped the attention of sizable pressure groups. Interpretations of public attitudes on foreign policy can almost never be drawn from election data."[69]

May was not saying that opinion could, much less should, be completely discounted; rather he was suggesting something else, that scholars detach themselves from their unfounded suppositions regarding public opinion, fuelled as these seemed to have been by a desire that policy be fashioned according to "some sort of general will," itself born of a national tradition in concordance with William of Malmesbury's understanding of vox populi, taken to be the closest thing imaginable to vox Dei. "American political leaders," chided May, "have hearkened to the voice of the people as their seventeenth-century forebears did to the voice of God. Perhaps scholars, instead of listening for these voices themselves, ought to begin by inquiring what it is that these men thought they heard."[70]

Over the ensuing decades, numerous research projects have been mounted whose aim has been to uncover the role of public opinion in foreign policy, as well as to discover whether national elections could be said to serve as the means by which the public's will became the state's obligations, and if so, how.[71] There has also, as we know, been a growing body of writing regarding that particular component of the public with which this book is concerned, ethnic diasporas. Notwithstanding all of this work, we are no closer than we have ever been to scholarly consensus regarding the importance of public opinion for foreign policy making, to say nothing of the role of elections in expressing the preferences of the public; this applies both to the generic study of opinion and policy as well as to this book's more focused concern upon ethnic diasporic lobbying broadly construed. Because attention is going to be directed, in chapters four and five, toward the mooted impact the "ethnic vote" has had upon foreign policy issues of great importance to what one scholar has rightly called America's "two king-sized minority groups—the Irish and the Germans,"[72] it is worth our spending a bit of time here on that scholarly discussion, prior to closing out this chapter with an assessment of ethnic lobbying *narrowly* construed.

Bernard C. Cohen is one of those scholars who think we do not know very much about the generic problem of public opinion and its presumed impact upon foreign policy making. Despite all the scholarly labor expended upon studying the topic, he concludes that "[w]hen we look at the area we variously call the nexus, or the linkages, or the impact of opinions on decision, . . . [w]e are left, along with V.O. Key, with the unsatisfactory conclusion that public opinion is important in the policy making process, though we cannot say with confidence how, why, or when." The reasons for this shortfall in usable knowledge, Cohen argues, can all be traced back to the unfortunate way in which most research projects have been framed, concentrated as they have tended to be upon a set of misleading categories of inquiry, predicated upon 1) "nonevidential assertions or implication of influence"; or 2) an "'osmosis' hypothesis," which basically treats the topic as self-evident, contained within some vague references to a "climate of opinion"; or 3) the "highly improbable relationship"—that is, an account that violates common sense in drawing an ostensive linkage between opinion and decision; or 4) the "empirically irrefutable proposition"—as, for instance, when someone such as Walter Lippmann pronounces, ex cathedra, that opinion is a "latent veto" no president can afford to overlook.[73]

As did May before him, so too did Cohen believe that the prevailing level of ignorance in respect of the impact that public opinion *might* be said to have upon policy making reflected too much faith in matters ideological, especially those rooted in the expectation of the citizen's right to have a voice in important decisions, accompanied by too little reliance upon good theory. His is not so much a counsel of despair as it is a reminder that the objective of scholars, when they seek to generalize upon the public's impact on policy, should always be to try to get inside the heads of decision makers, so that the scholars might understand how the latter actually perceived the linkage between public opinion and public policy. He concludes, sounding rather like Max Weber and other adherents to a heuristic (or "interpretive") epistemology, "I am concerned, thus, not to discover how officials perceive and react to what *I* may think of as public opinion, but to discover what aspects of the external environment come into *their* consciousness as politically relevant factors."[74]

I find this to be good advice, and in the first two case studies, chapters four and five, I will be attempting to take the measure of ethnic lobbying broadly construed, partly by looking at what was being alleged regarding the power of the ethnic vote to sway certain national elections, particularly from the point of the view of the central actors, both personal and institutional, involved in those foreign policy matters considered to be consequential for North American security cooperation (or the lack thereof). As we know, there have been many hypotheses advanced in recent years, growing in number since the ending of the Cold War for reasons related above, regarding the presumed influence of ethnic pressure groups upon foreign policy. Some assume that there *is* enhanced diasporic influence, and that it is not beneficial for American foreign policy writ large; others agree that diasporas *are* getting more voice in foreign policy, and that it is a good thing.[75] We also know that this renewed interest in the impact of ethnicity upon foreign policy represents but a resumption of a long-standing pattern of interrogation among those who study the connection between diasporas and policy making. In the concluding section of this chapter, I am going to concentrate upon lobbying in its narrower sense, whereby special interests petition governmental bodies for preferential treatment, usually (though not always) intended to advance interests of the kin-state (or ancestral homeland).

Before examining lobbying in its narrowest sense, however, let us close this section by canvassing the state of thinking (scholarly and otherwise) regarding the electoral power of the "ethnic bloc." The most recent U.S. presidential election, in 2012, appeared to give a fillip to those who believe that America's changing demographic mix has profound implications for electoral outcomes. In particular, the argument is that the Republican candidate, Mitt Romney, was severely handicapped by his and his party's inability to harvest enough votes from two increasingly important demographic cohorts, one of which was gender-specific (i.e., women) and the other ethnicity-specific (i.e., Latinos and especially Mexican Americans).[76] Usually, analysts who have looked at this and other presidential (and some congressional) elections spend most of their time upon ethnicity's consequences for *domestic* policy, but occasionally some have proffered views in recent years as to what America's shifting demography portends for its foreign policy.[77]

One such writer is Scott McConnell, who in 2009 sought to establish a connection between an America becoming increasingly multiethnic and a growing propensity toward noninvolvement in global affairs. McConnell was in no doubt as to whether ethnic-diasporic activism had been making a difference in foreign policy ever since the ending of the Cold War, for of this, he was certain. "Indeed," he asserted, "if one were to examine some of the major policy milestones of the Clinton era—active participation in the Northern Ireland peace process, the military occupation of Haiti, expanded trade embargoes on Cuba and Iran, the revelation of the Swiss banking scandals—it could be argued that ethnic lobbies were, as much as any coherent grand strategy, the era's prime movers." Not only this, but contrary to predictions that an increasingly multicultural America would imply good things for American global leadership because it would compel greater "internationalism," McConnell foresaw just the reverse occurring, a return, if not to isolationism then at least to an era when America's leaders had instinctively drawn back from ambitious foreign policies. In making this forecast, he detected a sublime irony: "On the basis of what is visible thus far, today's and tomorrow's Mexican-, Asian-, and Arab-Americans will more resemble the Swedes, Germans, and Irish of a century ago than the Poles, Balts, and Cubans of the Cold War era."[78]

What McConnell meant with his references to ethnic diasporas a hundred years ago—the "Swedes, Germans, and Irish"—was clear: these were all groups that militated, during the run-up to the First World War and from 1914 until 1917, for American nonparticipation in the global conflict, for reasons we will encounter (at least in respect of the Irish and

Germans) in chapters four and five. What was ironical could only be understood in the context of the past decade's debate within conservative circles about the wisdom of energetic "nation-building" promoted by the George W. Bush administration in the Middle East—a debate that pitted so-called neoconservatives favoring intervention against anti-interventionist paleoconservatives.[79] The former, children of immigrants themselves, had been among the prominent advocates of liberal immigration policies, while the latter championed restrictionism, and yet, as McConnell noted, "realists and America-Firsters will find their foreign policy aspirations at least partially satisfied via the unlikely avenues of immigration and multiculturalism. The paleoconservatives, losers in the immigration wars, will end up winners of an important consolation prize: the foreign policy of what remains of their cherished republic."[80]

In highlighting this irony, and in making explicit reference to diasporas a century ago who were thought to possess, through the ethnic vote, considerable leverage over U.S. foreign policy (viz., the Irish Americans and German Americans), McConnell leads his reader to the inference that the ballot box must be the mechanism that most successfully converts ethnic-diasporic preferences into policy outputs. Yet some of the examples he provides to substantiate his claim of ethnic clout (viz., Clinton policy initiatives on Haiti and the Swiss banking scandals) actually speak to that second aspect of lobbying introduced earlier, to be discussed below: the more narrowly focused activities of organized diasporas who seek positive policy results as a result of their assiduous petitioning of members of Congress, particularly those from the House of Representatives. This does not mean McConnell's assumptions about diasporic influence are misleading, but it does serve to remind us that the ethnic vote may not, after all, be the best place to look if one is seeking to assess foreign policy impact.

As with so much else appertaining to ethnic-diasporic activism, controversy reigns over exactly what can be deduced from the broad construe of lobbying as reflected in assumptions about the ethnic vote. Some scholars, for instance, take it as axiomatic that vote-focused diasporic activism can and does lead to policy change. Shortly after the Second World War, Samuel Lubell pronounced that ethnicity had precisely this effect, not only on America's domestic political arena, but on its foreign policy as well. In respect of the latter, he argued that it was ethnicity that had, prior to the war, made "isolationism" the default option of presidents fearful of alienating the large blocs of German, Irish, and Italian voters, and as a result suffering punishment on election day.[81] In stating this thesis, Lubell was challenging some assumptions about two particular foreign policy orientations, "isolationism" and "internationalism," which many scholars have been construing as primarily explicable in terms of *region* rather than ethnicity.[82] Lubell was hardly the first person to draw attention to the ethnic-vote thesis, nor would he be the last.[83]

Two decades later, Mark Levy and Michael Kramer would dramatically restate the thesis, only in a much more comprehensive and magnified version, when they basically pronounced the ethnic vote to be *the* single most important determinant of electoral outcomes in America.[84] And much more recently, ethnic voting has been again invoked as at least part of the explanation for such strategic decisions as, to take just one example, the enlargement of NATO in the mid-1990s.[85]

It is not my purpose here to debunk the ethnic-bloc thesis, simply to urge that we take such assumptions with more than the usual caution. There are three reasons for my saying this. The first is that foreign policy usually does not figure as the central issue with which the electorate grapples in presidential elections. The second is that even when it could be said that foreign policy did loom as a major concern, as for instance many think was the case in 1916 and again in 1920, it is far from clear that voter preferences were in any important way structured by concern with developments overseas rather than at home (a matter to which I will return in chapters four and five).[86] Third and most importantly, we have already experienced, above, some scholarly skepticism regarding claims that public opinion really does influence foreign policy making very much. To the extent that research calls into question broad-brush theories regarding the impact of public opinion upon policy, it must likewise cast into some doubt assumptions that the ballot box *is* the vector of most significance in converting diasporic activism into policy outputs—at least it must do so if we assume that opinion matters because it governs how the electorate responds to choices put before it at election time.

Yet if this is so, a recent study by two leading experts on public opinion throws some very cold water on assertions of ethnic voting power. Using data drawn from eight quadrennial pairs of surveys commissioned by the Chicago Council on Foreign Relations, and conducted between 1974 and 2002 by America's two leading opinion samplers (Gallup and Harris), authors Lawrence Jacobs and Benjamin Page sought definitively to answer the question of who influences the country's foreign policy. Their findings are, in their own word, "sobering," especially to advocates of "democratic theory," who hold that the public does and should govern the formation of foreign policy. Not so, say Jacobs and Page, noting that what their own research tells them flies in the face of commonly held assumptions that U.S. foreign policy is "substantially influenced" by public opinion.[87]

> Perhaps the most surprising finding in this whole set of analyses is the apparent weakness of public opinion. Even with these reduced and refined models, the public does not appear to exert substantial, consistent influence on the makers of foreign policy. . . . In short, in spite of generous model specifications, the effect of public opinion on the preferences of foreign policy makers appears to be—at best—modest, when critical competing variables are controlled for. In general, public opin-

ion takes a back seat to business and experts. These results challenge research that has suggested a generally strong public impact on foreign policy.[88]

LOBBYING NARROWLY CONSTRUED: THE "FOURTH BRANCH" OF GOVERNMENT

Lawrence Jacobs and Benjamin Page, in revealing the rather weak impact public opinion has upon foreign policy making, did not mean to suggest that the statist skeptics were correct all along, and that decision-making authority remained exactly where the realists hoped it should be, in the capable hands of those central authorities who were best positioned to interpret and promote the national interest. Quite the contrary, said Jacobs and Page; simply because the public did not have much of a constraining impact upon policy, it did not follow that the latter was under the control of central decision makers. Instead, they argued, in so many words, that Huntington's forebodings were actually reflective of contemporary reality, with one major exception to be discussed below: "special interests" were indeed exercising a growing impact upon foreign policy, and this was worrisome. "Our results," they concluded, "have some troubling normative implications. The apparently weak influence of the public will presumably disappoint those adherents of democratic theory . . . who advocate substantial government responsiveness to the reasoned preferences of citizens." But the realists should not derive too much comfort from this, given that the policy void is more than being filled by special interests, among which the most important, they argued, were *business* interests. "Competing political interests continue to fight over the national interest, and business often wins that competition."[89]

Note that Jacobs and Page did not follow Huntington totally; they refrained from according much (or any) weight to *ethnic* interest groups. Nevertheless, there are, as we are well aware, other students of foreign policy making who do stretch the envelope of curiosity further, so that ethnic-diasporic activism can be made to fit, sometimes almost exclusively so, into their own accounts of "lobbying" narrowly construed. Let us then, in this final section of the chapter, survey some of the claims and theories that have been advanced in respect of the influence attempts mounted by ethnic lobbies, as lobbying is traditionally employed, and not in the more expansive way in which I addressed the practice above. Just as the preceding discussion of lobbying (broadly construed) was nested in another debate, the one over the impact of public opinion as expressed through voting, so too will the following analysis of lobbying (narrowly construed) be contained within a wider body of scholarship regarding the generic category.

The place to start this analysis is with terminology. The English word "lobby" is a derivative of the Latin *lobium*, a covered walk in a cloister or a monastery, hence the ease with which it would come to find political application, initially in respect of the British House of Commons. In that initial political employment, a "lobbyist" was a journalist whose business entailed reporting, from the corridors of power, on the doings of government, while a "lobby-agent" was a different breed of cat altogether, someone who tried to *influence* legislators' decisions. Over time, that different breed would come to monopolize the label "lobbyist." This terminological alchemy was first performed not in a British but in an American context, specifically New York's capital city, Albany. Semantic alterations made there in the 1820s and 1830s caught on in the rest of the country, to such a degree that lobbying has ever since occupied a prominent place in debates about U.S. domestic and foreign policy making.

It is more than fitting that it should have been in the United States that both the word and the practice became so widespread. As was noted earlier in this chapter, American constitutional and demographic realities predisposed the country toward lobbying. The latter, demography, we have already discussed. As for the former, it needs to be said that the United States has been and remains structurally very accommodative of the practice, which it is why lobbyists are sometimes considered the "third house of Congress," or even the "fourth branch of government." The important point to keep in mind is that not only is lobbying perfectly legal, it is also, by some, revered, representing as it does a precious safeguard against the arbitrary exercise of (executive) power, and serving as the institutional embodiment of the constitutional right of Americans to *petition* government—a gift handed down to the present as a direct legacy from democracy's past, extending from the Magna Carta in 1215, through the Stamp Act Congress of 1765, the First Continental Congress, the Declaration of Independence, and finally coming to lodge in the First Amendment of the Constitution, granting the people the right "peaceably to assemble, and to petition the Government for a redress of grievances." [90] And while this hallowed right applies to all branches of government in theory, in practice it is almost exclusively the legislative branch to which the lobbyists pitch their woo. The lobbying of Congress takes three primary forms, the first and most important of which being direct contact with members of Congress or their staffers, the second being indirect (so-called grassroots) initiatives intended to secure influence on a member by public-relations campaigns in his or her district, and the third, even more indirect, finding its expression in the practice of "cross-lobbying," in which lobbyists approach other lobbyists to arrange mutual support on issues of concern to either (or the principle of "logrolling"). [91]

It is hardly surprising, given the centrality of Congress in the lobbying phenomenon, that the practice has far fewer fans than enemies, and this notwithstanding (perhaps because of?) the absolute explosion in the number of lobbying firms and individual lobbyists in Washington during the past several years, such that by the start of the current decade there were some 14,000 registered lobbyists in the capital, a considerable number of them being former congressional staffers.[92] At a time when many scholars are concluding that Congress has become severely dysfunctional (to say the least), and with polls continuing to show that most of the American public agrees with this assessment, one can understand why lobbying should be in such bad odor today.[93] Before endorsing the majority view about the pernicious impact of lobbying, though, let us take a quick look at some dispassionate arguments concerning issues of how, or even whether, lobbying does make an impact upon public policy.

The case against lobbying comes to rest upon a combination of assumptions, all predicated on the thought that lobbyists frustrate the "general will," and therefore are fundamentally antidemocratic agents. It is sometimes said that the House of Representatives, being the legislative chamber closest to the people, if for no other reason than its short (two-year) electoral cycle bids members to keep constant thumb-pressure on the public pulse, is the organ of government most reflective of this notional general will.[94] If this is so, then anything thought to distort the workings of that body must be said to tamper with the articulation and defense of the national interest in its most sensitive and legitimate forum. Presumably, lobbying in the Senate is less damaging, more a venial than a mortal sin. In either chamber, the transgression inheres in the cheapening and corruption of democratic governance. This happens because lobbyists frustrate the ability of the Congress to comprehend and to act upon its own "intentions." Even worse, they lubricate the decision-making process with filthy lucre.

What can we say about these claims? For starters, it is hard to disagree with one scholar's assessment that it is simply fallacious to impute "intent" to an institutional body such as the U.S. Congress, especially the House, with its collective ear so purportedly close to the people's lips. Not only is it fallacious, says Kenneth A. Shepsle, it is absurdly self-contradictory, for the notion of "legislative intent" is nothing other than an oxymoron. "[L]egislative intent, along with military intelligence, jumbo shrimp, and student athlete, belongs in this category. Legislative intent is an internally inconsistent, self-contradictory expression. Therefore, it has no meaning."[95] Much more important to the process of legislating than general preferences, either of the electorate or the members of Congress themselves, are the institutional norms and procedures that guarantee "there is no strong or obvious relationship between the exercisers of agenda power and the preferences of majorities. To the extent such exercises of agenda power affect the content of legislation [. . .], they cannot be traced to majoritarian preferences."[96]

If by definition there cannot be any general will animating legislative action, then it cannot be charged of lobbyists that they distort collective preferences, or at least that they are particularly culpable in this respect, given Shepsle's claim about the fictitious nature of legislative intent. But what of the argument that lobbying debases democracy because of the constant need of aspirants to legislative office to raise the funds they need to run for election in the first place, or to get themselves reelected? No one believes for a nanosecond that money is irrelevant to American (or other countries') electoral practices, and where there is money there will also be the danger of funds being misused. But are opinions being swayed, and House and Senate votes being bought, by the special interests? If they are today, it can at least be said that compared to the late nineteenth and early twentieth centuries, they are being purchased less, which is another way of putting forward the thought that however much the special interests, especially those supportive of "plutocracy," might be suborning American politicians today, they did far greater damage to democratic governance during the Gilded Age. This may be small comfort to those who hold high standards of democratic accountability,[97] but the more important issue here concerns whether, in fact, money is "talking" as much as it is sometimes maintained, with pernicious implications for democracy. And on this question, we once again find the scholars in their customary position of being divided. This is so, not only on the matter of money buying votes in elections, but also on its purchasing influence over legislation. As concluded by one student of the issue, lobbying presents the classic chicken-and-egg conundrum, to wit, "[d]o incumbents who receive money from special-interest groups cater to their wishes because they received campaign contributions, or do they receive campaign contributions because they are already committed to the interest group's point of view?"[98] On this important question, the best that can be said is that the evidence is mixed.

A few students of lobbying have even thought to portray it as something of a public good, an activity that far from damaging democracy actually strengthens it. This is the interesting claim by Richard Hall and Alan Deardorff, who reject traditional views that hold lobbying's primary logic to reside in the goal of getting legislators to alter their preferences. Instead, "[w]e propose a fundamentally different but fundamentally simple theory of lobbying. The main idea is that lobbying is primarily a form of legislative subsidy—a matching grant of costly policy information, political intelligence, and labor to the enterprises of strategically selected legislators. The proximate objective of this strategy is not to change legislators' minds but to assist natural allies in achieving their own, coincident objectives."[99] Rather than regarding them as the villainous pack they so often are imagined to be, why not think of lobbyists as legislators' unpaid (by them, at least) research assistants, enabling those who craft laws to do so with more information than they would possess in the absence of lobbying? Not miscreants but public-goods providers: this is how lobbyists ought to be comprehended, as people who "enlarge the resources that legislators have to work on behalf of their constituents. In this sense, lobbyists are actually good for representation."[100] Still, problems arise, particularly when one considers that resource-rich lobbies will inevitably have the upper hand in these subsidization sweepstakes. Money may not, in the end, talk, but it certainly mumbles fairly loudly, or at least indulges in stage whispers.

So much for this survey of lobbying as a generic enterprise; what can we say specifically about *ethnic* lobbying intended to make an impact upon foreign policy? How do the scholars assess the always difficult matter of demonstrating rather than merely assuming influence when they turn their attention to ethnic lobbies as narrowly construed? To begin with, some of them draw a firm line between lobbying's impact upon the domestic arena and its ability to sway decision makers on matters relating to foreign policy. The distinction, says one leading student of the lobbying phenomenon and his colleagues, inheres in two aspects of foreign policy that sets it apart from the hurly-burly of domestic politics: 1) the "centrality of the president" to foreign policy decision making, which renders Congress (and therefore lobbying of same) a much less relevant fact of political life; and 2) the sheer volume of policy in the foreign relations sphere that does not require being "legislated," and thus gets a considerable amount of freedom from the politics of pressure.[101]

Coupled with this, argues this same expert, Frank Baumgartner, is the American political system's fundamental bias in favor of the status quo, stemming from a surprising congruence in policy views (what he calls "shared information") emanating from the lobbying process itself, such that there emerges an epistemic community—"a policy community . . . made up of experts, and they were not born yesterday; naïve is not the operating rule within Washington, after all. . . . The broad base of participation in a policy community suggests that the stability that comes from the shared understandings of the current workings of a given public policy will likely be quite enduring." What change does come as a result of lobbyists' influence attempts, then, is usually at the margin, given that it is so hard to overturn, and easy to defend, the status quo. As Baumgartner and associates conclude: "Defenders of the status quo usually win in Washington."[102]

In partial agreement with the above-stated assertions is James M. Lindsay, who doubts that ethnic lobbies *have* been getting too great a voice in the foreign policy-making process. Nor does he believe that these lobbies have been able to steer the ship of state into waters it should never be plowing; when they do manage to have an impact upon policy making, it tends rather to reinforce the status quo than to reverse it. But Lindsay has a difficult time accepting that firm lines of demarcation hive off the foreign from the domestic policy arenas.[103] This is because, "[i]n

America, global politics is local politics—and local politics, often, is ethnic politics." That being conceded, it remains for policy analysts to try to understand why and how ethnic lobbies do manage, from time to time, to achieve influence over policy making, for he is certain that, "[o]n balance, ethnic groups matter, but not nearly as much or as often as people might suspect." It helps the cause of ethnic diasporas engaged in lobbying for foreign policy objectives if their ancestral homeland somehow is facing a threat that in some ways can also be construed as a threat to *American* interests, but congruent threat assessment is not enough to guarantee influence. "So when," he asks, "are ethnic lobbies likely to get their way? That depends on both the characteristics of the lobby itself and the broader political context in which it operates." In respect of the former, he lists four essential attributes of successful diasporic lobbying: 1) commitment, 2) unity, 3) resources, and 4) political skill. As for the latter, the broader political context, it very much matters whether the diaspora finds itself being opposed by "other powerful interests." [104]

Lindsay acknowledges that ethnic lobbies (viz., the earlier-cited criticism made by Huntington among others) attract their share of "passionate critics because of the lurking suspicion that they put the interests of their ancestral homeland before those of the United States. It is impossible to say whether this claim is true. The national interest and the best means for promoting it are not objective facts." Nevertheless, he is inclined to believe, on balance, that ethnic lobbying, when it is successful, is so because it advances America's national interests; it does not detract from them. Thus he is confident that, "in the main, the end result of ethnic lobbying will be not so much to capture American foreign policy as to enrich it." [105]

Charles McCurdy Mathias, whom we encountered briefly some pages back, was a U.S. senator who had direct experience with pressure politics exercised on behalf of ethnic diasporas. His views on the implication of such diasporic activism, like Lindsay's, were somewhat mixed, although less favorably disposed toward ethnic lobbies. And if he was certainly not prepared to claim that ethnic lobbying subverted the national interest, it could be said at times to have derogated from it. Mostly, though, he regarded diasporic activism's most "baneful" impact to be the manner in which emotion and incivility so often became infused into congressional debates that involved someone's ancestral homeland. Thus he found in emotionalism the answer to questions regarding the efficacy of ethnic lobbying. "The 'secret weapon' of ethnic interest groups," he argued, "is neither money nor technique, which are available to other interest groups as well, but the ability to galvanize for specific political objectives the strong emotional bonds of large numbers of Americans to their cultural or ancestral homes." [106] Importantly, Mathias appears to be isolating the "variable" of diasporic *size* as the most relevant consideration, which if true, suggests that variant of lobbying discussed in the preceding section, broadly construed so that it comes to depend upon one or another version of the "ethnic vote" argument, is what should be of most interest to us when we explore whether and how ethnic-diasporic activism can be incorporated into accounts about the rise and evolution of the North American security community.

Yet not all who study ethnic lobbies and foreign policy are prepared to give in to the temptation to grant to size alone the status of *primus inter pares*, when sifting through the necessary conditions held to account for influence. Some analysts take a counterintuitive tack in their bid to make lobbying correspond with influence. One such is Trevor Rubenzer, who has provided one of the few systematic attempts to assess the effectiveness of diasporic activism. For him, size alone is neither here nor there; much more important is the ability of diasporic groups to *organize* effectively, and the best way for them to do this is to mimic the manner in which other, nonethnic, pressure groups play the game. "Ethnic identity groups that are successful at influencing U.S. foreign policy," he tells us, "are successful because they operate well as interest groups. *Simply having a large number of potential members, even if these members are relatively unified, does not mean that influence will occur.*" [107] Although Rubenzer is not the only analyst to minimize the impact of a diaspora's size on its effectiveness, [108] his cautionary note here is apt, even if not totally persuasive, in light of what we shall discover in chapters four and five.

In those two chapters, we will learn why Rubenzer's stress upon interest-group effectiveness, its tautological nature aside (to wit, nothing succeeds like success), brings us back to where we started in this chapter's inquiry into ethnic-diasporic lobbying: the broad construe. There is a reason why so much attention used regularly to be paid, in the decades stretching from the Civil War to the Great War, to the two particular ethnic groups featured in chapters four and five, the Irish Americans and the German Americans: they were the two largest ethnic groups in the United States, apart from the English-descended Americans.

Although in the case of the first-named, the Irish Americans, great weight would come to be placed upon their presumed electoral preferences, it was ironically not really in the legal and constitutionally recognized aspects of ethnic-diasporic activism that they emerged as a complicating element in North American regional security, in the first place. Instead, it was primarily through extralegal influence attempts that depended upon force and the threat of force that Irish America began to be regarded, both in North America and Great Britain, as the principal element working against any fundamental improvement in the quality of interstate security relations within the Brebnerian "North Atlantic Triangle." [109]

Accordingly, the discussion of our first of the three case studies begins with an aspect of diasporic activism that decidedly should *never* be confused with the phenomenon of lobbying, no matter how broadly we construe the latter.

NOTES

1. John Mearsheimer and Stephen Walt, "The Israel Lobby," *London Review of Books* 28 (23 March 2006); and Mearsheimer and Walt, *The Israel Lobby and U.S. Foreign Policy* (New York: Penguin, 2007).

2. Michael Massing, "The Storm over the Israel Lobby," *New York Review of Books* 53 (8 June 2006).

3. Abraham H. Foxman, *The Deadliest Lies: The Israel Lobby and the Myth of Jewish Control* (New York: Palgrave Macmillan, 2007), pp. 55, 65. Also see the more restrained, yet still negative, assessment of the Mearsheimer-Walt thesis in Dore Gold, "Blaming Israel," *International Herald Tribune*, 17 October 2007, p. 6.

4. For the former critique, see Robert C. Lieberman, "The 'Israel Lobby' and American Politics," *Perspectives on Politics* 7 (June 2009): 235–57; for the latter, see the contribution by Mackubin Thomas Owens, of the Naval War College in Newport, Rhode Island, who wonders whether "aliens have taken over the bodies" of the two *ur*-realist professors, in "Debating the Israel Lobby," *Foreign Policy*, no. 156 (September/October 2006), p. 4.

5. Walter Russell Mead, "The New Israel and the Old: Why Gentile Americans Back the Jewish State," *Foreign Affairs* 87 (July/August 2008): 28–46.

6. Andrew J. Bacevich, "Review Essay," *Diplomacy & Statecraft* 19 (December 2008): 787–95, quote at p. 792.

7. Jennifer Schuessler, "A Bastion for Israel, Seething Inside," *New York Times*, 1 March 2004, pp. B1, B7. Also see n. 83, below.

8. Notes one historian of diaspora, we really think of Jews when we think of diaspora, following the destruction both of the first temple of Jerusalem (586 BCE) and of the second (70 CE); thus "[t]he Jewish diaspora, in my judgment, is quite literally incomparable to any other in its most salient characteristics," so much so that were it possible to police our terminology (it is not), he would plump for the concept's being "limited only to the ancient Hebrews and their descendants, the modern Jews." Donald Harman Akenson, "The Historiography of English-Speaking Canada and the Concept of Diaspora: A Sceptical Appreciation." *Canadian Historical Review* 76 (September 1995): 377–409, quote at pp. 378–79.

9. Gabriel Sheffer, *Diaspora Politics: At Home and Abroad* (Cambridge: Cambridge University Press, 2003), p. 33. Also see Milton J. Esman, *Diasporas in the Contemporary World* (Cambridge: Polity, 2009).

10. Robin Cohen, "Diasporas and the Nation-State: From Victims to Challengers," *International Affairs* 72 (July 1996): 507–20.

11. And in this respect, he pays heed to the cautionary advice tendered to those who might wish to loosen the denotative qualities of a concept, best expressed by Giovanni Sartori, "Concept Misformation in Comparative Politics," *American Political Science Review* 64 (December 1970): 1033–53.

12. Rogers Brubaker, "The 'Diaspora' Diaspora," *Ethnic and Racial Studies* 28 (January 2005): 1–19, quote at pp. 3–4.

13. Brubaker, "The 'Diaspora' Diaspora," pp. 11–13 (emphasis in the original).

14. On this group, see Patrick J. Haney and Walt Vanderbush, "The Role of Ethnic Interest Groups in U.S. Foreign Policy: The Case of the Cuban American National Foundation," *International Studies Quarterly* 43 (June 1999): 341–61.

15. See Louis R. Fraga et al., *Latinos in the New Millennium: An Almanac of Opinion, Behavior, and Policy Preferences* (New York: Cambridge University Press, 2011).

16. Laurence Halley, *Ancient Affections: Ethnic Groups and Foreign Policy* (New York: Praeger, 1985).

17. Here I adopt the usage of Henry Hale, who himself takes instruction from Max Weber on the matter of defining ethnicity: "By 'ethnic,' we follow Weber in referring to perceptions of common descent and culture along with at least some traits usually associated with those things, including shared language, physical resemblance, and common ritual regulation of life, including religion." Henry E. Hale, *The Foundations of Ethnic Politics: Separatism of States and Nations in Eurasia and the World* (New York: Cambridge University Press, 2008), p. 47.

18. See, for instance, Behrooz Ghamari-Tabrizi, "Loving America and Longing for Home: Isma'il al-Faruqi and the Emergence of the Muslim Diaspora in North America," *International Migration* 42 (June 2004): 61–86.

19. But for a dissenting view, predicated upon a looser understanding of diaspora than that offered by Brubaker, compare Mathias Schulze et al., eds., *German Diasporic Experiences: Identity, Migration, and Loss* (Waterloo, ON: Wilfrid Laurier Press, 2008). Also regarding them as an extant diaspora, but not a particularly relevant one, is Michael Lind, *The Next American Nation: The New Nationalism and the Fourth American Revolution* (New York: Free Press, 1995), pp. 286–87, where it is claimed that today, "Germany-in-America is . . . forgotten, even by German-Americans. At best, such diaspora enclaves are like television sets, receiving transmissions from the mother country but unable to transmit messages in return. At worst, they are mere curiosity shops."

20. On the dichotomous relationship between primordialists and optionalists, see Philip Gleason, "Identifying Identity: A Semantic History," *Journal of American History* 69 (March 1983): 910–31.

21. Notes one analyst, "[r]eal-world primordialists and constructivists agree that identities are constructed (i.e., that beliefs about primordiality are formed) during some identifiable period in history, that their symbolic content can vary to some degree over time, and that there is at least some variation in the intensity or nature of group identification across members." Henry Hale, "Explaining Ethnicity," *Comparative Political Studies* 37 (May 2004): 458–85, quote at pp. 461–62.

22. Quoted in Robert Gildea, *The Past in French History* (New Haven, Conn.: Yale University Press, 1994), pp. 3–4.

23. Cited by Perry Miller, *Errand into the Wilderness* (New York: Harcourt and Row, 1956), p. 169, quoting from Locke's *An Essay Concerning Human Understanding*, first published in 1690.

24. As is cogently argued in Francisco Gil-White, "How Thick Is Blood? The Plot Thickens . . . : If Ethnic Actors Are Primordialists, What Remains of the Circumstantialist/Primordialist Controversy?" *Ethnic and Racial Studies* 22 (September 1999): 789–820. Also see, on the difficulties constructivists encounter when they try to untangle themselves totally from primordialist categories, James D. Fearon and David D. Laitin, "Violence and the Social Construction of Ethnic Identity," *International Organization* 54 (Autumn 2000): 845–77.

25. Martin Bulmer and John Solomos, "Introduction: Re-thinking Ethnic and Racial Studies," *Ethnic and Racial Studies* 21 (September 1998): 819–37.

26. For a reminder of the ongoing capacity of ethnonationalism to foment violence, see Jerry Z. Muller, "Us and Them: The Enduring Power of Ethnic Nationalism," *Foreign Affairs* 87 (March/April 2008): 18–35. For critiques of the Muller thesis, as well as the latter's rebuttal of same, see "Is Ethnic Conflict Inevitable? Parting Ways over Nationalism and Separatism," *Foreign Affairs* 87 (July/August 2008): 138–50.

27. John Mueller, "The Banality of 'Ethnic War'," *International Security* 25 (Summer 2000): 42–70, quote at pp. 42, 53.

28. Bruce Gilley, "Against the Concept of Ethnic Conflict," *Third World Quarterly* 25 (September 2004): 1155–66, quote at p. 1160.

29. Charles King, "The Myth of Ethnic Warfare," *Foreign Affairs* 80 (November/December 2001): 165–70.

30. Hugh Donald Forbes, "Toward a Science of Ethnic Conflict?" *Journal of Democracy* 14 (October 2003): 172–77, quote at p. 175.

31. Stuart Kaufman, *Modern Hatreds: The Symbolic Politics of Ethnic War* (Ithaca, N.Y.: Cornell University Press, 2001); Daniel Patrick Moynihan, *Pandaemonium: Ethnicity in International Politics* (New York: Oxford University Press, 1993); Stephen Iwan Griffiths, *Nationalism and Ethnic Conflict: Threats to European Security* (Oxford: Oxford University Press, 1993).

32. See, for representative titles, Hazel Smith and Paul Stares, eds., *Diasporas in Conflict: Peace-Makers or Peace-Wreckers?* (Tokyo: United Nations Press, 2007); Stephen M. Saideman, *The Ties That Divide: Ethnic Politics, Foreign Policy, and International Politics* (New York: Columbia University Press, 2001); Myron Weiner, ed., *International Migration and Security* (Boulder, Colo.: Westview Press, 1993); and Will H. Moore, "Ethnic Minorities and Foreign Policy," *SAIS Review* 22 (Summer–Fall 2002): 77–91.

33. See, for instance, Gabriel Sheffer, "Ethno-National Diasporas and Security," *Survival* 36 (Spring 1994): 60–79.

34. Gil Loescher, "Refugee Movements and International Security," *Adelphi Papers* 268 (1992); Loescher, *Beyond Charity: International Cooperation and the Global Refugee Crisis* (New York: Oxford University Press, 1993); Paul Hockenos, *Free to Hate: The Rise of the Right in Post-Communist Eastern Europe* (New York: Routledge, 1993); Martin Baldwin-Edwards and Martin A. Schain, eds., *The Politics of Immigration in Western Europe* (Ilford, UK: Frank Cass, 1994).

35. Michael Mandelbaum, ed., *The New European Diasporas: National Minorities and Conflict in Eastern Europe* (New York: Council on Foreign Relations Press, 2000); and Charles King and Neil J. Melvin, "Ethnic Linkages, Foreign Policy, and Security in Eurasia," *International Security* 24 (Winter 1999–2000): 108–38.

36. See Yossi Shain and Aharon Barth, "Diasporas and International Relations Theory," *International Organization* 57 (Summer 2003): 449–79. For a comprehensive and balanced assessment of Armenian American diasporic activism, see Julien Zarifian, "Le 'lobby' arménien des États-Unis: Mythes et réalités," in *Minorités et pouvoir dans les pays anglophones*, ed. Taoufik Djebali (Paris: L'Harmattan, 2014), pp. 233–56.

37. As a descriptive term, "unipolarity" simply means, in the words of one leading theorist, "a structure in which one state's capabilities are too great to be counterbalanced." William Wohlforth, "The Stability of a Unipolar World," *International Security* 24 (Summer 1999): 5–41, quote at p. 9.

38. Melvin Small, *Democracy and Diplomacy: The Impact of Domestic Politics on U. S. Foreign Policy* (Baltimore: Johns Hopkins University Press, 1996), p. xvi.

39. Quoted in Thomas L. Friedman and Michael Mandelbaum, *That Used To Be Us: How America Fell Behind in the World It Invented and How We Can Come Back* (New York: Farrar, Straus and Giroux, 2011), p. 13.

40. See John Dumbrell, "America in the 1990s: Searching for Purpose," in *US Foreign Policy*, 2nd ed., ed. Michael Cox and Doug Stokes (Oxford: Oxford University Press, 2012), chap. 5. Also see, for this search, Michael E. Brown, Owen R. Coté Jr., Sean M. Lynn-Jones, and Steven E. Miller, eds., *America's Strategic Choices* (Cambridge, Mass.: MIT Press, 1997).

41. Running a close second to the political scientist Huntington was the historian Arthur Schlesinger Jr., for whom "it can scarcely be said that we have a foreign policy at all," so convinced had he become that subsequent to the disappearance of the Soviet Union the principal questions animating foreign policy making related to the most effective way ethnic constituencies could get America's backing for their particular demands. See his "Fragmentation and Hubris: A Shaky Basis for American Leadership," *National Interest*, no. 94 (Fall 1997), pp. 3–9, quote at pp. 3–4.

42. Samuel P. Huntington, "The Erosion of American National Interests," *Foreign Affairs* 76 (September/October 1997): 28–49, quote at p. 49.

43. Kenneth N. Waltz, *Theory of International Politics* (Reading, Mass.: Addison-Wesley, 1979).

44. See Robert Gilpin, *War and Change in World Politics* (Cambridge: Cambridge University Press, 1981), for a reminder that bipolarity might just be unstable and very dangerous.

45. Jeffrey Checkel, "The Constructivist Turn in International Relations Theory," *World Politics* 50 (January 1998): 324–48; Sujata Chakrabarti Pasic, "Culturing International Relations Theory: A Call for Extension," in *The Return of Culture and Identity in IR Theory*, ed. Yosef Lapid and Friedrich Kratochwil (Boulder, Colo.: Lynne Rienner, 1997), pp. 85–104; and Morris Dickstein, "After the Cold War: Culture as Politics, Politics as Culture," *Social Research* 60 (Fall 1993): 531–44.

46. Ted Hopf, "The Promise of Constructivism in International Relations Theory," *International Security* 23 (Summer 1998): 171–200.

47. John Gerard Ruggie, "The Past as Prologue? Interests, Identity, and American Foreign Policy," *International Security* 21 (Spring 1997): 89–125, quote at p. 112.

48. Samuel P. Huntington, *Who Are We? The Challenges to America's National Identity* (New York: Simon & Schuster, 2004), p. 8.

49. Optimistic assessments in the post-Cold War decade include Daniel Deudney and G. John Ikenberry, "The Logic of the West," *World Policy Journal* 10 (Winter 1993/94): 17–25; Ikenberry, "The Future of International Leadership," *Political Science Quarterly* 111 (Fall 1996): 385–402; and John Gerard Ruggie, "Multilateralism: The Anatomy of an Institution," *International Organization* 46 (Summer 1992): 561–98.

50. Huntington, *Who Are We?* p. 62.

51. Huntington, *Who Are We?* pp. 285, 291.

52. Will Kymlicka, "Being Canadian," *Government & Opposition* 38 (Summer 2003): 357–85, quote at pp. 374–75. On the negative assessment multiculturalism can receive from Québec policy intellectuals, see Kenneth McRoberts, "Canada and the Multinational State," *Canadian Journal of Political Science* 34 (December 2001): 683–713.

53. Ronald Takaki, *A Different Mirror: A History of Multicultural America* (Boston: Little, Brown, 1993).

54. Denis Lacorne, *La Crise de l'identité américaine: Du melting-pot au multiculturalisme* (Paris: Fayard, 1997), p. 20.

55. Leonard Dinnerstein and David M. Reimers, *Ethnic Americans: A History of Immigration*, 4th ed. (New York: Columbia University Press, 1999); Roger Daniels, *Coming to America: A History of Immigration and Ethnicity in American Life* (New York: HarperCollins, 1990); and Edward Prince Hutchinson, *Legislative History of American Immigration Policy, 1798–1965* (Philadelphia: University of Pennsylvania Press, 1981).

56. On that backlash, see John Higham, *Strangers in the Land: Patterns of American Nativism, 1860–1925* (New York: Atheneum, 1971); Tyler Anbinder, *Nativism and Slavery: The Northern Know Nothings and the Politics of the 1850s* (New York: Oxford University Press, 1992); Ray Allen Billington, *The Protestant Crusade, 1800–1860: A Study of the Origins of American Nativism* (New York: Rinehart, 1952; orig. pub. 1938); and Peter Schrag, *Not Fit for Our Society: Immigration and Nativism in America* (Berkeley: University of California Press, 2010).

57. Ernest R. May, ed., *The Coming of War, 1917* (Chicago: Rand-McNally, 1963), p. 1. Also see Louis L. Gerson, *The Hyphenate in Recent American Politics and Diplomacy* (Lawrence: University Press of Kansas, 1964); Joseph P. O'Grady, ed., *The Immigrants' Influence on Wilson's Peace Policies* (Lexington: University of Kentucky Press, 1967); Hélène Christol and Serge Ricard, eds., *Hyphenated Diplomacy: European Immigration and U.S. Foreign Policy, 1914–1984* (Aix-en-Provence, France: Publications Université de Provence, 1985).

58. Robert A. Divine, *American Immigration Policy, 1924–1952* (New Haven, Conn.: Yale University Press, 1957).

59. For a scathing critique of the restrictionist impulses of the 1920s, see Horace M. Kallen, *Culture and Democracy in the United States: Studies in the Group Psychology of the American Peoples* (New York: Arno Press, 1970; orig. pub. 1924).

60. See Robert W. Tucker, Charles B. Keely, and Linda Wrigley, eds., *Immigration and U.S. Foreign Policy* (Boulder, Colo.: Westview Press, 1990); and Ernest J. Wilson III, ed., *Diversity and U.S. Foreign Policy: A Reader* (New York: Routledge, 2004).

61. Arthur M. Schlesinger Jr., *The Disuniting of America: Reflections on a Multicultural Society*, new and rev. ed. (New York: W. W. Norton, 1998). Also see John J. Miller, *The*

Unmaking of Americans: How Multiculturalism Has Undermined the Assimilation Ethic (New York: Free Press, 1998).

62. Peter Brimelow, *Alien Nation: Common Sense about America's Immigration Disaster* (New York: Random House, 1995), p. xv.

63. Patrick J. Buchanan, *State of Emergency: The Third World Invasion and Conquest of America* (New York: Thomas Dunne/St. Martin's, 2006), pp. 11–12.

64. For rebuttals of the pessimistic claims advanced by Huntington et al., see John A. Hall and Charles Lindholm, *Is America Breaking Apart?* (Princeton, N.J.: Princeton University Press, 1999); Alfredo G. A. Valladão, The *Twenty-First Century Will Be American*, trans. John Howe (London: Verso, 1996); Alejandro Portes and Rubén G. Rumbaut, *Immigrant America: A Portrait*, 3rd ed., rev. and enl. (Berkeley: University of California Press, 2006); and Jack Citrin, Amy Lerman, Michel Murakami, and Kathryn Pearson, "Testing Huntington: Is Hispanic Immigration a Threat to American Identity?" *Perspectives on Politics* 5 (March 2007): 31–48.

65. Sometimes other tropes are used to suggest agency, for instance as with one author's choosing to replace the label "diaspora" with a different signifier, namely the "professional Irish"; see John P. Buckley, *The New York Irish: Their View of American Foreign Policy, 1914–1921* (New York: Arno Press, 1976), pp. 7–9.

66. Karl Schriftgiesser, *Lobbyists: The Art and Business of Influencing Lawmakers* (Boston: Little, Brown, 1951).

67. For case studies tending to demonstrate that diasporic influence correlates positively with state preferences, see Mohammed E. Ahrari, ed., *Ethnic Groups and U.S. Foreign Policy* (Westport, Conn.: Greenwood, 1987). In general agreement, though noting that there are some important exceptions to the rule of state dominance, see David M. Paul and Rachel Anderson Paul, *Ethnic Lobbies and US Foreign Policy* (Boulder, Colo.: Lynne Rienner, 2009).

68. See Brian J. Auten, "Political Diasporas and Exiles as Instruments of Statecraft," *Comparative Strategy* 25 (September 2006): 329–41. Theoretical works stressing the predominant role of central, "statist," decision making, albeit touching only very lightly (if that) on diasporas and foreign policy, include Stephen D. Krasner, *Defending the National Interest: Raw Materials Investments and U.S. Foreign Policy* (Princeton, N.J.: Princeton University Press, 1978); and Jonathan Paquin, *A Stability-Seeking Power: U.S. Foreign Policy and Secessionist Conflicts* (Montreal and Kingston: McGill-Queen's University Press, 2010).

69. Ernest R. May, "An American Tradition in Foreign Policy: The Role of Public Opinion," in *Theory and Practice in American Politics*, ed. William H. Nelson (Chicago: University of Chicago Press, 1964), pp. 101–22, quotes at pp. 116–17, 122.

70. May, "An American Tradition in Foreign Policy," pp. 101–22, quotes at pp. 116–17, 122.

71. Two standard references of these topics are Ralph B. Levering, *The Public and American Foreign Policy, 1918–1978* (New York: William Morrow, 1978); and Ole R. Holsti, *Public Opinion and American Foreign Policy*, rev. ed. (Ann Arbor: University of Michigan Press, 2004).

72. Lawrence H. Fuchs, "Minority Groups and Foreign Policy," *Political Science Quarterly* 74 (June 1959): 161–75, quote at p. 162.

73. Bernard C. Cohen, *The Public's Impact on Foreign Policy* (Lanham, Md.: University Press of America, 1983), pp. 7–18.

74. Cohen, *The Public's Impact on Foreign Policy*, pp. 26–27. On heuristics, see Georg Henrik von Wright, *Explanation and Understanding* (Ithaca, N.Y.: Cornell University Press, 1971); and Martin Hollis and Steve Smith, *Explaining and Understanding International Relations* (Oxford: Clarendon Press, 1990).

75. Expressing some concerns about the normative and empirical meaning of greater ethnic participation in foreign policy making is Tony Smith, *Foreign Attachments: The Power of Ethnic Groups in the Making of American Foreign Policy* (Cambridge, Mass.: Harvard University Press, 2000). Contrasted with this (moderate) pessimism is the claim that ethnic activism actually enhances the overall effectiveness of American

foreign policy, advanced most memorably by Yossi Shain, *Marketing the American Creed Abroad: Diasporas in the U.S. and Their Homelands* (Cambridge: Cambridge University Press, 1999), as well as Shain, "Ethnic Diasporas and U.S. Foreign Policy," *Political Science Quarterly* 109 (Winter 1994–95): 811–42.

76. For instance, see John Harwood, "For G.O.P., Hard Line on Immigration Comes at a Cost," *New York Times*, 8 March 2014, p. A12.

77. A good example of the latter being Brandon Valeriano, "The International Politics of New Latino America: The Foreign Policy Preferences of Latinos and the National Interest," *Journal of Latino-Latin American Studies* 2 (Spring 2007): 23–45.

78. Scott McConnell, "Not So Huddled Masses: Multiculturalism and Foreign Policy," *World Affairs* 171 (Spring 2009): 39–50, quotes at pp. 41–42.

79. On the distinction between the "neos" and the "paleos," which was apparent well before the Iraq war of 2003 and the ensuing controversy surrounding it, see John Ehrman, *The Rise of Neoconservatism: Intellectuals and Foreign Affairs* (New Haven, Conn.: Yale University Press, 1995).

80. McConnell, "Not So Huddled Masses," p. 50.

81. Samuel Lubell, *The Future of American Politics* (New York: Harper, 1952).

82. See, for some regionalist theses, Ray Allen Billington, "The Origins of Middle Western Isolationism," *Political Science Quarterly* 60 (March 1945): 44–64; Ralph H. Smuckler, "The Region of Isolationism," *American Political Science Review* 47 (June 1953): 386–401; and Marian D. Irish, "Foreign Policy and the South," *Journal of Politics* 10 (May 1948): 306–26.

83. For instance, see Louis H. Bean, Frederick Mosteller, and Frederick Williams, "Nationalities and 1944," *Public Opinion Quarterly* 8 (Autumn 1944): 368–75; John Snetsinger, *Truman, the Jewish Vote, and the Creation of Israel* (Stanford, Calif.: Hoover Institution Press, 1974); and John B. Judis, *Genesis: Truman, American Jews, and the Origins of the Arab/Israeli Conflict* (New York: Farrar, Straus and Giroux, 2014).

84. Mark R. Levy and Michael S. Kramer, *The Ethnic Factor: How America's Minorities Decide Elections* (New York: Simon & Schuster, 1972).

85. Although they were careful not to put too much weight upon the ethnic vote, both James Goldgeier and Ronald Asmus were certain that the electoral clout possessed by ethnic constituencies of Central and Eastern European origin was an important factor leading the Clinton administration to promote NATO's expansion. See James M. Goldgeier, *Not Whether but When: The U.S. Decision to Enlarge NATO* (Washington, D.C.: Brookings Institution Press, 1999); and Ronald D. Asmus, *Opening NATO's Door: How the Alliance Remade Itself for a New Era* (New York: Columbia University Press, 2002).

86. See, in particular, S. D. Lovell, *The Presidential Election of 1916* (Carbondale: Southern Illinois University Press, 1980); and R. A. Burchell, "Did the Irish and German Voters Desert the Democrats in 1920? A Tentative Statistical Answer," *Journal of American Studies* 6 (August 1972): 153–64.

87. Lawrence R. Jacobs and Benjamin I. Page, "Who Influences U.S. Foreign Policy?" *American Political Science Review* 99 (February 2005): 107–23, quotes at pp. 109, 119–20.

88. Jacobs and Page, "Who Influences U.S. Foreign Policy?" pp. 117–18.

89. Jacobs and Page, "Who Influences U.S. Foreign Policy?" p. 121.

90. Quoted in Charles McCurdy Mathias Jr., "Ethnic Groups and Foreign Policy," *Foreign Affairs* 59 (Summer 1981): 975–98, quote at pp. 975–76. It bears emphasis that the author, who was a Republican senator from Maryland at the time he wrote this article, was assuredly not an unalloyed enthusiast of lobbying!

91. James Deakin, *The Lobbyists* (Washington, D.C.: Public Affairs Press, 1966), pp. 54–55, 184–88. Also see Jeffrey M. Berry, *Lobbying for the People: The Political Behavior of Public Interest Groups* (Princeton, N.J.: Princeton University Press, 1977); and Russell Warren Howe and Sarah Hays Trott, *The Power Peddlers: How Lobbyists Mold America's Foreign Policy* (Garden City, N.Y.: Doubleday, 1977).

92. Francis Fukuyama, "The Decay of American Political Institutions," *American Interest* 9 (January/February 2014), pp. 6–19, cite at p. 13; Eric Lipton and Ben Protess, "Law Doesn't End Revolving Door on Capitol Hill," *New York Times*, 2 February 2014, pp. 1, 20.

93. See Thomas E. Mann and Norman J. Ornstein, *The Broken Branch: How Congress Is Failing America and How to Get It Back on Track* (New York: Oxford University Press, 2008); Francis Fukuyama, "American Political Dysfunction," *American Interest* 7 (November/December 2011): 125–27; and Fukuyama, "America in Decay: The Sources of Political Dysfunction," *Foreign Affairs* 93 (September/October 2014): 5–26.

94. For a thesis that is dubious about general will but nevertheless rests upon a conviction that the House is the entity most relevant for the expression of the national interest, see Peter Trubowitz, *Defining the National Interest: Conflict and Change in American Foreign Policy* (Chicago: University of Chicago Press, 1998).

95. Kenneth A. Shepsle, "Congress Is a 'They,' Not an 'It': Legislative Intent as Oxymoron," *International Review of Law and Economics* 12 (June 1992): 239–56, quote at pp. 239–40.

96. Shepsle, "Congress Is a 'They,' Not an 'It'," pp. 247–48.

97. For a fairly typical lament, see the special essay entitled "What's Gone Wrong with Democracy?" published in the *Economist* in late winter 2014: "[M]oney talks louder than ever in American politics. Thousands of lobbyists (more than 20 for every member of Congress) add to the length and complexity of legislation, the better to smuggle in special privileges. All of this creates the impression that American democracy is for sale . . . The result is that America's image—and by extension that of democracy itself—has taken a terrible battering." *Economist*, 1 March 2014, pp. 47–52, quote at p. 49.

98. Thomas Stratmann, "Some Talk: Money in Politics—A (Partial) Review of the Literature," *Public Choice* 124 (July 2005): 135–56, quote at p. 143.

99. Richard Hall and Alan V. Deardorff, "Lobbying as Legislative Subsidy," *American Political Science Review* 100 (February 2006): 69–84, quote at p. 69.

100. Hall and Deardorff, "Lobbying as Legislative Subsidy," pp. 80–81.

101. Frank R. Baumgartner et al., *Lobbying and Policy Change: Who Wins, Who Loses, and Why* (Chicago: University of Chicago Press, 2009), pp. 254–55. Also see Barbara Hinckley, *Less Than Meets the Eye: Foreign Policy Making and the Myth of the Assertive Congress* (Chicago: University of Chicago Press, 1994).

102. Baumgartner et al., *Lobbying and Policy Change*, pp. 239–40.

103. For an elaboration of this refusal to accept such a demarcation line, see James M. Lindsay, *Congress and the Politics of U.S. Foreign Policy* (Baltimore: Johns Hopkins University Press, 1994).

104. James M. Lindsay, "Getting Uncle Sam's Ear: Will Ethnic Lobbies Cramp America's Foreign Policy Style?" in Wilson, ed., *Diversity and U.S. Foreign Policy*, pp. 143–47, quotes at pp. 143, 145. This chapter was originally published as an article carrying the same title in the *Brookings Review* 20 (Winter 2002): 37–40.

105. Lindsay, "Getting Uncle Sam's Ear," pp. 146–47.

106. Mathias, "Ethnic Groups and Foreign Policy," pp. 996–97.

107. Trevor Rubenzer, "Ethnic Minority Interest Group Attributes and U.S. Foreign Policy Influence: A Qualitative Comparative Analysis," *Foreign Policy Analysis* 4 (April 2008): 169–185, quote at p. 183 (emphasis added).

108. For the case that smaller may be better, see Stephen M. Saideman, "The Power of the Small: The Impact of Ethnic Minorities on Foreign Policy," *SAIS Review* 22 (July 2002): 93–105.

109. The locus classicus for this metaphor is John Bartlet Brebner, *North Atlantic Triangle: The Interplay of Canada, the United States and Great Britain* (Toronto: McClelland and Stewart, 1966; orig. pub. 1945).

FOUR

Big Stick, or Splintered Shillelagh?

Irish America and Its Impact on the Canada-United States Security Relationship

PETER KING REVISITED

This book began with reference to New York congressman Peter T. King, whose committee hearings of March 2011 on homeland security so nicely managed to spotlight the conceptual and analytical "bookends," as it were, of this study on ethnic-diasporic activism and the Canada-United States security community. Those bookends are Irish America, and Muslim North America, the topics respectively of this chapter and chapter six. In between, we encounter German America, to be covered in chapter five.

Of the three chapters, the subject matter of the present one, dedicated to Congressman King's "own" ethnic group, that is to say Irish America, stands out. In part, it does so simply on the basis of "seniority" and longevity, for of our three cases, Irish America was the first to bestir itself in advancing a political agenda fraught with security consequences. Those consequences would persist for a considerable period of time, a span of some six decades during which security relations in North America—and, indeed, in the broader North Atlantic "triangle"—remained in a condition of flux. Partly, the case of Irish America stands out because of the methods adopted by diasporic activists in their myriad pursuits of political influence. Most importantly, though, the geopolitical significance of Irish American diasporic activism inheres in the unwavering goal that endowed it with its raison d'être: from the American Civil War through the ending of the First World War, that objective was to do what could be done to bring about a radical revision of the political status quo in the kin-country, Ireland. With some exceptions, those promoting this revisionist agenda operated upon the assumption that the delivery of harm to British interests, anywhere in the world, was bound to benefit Irish ones. Sometimes, Canada would be caught up *directly* in the Irish-British quarrel, with consequences of considerable magnitude for its immediate political future as well as for regional security in North America. At other times, the impact upon Canadian interests, as well as upon Canada-United States security cooperation, would be more indirect, though still far from inconsequential.

It will be recollected from the discussion toward the close of the previous chapter, regarding the narrow construe of ethnic lobbying, that a former U.S. senator from Maryland, Charles McCurdy Mathias, had some decidedly mixed views about the impact of ethnic-diasporic activism upon both the American legislative process and the country's foreign policy—views that he expressed in print a good decade prior to the ending of the Cold War, which so many analysts have interpreted, wrongly, as the start of an *unprecedented* era of interest-group activism in foreign policy. Mathias himself was too conversant with his country's history to be unaware of the earlier, lengthy, record of ethnic lobbying in the United States, and in this regard, he was certain that no other group could match the policy accomplishments of Irish America, which he considered to be the "oldest and most redoubtable of American ethnic interest groups. . . , credited with major historical exertions, and no little success prior to World War II, in setting the United States at odds with Great Britain. Irish-American as well as German-American opinion strongly resisted and probably delayed American intervention in both world wars."[1]

Senator Mathias is far from being alone in claiming that Irish America (aided and abetted by German American groups) had an important role in delaying American entry into the First World War, which if true would seem to have carried obvious consequences for Canadian security and defense interests, on the counterfactual assumption that had America entered the war at the same time Canada did in August 1914, the fighting would have progressed much more smoothly for the Allied side, and as a result fewer, likely *far* fewer, Canadians would have met their deaths on the killing fields in France. This counterfactual was very much on the minds of many policy intellectuals, in Canada as well as elsewhere in the North Atlantic triangle, in the period following the First World War. It was embedded within a cognitive framework that had, as its foundational logic, the Anglo-American rapprochement we encountered in chapter two. Readers will remember that two puzzles arose in respect of that rapprochement. One was its timing. The other was the more intriguing question as to why it did not spawn a full-blown alliance between the two great "Anglo-Saxon" powers, the United States and the United Kingdom, as so many contemporary enthusiasts of Anglo-American condominium had imagined and hoped it would do, in the early years of the twentieth century.

One of those enthusiasts, writing a few years prior to the Great War's outbreak, was Perry Robinson, a Briton with long experience in America, who summed up the promise of Anglo-American geopolitical community in words that deserve quoting here. The attainment of "Universal Peace" was fast approaching, of this Robinson was convinced. This was because

> [t]he ultimate domination of the world by the Anglo-Saxon (let us call him so) seems to be reasonably assured; and no less assured is it that at some time wars will cease. The question for both Englishmen and Americans to ask themselves is whether, recognising the responsibility that already rests upon it, the Anglo-Saxon race dare or can for conscience' sake—or still more, whether one branch of it when the other be willing to push on, dare for conscience' sake—hang back and postpone the advent of the Universal Peace, which it is in its power to bring about to-day, no matter what the motives of jealousy, or self-interest, or of self-distrust may be that restrain it.[2]

It was hardly necessary to put the finger upon the member of the race that was "hanging back" and failing to take up its duties on behalf of Anglo-Saxon geostrategic condominium; that laggard, clearly, was the United States. One might have thought that the Anglo-Saxon construction of world peace would have fallen victim to the war that was to have ended all war, but that is not how many observers in the English-speaking world regarded the matter, in that uncertain yet not unpromising postwar dawn. One such observer was the prime minister of Canada, Robert Borden, who in a June 1919 interview published in the *New York Sun* reflected on some of the lessons of the recent bloodletting in Europe, in which his own country had suffered fairly heavily (sixty thousand combatants dead in a total population of slightly fewer than eight million). Borden took comfort from the way in which the war had brought closer together the two largest English-speaking lands, and went on to assert that "these two nations have it within their power, if they are connected in purpose and in effort, to keep the peace of the world at all times in the future." Sadly, they could and should have been able to do exactly this during "the last weeks of July 1914, and spared the world all the sacrifices and sorrow that it has since endured."[3]

Borden did not elaborate upon what it was that kept the two English-speaking countries from doing their self-evident duty both to mankind and to themselves—to say nothing of to Canada, which for a short time during the early interwar years acted as if it, and *only* it, possessed the ability to foment Anglo-American unity, in an aspiration that would come to be remembered as the "linchpin" theory, briefly associated with a not altogether rational spirit one historian lampoons as "linchpin mania."[4] But had the prime minister bothered to spell out the causes preventing the condominium's formation in 1914, uppermost in his thinking would have been the political role played by powerful and highly mobilized ethnic diasporas in America, which not for the first time, and certainly not the last, were being said to exercise undue influence over its foreign policy, and therefore constituted—given the stakes in 1914 for Great Britain—an element that could not but make more difficult the task of maintaining world order. In short, what Robert Borden would have said, were we able to put his thoughts into the words of some of those more recent political scientists we met in this book's previous chapter, was that ethnic diasporas were injecting their preferences into the American foreign policy process, and thereby distorting the framing and promoting of the "national" interest, with unfortunate and possibly even calamitous results.

A Canadian prime minister may have been reluctant to name names, but the same cannot be said of a British prime minister and fellow member of the Imperial War Cabinet, David Lloyd George, who in his wartime memoirs cut to the chase in asserting that "[h]ad there been no Irish grievance, it is by no means improbable that America would have come much earlier into the war, and by so much shortened its duration."[5] When it came to bluntness, however, no one could top a high-ranking American naval officer and enthusiast of Anglo-American alliance, Admiral William Sowden Sims, who in an address to the London branch of the English Speaking Union in June 1921 made Lloyd George sound like a trafficker in euphemisms. Of two things, the admiral was certain. The first was the imminent construction of an Anglo-American strategic condominium, which would mean that the "English-speaking peoples . . . are going to run this round globe." The second was that try as they might, Irish American nationalists would not be able to prevent this from happening. Proclaiming that he had no desire to "touch on the Irish question," Sims nevertheless proceeded to do just that, declaring that "there are many in our country who technically are Americans, some of them naturalized and some born there, but none of them Americans at all." Indeed, he continued, they are "making war on America to-day. The simple truth of it is that they have the blood of British and American boys on their hands for the obstructions they placed in the way of the most effective operation of the Allied naval forces during the war."[6]

Sims might as easily have added the "blood of Canadian boys" to his list. So if we really wanted to pursue the counterfactual a bit further, we could say that absent the Irish American resistance to Anglo-American alliance, there would have emerged a security coupling capable of preserving, or restoring, the "universal peace," such that even if it did not take shape prior to the Great War but rather upon its outbreak in August 1914, America's rapid and effective resistance to aggression, from the very beginning of the fighting, would have had lasting beneficial impact upon international security at the war's conclusion. The "international community" of its day, epitomized in the new League of Nations with its revolutionary instrument of "collective security," would not have been handicapped at birth by America's absence, but would rather have gone on to become a bulwark against war's breaking out again in Europe. Thus if one takes the consequences of America's *late* entry into the war to include the seeds of its own subsequent disenchantment with both the League and collective security, then the counterfactual, America at war in August 1914, would have implied a far happier outcome for Canada, the United States, and the United Kingdom—to say nothing of much of the rest of the planet! America's interwar infatuation with isolationism would never have transpired, and neither, therefore, would another great-power war have taken place. Seen in this way, the impact of Irish America upon Canadian regional and global security interests could not have been more profound.

There is much to be said on behalf of counterfactual reasoning when applied to matters of international peace and security, even if it is true that, as Arthur Burns reminded readers long ago, "[t]o supplement an account of what *did* happen with a number of sketches of what *might* have happened is certainly not to provide additional explanations." Nevertheless, there is value in the exercise, because "it does allow one to say whether what happened was to be expected or was unexpected on the basis of theory."[7] Quite so, and Burns does well to underscore the utility of counterfactual reasoning, a form of reasoning to which I will myself allude in this chapter's final paragraphs, in hopes of making an important point. For the most part, though, I am going in these pages to hold my own counterfactual impulses in check as much as I can, out of recognition of the pitfalls necessarily awaiting those of us who might otherwise be tempted to make sweeping claims about a better future we could and should have had, if only we had not been deprived of a different past.

In this chapter, therefore, I deal mostly with the past we *did* have. And when it comes to the record of Irish American diasporic activism, there is more than enough empirical grist for anyone's mill. Thus while this account of Irish America's impact(s) will not be completely indifferent to Canada's and other countries' world-order interests (what Arnold Wolfers would have labelled their "milieu goals"[8]), mostly the analysis here will concentrate upon those *regional* security consequences that might plausibly be associated with Irish America's exertions. In particular, we want to examine the extent to which the latter could credibly be said to have had an effect upon the origins of the Canada-United States security community, during the decades between the American Civil War and the interwar period.

Irish American diasporic activism in that period manifested itself in various ways, but always there was one overarching goal being pursued:

the creation of a new political order in the ancestral homeland, in which "Irish freedom"[9] would be attained either by outright separation from the UK or by some variant of "home rule," perhaps along lines of what British North America had achieved in the run-up to Confederation in 1867.[10] Usually, particularly insofar as concerned Irish America, it was the former (separatism) rather than the latter (home rule) that provided the most inspiration, even though we would be unwise to ignore the allure that home rule would sometimes possess in Ireland and even in America, never more so than during the early years of the twentieth century.[11] Plus, it needs always to be kept in mind that the boundaries between home rule and separatism could, at times, be blurred, with the best illustration of this being the occasional tactical alliances crafted between proponents of the two tendencies, to say nothing of the ongoing debate as to whether the preeminent exponent of home rule, Charles Stewart Parnell, had not himself been prepared to embrace the republican cause.[12]

Some scholars have remarked, persuasively in my view, upon a difference between Irish and Irish American nationalisms.[13] Among the many implications of this differentiation was a consistency in Irish American diasporic activism that at times was lacking among nationalists back home, meaning that vigorous opposition to British interests, in Canada and elsewhere, would pretty well be the order of the day, as far as concerned the former. Activists in the diaspora, even more than their kinfolk across the sea, put great stock in the national axiom that "England's difficulty is Ireland's opportunity."[14] Thus could one leading student of Anglo-American relations whimsically express this chapter's *problématique* in the form of a rhetorical question: "To what extent," asked Harry Cranbrook Allen, "can the Irish Americans, who were thus so numerous, be reckoned an agent of co-operation between Britain and America? Not in the very least, it would seem at first sight, but rather the reverse. . . . It is probable that the Irish group had more influence upon American foreign policy than any other body of opinion, and that influence was usually anti-British."[15]

Admittedly, even Allen was moved to append a slight qualification to his otherwise blanket assertion, conveyed through his remarks about "at first sight" and "usually." These alluded to the countervailing pressure that *some* Irish Americans (the so-called Scotch Irish) could occasionally exert upon the general tone of Anglo-American relations, working as they did to foment rather than to frustrate Anglo-American condominium.[16] With this aside, Allen was alerting his readers to the need for precision in the matter of discussing the identity grouping we call Irish America, a good reminder, and one to be revisited in the following section of this chapter. In the main, though, his ascription of anti-British, and a fortiori anti-English, sensibilities to the vast majority of Catholic Irish Americans would not be a candidate for successful contradiction, nor will

I dispute it in these pages; "rather the reverse," to quote Allen once more. This is because Catholic Irish emigrants to the United States in the nineteenth century possessed, in the words of George Potter, a "strong cultural identity shared through the patron saint, a deep devotional faith and a *hatred of England.*" [17]

"GREATER IRELAND": THE IRISH DIASPORA IN AMERICA

Recall from the previous chapter's discussion that scholars have divergent positions, sometimes wildly so, regarding the mooted influence ethnic diasporas might be said to exert upon U.S. foreign policy. Let us, for our purposes in this chapter, dismiss outright the claims of some, to the effect that ethnic interest groups are generally without much if any causal significance: more objects to be affected by the decisions of central state actors than subjects in their own right. Instead, we concentrate in these pages not on whether but on how Irish America has so frequently been held to have exerted a powerful impact upon U.S. diplomacy, particularly in the all-important matter of the Anglo-American relationship, pregnant as the latter had been with significance for both global security and North American security, from the late 1860s until the early 1920s. Recall, too, that to the extent something approaching a consensus view might exist on the matter, it is usually said that three ingredients are especially relevant to diasporic success in pursuing policy objectives. To say again, these are size, social status, and effective organization as a pressure group. In the case of Irish America, this first criterion has been amply fulfilled from the earliest stages of American political development, while the second would become satisfied by the turn of the twentieth century at the latest. As for the third, this is more contentious given the legendary squabbles that continuously roiled relations within the Irish American leadership ranks.

   This chapter mainly explores that initial criterion, size, with the other two criteria becoming folded into the analysis of chapter five, for reasons that will be explained therein. Already by the time of the first federal census produced by the newly independent United States, in 1790, the Irish constituted between 14 and 17 percent of the country's total non-slave population of 3.3 million (adding slaves brought the total to 3.9 million), with Ulster alone providing 10 percent of the American total. The Irish had begun to settle in America well before there even *was* a United States, and during the course of the seventeenth century between 50,000 and 100,000—most of whom in these early years actually were Catholic—left Ireland for Britain's North American colonies, which at that time were, with the exception of Newfoundland, to be found to the south, rather than the north, of the boundary today separating Canada and the United States. They would be followed, in the eighteenth century, by a much larger cohort of Irish emigrants, estimated between 250,000 and 400,000 and this time, largely Presbyterians from Ulster.[18]

These latter came in four successive waves that had their origins in changes in British policies of economic, cultural, and political provenance, between 1717 and 1775. Until the fourth decade of the nineteenth century, when large numbers of Irish Catholics started to arrive in America, the Ulster emigrants had been content enough to be known simply as "Irish," which is how they saw themselves, even if so many (but not all) of them had descended from Lowland Scots who had transited the North Channel of the Irish Sea in the seventeenth century in quest of a better life in Britain's Irish dominion.[19] In a bid to differentiate themselves from their Catholic "kinfolk" in heavily Protestant America, the Ulster Irish took, in the two decades before the Civil War, to calling themselves "Scotch Irish," and while this new identity grouping of Ulster origin would come to play a considerable role in American societal and policy debates, with interesting implications for the evolution of the country's military doctrine (the Scotch Irish being said to constitute America's "warrior caste"),[20] it would be the Catholic Irish who turned out to have greater relevance for American foreign policy, and especially for Canada-United States regional security, during the years spanning the Civil War and the First World War. Thus, we will leave the Ulster Irish at this point, and concentrate mainly on the nineteenth-century stream of immigration from the Emerald Isle's other three provinces of Leinster, Munster, and Connaught—a stream that was becoming, after the 1830s, a heavily Catholic one.

There was a third category of Irish emigrants, distinguished less by religious than by ideological orientation, who would make a mark for themselves in the domestic political debates of the American host-state. These were the political refugees who came seeking asylum in the newly independent United States following the failed 1798 uprising of the United Irishmen, which had been led by the Anglo-Irish Protestant Theobald Wolfe Tone, but among whose ranks could also be found Catholics and Presbyterians.[21] The struggle for Irish independence resulted in their becoming associated with republican and revolutionary movements elsewhere in Europe, nowhere more so than those in France. Thus was established an early "French connection" with Irish nationalists, which would sustain itself well into the nineteenth century. As a result, a myth was developed that there existed—to some, had *always* existed—a strong ideological and even ethnic bond between the Irish and the French, cognate folks if ever such were thought to exist anywhere on earth. As with all myths, this one had only an irregular correspondence with empirical realities, such that as time went on, it would effectively become a poorly cloaked falsehood. By the early twentieth century, given the aforementioned nationalist axiom about England's difficulty being Ireland's opportunity,[22] there arose a growing pro-German trend among nationalist elites in both Ireland and the diaspora, with profound if unintended negative consequences for Britain's post-1904 European security partner and soon-to-be military ally, France.[23]

During the formative years of the American republic, revolutionary France did have an obvious appeal to Irish nationalists struggling against British rule, and political developments in France would continue to have reverberations for Ireland well into the middle of the nineteenth century, as we will find in the next section of this chapter. But the political exiles who had ventured to America following the 1798 uprising arrived in a country governed by Federalists and at a moment when the American domestic political arena was the scene of bitter tension between this dominant party, highly dubious about France at the best of times, and its more Francophile Democratic-Republican (Jeffersonian) foes.[24] Thus it was hardly unexpected, in light of those raging political controversies in their new host-state, that the Irish should have found themselves routinely being denounced by Federalists as subversives and, worse, pro-French ones in the bargain![25]

Notwithstanding the controversy that swirled for a time around Irish activism during the late eighteenth century and early period of the nineteenth century, years when Irish nationalism could draw attention to itself because of an *ideological* orientation toward a country (France) that inspired conflict within the United States, by the late 1830s and early 1840s the Irish American diaspora would begin to garner attention much more for its *religious* than its ideological dimension. Emanating from an overwhelmingly Protestant American society, this attention could hardly be welcoming. The political exiles of the immediate post-1798 years had, as noted above, included a good many Irish *Protestants* who had gotten mixed up in republican struggles back home. With the changing religious composition of Irish immigration into the United States, becoming predominantly Catholic in the 1830s and remaining so thereafter, there developed an alteration in the tenor of domestic debates as to the meaning of this newly forming diaspora for American society, with many prepared, on religious grounds, to conclude that the influx boded nothing but ill for the future of a still largely anti-Catholic republic.

It has been said of the Irish Americans, primarily because of this shift in their religious composition, that they were the "first major immigrant group seriously to threaten the stability of American society."[26] The rise of anti-Catholic nativism was an immediate response to the growth in the country's Catholic population, with a powerful impact on political developments at both the federal and state levels in the pre-Civil War period.[27] On the federal level, anti-Catholicism was to find its home principally in the Whig Party. Not surprisingly, the major rival party in the 1840s, the Democrats, were quick to sense that electoral gain might be had by offering a helping hand to the new arrivals from Ireland, as well as to their American-born offspring. In exchange for this solicitude, the party sought and received support at the polls from the Irish American electorate, to such an extent that by the time of the 1844 national election, Irish Catholics were said to constitute the largest solid bloc of "ethnic" voters in the United States. Thus began a long period in which it was axiomatic that the Irish Catholic could be counted upon to be a Democratic voter, with implications for unfolding debates regarding the "influence" wielded by diasporas over not just America's domestic politics, but its foreign policy as well. In the 1840s, however, those latter kinds of debates were still a few years in the future, so that while it was widely, if probably incorrectly, assumed in the 1844 election's aftermath that James Knox Polk had owed his victory to the Irish Catholic vote, no one at the time argued that the electoral harvest had in any way depended upon arguments related to foreign policy.[28]

The period during which diasporic activism—indeed the very meaning of the diaspora for America—would be primarily if not totally associated with *domestic* rather than foreign policy agendas turned out not to last very long, and for the six decades upon which I focus in this chapter, stretching from 1861 to 1921, Irish American diasporic activism was so freighted with implications for foreign and security policy that it is almost, though not quite, possible to overlook the domestic side of the activist agenda altogether. Whether we focus upon the foreign or the domestic dimension of Irish diasporic activism, however, we must never lose sight of one unique characteristic of Irish demographic fluxes during the century of heaviest emigration from Ireland and other parts of Europe to America.

What *was* this unique attribute of Irish emigration patterns? Let us start out with what was *not* unique about the Irish demographic presence in the United States: its size. As impressive as was the Irish demographic weight in American demography by the latter part of the nineteenth century and the early part of the twentieth century, some other Europe-descended groups had an even larger presence in America. Irish America never did constitute the largest "non-English"[29] European diaspora living within the borders of the American host-state during the years I cover in this book, but it was always a close second to the group that did occupy the pole position, the German Americans, with whom we will become more familiar in chapter five. But unlike either the German Americans or the group Horace Kallen referred to as the "Brito Americans,"[30] the Irish Americans stood apart as a result of one singularly distinctive demographic feature, namely the proportionally huge share of those identifying, globally, as Irish who would end up residing outside the borders of the kin-country.

With reason, it has been said of migration from Ireland over the past two centuries that it "represents one of the most significant dispersals of population in European history."[31] Altogether, in the period 1800 to 1920, some five million Irish would resettle in the United States. The first U.S.

federal census taken in the twentieth century (in 1900) revealed an Irish content to American demography that came close to matching the German one, with 4,826,904 listed as Irish, meaning either that they themselves had been born in Ireland or that they had at least one parent born there. Usually, these two categories are referred to in the United States, respectively, as "first-generation" and "second-generation" immigrants, who together might be said to have represented the Irish "stock" in the host-country. But Irish American nationalist leaders were not slow to seize upon a much larger figure, one that represented an Irish "element" extending well beyond the second generation and embracing the descendants of those Irish who had been resident in America since the colonial era. Thus did it become possible for Irish American activists regularly to claim to be speaking on behalf of some twenty million Irish Americans, a century or so ago.[32]

As we will discover in chapter five, German Americans were somewhat more numerous than Irish Americans (to say nothing of English-descended Americans, still in the majority at this time). However, because Germany itself would remain so heavily populated even during the era of heaviest emigration, the numbers of its people who left the homeland during the nineteenth century never constituted more than a small slice of the overall population, with the result that the German "nation" continued to reside within the boundaries of the German states-system and, most importantly, within those of that new German state fashioned in the wake of Prussia's victory over France in 1871, Bismarck's Reich. In stark contrast to this was the experience of the Irish, second only to the Jews as "the chronic exiles of this world," with more of them living outside of the kin-country than inside it by the twentieth century—if by "them" we mean not just the Irish-born, but the Irish-*descended* as well.[33] Even among the more restrictive, first-generation, category, an astounding 43 percent of the Irish-*born* were living outside the country by 1920, more than a million in the United States alone. This put Ireland in a class by itself, from which were excluded even such otherwise heavy emigration countries in Europe a century ago as Norway (with 14.8 percent of its native-born living elsewhere), Scotland (14.1), and Sweden (11.2)—each of whose percentage shares dwarfed the overall European average in that era, of 4 percent. As a result of this "continuous Irish diaspora," the country's population would remain stable throughout the twentieth century, rather than growing, as would the population of almost all other European lands.[34]

Let us pause a moment to reflect upon the geopolitical significance of this last observation. The Republic of Ireland today is hardly a populous place, containing roughly the same number of inhabitants as are to be found within the metropolitan boundaries of Mexico's second-largest city, Guadalajara—around 4.6 million. (Bringing in Northern Ireland would increase the Irish total to 6.4 million.) Its small demographic profile stands in sharp contradistinction to Ireland's considerable geopolitical profile over the centuries, and never more than during the six decades following America's Civil War, when the "Irish Question" regularly could be counted upon to present interesting dilemmas for transatlantic as well as North American security. If ever a country could be said to have produced more history than it was capable of consuming, then that country is Ireland. In this respect, George Bernard Shaw was hardly exaggerating when he observed, in a November 1928 article published in the *Irish Statesman*, that "[i]n the nineteenth century all the world was concerned about Ireland. In the twentieth, nobody outside Ireland cares twopence what happens to her."[35] Far from exaggerating, the great Irish playwright was actually understating the impact of his native country upon global affairs, for during the first two decades of the twentieth century the Irish Question would retain, perhaps even in augmented fashion, its strategic salience, especially if we are to credit the abovementioned observations of David Lloyd George and William Sowden Sims.

The discrepancy between Ireland's demographic and its geostrategic weight was not always as glaring as it would become by the late nineteenth and early twentieth centuries. For sure, in view of the tremendous disparity today between an America with nearly 320 million inhabitants (including so-called illegals) and an Ireland with fewer than 5 million (again, excluding Northern Ireland), it is difficult to recall that prior to the phenomenal spike in the rate of outmigration triggered by the famine of the late 1840s, the Emerald Isle's population of 8 million had been nearly *half as large* as America's own, of 17 million (including 2.5 million slaves). And if one were to go back two decades prior to the famine years of the late 1840s, the gap between Ireland and America was even smaller, the island's 7 million people almost equalling the total non-slave population of America in 1820, roughly 8 million (to which were added 1.5 million slaves).[36]

There had been intermittent problems with the potato crop in Ireland and elsewhere in Europe prior to the mid-1840s, for instance in 1822, 1831, 1835, 1837, and 1842, but nothing on the scale associated with the carnage inflicted by the potato blight, *Phytophthora infestans*, in 1845 and the subsequent half decade. During those six long years, some two million souls simply disappeared from the island's demographic mix, half of them perishing from starvation and disease (mostly the latter), the other half emigrating.[37] In fact, more people quit Ireland during the 11 years following this latest famine than had left it over the previous 250 years.[38] Of the 2 million or so who departed between 1845 and 1856, some 1.5 million went to the United States, with another 340,000 bound initially for Canada, many of these latter eventually ending up in the United States, as well. Nor would the demographic hemorrhage halt in that latter year. Far from it: between 1856 and 1921 at least a further four million would emigrate, again mainly to North America and especially to the United States.[39]

It is difficult to overstate the impact of the great famine upon the subsequent development of Irish American nationalism, and to the extent that the latter can be distinguished from Irish nationalism generically, it has much to do with the way in which post-famine Irish Catholic immigrants to America would come to style themselves. Although not the entire source of the differentiation between the two streams of Irish nationalism, the great famine reinforced a preexisting, and acute, sense of what might today be called "ontological insecurity"[40] among an Irish American diasporic community burning with a craving to enhance its collective self-esteem. This quest for status, fuelled partly in reaction to the nativist anti-Catholic agitation that had preceded the famine immigration but had been exacerbated greatly by the latter, is what Thomas N. Brown had in mind when he observed that the "immigrant's nationalism was too fierce an enthusiasm to derive simply from the passivity of a nostalgia for the Old Country. Indeed, it was the ruling passion for many of the second and third generation who knew only America. Like the almost mythic Captain William Mackey Lomasney, who was born in Ohio and blown to bits by his own dynamite under London Bridge in 1883 [*sic*], the fiercest nationalists were often the sons of immigrants."[41]

The nationalistic sensibilities of the Irish immigrants in America would set them apart from other European immigrant groups, especially from the German Americans until this latter group became politicized around foreign policy in the years preceding the First World War. It is doubtful that very many, if any, Irish nationalists, whether at home or in America, would have entirely agreed with the observation made by the Anglo-Irish writer, Oscar Wilde, in the 1880s, on the topic of relations between England and Ireland, that "[i]f in the last century she [England] tried to govern Ireland with a violence that was intensified by race hatred and religious propaganda, she has sought to rule in this century with a stupidity that is aggravated by good intentions."[42] Admittedly, the comment about stupidity would have been accepted readily enough in Irish-nationalist circles, but *not* the one about good intentions, for in the decades following the great famine it was widely held that Britain had intended to starve to death a people it had been incapable of subjugating throughout the centuries of rule from England. In short, it was believed by many that Britain had perpetrated a policy of genocide in Ireland—a belief that was itself easily derivative of a corollary mistaken conviction, to wit, that the island's political history since the late twelfth century had been an unbroken tale of bitter enmity between English rulers and Irish subjects. The reality was otherwise, for as one historian of medieval Ireland has put it, though the "seven centuries of solid and unbroken military resistance are the accepted back-drop to the drama of Irish history, . . . [t]he truth is very different." At no time, writes Francis Shaw, could medieval conflict be characterized as a "straightforward" affair pitting all Irish against all English (or, as the latter were sometimes known, Anglo-Norman). "As often as not there were more Irishmen fighting with the English than against them. . . . In the English army which opposed Hugh O'Neill in 1598, two-thirds were Irishmen, 1700 being Palesmen and 2,500 Gaelic Irishman."[43]

Still, it is not what actually *does* transpire so much as what is believed to have transpired that turns out to be instrumental in setting a political agenda, given the familiar tendency of activists everywhere to search for a "usable past" capable of inspiring present and future action. Thus it was hardly unexpected that, following the famine, so many recent Irish arrivals in America could easily consider themselves to be "involuntary exiles," forced to leave hearth and home by the dastardly English, a vile breed that had attempted *deliberately* to starve them during what nationalists preferred to term the "great starvation" or the "great hunger"—in Irish, *an gorta mór*—instead of the great famine. It was not just the famine that was remembered in this way, for as one historian notes, "[c]ontemporary records emphasize anger and frustration at the daily lot in Ireland—neighbours, debts, weather, bad luck. Memory, however, prioritizes the sense that cruel England drove them from their home."[44] And so it was that the Irish diaspora, nowhere more so than in America, would be stamped with what David Doyle has called a "self-indulgent communal morbidity."[45] With this came an unslakeable thirst for revenge.

No one, these days, takes seriously the earlier claim about British *intent* to starve the Irish into submission in the late 1840s. Historians and others have successfully debunked the genocide thesis; of this there can be no dispute.[46] By the same token, few would contend that the lengthy period of British rule of Ireland represented the epitome of "best practices" in the arts of governing, considering that the state's response to the famine was colossally inadequate, so much so that it could without difficulty be categorized as among Britain's "worst" governance practices imaginable. That so many could perish in so short a time in what was, be it recalled, an intrinsic part of the world's most developed polity, really does signify a colossal failure of state capacity to respond to crisis within its own borders. But it was not just the matter of British rule as exemplified by the famine; more generally, there has grown up a fairly consensual view that Britain's lengthy experience with governing (or, better, trying to govern) Ireland can most realistically be captured in one word, "misrule."[47] Commentators, including not a few English ones, have noted major divergencies in the manner in which London chose to administer its divers territorial holdings, both inside and outside of the United Kingdom itself, ranging at one extreme from the willing concession of self-government to the "white dominions" that had become affixed to the empire subsequent to the American departure therefrom,[48] to the other extreme of direct, and not-so-benign, colonial rule of nonwhite territories in what today would be called the "global south." Somewhere in between these positive and negative governance poles could be found Ireland, which had been affixed to the United Kingdom in 1800 but had throughout the nineteenth century remained fairly unstable outside of Ulster, until the eventual separation of the three other provinces from the union altogether, shortly after the First World War.

In this regard, the judgment rendered by one English writer in the early twentieth century, commenting upon his country's experience running Ireland, could not have been more apposite. "The Turks in Macedonia, the Germans in Poland, the Austrians in Southern Italy, even the Americans in their dealings with the Red Indians," observed Sydney Brooks, "have scarcely failed more wretchedly than we, the champion colonisers and rulers of the earth, have failed in Ireland. . . . [T]here are few defects in the Irish state, and few shortcomings in the Irish character, which cannot be traced back originally to English misgovernment, or which have not, at any rate, been intensified by that misgovernment."[49] The situation was aggravated by one important feature of British-Irish relations: territorial proximity. This feature resulted in Ireland's possessing, in the words of Donald Akenson, "a strategic significance in relation to England which is out of all proportion to its own size. From a military point of view, Ireland stands poised as a knife in England's back."[50]

Nor was this all. More noteworthy from the strategic point of view even than proximity was a second feature, demographic rather than geographic. As we know from the earlier discussion in this chapter, the Irish "nation" elsewhere was becoming, after the midpoint of the nineteenth century, an ensemble that would approximate, in size as well as in importance, the Irish who remained in their homeland. In ways that were becoming ever more difficult to ignore during the latter decades of the nineteenth century and opening ones of the twentieth century, there had been arising a "Greater Ireland" on the Atlantic's distant shores. Sir William Harcourt, home secretary of the Gladstone government in the early 1880s—years during which "Ireland was in a fierce stage of revolution,"[51] associated with widespread agrarian unrest (the "Land War" of 1879–1882) and an urban-terrorist campaign featuring dynamite attacks on British cities[52]—astutely noted that "[i]n former Irish rebellions, the Irish were in *Ireland* . . . Now there is an Irish nation in the United States, equally hostile, with plenty of money, absolutely beyond our reach and yet within ten days' sail of our shores."[53] To another English observer during this same tense period of the early 1880s, "the Irish in America were, in fact, an *imperium in imperio*—a great and powerful nation with unlimited resources by sea and land, and ready and willing to give important material aid, and troops and arms, with the connivance, or even in spite, of the United States government. . . . Looking across the Atlantic to what is sometimes called Greater Ireland, we see a vast population of

Irish, divided into sections among themselves, but united as one body in their desire to inflict injury on England."[54]

It was not only England that would feel the impact of this "transcendental" Irish republic abuilding in the United States.[55] For a while, Irish American nationalists also had Canada high on their list of preferred targets, with obvious, and unpleasant, implications for the quality of security arrangements within North America. Let us turn to these implications, starting with the following section's discussion of influence attempts launched by diasporic activists whose proclivities ran much more to "physical force" nationalism than they did to its constitutional-nationalist counterpart.

NORTH AMERICAN "WAZIRISTAN": THE UNITED STATES AS A THREAT TO CANADIAN (AND BRITISH) SECURITY

If meiosis, as some grammarians instruct us, can be an antonym for hyperbole,[56] then the verdict rendered by Mabel Gregory Walker on Irish American diasporic activism surely represents the apex of geostrategic meiosis. Writing more than four decades ago, she noted that while Irish Americans had, along with other ethnic groups, contributed to enriching American society, they had also, more than any other such group, "occasionally complicated affairs, both domestic and foreign, for the land of their adoption."[57] In chapter two, we saw why the celebration of North America's "long peace" as somehow being directly dateable from the Treaty of Ghent in 1814 is so woefully anachronistic. Geopolitically speaking, what happened that year in Ghent, *stayed* in Ghent. It would take nearly an entire century for anyone credibly to argue that a North American security community either was emerging or had already emerged. Though not the only reason for their security community's tardy appearance on the regional scene, Canadians' and Americans' rather differing assessments of the merits of the continent's Irish diaspora had more than a little to do with delaying the onset of healthier security cooperation between the two countries.

In the preceding section, we looked at the Irish diaspora in the United States. Here, a word or two must be offered in respect of the Irish diaspora in Canada, which was not only much smaller than that in the neighboring United States, but also tended, as time went on in the nineteenth century, to be relatively more Protestant in religious orientation than the increasingly Roman Catholic one to the south. This does not mean that the kind of diasporic activism associated with the generic brand of Fenianism, about which we will shortly learn a bit more, had no impact upon Canada; it is simply to recognize that to the extent a North American-based Irish diaspora was to trouble (or, to use Mabel Walker's emollient variant, "occasionally complicate") Anglo-American and therefore Canadian-American security relations, it was almost entirely due to the exertions of Irish-American activists. There had been a not insignificant outflow from Catholic counties of Ireland to Canada during the time of the great famine, but after the mid-1850s Irish emigration to Britain's North American provinces would greatly subside, and this, coupled with the fact that pre-famine Irish inflows to Canada had consisted mainly of Protestants, made Canada's Irish reality greatly different from America's. And to the extent that Irish Catholic nationalist impulses could be felt north of the U.S. border, as they could, especially in the large cities of Canada,[58] these manifested themselves mostly through a general preference for solving the Irish Question through constitutional means instead of violent ones. As David Wilson has written, a constant refrain would be heard when Irish-Catholic Canadians took to proffering policy advice: "From the late 1840s, the same message was repeated over and over again: if Ireland could get what Canada already had . . . then Ireland would be satisfied."[59]

There was an additional, highly noteworthy, political consideration. North of the Canada-U.S. border, the use of violence to promote Irish nationalist ends could easily be regarded as sedition or even treason, and could in theory cost proponents their lives. In theory, because the only Irish-Catholic extremist ever to be executed by Canada was put to death not for treason but for murder, in the April 1868 assassination of Thomas D'Arcy McGee, an exile from the "Young Ireland" uprising of 1848 who became, in Canada, a prominent politician in the new federation, espousing constitutional nationalism in Ireland and opposing physical-force nationalism in North America.[60] South of the border, however, depending upon the climate of Anglo-American relations in the post-Civil War years, physical-force initiatives might meet either with mild reproval from the U.S. government, or at times even with thinly veiled satisfaction, reflecting a sense that England's difficulty might not just be Ireland's opportunity, but America's as well. Gradually, Washington would shed this latter conceit, of being able to extract some gain from Irish America's physical-force exertions, but for a brief period during the last half of the 1860s, it looked very much to the British (and the Canadians) as if the U.S. government was quite happy to countenance the country's Irish diaspora being put to the service of the American "national interest," by stirring up trouble, both in North America and in the UK.

The United States did not merely stand as a model for those seeking Ireland's outright independence, according to republican principles and institutions. It also constituted, in many instances, a springboard from which physical-force nationalists could seek to achieve Irish freedom, either by taking Britain's North American possessions away from it and perhaps "swapping" them in exchange for Irish independence, or by aiding directly the cause of insurrection in the British Isles through bases of operation on American soil. Therefore, when glimpsed from a Canadian (or British) coign of vantage, the United States in the immediate post-Civil War period looked to policy makers not so unlike the way that contemporary Pakistan's federally administered tribal areas, especially Waziristan, have appeared to American, Canadian, and other NATO allies' defense policy makers over the course of the last decade—as a dangerous safe haven from which attacks against them could be mounted, more or less with impunity.[61]

On either side of the Atlantic, the most consequential of all physical-force groupings was known, generically, as the Fenians. About this political grouping, or better, orientation, a great deal has been written, much of it suffused with normative content intended to minimize, and more often than not trivialize, the aspirations and accomplishments of those committed to physical force as a means of obtaining Irish freedom. There is much merit in the negative assessment of the phenomenon, for it would be hard to find a more fractious political movement anywhere in the Western world than that associated with the cause of Irish independence; in the colorful phrase of one Irish writer, litigiousness within the movement could, and often did, readily conjure up the "oldest national cliché. What time are we having the split?"[62] Typical in this regard is the judgment of one Canadian specialist on Fenianism, who notes that the movement's leaders "were too often violent, emotionally unstable, and incompetent conspirators who were careless about financial matters and appeared, at times, to be exploiting nationalist sentiments among poor and excitable Irish immigrants for the sake of ill-defined personal ambitions."[63]

Besides, Fenianism's *North American* exertions, which some had thought would blaze the trail to independence, turned out instead to be roads to nowhere; as such, these failures between 1866 and 1870 (discussed below) could easily be interpreted as having discredited Fenianism in its entirety. Thus has it been easy to caricature the Fenians who dreamed of taking Canada from British control as little more than buffoons. "Could anything," wondered one American historian in the immediate post-First World War period, "have been more fatuous, more grotesquely doomed to failure," than the raids on Canada following the Civil War? If Irish American activists were banking on general American support for Irish independence, they were in for serious disappointment, because "while there were here many who sympathized, more or less openly, with the cause of Ireland, very few of those sympathizers were so deluded as to see any possibility of success in the attempt. . . . The entire story of Fenianism is a record of ineptitudes; of costly and laborious organization, conceived in secrecy and shrouded in mystery, which was no sooner achieved than it vanished, with nothing to show as fruit for all its travail."[64]

Sometimes, however, the critics go overboard, and forget that there was a highly important *transatlantic* dimension of Fenianism, one that in the end would actually determine the outcome of the lengthy independence saga, notwithstanding the near-constant turmoil and frequent and successive frustrations physical-force elements would experience throughout the six decades following the American Civil War. And even though the efforts to take Canada failed so spectacularly, this did not at all negate the significance of the Waziristan analogy. To the contrary: in that long period stretching from the middle of the 1860s to the beginning of the 1920s, it was all too easy, as well as eminently realistic, for observers to imagine that the future of Ireland would ultimately be settled in America, with Irish American nationalists taking the lead role. Whether they were going to use their assumed voting power to "capture" the American state and therefore dictate the country's foreign policy, or whether they would constitute a large and effective fighting force kept safe from British military reprisals by dint of their American safe haven, remained to be determined. But on the strategy, as opposed to the tactics, of trying to winkle Ireland from British control, few were prepared to concede that the "Greater Ireland" located in the United States would be anything other than centrally involved in the struggle.[65] Just how successful its involvement would turn out to be, though, depended very much upon the fortunes of the UK-based branch of the Fenian family.

From its very inception, generic Fenianism had been a transatlantic manifestation, as well as a transnational one, owing a great deal ideologically and practically to the predecessor vogue of revolutionary movements in Western Europe during the second half of the 1840s. As one enthusiast of the phenomenon relates, the concept itself can be grasped in two dimensions, one narrow, the other broad. "In its simplest and purest form," writes Joe Ambrose, "it refers to an ideology which seeks to remove the British presence from Irish affairs by force of arms. In a slightly expanded form, it refers to a huge cultural empire which involves the Irish language, an interpretation of Irish history, the pursuit of Irish music and, most successfully, the propagation and playing of Irish games."[66] For my purposes in this chapter, I address generic Fenianism in the narrower sense, which stresses the central aspect of *insurrectionary* violence, though clearly Ambrose has a good point in drawing our attention to the nexus between Fenianism and cultural nationalism.[67]

Some participants in Ireland's own abortive insurrection during the revolutionary year 1848 were banished by Britain to the other side of the world (Van Diemen's Land, i.e., today's Australian state of Tasmania), with many of these subsequently making their way to the United States; others avoided arrest and fled into exile, to both the United States and the continent of Europe.[68] The most prominent of the exiles, James Stephens, sought and obtained refuge in Paris, where he mixed with and absorbed ideas from like-minded political activists from France and other European lands.[69] It was Stephens who, upon his return to Ireland nearly a decade later, founded the organization that for a while would come to symbolize Fenianism, although he himself was careful, for reasons of security, not to give any name to the new and very secretive society he established in Dublin on St. Patrick's Day 1858. Others, though, soon took to referring to this organization as either the Irish Revolutionary Brotherhood or the Irish Republican Brotherhood, and over time it would be the latter name that stuck, such that between 1867 and the start of the Anglo-Irish war in 1919 the IRB was always to be found among the groups eager to free Ireland by violent, usually insurrectionary, measures. It was not the only institutional player within the physical-force community, and by the early twentieth century it would not even be the most important such player in Ireland; still, it maintained a constant presence on the scene from its 1858 founding until the Irish civil war of the early 1920s.[70]

Whatever Stephens might have thought his new organization should be called, it was not long before it got attached to it the umbrella label of "Fenianism." This was as a result of a branding effort undertaken by Stephens's New York-based associate John O'Mahony, who named the American affiliate of the new organization the Fenian Brotherhood. Fenianism would end up long outliving that America-based affiliate itself, which as early as 1867 began to bleed membership to a new organizational embodiment of generic Fenianism, the Clan na Gael.[71] O'Mahony, like his Young Ireland comrade, Stephens, had left for Parisian exile following the failed 1848 uprising, and had remained in France for half a dozen years, before departing for New York.[72] Unlike Stephens, however, O'Mahony was a scholar as well as a revolutionary, someone who even managed to establish for himself something of a reputation among the limited circle of specialists in Gaelic lore, through his translation into English of Seathrún Céitinn's *Foras feasa ar Éirinn*.[73] Being well-versed in the early history of Ireland, O'Mahony knew that back around 300 CE the high king of Ireland, a Connaught monarch named Cormac Mac Airt, had established a standing army to protect his kingdom from the Romans, conquerors of neighboring Britain. This army was commanded by the king's eponymous son-in-law, Finn Mac Cumhail, hence the force's being called the Fianna. As one chronicler explains, "the Romans were already in decline, no invasion of Ireland occurred, and the Fianna, with little to do, degenerated—but not before their deeds had been sung in heroic fashion by the poet Oisín, son of Finn, in epics or sagas that have been transmitted through centuries by word of mouth alone."[74]

More than a millennium and a half later, the American Civil War would provide the latter-day Fianna with plenty to do. The stars seemed in the early 1860s finally to be in alignment for Irish nationalist elements, on both sides of the Atlantic, given that the vicissitudes of America's internecine conflict were slowly but surely ensnaring the American and British governments in a web of increasingly strained relations. When in November 1861 the USS *San Jacinto* intercepted the RMS *Trent* on the high seas and removed two Confederate diplomats bound for Europe, war between the North and the British loomed as a distinct prospect. Though combat was averted as a result of a diplomatic climb-down by the government of Abraham Lincoln, tensions remained, and would continue into the early postwar period, before finally being somewhat appeased with the Treaty of Washington of 1871, about which one Canadian commentator wrote, suggestively (if possibly prematurely), that it marked the end of the Anglo-American "Hundred Years' War."[75]

Rumors of Anglo-American rancor always came as unalloyed glad tidings to Irish nationalist ears. Why not? For as a leading authority on Fenianism has sagely noted, the "consortium of Stephens and Company Ltd. and O'Mahony Inc." needed to establish credibility in the marketplace for its wares, and what could be better than an Anglo-American war for accomplishing just this? "The one genuine basis of credibility available to [F]enianism was the prospect of Britain being embroiled in a major war."[76] Less joyous, admittedly, were the tidings of combat emanating from America's own battlefields, where as many as 200,000 Irish Americans would see service between 1861 and 1865, the majority (around 150,000) wearing Union blue.[77] The Union and the Confederacy each had its illustrious Irish American units—the famed "Fighting 69th" from New York even said to be a regiment "composed entirely of Fenians."[78] Regrettable though it might be that Irish blood was, in the course of things, getting spilled—and by Irish hands, at times!—there was a promising upside to this temporary downside: Irish American gallantry in combat, never more fulsomely on display than at the Battle of Fredericksburg in late 1862,[79] would be bound to be repaid after the war by a grateful American (or at least, Northern) public prepared to think much more kindly of Fenianism—and of Irish Catholicism—than it had been, prior to the war.

Not only this, but there was a second, likely even more important, legacy of the Irish combat experience between 1861 and 1865: tens of thousands of Irish American nationalists had been transformed into battle-hardened veterans who could be mobilized, after Appomattox, for the *good* war, the one that would at last free Ireland from Britain's embrace. Nor was it even necessary for the current, unfortunate, North-South strife to draw to an end before permitting one's thoughts to dwell upon the more pleasant battles to come. For instance, during the Atlanta Campaign in the summer of 1864, the most prominent Irish American general in the Union army, Thomas W. Sweeny, contacted his Confederate opposite number, General Patrick Cleburne, with the suggestion that once the Civil War was over, they should team up in the struggle against the common British foe.[80] Clearly, not all of the 200,000 Irish veterans would, or could, be tapped for the anti-British jihad. Nevertheless, it was reliably accepted that at least 10,000 and possibly as many as 50,000 soldiers, from both sides, had become converts to Fenianism during the course of the fighting; thus it was hardly far-fetched for observers in lands that Fenians had within their crosshairs to perceive the threat as being a rather grave one, and not at all like the trivial business that some subsequent recounts of Fenianism would dismiss it as having been.[81]

While everyone in Irish nationalist ranks whose tastes ran to what one scholar refers to as "advanced" nationalism[82] (i.e., reliance upon violent as opposed to constitutional methods of altering the political status quo) might have clearly grasped the identity of the foe to be combatted, it was much less obvious where to land the blow against Britain. For the IRB founder, Stephens, as well as for O'Mahony, it had to be in Ireland that the insurrection would be mounted. Others were not so sure, and a major rift soon opened within Fenianism over where to strike. A group of American-based militants known as the "Senate," and led by William Randall Roberts and the aforementioned General Sweeny, were convinced that an armed uprising in Ireland was doomed in advance, and would be nothing short of a bloodbath. From their perspective, far better would be the chances of striking successfully at British rule through *Canada*. As we saw in chapter one, the border separating Canada from the United States had known its fair share of combat over the long period during which North America was a "dominion of war."[83] And even with the cessation of interstate conflict subsequent to the termination of the War of 1812, filibustering incidents continued to occur from time to time during the 1830s and 1840s, reminders that North America had yet to become a zone of peace.

Already, by 1848, some British colonial officials had been evincing concern about a serious *Irish* complication getting introduced into continental security affairs, and doing so in the rudest possible manner, via cross-border aggression.[84] In that year, the newly appointed governor general of Canada, Lord Elgin (otherwise known as James Bruce), drew specific attention to one possible implication of the recent ending of the Mexican War—the prospect of Irish American "fanatics" who had recently been serving with U.S. forces in Mexico entering Canada to stir up opposition to continued British rule in the country.[85] Nothing came of these fears at the time, but it would not be long before similar anxiety was again expressed, only in greatly magnified fashion, given that this time the numbers of Irish American veterans bearing historic grudges against Britain would be vastly larger than they had been two decades earlier.

Ironically, in light of his known antipathy to the Canadian option, it was O'Mahony's faction that struck the first blow against British North America, when in April 1866, in a bid to spike accusations that he and his supporters were partisans not of action but of its opposite, an attempt was made to seize and hold Campobello Island, in Passamaquoddy Bay, off New Brunswick.[86] It was a disaster for the Fenians, but it had the political effect of rallying support in the province for a confederation of Britain's North American holdings. The ease with which the raid had been repulsed tended to give the impression that Fenianism was a paper tiger, notwithstanding the alarmism of just a few months before. Some even imagined that the threat of armed incursions north of the border had been seen off entirely. It had not. The Campobello caper actually fortified the anti-O'Mahony faction in its conviction to try to seize a prize far more important than an irrelevant island off New Brunswick. That prize was the United Province of Canada, soon to become (thanks in no small part to the Fenians!) the heartland of the federation that would, starting in 1867, bear the name Canada.[87]

With the O'Mahony faction being so discredited, the field was open in mid-1866 for the Roberts-Sweeny camp to put into effect its plan for a three-pronged offensive against both parts of the United Province, Canada West (today's Ontario) and Canada East (Quebec). Sweeny's western-most wing was supposed to commence action against the Ontario town of Stratford and proceed therefrom to take London. His center wing was to seize Port Stanley, on the north shore of Lake Erie, and establish itself as a threat to Toronto to the east, in hopes of drawing defenders from that city toward it. This would then allow the eastern wing to conduct the brunt of the offensive, marching into Quebec from its base in St. Albans, Vermont, with the full expectation of being joined in the campaign by both the Montreal Fenians and an undetermined number of French Cana-dians, presumably as eager as the radical Irish in Canada to throw off the British yoke. Needless to say, much of this planning went awry, in no small measure because it was based on faulty expectations of mustering support from discontented elements within Canada. However, a Fenian force led by Colonel John O'Neill did manage to defeat a contingent of Canadian militia at the Battle of Ridgeway on the Niagara Peninsula, in early June 1866, before returning to sanctuary in the United States, where the federal government somewhat gingerly apprehended the raiders.[88]

Invasive Fenianism was nearly down for the count in North America (though there would be one more foray into Canada from Vermont, in 1870),[89] and it is hard to argue against the verdict that Canada emerged stronger, both politically and militarily, thanks to this kinetic manifesta-tion of Irish American diasporic activism.[90] But if the armed (and, after a fashion, "organized") Fenian challenge had been dissolved in North America, diasporic activism would remain to complicate Canadian-American relations for many years to come. Most immediately, it would take the form of a sustained public relations campaign against an "op-pressive" Canadian state that had sentenced to death more than a score of Fenians taken prisoner in the 1866 events, and that was now threaten-ing to carry out the sentences, notwithstanding American and British governmental appeals for clemency.[91] And even when the sentences were commuted, as they all would be by the end of December 1866, an ongoing publicity campaign against Canada's equivalent of Guantánamo Bay, the Kingston Penitentiary, continued to nourish an undercurrent of anti-Canadianism among a sizeable, and vocal, segment of American public opinion.[92]

THE "MCDOWELL-BAGENAL" THESIS

It would be tempting, but wrong, to imagine that with the disappearance of any further prospect of a Fenian invasion of British North America, the Waziristan analogy would similarly have vaporized. There are two reasons, however, why the analogy remains apt, and would continue to be so, for several more decades. First, while Fenian armed violence in North America would not directly disturb continental security any longer (with some minor exceptions, to be discussed below), Fenian activity in the UK itself actually became a growing, and near-constant, worry for British officials, beginning in the latter months of 1867, despite the easy quelling of a Fenian rising in Ireland the previous March.[93] The onset of "Fenian Fever" in the UK, with all the challenges posed thereby for the balancing of civil liberties with the requirements of British homeland security, became a recurring rallying opportunity for diasporic activists in the United States, such that the institutional wilting of the Fenian Brotherhood (begun in 1869 and completed by 1886) would not fundamentally affect the way in which British security officials would continue, for decades, to assess the meaning of Irish American diasporic nationalism.[94]

Writing at the outset of the 1920s, one British security official expressed his skepticism about the Irish Question's resolubility, due to the safe harbor offered in America to those plotting mayhem against Britain. There could be no mistaking Hugh Campbell's dudgeon, even if his predictive skills left something to be desired, because even as the ink was drying on his book's page-proofs, the Free State was being created: "[s]o long as there exists a powerful criminal organization rooted in the United States, as well as in Ireland, . . . whose avowed object is the establishment of an independent Irish Republic by methods of political assassination and secret murder," nothing would change for the better. It certainly was true that many Irish had been in near-perpetual insurrection against British rule for centuries, but shifting demographic realities had radically altered the security environment in the Emerald Isle. Ever since the 1860s, the "source of infection has been external, and the Irish of the United States have been responsible for energising the Irish of Great Britain and Ireland into active crime."[95]

Given Campbell's police background (for a time he had been a staff officer for the chief of Irish police), it is understandable that he would discuss political violence in the language of crime fighters everywhere, as criminal behavior and nothing but. Usually, however, the framing of narratives involving the use of physical (as opposed, as it sometimes was, to "moral") force, takes place against a broader political debate, over whether Fenianism can be equated with terrorism.[96] If it can be (and on this point, the scholars are, not surprisingly, divided), then it is easy to understand the ire felt by so many in the UK and Canada during the course of the lengthy period in which American governments, either by commission or omission, were argued to be complicit in terrorism. In the judgment of Lindsay Clutterbuck, while "Ireland and its future provided their rationale for violence, the immediate threat they posed to life and limb came from operations planned, initiated, and supported from the USA."[97] Obviously, as time went on, administrations in Washington grew ever more uneasy about even the suspicion of their being enablers or (much worse) promoters of terrorism, and at least one scholar has suggested that the combating, or at least condemning, of such Irish American violence provided a means not of driving the "Anglo-Saxon" powers further apart, but of actually fostering greater cooperation between them, for in Jonathan Gantt's words, "Irish terrorists were powerful non-state actors who helped shape the Atlantic community."[98]

This thesis—let us call it the therapeutic thesis—would have surprised contemporary British (and Canadian) observers of the American scene, who instead reacted at the time in a manner not unlike that in which more than a few American official and nonofficial observers would, during the immediate post-9/11 period, focus a critical gaze upon a Canadian government that they considered to be wantonly inattentive to the risks presented by radical Islamists to America's physical security. During the late 1860s and for many years thereafter, British and Canadian officials were stupefied by what they considered to be the reckless insouciance of Washington in the face of mountains of evidence that missions of destruction were being financed and planned in America, and carried out by Irish extremists operating from an American sanctuary.[99]

If the Waziristan comparison is apt, so too is another analogy: Brooklyn, New York, as America's Swat Valley. It was the cynosure for hatching one of the more imaginative, if bizarre, campaigns of violence to be mounted against British targets: the Dynamite War of the 1880s. At the start of that decade, Brooklyn was America's third-largest city, surpassed in size only by New York City, into which it would become incorporated in 1898, and Philadelphia. In addition to boasting the third-largest Irish-born community in the United States, Brooklyn was the home of what was dubbed the "Dynamite School of Instruction," run out of the Greenpoint section of town, which gave thirty-day courses to bomb makers in the arts of safely assembling explosives. Tuition for the course was $30, which included room and board, but all fees were waived for anyone agreeing to become a "missionary" to Britain. The legal name of the enterprise was the Mansonitor Manufacturing and Experimental Chemical Company, whose president, Richard Rogers, was a New York City-born son of Russian and Scottish immigrant parents, and who went under the pseudonym of "Professor Mezzeroff." We will come upon the not-so-good professor again, in chapter five, in connection with his collaboration with a leading German anarchist based in New York, Johann Most.[100]

The school's purposes were hardly a secret to the American authorities, not with dynamiting itself being so publicly championed by leading figures in Irish America, including Patrick Ford, publisher of the *Irish World*, and John Devoy, founder of the Clan na Gael, the principal organizational successor of the Fenian Brotherhood, and a leading Irish American journalist in his own right.[101] The object of their praise was a campaign hatched in the aftermath of the failed attempts at insurrectionary violence both in Britain and British North America in the late 1860s, and it frankly divided Fenians, many of whom insisted that the only "honorable" way to fight the British foe was to target, in a more or less conventional manner, his armed forces. But dynamiters, whose programmatic and very "asymmetric" tactics found expression for a time through the euphemism of "skirmishing," believed that the latest explosive technologies could bring about a quick, if necessarily somewhat bloody, end to the long struggle against English rule, and do so on Irish terms. Some of the more deluded advocates of this form of urban guerrilla even convinced themselves that dynamite—whose quasi-religious properties were also being embraced by radical elements associated with the German American diaspora[102]—would be the deus ex machina bringing to a happy ending that struggle, though the reduction of Britain's principal urban centers to heaps of ember and ash.

Knowing what we do today about the extreme allergy to terrorism of a security-conscious American state, it can seem a bit surprising—even shocking—to discover just how blasé the country's political elites (with some notable exceptions, such as Charles Francis Adams, U.S. minister to Britain from 1861 to 1868) could be in the face of what were palpable breaches of the legal, not to say moral, obligations of governments to refrain from allowing their territory to be used to attack countries with which they were not at war. How, then, to explain what appears to be an anomaly? Partly, of course, the explanation can be glimpsed in the above-mentioned imagery of Frank Underhill, the Anglo-American "Hundred Years' War." With the enemy of one's enemy almost always ranking as one's friend, it is not terribly surprising that American officials should have looked almost fondly on Irish American influence attempts that put a premium upon violence, for even though there may not have been a state of war between the Anglo-American powers during the 1860s and for some time thereafter, there was certainly nothing remotely approximating a stable peace between them, until the century drew to a close. The historic grudge carried by so many Americans had become magnified by the diplomatic frictions stirred up by the Civil War, manifested as these were in the victorious Union by the conviction that Britain had *itself* blatantly violated the canons of neutrality through the aid and comfort bestowed upon the Confederacy during the conflict.[103] Thus, turnabout could only be the fairest of play, especially in light of the postwar demand for compensation for damages to Northern shipping inflicted by the British-built and equipped commerce raider, the CSS *Alabama*.[104]

But there was more to it than interstate grudges. There was also a singularly *intrastate* component endowing Irish American diasporic activism with the appearance, if not reality, of being a powerful element in the shaping of the overall American national interest.[105] It will be recalled from chapter three's discussion of the phenomenon of ethnic "lobbying" broadly construed, emphasizing as it did the perceived voting power of ethnic constituencies within the United States, that a diaspora's size has had a way of being taken into consideration in discussions of electoral outcomes, and this even though it would not be until halfway through the twentieth century that psephologists would begin to develop the capability of doing other than simply making ballpark estimations of that mooted voting power.

In chapter five we are going to revisit two important contests, the presidential elections of 1916 and 1920, about which it used to be claimed that the "ethnic vote" was a decisive consideration in the campaigns and their outcomes. I put this analysis off until we reach the next chapter's inquiry into German American diasporic activism because in those two elections, Irish and German American voters were widely regarded as tantamount to Tweedledum and Tweedledee: each constituency being said to have wanted the same thing, even if not for the same reason. The two diasporas, in this respect at least, really are nearly impossible to disaggregate for purposes of assessing the ethnic-vote thesis.

In what remains of this chapter, let us instead tie up the discussion regarding physical-force methods in such a way as to show how it can so easily be melded into an analysis of ethnic lobbying, that other principal means through which the impact of Irish American diasporic activism was believed to have manifested itself in North American and transatlantic security affairs. To make the connection, I am going to focus upon one particular case, adumbrated earlier in this chapter. This was the case of Luke Dillon, who if remembered at all today (and this is doubtful) is known for his involvement in the final attempt by Irish American nationalists to exploit American territory for staging an attack against a Canadian target. Although the practice of striking at Canada had been mainly abandoned following the Clan na Gael raid in Quebec in 1870, the dream continued to inspire a few imaginations. In December 1884, for instance, one of the veterans of the Dynamite War in the UK, a "graduate" of the aforementioned Brooklyn academy of explosive arts named Thomas Mooney (who occasionally sported the alias "Professor Armstrong") is reported to have detonated explosive devices in the provincial government building then in the final stages of construction in Quebec City.[106] More to the point, and the most important of the post-1870 incidents involving Canada, would be another Dynamite War veteran's attempt, during the Boer War, to disable the Welland Canal. This incident reflected, and was motivated by, the familiar logic entertained by many diasporic activists in Irish America, of Britain's wars holding out the prospect of Irish advantage.

The main protagonist in this last gasp of physical-force nationalism to directly implicate Canada was Dillon, who with two comrades detonated a dynamite package affixed to the gates of the canal's Lock 24, in Thorold, Ontario, on 21 April 1900. The damage was minimal, though things might have been different had the charge been planted on the other side of the lock's gates, forcing them apart rather than more closely together. Ironically, the Dillon case is much more significant for what it tells us about lobbying rather than about dynamiting, even though Dillon himself had made his mark in that more explosive realm, having been one of the bombers of the House of Commons in London in January 1885, prior to finding his way safely out of the UK and back to America. Dillon, sentenced along with his two colleagues, John Nolan and John Walsh, to life imprisonment in Kingston Penitentiary, became very much a cause célèbre among certain circles of opinion in the United States—not unlike the way another famous prisoner a century later, Omar Khadr, would mutatis mutandis serve as a rallying focus for some Canadians objecting to Americans' incarcerative practices, to be discussed in the concluding chapter.

From the afternoon of Dillon's sentencing until the morning, fourteen years later, of his release, his supporters within Irish America kept up a steady refrain about his being an innocent man held in subhuman captivity by an oppressive government, obsessed as it was with homeland security and only too willing to violate basic human rights. The lobbying efforts mounted on his behalf constantly featured threats that if Washington did not intervene to get him released from prison, elected officials could expect to pay the price on voting day. Threats such as this had, of course, been well-rehearsed long before Dillon's time, and were particularly conspicuous immediately after the Civil War, when many observers, especially in Britain and Canada, tended (in their charitable moments, that is) to chalk up America's laxity in cracking down on Fenians who violated the country's neutrality law to a concern, on all sides of the political house in the American capital, with the "Irish vote"—and not to any particular hostility to Canada or Britain.

To be sure, as we have already discovered, in the immediate aftermath of the Civil War there was no great love lost between the American and British governments, and this had obvious implications for U.S. relations with Canada. But by the time Dillon would experience his moments in the continental security spotlight, much had changed, what with the two English-speaking powers basking by the turn of the century in the unwonted but warming glow of balmy bilateral relations, traced to those events between 1895 and 1898 that sealed the Great Rapprochement, and were covered in some detail in chapter two. Although by 1900 there could no longer be any conceivable geostrategic gain to be found in an

American administration's intervening on behalf of Dillon or anyone like him, there was still the matter of domestic *political* gain to consider. Depending upon the context, this could make a difference, and though it is true that neither William McKinley nor his successor in 1901, Theodore Roosevelt, saw any great need to cater to the presumed Irish vote, matters would be otherwise for William Howard Taft, in the approach to the 1912 election.

Roosevelt's successor and quondam friend faced a much more difficult prospect than Republican candidates for election or reelection to national office had been used to confronting. Thus it came as no great surprise that he should, as the 1912 election drew nearer, be attentive to requests that he intercede on Dillon's behalf, all the more so because the coming election was shaping up to be no typical presidential contest, with the likelihood growing that if the former president, Roosevelt, did not wrest the nomination away from Taft he might bolt the party altogether, throwing into jeopardy the latter's reelection chances.[107] The year prior to the election, the president had been approached by, of all people, the Republican governor of Rhode Island, Aram J. Pothier, urging him to "restore freedom to Luke Dillon," because there were a great many "progressive" (read: Irish American) voters, both in the Ocean State and nationwide, with a strong emotional stake in this case. Taft was not slow to seize the point, and he instructed his secretary of state, Philander C. Knox, to broach the issue directly with Canadian officials. The president was hoping that a pardon for Dillon would help him politically, in two ways. First, he thought it would dissipate Irish American opposition to his proposed arbitration treaty with Great Britain, it being widely believed at the time that the Irish Americans had somehow been chiefly responsible for scuppering a previous treaty in 1897 intended to bring the United States and the UK into a more cooperative relationship, inter alia through the promotion of arbitration.[108] Second, he felt it might strip enough Irish American voters away from the Democratic Party in the upcoming election to enable him to remain in the White House. On neither of these counts was he successful, though the new government in Canada headed by Robert Borden, winner of the 1911 federal election, would show itself more disposed than the previous government of Wilfrid Laurier had been to setting Dillon free, something that would eventually be done, to little fanfare, on 12 July 1914.[109]

It is more than telling that Dillon should have become transformed from paladin of physical-force militancy to token of the ethnic vote, for such had been the transformation of Irish American diasporic activism itself, at least insofar as concerned the North American continent: the more that violent solutions there receded into the realm of impracticality, the more pronounced became appeals to the legal and constitutional path toward influence over U.S. foreign policy—a path to be cleared, it was thought by many, through the wonder-working properties of the threat

to visit electoral retribution upon any politician foolish enough to frustrate the activists' wishes. We can even give a label to this vision of
diasporic influence made manifest in the voting booths of the land: the
"McDowell-Bagenal" thesis. Unlike the other thesis we encountered earlier in this section, the so-called therapeutic one holding that the net effect
of Irish terrorism in the Atlantic world was to bring closer together the
two leading English-speaking powers, the McDowell-Bagenal thesis as-
serts just the opposite. Its logic resides in the assumption that in a liberal
democracy such as America's, with constant striving for electoral advantage often trumping a political aspirant's personal better judgment, there
would be an inevitable tendency to "pander" to the ethnic vote, assuming
of course that it was a sufficiently large and alluring one, as the Irish vote
was routinely considered to be.

The McDowell-Bagenal thesis owes its name to the twinning of two
rather bold assertions, made at nearly a half century's remove from each
other. The first element of the compound label is actually the more recent
of the two, stemming from a speaking engagement during the summer of
1919 of the newly chosen "president" of a very provisional Irish Republic,
Éamon de Valera, who was in America to raise funds for the republican
cause, on behalf of an independent country yet to be born. De Valera, a
fugitive from British justice in Ireland, had slipped into the United States
in June, aboard the SS *Lapland*, and would remain in the land of his birth
until December 1920, a period of some nineteen months.[110] During the
first few weeks of his sojourn, de Valera would log some six thousand
miles, and address close to half a million people in seventeen locales. One
of those spots was Butte, Montana, which somewhat improbably boasted
the largest proportional share of Irish American residents of any city or
town in America at the time, with 26 percent of the townsfolk being
either Irish-born or the children of Irish-born.[111]

It was in the Montana mining town that one of the "home-truths"
about the alleged impact of the Irish American diaspora on domestic,
and—who could say?—possibly even on transatlantic affairs was recited,
during the welcoming remarks extended by one of the state's leading
politicians, Lieutenant Governor William Wallace McDowell, who was
filling in for Governor Sam Stewart. To a crowd of around ten thousand
who had gathered in the city's Hebgen Park to hear de Valera, McDowell
remarked that "[t]hey tell us that the Irish cannot govern themselves. I
can tell you Mister President that while I know nothing of what the Irish
do in Ireland, in this country they run the American government."[112]

McDowell's comment might have seemed an exaggeration, but if so it
was not much of one, as far as many contemporary observers were concerned. Indeed, ever since they began to arrive in America in large numbers in the quarter century preceding the Civil War, America's Irish Catholics had for many students of the country's domestic politics loomed as
an electoral force to be reckoned with—a force that only grew over time,

so that eventually Irish America would find itself dubbed by some analysts as the country's "political class."[113] Nor was this characterization anything novel, for one English writer had even made an assertion similar to McDowell's nearly four decades previously, although it did not attract the same attention as the Hebgen Park comment. It is to that writer, Philip Bagenal, that the second element in the thesis finds its origins, specifically to his 1882 book entitled *The American Irish and Their Influence on Irish Politics*, in which attention was drawn to one aspect of American electoral reality that in more recent times has found expression through the political scientists' concept of the "swing state"—that is, a state said to be, by dint of its weight in the electoral college as well as certain other demographic peculiarities, capable virtually on its own of determining the outcome of presidential elections. In Bagenal's opinion, New York was just such a state, "the empire state of the Union, which is governed almost entirely by the Irish vote."[114]

DÉNOUEMENT: THE WARTIME EXPERIENCE AND AFTER

The Irish Americans, of course, did not "run" the American government, but the Irish vote certainly had appeal to politicians aspiring to high office; it would be unusual were this not to have been the case, given that a politician's immediate objectives must always include the important business of getting elected. Still, not all presidents proved as solicitous as William Howard Taft of assuaging Irish American feelings, and sometimes Irish diasporic activists' entreaties would receive a frosty response from on high, never more so, ironically, than from Theodore Roosevelt and Woodrow Wilson—ironically given what we know about how little common ground existed between these legendary political enemies, each possessed of an ample portion of loathing for the other.[115] Nevertheless, as far as British and Canadian officials were concerned, there was an ever-present presumption that the Irish vote *must* be exercising undue (and unholy) influence over American foreign policy, and this presumption had a way of coloring relations between the three members of the North Atlantic triangle for the entire period I cover in this chapter—if anything, becoming even more pronounced during the First World War, given the grave consequences of that struggle.[116] So to the extent that British and Canadian officials vested the Irish Americans with "influence" during these years, it could be said that the diaspora possessed such influence, even if it is hardly easy to demonstrate that the same degree of sway existed over *American* policy making itself.[117]

Even today, after the passage of nearly a century, it is hard to gauge with any accuracy the claims highlighted at the beginning of this chapter, in which allegations were made, implicitly in the case of Robert Borden, more directly in the cases of David Lloyd George and William Sowden

Sims, to the effect that Irish Americans bore great responsibility for delaying U.S. entry into the First World War, and as a result imposed real costs on both British and Canadian military forces, prevented as each was from having the United States as an ally until the third year of the war, with all that this implied for casualty rates as well as other costs imposed by the fighting between August 1914 and April 1917.

The events of the First World War will be covered in greater detail in the following chapter, in an analysis that, as previously noted, requires a certain amount of blending of the influence attempts made by both of the large diasporas, the Irish American and German American ones.[118] This is due not only to the tacit and in some instances formal alliances struck between lobbying organizations claiming to represent the two ethnic groupings during the decade preceding American entry into the war, but also because of the basal congruence in the groups' objectives—up, that is, to April 1917. For sure, it had been one thing during the preceding decade for Irish American nationalists to muse about the benefits a war between Britain and Germany would bring Ireland's way, and the Irish American *Chicago Citizen* was not very far off the mark when it enthused, in a July 1908 editorial, that "[t]here is not an Irishman in America today, in whose veins good red blood is flowing, who would not rejoice to hear that a German army was marching in triumph across England from Yarmouth to Milford Haven."[119] But once America itself had joined the war, things changed radically for diasporic activists in America, the Irish Americans throwing themselves fully behind the war effort in a way that was hardly replicable by German Americans. Irish American activist Edward F. Dunne may have been overstating things, albeit only slightly, when he commented that "[n]o element in the United States entered more heartily into the prosecution of that war than did the American citizens of Irish descent."[120] In becoming converts to an agenda they had so recently and ferociously opposed, diasporic activists would, however, do so on their own terms, as they seized upon using President Wilson's subsequent commitment to the noble principle of the "self-determination" of small nations, made in his "fourteen points" address early in 1918, as a more than convenient way to marry the "Americanism" of Irish Americans' rallying around the Stars and Stripes with the commitment to Irish freedom.[121] Throughout the war's final year it was well understood by Irish American nationalist elites that Ireland was bound to find itself at the head of the line of deserving recipients of whatever self-determination the war's victors would be willing to bestow. Unfortunately for them, neither the British nor the American governments shared that same passion.[122]

In the end, self-determination would come Ireland's way, though not through concessions made by the British at the Paris peace negotiations that followed the Great War. Nor would Woodrow Wilson be recalled very fondly by Irish nationalists, including and especially in the United

States itself, once it became clear that the president had been unable or unwilling, or both, to force Britain to grant self-determination to Ireland at Paris.[123] It took a violent, nasty, struggle with Britain for Ireland, or at least for the three provinces outside of Ulster, to achieve self-governing status, initially with the establishment of the Irish Free State in 1921, and then late the following decade, with the creation of the Republic. Upon the winning of self-determination, even in the qualified form of the Free State, Irish American diasporic activism would begin its inevitable decline.[124] Starting with the Anglo-Irish treaty of December 1921, and gaining momentum with the obviously confusing episodes of the Irish civil war of mid-1922 to mid-1923, the bottom would drop out of the one foundational element that had sustained for so long a sense of purpose and unity in an otherwise fractious Irish American diaspora: Anglophobia, and its foreign policy corollary of eschewing closer security cooperation between the United States, Britain, and Canada. By the end of the 1920s, there was hardly anything left to serve as a rallying point for the dwindling band of diasporic activists, whose constant critique of U.S. foreign policy would lose its "special audience since the majority of Irish Americans, having accomplished the distinctive group goal of Irish independence, had become largely indistinguishable from their fellow Americans."[125]

And though there would be, toward the end of the twentieth century, a minor revival of Irish American interventionism in the affairs of the UK (the so-called troubles in Ulster),[126] this diasporic activism paled in significance compared to what had gone before, in the six decades covered in this chapter. Not only was Irish American involvement in support of the IRA—involvement that also featured, as we have seen, Peter T. King's participation—small beer compared to earlier generations of Irish Americans' support of nationalist causes, but unlike many of those earlier influence attempts, by the late twentieth century no one could argue that whatever Irish diasporic activists might desire could have any possible bearing upon the quality of the Canada-United States security community. This brings us back to the major question pursued in this book: what can we deduce about the impact that Irish American diasporic activism had upon the quality of security relations between the United States and Canada, especially as regards the rise and evolution of their regional security community?

I think there can be no disputing that during the long period when U.S. relations with Britain were tenuous *and* when Canadian security was intimately bound up with British security, Irish America certainly made its "contribution" to minimizing the potential of healthy cooperation between the United States and Canada. Indeed, security relations between neighbors do not get much worse than in those instances when the territory of one is being used to strike at the territory of the other. In this concrete way, then, we can hypothesize without too much risk of contradiction that the era of physical-force (or "advanced") Irish nationalism *within North America* must, at minimum, be taken as prima facie evidence of the nonexistence of a security community. It does not follow, however, that Fenianism was the cause of this unfortunate manifestation of "bad neighborly" relations on the continent; the best that can be said is that the poor relations between the United States and Britain (and by extension, Canada) gave Fenianism certain opportunities.

Much more important, and interesting, though, is the impact of Irish American "ethnic lobbying," broadly construed, on the North American security community, as well as upon that other security dispensation that has come to be an ever-present condition of Canada-United States relations, their alliance. One view, which seems to be the dominant one (witness the comments cited at the beginning of this chapter of Borden, Lloyd George, and Sims, to say nothing of those of Charles McCurdy Mathias), is that in the absence of the Irish American diaspora, with its passionate commitment to the revision of the Irish status quo, one might easily have anticipated not just an earlier arrival on the scene of the Canada-United States security community, but even more importantly, of the construction of the Anglo-American and Canadian-American alliances. Against this dominant view, however, there is another possibility that suggests itself, one I revisit in the next chapter—the possibility that, completely without intending or desiring this outcome, Irish American opposition to Anglo-American (and by extension Canadian-American) condominium, assisted as this was by German American diasporic opposition to this same outcome, actually contributed to, rather than retarded, the formation of alliance between the United States, the UK, and Canada.

To get a sense of how this perspective, which is not just counterintuitive but implicitly counterfactual (in positing American neutrality even in the absence of ethnic-diasporic activism), let us now turn our attention, in chapter five, to the case of the German American diaspora.

NOTES

1. Charles McCurdy Mathias Jr., "Ethnic Groups and Foreign Policy," *Foreign Affairs* 59 (Summer 1981): 975–98, quote at p. 982.

2. H. Perry Robinson, *The Twentieth Century American: Being a Comparative Study of the Peoples of the Two Great Anglo-Saxon Nations* (Chautauqua, N.Y.: Chautauqua Press, 1911), p. 19.

3. Quoted in Justin Massie, *Francosphère: L'importance de la France dans la culture stratégique du Canada* (Montréal: Presses de l'Université du Québec, 2013), p. 174.

4. The term is Robert Bothwell's; see his "Has Canada Made a Difference? The Case of Canada and the United States," in *Making a Difference? Canadian Foreign Policy in a Changing World*, ed. John English and Norman Hillmer (Toronto: Lester, 1992), pp. 8–9.

5. Quoted in Thomas J. Noer, "The American Government and the Irish Question during World War I," *South Atlantic Quarterly* 72 (Winter 1973): 95–114, quote at p. 98. British leaders had for some time been convinced that Irish America was the single

biggest obstacle to closer security relations between the United States and the UK. In 1900, two years before he became prime minister, the home secretary, Arthur Balfour, told Henry White that "harmonious cooperation between the two great Anglo-Saxon states" would always be hard to arrange, because "large numbers of the most loyal citizens of America . . . come from that part of Ireland which has never loved England." Quoted in Stephen Hartley, *The Irish Question as a Problem in British Foreign Policy, 1914–18* (London: Macmillan, 1987), p. 3.

6. Quoted in "Sinn Fein and the Admiral," *Literary Digest* 69 (25 June 1921): 7–9, quote at p. 7.

7. Arthur Lee Burns, "International Theory and Historical Explanation," *History and Theory* 1, 1 (1960): 55–74, quote at pp. 73–74. But for a more direct defense of counterfactuals, compare Philip E. Tetlock and Aaron Belkin, "Counterfactual Thought Experiments in World Politics: Logical, Methodological, and Psychological Perspectives," in *Counterfactual Thought Experiments in World Politics: Logical, Methodological, and Psychological Perspectives,* ed. Tetlock and Belkin (Princeton, N.J.: Princeton University Press, 1996), pp. 3–38. For a very creative application of counterfactual reasoning to an important recent debate in international security, the one over the 2003 Iraq war, see Frank P. Harvey, *Explaining the Iraq War: Counterfactual Theory, Logic and Evidence* (Cambridge: Cambridge University Press, 2012).

8. Arnold Wolfers, *Discord and Collaboration: Essays on International Politics* (Baltimore: Johns Hopkins Press, 1962).

9. See Richard English, *Irish Freedom: The History of Nationalism in Ireland* (London: Macmillan, 2006). The English invasion of 1169 is often regarded to be the starting date for Ireland's lengthy period of subjugation, though it took a few centuries for English rule to become consolidated, something finally accomplished through the intensification of the campaign, running from the middle of the sixteenth until the end of the seventeenth centuries, to make of Ireland a Protestant as well as an English domain. See Thomas Bartlett, *Ireland: A History* (Cambridge: Cambridge University Press, 2010), chap. 3: "The Making of Protestant Ireland, 1541–1691."

10. See Alvin Jackson, *Home Rule: An Irish History, 1800–2000* (Oxford: Oxford University Press, 2003); and Michael Laffan, "John Redmond (1856–1918) and Home Rule," in *Worsted in the Game: Losers in Irish History,* ed. Ciaran Brady (Dublin: Lilliput Press, 1989), pp. 133–42.

11. Noted one English sympathizer with home rule shortly before the outbreak of the First World War, "[t]here is at present a peace in the country such as Ireland has not known for more than a century," largely because of recent land-reform legislation that greatly improved the lot of the country's agrarian population and extirpated the problem of "landlordism." This author went on to claim—and this a mere four years before the Dublin Easter Rising of 1916!—that physical-force nationalism had gone onto life support, such that "the whole Irish agitation is thoroughly peaceful and constitutional." Sydney Brooks, *Aspects of the Irish Question* (Boston: John W. Luce, 1912), pp. 41, 210–11.

12. On this last point, see Patrick Maume, "Parnell and the I.R.B. Oath," *Irish Historical Studies* 29 (May 1995): 363–70. For the sometimes indistinct line separating those who preferred a separation brought about through violence from advocates of a peaceful transition to home rule, see T. W. Moody, *Davitt and the Irish Revolution, 1846–82* (Oxford: Clarendon Press, 1981).

13. Insightful variations on the theme of Irish nationalism(s) are provided in Thomas N. Brown, *Irish-American Nationalism, 1870–1890* (Philadelphia: J. B. Lippincott, 1966); Brian Jenkins, *Irish Nationalism and the British State: From Repeal to Revolutionary Nationalism* (Montreal and Kingston: McGill-Queen's University Press, 2006); and D. George Boyce, *Nationalism in Ireland,* 2nd ed. (London: Routledge, 1991).

14. Quoted in Sean O'Faolain, *The Irish: A Character Study* (Old Greenwich, Conn.: Devin-Adair, 1979; orig. pub. 1949), pp. 109–10. Also see Robert J. Thompson and Joseph R. Rudolph Jr., "Irish-Americans in the American Foreign-Policy-Making Pro-

cess," in *Ethnic Groups and U.S. Foreign Policy*, ed. Mohammed E. Ahrari (Westport, Conn.: Greenwood, 1987), pp. 135–53.

15. Harry Cranbrook Allen, *Great Britain and the United States: A History of Anglo-American Relations, 1783–1952* (London: Oldhams, 1954), pp. 101–2.

16. Also known in North America as "Scots-Irish" and, in the north of Ireland, as "Ulster Scots." See Patrick Griffin, *The People with No Name: Ireland's Ulster Scots, America's Scots Irish, and the Creation of a British Atlantic World, 1689–1764* (Princeton, N.J.: Princeton University Press, 2001); and Leroy V. Eid, "Irish, Scotch and Scotch-Irish: A Reconsideration," *American Presbyterians* 64 (Winter 1986): 211–25. But for the reminder that, in the South at least, the distinction between the unalloyed and modified Irish identities was not always evident, see David T. Gleeson, "Smaller Differences: 'Scotch Irish' and 'Real Irish' in the Nineteenth-century American South," *New Hibernia Review* 10 (Samhradh/Summer 2006): 68–91.

17. George Potter, *To the Golden Door: The Story of the Irish in Ireland and America* (Boston: Little, Brown, 1960), p. 3 (emphasis added).

18. Kevin Kenny, *The American Irish: A History* (New York: Longman, 2000), pp. 7–8.

19. James G. Leyburn, *The Scotch-Irish: A Social History* (Chapel Hill: University of North Carolina Press, 1962), pp. 142–43.

20. For the Scotch Irish impact on U.S. foreign policy, see the discussion of "Jacksonianism" in Walter Russell Mead, *Special Providence: American Foreign Policy and How It Changed the World* (New York: Knopf, 2001); as well as David Hackett Fischer, *Albion's Seed: Four British Folkways in America* (New York: Oxford University Press, 1989); and James Webb, *Born Fighting: How the Scots-Irish Shaped America* (New York: Crown, 2004).

21. See David A. Wilson, *United Irishmen, United States: Immigrant Radicals in the Early Republic* (Dublin: Four Courts Press, 1998). In that era in Ireland, it was common to distinguish between "Protestants" (i.e., members of the Church of England, which in Ireland was, and is, the Church of Ireland) and "dissenters" (i.e., Presbyterians).

22. The first president of the Irish Republic, Douglas Hyde, would comment upon his countrymen's collective psyche that they possessed "a dull, ever-abiding animosity" in respect of England, so much so that they "grieve when she prospers and joy when she is hurt." Quoted in Jeremy Paxman, *The English: Portrait of a People* (London: Penguin, 2007), p. 49.

23. The Entente Cordiale of 1904 may not have been an alliance, but it certainly hinted at the future existence of such a collective-defense arrangement between Britain and France. For a critical assessment of Irish sentimentality in respect of France during the late nineteenth and early twentieth centuries, see Pierre Ranger, *La France vue d'Irlande: L'histoire du mythe français de Parnell à l'État Libre* (Rennes: Presses Universitaires de Rennes, 2011).

24. See Meade Minnigerode, *Jefferson, Friend of France, 1793: The Career of Edmond Charles Genet* (New York: G. P. Putnam's Sons, 1928); and Claude Fohlen, *Jefferson à Paris, 1784–1789* (Paris: Perrin, 1995).

25. Jay P. Dolan, *The Irish Americans: A History* (New York: Bloomsbury Press, 2008), pp. 31–32. Although the Federalists had little love for revolutionary France, the principal target after June 1798 of the four measures that came to be known as the Alien and Sedition Acts, they also worried about the Irish in America, whose anti-British activities it was feared made them cat's paws for French interests. See Alexander De Conde, *The Quasi-War: The Politics and Diplomacy of the Undeclared War with France, 1797–1801* (New York: Charles Scribner's Sons, 1966), pp. 94, 98–100; James Banner, "France and the Origins of American Political Culture," *Virginia Quarterly Review* 64 (Autumn 1988): 651–70; and Edward C. Carter, "A 'Wild Irishman' under Every Federalist's Bed: Naturalization in Philadelphia, 1789–1806," *Pennsylvania Magazine of History and Biography* 94 (July 1970): 331–46.

26. Patrick J. Blessing, "Irish Emigration to the United States, 1800–1920: An Overview," in *The Irish in America: Emigration, Assimilation and Impact*, ed. P. J. Drudy (Cambridge: Cambridge University Press, 1985), pp. 11–37, quote at p. 31.

27. See Ray Allen Billington, *The Protestant Crusade, 1800–1860: A Study of the Origins of American Nativism* (New York: Rinehart, 1952; orig. pub. 1938); and Tyler Anbinder, *Nativism and Slavery: The Northern Know Nothings and the Politics of the 1850s* (New York: Oxford University Press, 1992).

28. Noel Ignatiev, *How the Irish Became White* (New York: Routledge, 1995), pp. 75–76.

29. Some find the very thought of the English in the United States constituting a "diaspora" to be close to a contradiction in terms, for as Samuel Huntington and others have argued, they were a "settler" not an "immigrant" group of people, and only the latter can be considered diasporic. Samuel P. Huntington, *Who Are We? The Challenges to America's National Identity* (New York: Simon & Schuster, 2004). Many others have rejected this assertion, though, and they rest their case on there being no logical or empirical reason to exclude a priori the English from diasporic consideration, with some scholars even referring to them as the "hidden diaspora." For critiques, explicit and implicit, of the Huntingtonian perspective, see respectively Alexander De Conde, *Ethnicity, Race, and American Foreign Policy: A History* (Boston: Northeastern University Press, 1992); and Tanja Bueltmann and Donald M. MacRaild, "Globalizing St George: English Associations in the Anglo-World to the 1930s," *Journal of Global History* 7 (2012): 79–105.

30. Horace M. Kallen, *Culture and Democracy in the United States: Studies in the Group Psychology of the American Peoples* (New York: Arno Press, 1970; orig. pub. 1924), p. 99.

31. Enda Delaney, "The Irish Diaspora," *Irish Economic and Social History* 33 (2006): 35–45, quote at pp. 38–39.

32. Ever since the 1980 census, Americans have been able to answer subjective questions regarding ethnic identity, and to self-identify accordingly. That 1980 census revealed that the number of Irish Americans had more than doubled since the era of the First World War, due to processes related to natural as well as "social" increase; see Michael Hout and Joshua R. Goldstein, "How 4.5 Million Irish Immigrants Became 40 Million Irish Americans: Demographic and Subjective Aspects of the Ethnic Composition of White Americans," *American Sociological Review* 59 (February 1994): 64–82.

33. Brian Inglis, *The Story of Ireland* (London: Faber and Faber, 1956), p. 27.

34. Terence Brown, *Ireland: A Social and Cultural History, 1922–2002* (London: Harper Perennial, 2004), p. 10. Also see Patrick Fitzgerald and Brian Lambkin, *Migration in Irish History, 1607–2007* (London: Palgrave Macmillan, 2008), pp. 190–92.

35. Quoted in Brown, *Ireland*, pp. 124–25.

36. Blessing, "Irish Emigration to the United States," pp. 15–17.

37. Blessing, "Irish Emigration to the United States," pp. 15–17.

38. S. H. Cousens, "Emigration and Demographic Change in Ireland, 1851–1861," *Economic History Review*, new ser., 14, 2 (1961): 275–88.

39. Fitzgerald and Lambkin, *Migration in Irish History*, pp. 172–74.

40. An excellent introduction to this concept is Jennifer Mitzen, "Ontological Security in World Politics: State Identity and the Security Dilemma," *European Journal of International Relations* 12 (September 2006): 341–70.

41. Thomas N. Brown, "The Origins and Character of Irish-American Nationalism," *Review of Politics* 18 (July 1956): 327–58, quote at p. 331. Lomasney was actually killed in mid-December 1884.

42. Quoted in Padraic Colum, *Arthur Griffith* (Dublin: Browne and Nolan, 1959), p. 71.

43. Francis Shaw, "The Canon of Irish History—A Challenge," *Studies* 61 (Summer 1972): 113–53, quote at pp. 141–42. "Palesmen" refers to inhabitants living within the part of medieval Ireland most directly under English control, basically a small area embracing all or most of the counties of Dublin, Leith, Meath, and Kildare. Seán Duffy, ed., *Atlas of Irish History*, 2nd ed. (Dublin: Gill and Macmillan, 2000), pp. 46–47.

44. R. F. Foster, *The Irish Story: Telling Tales and Making It Up in Ireland* (Oxford: Oxford University Press, 2003), p. 97.

45. Kerby A. Miller, with Bruce Boling and David N. Doyle, "Emigrants and Exiles: Irish Cultures and Irish Emigration to North America, 1790–1922," *Irish Historical Studies* 22 (September 1980): 97–125, quote at p. 100. Also see Paul Arthur, "Diasporan Intervention in International Affairs: Irish America as a Case Study," *Diaspora: A Journal of Transnational Studies* 1 (Fall 1991): 143–62, citing at p. 144.

46. See James S. Donnelly Jr., "The Construction of the Memory of the Famine in Ireland and the Irish Diaspora, 1850–1900," *Éire-Ireland* 31 (Spring–Summer 1996): 26–61.

47. One does not have to be an Anglophobe to subscribe to the "misrule" thesis, as evidenced by this trenchant assessment of an American commentator who is much more inclined toward Anglophilia than Anglophobia: "In peace and war England's policies in Ireland were a shame and a horror for most of modern times." Walter Russell Mead, *God and Gold: Britain, America, and the Making of the Modern World* (New York: Alfred A. Knopf, 2008), p. 60.

48. See Vincent Todd Harlow, *The Founding of the Second British Empire, 1763–1793*, 2 vols. (London: Longmans, Green, 1952).

49. Sydney Brooks, *The New Ireland*, 2nd ed. (Dublin: Maunsel, 1907), pp. 92, 107. This English reformer's tone would change over the subsequent five years, as evidenced by his more upbeat assessment in his 1912 book on the Irish Question, cited in n. 11, above.

50. Donald Harman Akenson, *The United States and Ireland* (Cambridge, Mass.: Harvard University Press, 1973), p. 5.

51. Stephen Lucius Gwynn, *Dublin Old and New* (Dublin: Browne and Nolan, [1937]), p. 105.

52. On the agrarian unrest, see Moody, *Davitt and the Irish Revolution*; and Anne Kane, "Narratives of Nationalism: Constructing Irish National Identity during the Land War, 1879–82," *National Identities* 2 (November 2000): 245–64; for the urban bombings (to be discussed below), see Kenneth R. M. Short, *The Dynamite War: Irish American Bombers in Victorian Britain* (Atlantic Highlands, N.J.: Humanities Press, 1979).

53. Quoted in Christy Campbell, *Fenian Fire: The British Government Plot to Assassinate Queen Victoria* (London: HarperCollins, 2002), p. 7.

54. Philip H. Bagenal, *The American Irish and Their Influence on Irish Politics* (London: Kegan Paul, Trench, 1882), pp. 151, 244–45.

55. J. Bowyer Bell, "The Transcendental Irish Republic: The Dream of Diaspora," in *Governments-in-Exile in Contemporary World Politics*, ed. Yossi Shain (New York: Routledge, 1991), pp. 202–18.

56. On this point of grammar, see H. W. Fowler, *A Dictionary of Modern English Usage*, 2nd ed., rev. Ernest Gowers (Oxford: Clarendon Press, 1968), pp. 356–57. Meiosis can be considered as a form of expressive understatement.

57. Mabel Gregory Walker, *The Fenian Movement* (Colorado Springs: Ralph Myles, 1969), pp. 100–1.

58. See Rosalyn Trigger, "The Geopolitics of the Irish-Catholic Parish in Nineteenth-Century Montreal," *Journal of Historical Geography* 27 (January 2001): 553–72; Robert J. Grace, "Irish Immigration and Settlement in a Catholic City: Quebec, 1842–61," *Canadian Historical Review* 84 (June 2003): 217–51; and Cecil J. Houston and William J. Smyth, *Irish Emigration and Canadian Settlement: Patterns, Links and Letters* (Toronto: University of Toronto Press, 1990).

59. David A. Wilson, "Introduction," in *Irish Nationalism in Canada*, ed. Wilson (Montreal and Kingston: McGill-Queen's University Press, 2009), pp. 3–21, quote at p. 8. Also see Peter M. Toner, "The Home Rule League in Canada: Fortune, Fenians, and Failure," *Canadian Journal of Irish Studies* 15 (July 1989): 7–19.

60. D. C. Lyne and Peter M. Toner, "Fenianism in Canada, 1874–84," *Studia Hibernica*, no. 12 (1972), pp. 27–76, citing from pp. 27–28. McGee's assassin presumptive, Patrick James Whelan, was hanged on 11 February 1869 in what turned out to be Canada's last political execution. See David A. Wilson, "The Fenians in Montreal,

1862–68: Invasion, Intrigue, and Assassination," *Éire-Ireland* 38 (Fall–Winter 2003): 109–33; and Wilson, "Was Patrick James Whelan a Fenian and Did He Assassinate Thomas D'Arcy McGee?" in *Irish Nationalism in Canada*, pp. 52–82. Also see this same author's two-volume biography of McGee, *Thomas D'Arcy McGee* (Montreal and Kingston: McGill-Queen's University Press, 2008–11).

61. For an insightful assessment of Western perspectives on today's Pakistan, see T.V. Paul, *The Warrior State: Pakistan in the Contemporary World* (Oxford: Oxford University Press, 2014).

62. Dave Hannigan, *De Valera in America: The Rebel President's 1919 Campaign* (Dublin: O'Brien Press, 2008), p. 212.

63. Hereward Senior, "Quebec and the Fenians," *Canadian Historical Review* 48 (March 1967): 26–44, quote at p. 26.

64. Frank H. Severance, "The Fenian Raid of '66," *Publications of the Buffalo Historical Society* 25 (1921): 263–85, quote at pp. 266–67.

65. See the comprehensive, though not unbiased, account of Charles Callan Tansill, *America and the Fight for Irish Freedom, 1866–1922: An Old Story Based upon New Data* (New York: Devin-Adair, 1957).

66. Joe Ambrose, *The Fenian Anthology* (Cork: Mercier, 2008), p. 10.

67. Others making this connection include Patrick McCartan, "William Butler Yeats — The Fenian," *Ireland-American Review* 1, 3 (1938): 412–20; Tom Garvin, *Nationalist Revolutionaries in Ireland, 1858–1928* (Dublin: Gill and Macmillan, 1987); and M. J. Kelly, *The Fenian Ideal and Irish Nationalism, 1882–1916* (Woodbridge, UK: Boydell Press, 2006).

68. John Belchem, "Nationalism, Republicanism and Exile: Irish Emigrants and the Revolutions of 1848," *Past & Present*, no. 146 (February 1995), pp. 103–35.

69. John Newsinger, "Old Chartists, Fenians, and New Socialists," *Éire-Ireland* 17 (Summer 1982): 19–45. On Stephens's political career, see Desmond Ryan, *The Fenian Chief: A Biography of James Stephens* (Dublin: Gill and Son, 1967); and Marta Ramón-García, *A Provisional Dictator: James Stephens and the Fenian Movement* (Dublin: University College Dublin Press, 2007).

70. For the rise, decline, partial re-rise, and ultimate demise of the IRB, see Owen McGee, *The IRB: The Irish Republican Brotherhood from the Land League to Sinn Féin* (Dublin: Four Courts Press, 2005); John O'Beirne-Ranelagh, "The IRB from the Treaty to 1924," *Irish Historical Studies* 20 (March 1976): 26–39; and J. M. Curran, "The Decline and Fall of the IRB," *Éire-Ireland* 10 (Spring 1975): 14–23.

71. William D'Arcy, *The Fenian Movement in the United States: 1858–1886* (New York: Russell and Russell, 1971; orig. pub. 1947), pp. 385–86.

72. On the ideals that animated Young Ireland's republican agenda, see Patrick Maume, "Young Ireland, Arthur Griffith and Republican Ideology: The Question of Continuity," *Éire-Ireland* 34 (Summer 1999): 155–74.

73. Or, Geoffrey Keating's *History of Ireland*.

74. Seán Jennett, *Connacht: The Counties Galway, Mayo, Sligo, Leitrim and Roscommon in Ireland* (London: Faber and Faber, 1970), pp. 24–25.

75. Frank H. Underhill, "Canada and the North Atlantic Triangle," in *In Search of Canadian Liberalism*, comp. Underhill (Toronto: Macmillan of Canada, 1961), quote at pp. 256–57. On the delicate state of Anglo-American relations during and shortly after the Civil War, see Kenneth Bourne, "British Preparations for War with the North, 1861–1862," *English Historical Review* 76 (October 1961): 600–32; and especially Amanda Foreman, *A World on Fire: Britain's Crucial Role in the American Civil War* (New York: Random House, 2010).

76. R. V. Comerford, *The Fenians in Context: Irish Politics and Society, 1848–82* (Dublin: Wolfhound Press, 1985), pp. 119–20.

77. Cal McCarthy, *Green, Blue and Grey: The Irish in the American Civil War* (Cork: Collins Press, 2009); Susannah Ural Bruce, *The Harp and the Eagle: Irish-American Volunteers and the Union Army, 1861–1865* (New York: New York University Press, 2006); David T. Gleeson, *The Green and Gray: The Irish in the Confederate States of America*

(Chapel Hill: University of North Carolina Press, 2013); and Sean Michael O'Brien, *Irish-Americans in the Confederate Army* (Jefferson, N.C.: McFarland, 2007).

78. Michael V. Hazel, "First Link: Parnell's American Tour, 1880," *Éire-Ireland* 15 (Spring 1980): 6–24, quote at p. 23.

79. For the savage Fredericksburg fighting in December 1862, in which an all-Irish Union brigade led by General Thomas Francis Meagher saw its effectives reduced in one day from 1,200 to fewer than 300 men, in a failed attempt to take Marye's Heights, see Robert G. Ahearn, *Thomas Francis Meagher: An Irish Revolutionary in America* (Boulder: University of Colorado Press, 1949), pp. 118–21. Also see Daniel M. Callaghan, *Thomas Francis Meagher and the Irish Brigade in the Civil War* (Jefferson, N.C.: McFarland, 2006).

80. Jack Morgan, *Through American and Irish Wars: The Life and Times of General Thomas W. Sweeny, 1820–1892* (Dublin: Irish Academic Press, 2005), pp. 108–9. Also see Muriel Phillips Joslyn, ed., *A Meteor Shining Brightly: Essays on Major General Patrick R. Cleburne* (Macon, Ga.: Mercer University Press, 2000).

81. For an account stressing the perceived gravity of the threat, see Arthur Mitchell, "The Fenian Movement in America," *Éire-Ireland* 2 (Winter 1967): 6–10.

82. For this usage, see Matthew Kelly, "'Parnell's Old Brigade': The Redmondite-Fenian Nexus in the 1890s," *Irish Historical Studies* 33 (November 2002): 209–32, quote at p. 209.

83. See Fred Anderson and Andrew Cayton, *The Dominion of War: Empire and Liberty in North America, 1500–2000* (New York: Viking, 2005).

84. Marta Ramón-García, "Square-Toed Boots and Felt Hats: Irish Revolutionaries and the Invasion of Canada (1848–1871)," *Estudios irlandeses* 5 (2010): 81–91.

85. Quoted in Brian A. Jenkins, *Fenians and Anglo-American Relations during Reconstruction* (Ithaca, N.Y.: Cornell University Press, 1969), quote at pp. 14–15.

86. See Harold A. Davis, "The Fenian Raid on New Brunswick," *Canadian Historical Review* 36 (December 1955): 316–34; Maxwell Vesey, "When New Brunswick Suffered Invasion," *Dalhousie Review* 19 (1939–40): 197–204; and Robert L. Dallison, *Turning Back the Fenians: New Brunswick's Last Colonial Campaign* (Fredericton, NB: Goose Lane Editions, 2006).

87. One scholar's assessment of the unintended consequences, for Canada, seems particularly apt: "perhaps the most important result of Fenianism was the impetus it gave to the development of Canadian nationalism. . . . In British North America, nationalism was at its highwater mark in the mid-1860s, and much of this was the result of the Fenian menace. . . . Canadians, on the whole, profited considerably from the Fenian experience." Wilfried Neidhardt, *Fenianism in North America* (University Park: Pennsylvania State University Press, 1975), p. 135.

88. See Peter Vronsky, *Ridgeway: The American Fenian Invasion and the 1866 Battle That Made Canada* (Toronto: Allen Lane, 2011).

89. Hereward Senior, *The Last Invasion of Canada: The Fenian Raids, 1866–1870* (Toronto: Dundurn Press, 1991).

90. See in particular, Hereward Senior, *The Fenians and Canada* (Toronto: Macmillan, 1978); Charles P. Stacey, "The Fenian Troubles and Canadian Military Development, 1865–1871," *Canadian Defence Quarterly* 13 (April 1936): 270–79; and Stacey, "Fenianism and the Rise of National Feeling in Canada at the Time of Confederation," *Canadian Historical Review* 12 (September 1931): 238–61.

91. Joseph A. King, "The Fenian Invasion of Canada and John McMahon: Priest, Saint or Charlatan?" *Éire-Ireland* 23 (Winter 1988): 32–52, citing from pp. 43–45.

92. In total, twenty-four death sentences were meted out, all but three of them in Ontario courtrooms. None of the commuted prisoners even came close to serving his full term of twenty years' hard labor, and only one of them (Thomas Maxwell) died in prison, of illness. The rest were freed over a period running from April 1867 through July 1872. See Wilfried S. Neidhardt, "The Fenian Trials in the Province of Canada, 1866–7: A Case Study of Law and Politics in Action," *Ontario History* 66 (1974): 23–36.

93. Shin-Ichi Takagami, "The Fenian Rising in Dublin, March 1867," *Irish Historical Studies* 29 (May 1995): 340–62.

94. Leon Ó Broin, *Fenian Fever: An Anglo-American Dilemma* (New York: New York University Press, 1971); Brian A. Jenkins, *The Fenian Problem: Insurgency and Terrorism in a Liberal State, 1858–1874* (Montreal and Kingston: McGill-Queen's University Press, 2008); and John Newsinger, *Fenianism in Mid-Victorian Britain* (London: Pluto Press, 1994).

95. Hugh Bertie Campbell Pollard, *Secret Societies of Ireland: Their Rise and Progress* (London: Philip Allan, 1922), pp. ix–xi.

96. See Maureen Hartigan, Alan O'Day, and Roland Quinault, "Irish Terrorism in Britain: A Comparison between the Activities of the Fenians in the 1860s and Those of Republican Groups Since 1972," in *Ireland's Terrorist Dilemma*, ed. Yonah Alexander and Alan O'Day (Dordrecht: Martinus Nijhoff, 1986), pp. 49–60.

97. Lindsay Clutterbuck, "Countering Irish Republican Terrorism in Britain: Its Origin as a Police Function," *Terrorism and Political Violence* 18, 1 (2006): 95–118, quote at p. 117.

98. Jonathan Gantt, *Irish Terrorism in the Atlantic Community, 1865–1922* (New York: Palgrave Macmillan, 2010), p. 5. For a somewhat similar assessment of Irish American diasporic activism as contributive to better Anglo-American relations, see David Sim, *A Union Forever: The Irish Question and U.S. Foreign Relations in the Victorian Age* (Ithaca, N.Y.: Cornell University Press, 2013).

99. On that insouciance, see Wilfried S. Neidhardt, "The American Government and the Fenian Brotherhood: A Study in Mutual Political Opportunism," *Ontario History* 64 (1972): 27–44.

100. Niall Whelehan, *The Dynamiters: Irish Nationalism and Political Violence in the Wider World, 1867–1900* (Cambridge: Cambridge University Press, 2012), pp. 157–60.

101. J. Paul Rodechko, "An Irish-American Journalist and Catholicism: Patrick Ford of the *Irish World*," *Church History* 39 (December 1970): 524–40; James Reidy, "John Devoy," *Journal of the American Irish Historical Society* 27 (1928): 413–25; Terence Dooley, *The Greatest of the Fenians: John Devoy and Ireland* (Dublin: Wolfhound Press, 2003).

102. See Tom Goyens, *Beer and Revolution: The German Anarchist Movement in New York City, 1880–1914* (Urbana: University of Illinois Press, 2007).

103. See George Herbert Adams, *Why Americans Dislike England* (Philadelphia: Henry Altemus, 1896).

104. See Adrian Cook, *The Alabama Claims: American Politics and Anglo-American Relations, 1865–1872* (Ithaca, N.Y.: Cornell University Press, 1975); and Frank J. Merli, *The Alabama, British Neutrality and the American Civil War* (Bloomington: Indiana University Press, 2004).

105. For the claim that Irish American diasporic activism has been greatly overstated as a source of tension between the United States and the UK during the post-Civil War decades, see Donald M. MacRaild's review of the book by David Sim (n. 98, above), in the *Times Higher Education* supplement of 2 January 2014, available at http://www.timeshighereducation.co.uk/books/a-union-forever-the-irish-question-andus-foreign-relations-in-the-victorian-age-by-david-sim/2010112.article.

106. Whelehan, *Dynamiters*, pp. 164–65.

107. Which is what happened, Taft finishing third behind Woodrow Wilson and Roosevelt, but ahead of the Socialist candidate, Eugene V. Debs; see James Chace, *1912: Wilson, Roosevelt, Taft & Debs—the Election That Changed the Country* (New York: Simon & Schuster, 2004).

108. This previous treaty failed of ratification due to opposition not only from Irish America, but more importantly from "silverite" agrarian forces in western states; see Nelson Manfred Blake, "The Olney-Pauncefote Treaty of 1897," *American Historical Review* 50 (January 1945): 228–43. On the Taft arbitration treaties, see Richard Olney, Jackson H. Ralston, and W. C. Dennis, "Address of Honorable Richard Olney, Formerly Secretary of State, on General Arbitration Treaties," *Proceedings of the American*

Society of International Law at Its Annual Meeting (1907–1917), vol. 6 (25–27 April 1912): 102–14.

109. For the Dillon saga, see Colm J. Brannigan, "The Luke Dillon Case and the Welland Canal Explosion of 1900: Non-Events in the History of the Niagara Frontier Region," *Niagara Frontier* 24 (Summer 1977): 36–44.

110. Dennis M. Sullivan, "Éamon de Valera and the Forces of Opposition in America, 1919–1920," *Éire-Ireland* 19 (Summer 1984): 98–115.

111. Kenny, *American Irish,* p. 190.

112. Quoted in Hannigan, *De Valera in America,* pp. 83–84.

113. James P. Walsh, ed., *The Irish: America's Political Class* (New York: Arno Press, 1976).

114. Bagenal, *American Irish and Their Influence on Irish Politics,* pp. 61–62.

115. See John Milton Cooper, *The Warrior and the Priest: Woodrow Wilson and Theodore Roosevelt* (Cambridge, Mass.: Belknap Press, 1983); and J. Lee Thompson, *Never Call Retreat: Theodore Roosevelt and the Great War* (New York: Palgrave Macmillan, 2013).

116. Thomas E. Hachey, "The British Foreign Office and New Perspectives on the Irish Issue in Anglo-American Relations, 1919–1921," *Éire-Ireland* 7 (Summer 1972): 2–13.

117. For a theoretical foray into this means of construing the sometimes ineffable quality of "influence," see Bas Arts and Piet Verschuren, "Assessing Political Influence in Complex Decision-making: An Instrument Based on Triangulation," *International Political Science Review* 20, 4 (1999): 411–24.

118. For the tight correspondence between Irish American and German American interests and projects, see Edward Cuddy, "Irish-American Propagandists and American Neutrality, 1914–1917," *Mid-America* 49, 4 (1967): 252–75.

119. Quoted in Alan J. Ward, "America and the Irish Problem, 1899–1921," *Irish Historical Studies* 16 (March 1968): 64–90, quote at pp. 73–74.

120. Edward F. Dunne, *What Dunne Saw in Ireland: The Truth about British Militarism in All Its Brutality* (New York: Friends of Irish Freedom, 1919), p. 3.

121. See, for the growing "Americanism" of Irish American mass opinion, Thomas J. Rowland, "Irish-American Catholics and the Quest for Respectability in the Coming of the Great War, 1900–1917," *Journal of American Ethnic History* 15 (Winter 1996): 3–31.

122. On the peace conference and the Irish situation, see James P. Walsh, "Woodrow Wilson Historians vs. the Irish," *Éire-Ireland* 2 (Summer 1967): 55–66.

123. See William E. Leary, "Woodrow Wilson, Irish Americans, and the Election of 1916," *Journal of American History* 54 (June 1967): 57–72; Ronan Brindley, "Woodrow Wilson, Self Determination and Ireland, 1918–1919: A View from the Irish News-papers," *Éire-Ireland* 23 (Winter 1988): 62–80; and John B. Duff, "The Versailles Treaty and the Irish-Americans," *Journal of American History* 55 (December 1968): 582–98. But for a rejoinder that, if anything, Wilson was actually sympathetic to Ireland, compare Hans Vought, "Division and Reunion: Woodrow Wilson, Immigration, and the Myth of American Unity," *Journal of American Ethnic History* 13 (Spring 1994): 24–50.

124. For the impact of Irish self-determination on the collapse of diasporic activism in the United States, see Michael Doorley, *Irish-American Diaspora Nationalism: The Friends of Irish Freedom, 1916–1935* (Dublin: Four Courts Press, 2005), pp. 153–54; and Laurence Halley, *Ancient Affections: Ethnic Groups and Foreign Policy* (New York: Praeger, 1985), p. 162.

125. John P. Buckley, *The New York Irish: Their View of American Foreign Policy, 1914–1921* (New York: Arno Press, 1976), pp. 389–90.

126. See Adrian Guelke, "The United States, Irish Americans and the Northern Ireland Peace Process," *International Affairs* 72 (July 1996): 521–36; and Andrew J. Wilson, *Irish America and the Ulster Conflict, 1868–1995* (Washington, D.C.: Catholic University Press, 1995).

FIVE

"Do the German Americans Dictate Our Foreign Policy?"

The Principle of the Opposite Effect, Applied

DEUTSCH-AMERIKA MOBIL!

In the second year of the Great War, a book was published in Berlin that highlighted some robust assertions about ethnicity's impact upon security, broadly similar in concept to asseverations made over the past two decades, during the American debate redux over ethnic diasporas, which as we remember from chapter three has featured a lively dispute as to whether "ethnic lobbies" were capturing the foreign policy process in the United States, thereby distorting the articulation and promotion of the national interest. In addition, this wartime book contributed one highly idiosyncratic assessment, to be discussed below, of the impact that diasporic activism, in this case that of German America, might have upon the regional security setting in North America. The book was written by Karl Jünger, and it bore the title *Deutsch-Amerika mobil!*[1]

The ending of the Cold War, as we know, resulted in a veritable flood of scholarly and other publications addressing the potential significance of diasporas for American foreign policy, and because of this, for regional and global security writ large. Although many analysts, during the past two decades, have professed themselves to be shocked at discovering that ethnic (and other) pressure groups might be competing to gain a voice in discussions of America's foreign policy, their surprise is difficult to understand. The phenomenon of ethnic lobbying is nothing if not old hat in the American context, and even the laziest observer of America's foreign policy a century or so ago, when Jünger was writing, would have

been familiar with the claims and counterclaims swirling around the postulated, and frequently controversial, linkages between ethnicity, the national interest, and America's grand strategy. Nor were these discussions
solely a consequence of the long-standing Irish Question in transatlantic
affairs, as important as that interrogation so obviously was, because of its
impact upon America's relations with Great Britain and Canada.

As we discovered in the previous chapter, large as that Irish diaspora
was in the United States during the late nineteenth and early twentieth
centuries, there was another non-English ethnic group that was even
larger. That group was the German Americans. Although this ethnic
community did not bring with it to the new host country anything remotely approaching the kind of nationalist baggage that countless Irish
immigrants to America held so firmly in their grip as they tramped down
the gangplank, German America would not forever remain a geopolitically inert identity grouping. During the decade preceding the First
World War and for the three years between 1914 and 1917, German
America bid fare to dislodge Irish America as the most strategically consequential ethnic grouping in the United States, or anywhere else in the
world, and this because of a burgeoning transatlantic collective identity,
rooted in German nationalist sensibilities. There were a few reasons for
this diaspora's new significance in regional and global security affairs,
but one in particular stood out. It was the expectation that animated the
publication of Karl Jünger's monograph—the expectation that America's
large German population would prove to be sufficiently powerful to halt
in its tracks any prospect of Anglo-American strategic condominium,
with all that this might imply for the European balance of power at a time
when Germany was clearly on the ascendancy in the global pecking order, and the overburdened British were casting hopeful glances in America's direction.[2]

This assumption that German America could prevent Anglo-
American alliance coursed like an electric current through the pages of
Jünger's book, starting with its preface, penned by a retired Kaiserliche
Marine admiral and longtime enthusiast of German colonialism, Eduard
von Knorr. England, prophesied von Knorr, was destined to go down to
defeat at the hands of Germany, because America was bound to remain
neutral in the World War, and it would do so as a result of the activities
of the German diaspora there, working so tirelessly and effectively to
promote the interests of the Fatherland. England had no one to blame for
this state of affairs but itself, for its aggression had stirred a slumbering
demographic giant, the worldwide German diaspora (*das Deutschtum der
ganzen Welt*), fusing it into a powerful asset for German foreign and security policy, nowhere more so than in the United States, where 90 percent of the diaspora could be found (a further 4 percent lived in Canada).[3]

Jünger not only echoed the admiral's enthusiasm, he outdid it, in conjuring up a particularly North American security dimension, one that would supply the icing on the cake of diasporic activism. Clearly, there were limits to what even German America might accomplish, and Jünger was not so deluded as to imagine the diaspora could shake the United States from its tradition of isolation from the European balance of power, however otherwise desirable the fostering of an alliance between America and *Germany* might be. Still, it ought reasonably to be expected of the German Americans that they could render a great favor to both their old and new homelands, by staging a geopolitical coup that Jünger imagined all Americans desired, a North American *Anschluß*, through the forcible annexation of Canada. How might they provide this service? The answer was to be found in the statistics revealing that there were apparently more than half a million German "reservists" residing in the United States when the war broke out. Since they might have difficulty crossing an Atlantic controlled by the Royal Navy, a better way to get them into combat would be to unleash them against Canada. Add to their ranks the considerable numbers of Germans (including Austrians) dwelling in Britain's northern dominion, and it could appear that North American "unification" would be a mere matter of marching.[4]

Apart from Jünger, there were some other, though not very many, enthusiasts for this extreme vision of Fenianism *auf deutsch*. It is known that during the war years German agents did indeed plan and encourage plotting against Canada, and though some small-scale sabotage campaigns would eventually see the light of day, the most grandiose of plots never came close to fruition.[5] Nevertheless, it was not at all illogical for many contemporary observers to imagine that German American diasporic activism might, in a rather different way, have an impact upon global and regional security by keeping the United States out of any European war. Those analysts in Germany who professed expertise in American affairs during the prewar years blithely shared a great many "untested" assumptions about that country, none more pregnant with geopolitical purport than, in Earl Beck's words, their "exaggerated impression of the role of German Americans in the life of the nation."[6] In fairness, so too did many German American participants in the era's policy debates share these assumptions.

After all, the idea of German American diasporic energies being applied to prevent any American participation in the European balance of power had been making the rounds for more than a decade prior to the eructations of the guns in August 1914. A few years previous to the war's outbreak, the editors of a pro-British publication, the *American Review of Reviews*, had published a provocative essay questioning whether the American foreign-policy dog was really being wagged by a German American tail, a contention that had been advanced earlier in the decade, in an article written by a German American activist from Pennsylvania,

William Weber, who had broached the thesis in the pages of the *Preussis-che Jahrbücher*. Due to the sheer size of the German vote in the United States, Weber was convinced no American government would dare run the risk of forging an alliance between the world's two leading "Anglo-Saxon" powers. From this, he concluded that the peace of Europe would be kept, because without American support, Britain would be unwilling to challenge Germany military—and Germany, as Weber and those who read him knew, only wanted peace.[7]

In official circles in Berlin the view would from time to time get expressed that Germany indeed did possess an inestimable asset in the large German American diaspora. Kaiser Wilhelm was prone to assess the German American community in terms of the service it might render the Fatherland, and he was hardly alone. For instance, at Potsdam in June 1908 he was reported to have said that "[e]ven now I rule supreme in the United States, where almost one-half of the population is either of German birth or of German descent, and where three million voters do my bidding at the Presidential elections. No American administration could remain in power against the will of the German voters."[8] It is possible, perhaps even likely, that the Kaiser did not actually choose such a provocative way to make his point at Potsdam, though clumsiness in speech was never something he could easily avoid, if given half a chance, a foible that some years earlier had prompted his mother to remark, "I wish I could put a padlock on his mouth for all occasions where speeches are made in public!"[9] Whatever his means of expression, there was no question where his heart lay, as it was hardly unknown for him to make public, and wistful, reference to the German American diaspora when discussing foreign-policy topics, as he did on so many occasions.[10] Comments along these lines regularly found their way into the world's English-language press, ensuring that the Kaiser's views on demography and security became familiar enough to Americans.

One such American was Theodore Roosevelt. While still serving as governor of New York, he had been known occasionally to express his own indignation about a growing sense of expectancy in Berlin that the German Americans could somehow be counted upon to serve as a check on any Anglo-American strategic condominium. Writing to an English correspondent in January 1900, Roosevelt confessed to being "amused when I see the Kaiser quoted as saying that the German-Americans would not allow us to go to war with Germany. Those that are born here would practically without exception back up America in the most enthusiastic way were we to get into a struggle with Germany."[11] A decade and a half later, Roosevelt's tune would change considerably, as he threw himself behind an immediate American entry into the war following the sinking of the *Lusitania*, launching a full-throated campaign on behalf of preparedness and Americanization, the latter in explicit opposition to

German Americans and other so-called hyphenates (but principally the German Americans).[12]

The Kaiser, as did other German political figures during the run-up to the First World War, regarded the German American diaspora as a geo-strategic ace in the hole, and why should he, and they, not have? During the period from the American Civil War through practically the entirety of the Bismarckian era, German leaders had routinely been expecting good things to result from the fact that, as Bismarck once put it, "Germany had in the United States her second largest state after Prussia."[13] Moreover, as we learned in chapter three, many scholars are convinced that influence comes to those ethnic lobbies that can boast of three qualities: size, social standing, and skillful organization. It seemed that by the dawn of the twentieth century the German Americans, unlike the Irish Americans, could lay claim to all three components of this ethno-politico trifecta, whereas the Irish could, at best, fulfill only the first two conditions, given the well-advertised penchant for factionalism within the Irish American activist diaspora throughout the entire period between 1861 and 1921. Was it so wrong, then, for some to detect in German America precisely those qualities required to obtain influence over American foreign policy, especially if it was going to work closely with Irish America, whose fractious tendencies could be moderated by sound German management skills?

And even though the idea of mobilizing German reservists to seize Canada for delivery to an expansionist, and presumably grateful, United States verged on lunacy, there was still an important way that German-diasporic activism could be said to possess very negative implications for Canadian security interests. We have already glimpsed this negative connotation of diasporic activism when, at the start of the previous chapter, we canvassed some of the counterfactual arguments that had been made in the early postwar period, regarding the costs absorbed by British and Canadian society as a result of the American delay in entering the fighting. Whatever was said by personages such as Admiral Sims about Irish America's responsibility for imposing those costs had, a fortiori, also to be said of German America. The assumption is that had those two large diasporas not been such a presence in prewar American demography, many British and Canadian combat deaths would have been avoided. Not only this, but as we also saw in chapter four, some champions of Anglo-American condominium were prepared to charge the two diasporas, whether working singly or in tandem, with having created the permissive conditions for the war to have broken out in the first place, thus laying at their doorstep all of the death and destruction of the 1914–1918 period.

This is to say that just because German Americans might never have succumbed to the charms of a Fenianismus of their own, notwithstanding those few incidents during the First World War in which Germans (and

German Americans) sought to use U.S. soil to conduct sabotage against Canadian—and sometimes *American!*—targets during the period of American neutrality,[14] it does not absolve them from the charge that they too proved to be a divisive element in continental security affairs, one that could even be remarked to have done more damage to Canadian interests than Irish America had. This is a charge, however, that is easy to make but difficult to substantiate, not least because it overlooks the possibility, to which I return in this chapter's concluding section, of German-diasporic activism backfiring, and making American participation in the war more rather than less likely. For the moment, though, let us give counterfactuals a wide berth, and concentrate instead upon some empirical considerations pertaining to German America, starting in the section immediately below with its size.

ARE AMERICANS MORE GERMAN THAN ENGLISH?

In the same year that saw the publication of Karl Jünger's melodramatic vaunting of German America's ability to keep the United States out of the war, a pro-British publication in the United States broached a related hypothesis, in effect wondering whether the country's population might not just be too "German" for Britain's, or possibly even America's, good. The hypothesis was presented through this query, expressed by author James Middleton: "Are Americans more German than English?"[15] It was a good question, and this was hardly the first time anyone had ventured to ask it. Just a few years earlier, another American, Homer Lea, had thrown a bucket of exceedingly cold water on what was considered by many in the English-speaking transatlantic world to be a very comforting policy conceit, namely the anticipation that the "race patriotism" subsumed under the category of "Anglo-Saxonism" was on the verge of developing into a major geostrategic asset for Great Britain and other English-speaking countries, not excluding the United States itself, as the latter began to take its place alongside the world's acknowledged great powers.

For those who were counting on this new collective identity to yield exactly that Anglo-American strategic condominium whose advent many in Britain, and a few even in North America, were beginning to champion at the turn of the century,[16] Lea's analysis could hardly have been more unwelcome. It had everything to do with people in motion, for as Lea saw matters the inexorable demographic trends of the previous century pointed to one conclusion and one conclusion only: Americans would soon be dropping out of the category of Anglo-Saxondom altogether, and this because of the immigration patterns from the early nineteenth century on, which had featured such a paltry British share (only a quarter) of the new arrivals to the country. From those migratory trends it was all too easy to predict that the "day of the Saxon," pace the Perry Robinsonses and William Sowden Simses of the Atlantic world, was drawing to an end, it being only a matter of time before America's demographic tipping point would be reached, and the country's English-descended citizens found themselves in the minority. Not only, then, should Britain refrain from betting too heavily on America's rallying to its side in any future clash of civilizations, but it was conceivable that America and Britain might themselves come to blows, in no small part as a result of their growing ethnic divergencies.[17]

There was no shortage of evidence to buttress this kind of somber analysis, should one wish to search for it. By way of illustration, let us work backward, and begin by citing some very recent statistics, prior to surveying the historical development of German America. As was noted in the previous chapter, ever since 1980, Americans have been able, in their decennial census reporting, to indicate the ethnicity (or ethnicities) with which they identify. The most recent census, in 2010, shows what the three previous ones also revealed, and even though this news continues to come as a surprise to many, the category "German" regularly ranks *first* among the ethnic self-ascriptions of Americans. In 2010, for instance, some 49.8 million of the country's population of around 313 million claimed to be German; followed by Irish, at 35.8 million; Mexican, at 31.8 million; English, at 27.4 million; and Italian, at 17.6 million.[18]

One would think that with numerical representation such as this, it must necessarily follow that the answer to the query put by James Middleton could only have been in the affirmative, for if Americans are clearly so much more German than English today, they must equally have been so a century ago, with geopolitical implications impossible to overlook. Before settling into this conclusion, though, we would do well to consider two important aspects of American demography, then as well as now. The first is that sheer numbers alone do not a "diaspora" make, for as we realize from chapter three, many scholars insist that there must as well be a significant emotional attachment between the diaspora and the kin-state, construed in terms of a "homeland orientation." Usually, this latter is of a positive nature, though as we realize, it is not always so, given that occasionally diasporas have been characterized more by repulsion than by affection toward the government of the land whence they (or their forebears) originated.

The second, more important, thing to keep in mind about American demography, not just a century ago but also today, is that the numbers sometimes dissemble. Prior to 1980 and its amplification of subjective considerations related to the counting of heads, which is what occurs with questions that invite respondents basically to self-select their ethnicity, other techniques, analytico-deductive in nature, were employed by experts interested in gauging Americans' ethnic origins. Usually, these techniques depended upon genealogical data, supplemented by available government statistics related to immigration. Importantly, before the era of self-ascription began, it was still possible to claim that the largest single "ethnicity" in the United States was the one whose origins could be traced to either England itself or the *geographic* entity we know of as Great Britain—that is, the island that contains England, Scotland, and Wales, but excludes "John Bull's other island,"[19] Ireland.

Moreover, since 1980 the "English" aspect of Americans' ethnicity consistently has been underreported, for the good reason that so many opting to self-identify on the census form have chosen for themselves a different category, "American," even though it can logically be assumed that the vast proportion of this group in fact are descendants of people who consider their ancestors to have been "settlers" rather than "immigrants." Notwithstanding the conceptual difficulties with such a distinction, encountered earlier in this book, it is obvious that the overwhelming majority of the former, the so-called settlers, came to America from Britain, and mostly from England. According to Samuel Huntington, perhaps the most well-known propounder of the settler-immigrant dichotomy, had there been no further demographic influxes into the United States after 1790, the country's population two centuries later would have grown to 122 million instead of to the level it actually did reach in 1990, 249 million. And even with the vast immigration waves that broke so repeatedly on American shores from the country's origins until the restrictionist 1920s, descendants of the "settlers" still made up almost *half* (49 percent) of those 249 million.[20] What this means is that the "English" element in America today remains the largest single ethnic grouping in an objective (i.e., genealogical), even if not a subjective, sense. And more importantly, given this chapter's inquiry into the geopolitical implications of German America in the era of the First World War, it means that the answer to James Middleton's question must be a rather emphatic "no." Americans at that time were actually much more English than they were German, no matter what they might otherwise have believed before the fighting in Europe began.

Still, there can be no denying that German Americans were, in their own right, a substantial identity grouping in the America of a century ago. They were also becoming, as we are going to find out, a highly mobilized identity grouping, quite unlike today's German Americans, who possess little knowledge of, and even less sentimental attachment to, the so-called ancestral homeland. Germans had begun arriving in America during the late seventeenth century,[21] although there was one famous scholar who ventured to state that their presence actually predated the age of European colonization. This was none other than Hugo Grotius, who three years before his death in 1645 made so bold as to claim, in a tract entitled *On the Origin of the Native Races of America*, that America's indigenous population was largely descended from the Chinese—and the *Germans!*[22] This eminent jurist's bizarre assertion may have been inaccurate insofar as concerned the timing of the Germans' arrival on American soil, but there can be no gainsaying the numbers who did turn up, starting in the 1680s, such that by the onset of the American Revolution in 1775, Germans were already accounting for nearly 10 percent of the total population of England's seaboard colonies.

Their presence was particularly marked in Pennsylvania, where around the midpoint of the eighteenth century it had been known to trigger anxiety among some of the colony's English-descended denizens, including Benjamin Franklin, who had been fretting not just about the Germans' assimilability, but also about their reliability in helping assure the colony's defenses against its French and indigenous adversaries.[23] Germans were to be found not just in Pennsylvania, where they were incorrectly, often derisively, known as the "Pennsylvania Dutch."[24] They could be encountered almost everywhere in the new American republic, where with the exception of the English themselves, they would usually constitute the largest ethnic group of European origin, though at times the Irish would nudge them temporarily from this second-ranking position, as was noted in the previous chapter. By the latter half of the nineteenth century, massive migration from Germany had made of the United States the "home of the third largest number of German-speaking people in the world."[25]

Consider the following: between the ending of the Napoleonic Wars and the beginning of the First World War, some thirty-seven million Europeans would quit their homelands for a life elsewhere, and of this total, all but three million headed for the New World.[26] Amid this migratory flux, Germans were conspicuous, travelling in such quantities as to make the *"Völkerwanderung* of the Germanic tribes in the early Christian era sink . . . to insignificance."[27] Successive bursts of heavy immigration during the eight decades following 1830 brought roughly six million Germans to American shores.[28] The last federal census prior to the First World War, in 1910, revealed that out of a total American population of 92 million, some 2.5 million had been born in Germany, with another 5.8 million being "second-generation." Combining first and second generations yielded the category known as "stock," within which were included 8.3 million German Americans, a total about a third again as large as the stock of the next-ranking immigrant group, the Irish Americans, such that a century ago Germans comprised 26 percent of the country's total "foreign" (taken to mean *not* English-descended) stock.[29]

Yet even this understated the German presence in American demography, for to the first- and second-generation Germans had to be added those whose forebears had been in the country longer, and who continued to identify themselves as German and to live, as much as possible, a German life in America. And such a life was indeed possible for them to live, for as James Berquist has noted, even as recently as the early twentieth century every large U.S. city had a German district, wherein could be discerned a "pervasive 'foreignness' . . . reinforced by the sight of shops bearing signs in German, restaurants and public houses advertising their German fare, German bookshops and newspaper offices, German physicians, grocers and banking houses—all the elements of a rather complete and self-contained community." [30] Thus it could be, and frequently was, argued that there existed a German "element" in America (usually construed as meaning anyone with a significant admixture of German blood flowing through their veins) accounting for no less than 27 percent of the country's *total* population in the years just prior to the First World War! [31]

Though the German Americans may have been a bit more numerous than the Irish Americans, there was a major political and even *strategic* distinction to draw between the two ethnic groupings. Indeed, for most of the time prior to the early twentieth century, it was hard to conceive of German America as constituting much of a "diaspora" at all, if by that term we assume the existence of a homeland orientation laden with political signification. Unlike the Irish Americans, the German Americans lacked a single "kin-state," real or imagined, to inspire them to political activism, until, that is, the founding of Bismarck's Reich following the Franco-Prussian War of 1870–1871. [32] Moreover, while there no doubt was a great deal of sentimentality felt by many immigrants toward their "homeland" (*heimat*) left behind, it was not easy to transmute this emotionalism into the powerful ideology we know of as "nationalism." [33]

This is because the German Americans, until the 1870s, could not comprehend what for the Irish Americans could never be forgotten— namely, the identity of the foreign "enemy" that did so much to invigorate their own collective self-understanding. Like the vast majority of all immigrants (including the Irish) to the United States, Germans who chose to settle there did so for economic reasons, and even the group who had sought American exile for mainly political reasons, the so-called Forty-Eighters who arrived following the failure of the 1848 liberal revolution in Germany, [34] lacked any external foil for their own group identity. In the absence of any foreign state to stand as surrogate "oppositional other," German American diasporic identity tended to be a longer time in the making than had been its Irish American counterpart, which is another way of saying that the German Americans could not be expected to become nationalists until the Germans themselves had. A necessary consequence of this was that German America could not really be regarded as much of a factor in security arrangements appertaining to either North America or the broader North Atlantic triangle for almost the entirety of the nineteenth century.

And even when German America began feeling its nationalistic oats during the decade following the Civil War, the "objective correlative" for this newly established collective sentimentality was hardly the object of Irish America's loathing, Britain. Instead, it was upon Ireland's (and Irish America's) favorite European land, France, that German Americans cut their ontological teeth. Given their antipathy to France, a country that had long ago ceased to figure as a complicating element in North American regional security (at least insofar as concerns Canada-U.S. relations),[35] it is easy to see why German diasporic activism in 1870 and 1871 could not possibly possess anything remotely approaching the geopolitical significance of the Irish American diaspora. Nor was it the case that German American activism at the time of the Franco-Prussian War mattered very much to anyone save the German Americans themselves.

In later decades, a view would develop in certain French policy circles that Paris used to suffer from a severe comparative disadvantage vis-à-vis Berlin and some other European capitals when it came to the global balance of power. It did so because, alone among the major European countries, France lacked a sizeable diaspora in the United States, and as a result of this it was harder for it to avail itself of sympathy and support from Washington, especially at moments when it most needed these, such as when it was locked in dispute with a European rival that *did* happen to possess a large America-based diaspora. Just as in the previous chapter, when a pair of labels was affixed to "theses" purporting some tangible linkage between ethnicity and security, we might continue the practice here and refer to the supposition that France suffered as a result of the German America diaspora as the "Duroselle-Tardieu" thesis.[36]

The first element in this label stems from a comment made by the great French historian Jean-Baptiste Duroselle, to the effect that among the major European powers in the early twentieth century, the only one not to be represented in the United States by a large diaspora was France. This, he added, was bound to have a negative impact upon the quality of France's relationship with America and, by extension, France's broader interests in global security.[37] It was an assertion that a few others had made before him, most memorably André Tardieu, who in an important book on Franco-American relations written in the late 1920s, lamented that the dismal state into which the bilateral relationship had tumbled following the First World War was in no small measure due to the fact that too few French had ever chosen to settle down in the United States. From his coign of vantage in Paris, Tardieu expressed understanding of why young Americans should have been finding it so difficult to warm to "the only country which has given them no schoolmates. . . . France has contributed nothing to the melting-pot. France has not woven itself into American life by immigration."[38]

Whatever validity the Duroselle-Tardieu thesis may possess as a general comment upon France's relationship with the United States and its bearing upon French security interests, there really is little of consequence to have stemmed from the emotional reaction of German Americans to the news arriving from the battlefields of the Franco-Prussian War. It is not that Prussian military success left German Americans unmoved; quite the contrary, it gave a fillip, albeit only briefly, to their self-esteem in the American host country, and supplied a foretoken of what was in store for German diasporic activism, once it became reengaged on a foreign policy issue, in the early twentieth century.[39] It also provided the occasion for a colossal street party in New York City, where in the wake of the Prussians' triumphal entry into Paris and proclamation of the Reich, a monster rally took place in celebration of the war's ending, during which some 400,000 marched in what the New York *Tribune* labeled the "largest parade that New York had ever seen."[40]

But no one should ever make the mistake of assuming that German America played any role of importance in the war's outcome, or even that somehow this ethnic community occasioned an American "tilt" toward the Prussian side in the conflict, though such a tilt there was. The Prussians did not need any U.S. support, and the German Americans had little if anything to do with Washington's preferring Prussia to France. By the time the war broke out in 1870, there was precious little love lost in the United States for the country's ostensive "oldest ally," France. There were many reasons for this estrangement, but one was certainly of very current vintage: the perception (more correct than not) that the French had sympathized with the South in the recent Civil War, while the Prussians had stood out as a rare European state supportive of the North.[41] Thus when the European fighting began in 1870 the hour of "payback" had arrived, as far as the Republican administration in Washington was concerned—an administration, for good measure, presided by the last commander of the Union Army, Ulysses S. Grant.

Given not only the gratitude for Prussia's stance during America's recent internecine agony, but also the high regard in which it was held by America's politically informed elites (especially those living in the northeastern states)—Prussian administrative practices being considered the epitome of European public virtue and good governance—it only made sense for praise to be heaped upon the country that was waging war against France. It is hardly coincidental that so many of these "politically informed elites" were English-descended Americans themselves, for nowhere did the German image shine more brightly in American eyes than among the cultural and intellectual vanguard who propelled the "New England renaissance" from the 1830s onward. In the estimation of one prominent historian of German relations with the United States, Manfred Jonas, it was in the realm of culture and education far more than in commerce and security that Germany made its greatest impact upon nineteenth-century America. "The debt of Ralph Waldo Emerson to Immanuel Kant and Georg Wilhelm Friedrich Hegel, and of George Bancroft and John Lothrop Motley to German historical scholarship, formed part of a cultural bond that was to leave a permanent impress on American thought."[42]

Thus it was only natural for James Russell Lowell to write to fellow New England highbrow, Charles Eliot Norton, at the outbreak of hostilities in 1870, "as against the Gaul, I believe in the Teuton. And just now I wish to believe in him, for he represents civilization. Anything that knocks the nonsense out of Johnny Crapaud will be a blessing to the world." In the same vein, Louisa May Alcott could exult, "I side with the Prussians, for they sympathized with us in our war. Hooray for old Pruss!"—a sentiment that to American opinion shapers four decades hence would admittedly sound suspicious, even to some, treasonous.[43] But for much of the post-Civil War period, until such time later in the century as geopolitical rivalries over Samoa, China, and especially the Philippines would begin to sour the bilateral mood, Germany did represent to many Americans the most progressive, wholesome spot on the European map; in Lowell's word, it *was* civilization.[44] Nor could it be overlooked in Berlin that the American minister, George Bancroft, was so much a Gemanophile that fellow historian Leopold von Ranke was able affectionately, and not inaccurately, to refer to him as "one of us Germans."[45]

It is one thing, therefore, to note that the German diaspora in America certainly rallied behind Berlin during the war with France; it is quite another to argue that it also played a role in getting Washington to look with favor upon the Prussian side. U.S. pro-German policy in 1870 and 1871 was "overdetermined," and hardly needed pressure from German Americans to bring it about; in this case, the latter were pushing against an open door, rather than flexing their "lobbying" and electoral muscles, as some have suggested.[46] A far more interesting test of the Duroselle-Tardieu thesis, however, would not be long in the making. This test would come in the first two decades of the new century, with the efforts of German America, along with its newly discovered Irish American allies, to make real the hopes entertained by so many, both in Germany and in America, that ethnic lobbying *could* guarantee that in any future European war, American power would not be made available for British (and Canadian) strategic purposes.

STATUS AND THE DEBATE OVER AMERICA'S NATIONAL IDENTITY

Obviously, assessing the German Americans simply in quantitative terms, irrespective of the method of calculation—German-born? German stock? German element?—could easily yield the conclusion that they certainly possessed considerable demographic heft. But as we found in chapter three's analysis of the ingredients of diasporic "influence," size alone, no matter how important, is not enough. To numbers must be added a pair of further considerations. The first of these is the ethnic group's perceived social status within the host country, and the second is its ability to mobilize itself organizationally in such a manner as to capitalize upon both its numbers and its social recognition. In this section we explore the issue of status, which in turn leads us into a much broader debate involving nothing other than the American "national identity" itself—a debate that would have a tremendous impact on how the United States would come to gauge its "interests" in the European balance of power.

Social status is nothing if not an ambiguous category, so in a bid to delimit its connotations I will structure this section's analysis around two factors said to contribute to the way in which a community (ethnic or otherwise) comes to find itself adjudged by society. The first factor is economic in nature, and manifests itself in statistical assessments of, in our case, an ethnic group's general level of prosperity; by this measure, German Americans did well, consistently ranking among the most prosperous of the country's ethnic groups, even when compared with their English-descended countrymen. The second factor is much more subjective, and entails judgments of the ethnic group's "cultural capital," as these become woven into larger narratives regarding the group's contributions to the social and political development of the host country; in sum, this factor turns out to be a judgment of their "American-ness." Even here, German Americans would, by the late nineteenth century and through the first decade of the twentieth century, find themselves on the receiving end of a good measure of deference from American society in general. In retrospect, we can now say that the decade prior to the First World War represented the high point for the reputation of German Americans, and to a lesser degree of that of Germany itself. In the words of one scholar who has concentrated upon that reputation, "[w]hether seen in their newly unified nation or in this country, the Germans were generally regarded as methodical and energetic people. Their discipline, efficiency, and industry made them models of progress. In their devotion to music, education, science, and technology they aroused the admiration and emulation of Americans."[47]

Notwithstanding that this was an era in which "nativist" voices were once again beginning to attain resonance in American debates about immigration, German America was relatively exempt from charges of contaminating the American way of life—relatively exempt, because in more puritanical parts of the country, German Americans were sometimes seen as having too much respect for beer halls and not enough for "proper" observance of the Sabbath.[48] In the main, though, the revival of nativism did not present much of a problem for German America. This is because, unlike the earlier manifestation of nativism prior to the Civil War, this latter one featured debates highlighting "race" and geography much more than religion, with a clear distinction being postulated between the "new" (and bad) immigration stemming from unfamiliar parts of eastern and southern Europe and the "old" (and good) immigration hailing from the continent's northwestern vicinages, suitably expanded so as to comprise not only the British Isles, but also Scandinavia, the Netherlands, and *Germany*. So the "new nativism" associated with the new immigration actually worked, for a time, in the German American diaspora's favor.

Thus what Josiah Flynt had to say about them could pass muster as a reasonable approximation of a general American image of German Americans at the turn of the century: they were a hardworking folk who, despite some rough edges and occasional tendencies to perfectionism and emotionalism, remained utterly incorruptible and eminently assimilable into broader American society. In short, if any ethnic group needed to be found to substantiate the contributions immigrants were capable of making to their host country ("immigrant gifts," in the jargon of the day), it would be hard to top the German Americans. "Morally our Germans are a distinct improvement on those in Germany. Perhaps they are not more honest, but they are just as honest, and they are decidedly more virtuous," asserted Flynt. Likely their most impressive attribute, he continued, was the "ease and almost eagerness with which they throw off their nationality. Except possibly the Irish, there is no other race which so quickly becomes American and anti-European."[49]

We are going to see how off the mark this latter observation would shortly come to seem, during the highly emotional debates about American identity that exploded on the outbreak of the war in 1914. For the moment, though, nearly everything Josiah Flynt wrote in 1896 would have been regarded as sensible enough to American readers. Historian John Higham seconds this verdict, noting that prior to the war, "[p]ublic opinion had come to accept the Germans as one of the most assimilable and reputable of immigrant groups," a people whom one Boston sociologist had even, in 1903, deemed the best ethnic group in all of Beantown.[50] Many other observers would have been prepared to say roughly the same about them no matter in which U.S. city they happened to reside. Indeed, as late as the wartime years, some demographic researchers could continue to assert that German Americans remained the cream of the country's immigrant crop, ranking according to one 1916 study ahead even of immigrants from England.[51]

To be sure, things had not always gone so smoothly for the image of German immigrants in the United States, and they had not escaped completely unscathed from the first nativist outbreak during the 1850s, triggered as this had been by Europe's agricultural crisis of the late 1840s, with the subsequent increase in Catholic (including German Catholic) immigration into Protestant America.[52] Apart from that interlude, the only impediment on the German Americans' road to enhanced social standing, more like a pothole than anything else, was their being associated with a new, and troubling, political phenomenon reaching post-Civil War America from European shores: anarchism. Socialism, along with its anarchist spawn, had been closely linked in the America of the second half of the nineteenth century with *German* Americans, not that the majority of the latter were either socialists or anarchists, for they assuredly were not, but rather that both political trends owed much to German, and German American, inspiration. Anarchism on its own could reflect any number of political practices and beliefs, but it was its growing connection with terrorism starting in the 1870s that would prove to be somewhat problematical, if only for a while, for German America's status within the host society. As James Joll relates, "[f]rom 1870 on there was always to be a section of the anarchist movement ready to commit acts of terrorism, if not for their own sake at least to symbolize a total revolt against society . . . All over Europe and elsewhere, terrorism was to become an accepted political weapon."[53]

Just as not all anarchists were terrorists and vice versa, neither were all anarchists in the United States German Americans, and by the early decades of the twentieth century anarchism in the country would come increasingly to be associated with Italian Americans. But to the extent that, during the first flush of anarchism in America, an anarchist hearthstead could be found anywhere in the country, it was decidedly in a German American part of what was turning into a fairly important German American city. That city was New York, the German American heartland of which was known as Kleindeutschland, a district in Manhattan's lower east side embracing the city's 10th, 11th, 13th, and 17th wards (between 14th St. on the north, 3rd Ave. and the Bowery on the west, Division St. on the south, and the East River). In this part of town, one contemporary observer noted, "more people spoke the Saxon tongue than the Anglo-Saxon."[54] Metropolitan New York itself was home to more than half a million Germans, making it in a way "a third German capital, larger than any German city other than Berlin or Vienna."[55]

One German who lived and worked in Kleindeutschland was the anarchist theoretician and activist Johann Joseph Most. It would be he who more than any other single individual would contribute to instilling, for a short period of time, a different and less glowing image of German America in the minds of the country's Anglo-descended majority. The perturbing impact of Most upon that image was due to his unabashed and undisguised advocacy of violence for revolutionary ends. A onetime social democratic politician in Germany, Most had quit both his party (the SPD) and his homeland in the wake of Bismarck's crackdown on socialists, eventually establishing himself in New York, where he edited the city's most important anarchist journal, *Freiheit*.[56] In the previous chapter's discussion of Irish American "physical-force" activities we encountered one of that journal's occasional contributing writers, the pseudonymous "Professor Mezzeroff," better known as Richard Rogers, president of the Mansonitor Manufacturing and Experimental Chemical Company in Brooklyn, which had offered so much "pedagogy" in the explosive arts to combatants of the United Kingdom's Dynamite War.[57]

The affinity between Rogers and Most was hardly surprising, in light of their common, and profound, reverence for dynamite. Most owed much of his renown to a very peculiar little tract he brought out in July 1885, extolling the wonder-working properties of this and other explosive technologies, said to hold the key to righting all social wrongs in the capitalist world, and even (as we saw in the last chapter) to ushering forth the independence of Ireland. Its German title was rendered into English as "The Science of Revolutionary Warfare: A Little Handbook of Instruction in the Use and Preparation of Nitroglycerine, Dynamite, Gun-Cotton, Fulminating Mercury, Bombs, Fuses, Poisons, Etc., Etc."[58]

This image of Most as the evil genius of terrorist anarchy became firmly fixed in mainstream American consciousness as a result of an incident that would occur during the year following the publication of this seventy-four-page panegyrical manual. This was the Haymarket affair in early May 1886 in Chicago, during which a labor dispute escalated into violence in the city's Haymarket Square that led to sixty-seven police officers being injured, with eight eventually dying, in a melee that followed someone's tossing a bomb into their ranks. A similar number of civilians in the crowd also died, with upwards of thirty more being wounded. Significantly, most of this carnage was a result not of the explosive device thrown, but of the police gunfire that followed the blast; as one chronicler of the affair put it, "[t]here can be little doubt, therefore, that most if not all of the officers had been wounded by their own comrades, who fired indiscriminately in the panic that followed the explosion."[59]

Over the next two years the Haymarket incident would continue to reverberate in an America that had been growing more and more familiar with industrial unrest, and at a time when it and other parts of the Western world were coming face-to-face, as they would not again come until the early twenty-first century, with international terrorism. In the end, after a long and controversial trial, eight anarchists were sentenced to death for their part in the Haymarket events, notwithstanding the spotty and even contradictory nature of much of the "evidence" presented against them. Four were hanged in November 1887, with a fifth committing suicide in his prison cell on the eve of the execution; the remaining three would be pardoned by Illinois governor John Peter Altgeld, in 1893. Of the five who died (Albert Parsons, August Spies, Georg Engel, Adolph Fischer, and Louis Lingg, who took his own life) all but Parsons were German.[60]

In the context of the times, it cannot be too surprising to learn that the Haymarket incident stimulated a bout of antiradicalism as well as xenophobia in the United States. Terrorist incidents had been occurring intermittently during the 1870s and 1880s, in the United States as well as in Europe, and these included the assassination of the country's president, James A. Garfield, as well as highly publicized killings of two British officials in Dublin's Phoenix Park, to say nothing of the Dynamite War being conducted in the UK during the first half of the 1880s, though none of these killings could be chalked up to anarchism itself. Nevertheless, starting at the end of the 1870s, the connection between terrorism and anarchism would become more firmly rooted in the public mind throughout the transatlantic world.[61]

During the period prior to and subsequent to Haymarket, assassinations of political leaders became commonplace on either side of the Atlantic. In 1879, Prince Dmitry Kropotkin of Russia was murdered. Two years later came the turn of Czar Alexander II. The 1890s saw further European leaders cut down by anarchist violence. In 1894 the French third republic's fourth president, Marie-François Sadi Carnot, was killed. His death was followed three years later by that of the Spanish prime minister, Antonio Canovas del Castillo. In 1898 Elisabeth of Bavaria was assassinated, a fate that met King Umberto of Italy a year hence. In 1901, America's president, William McKinley, would be mortally wounded by an anarchist gunman while attending the Pan-American Exposition in Buffalo, New York—an assassination that may have been carried out by a Polish American, Leon Czolgosz, but one that some in the United States were blaming on the German American, Most, though by this time the former firebrand had forsaken revolutionary violence.[62] In short, for close to half a century the transatlantic world grappled with terrorist mayhem increasingly associated with the anarchist brand, and comprising what one analyst has termed a "loose international network" of ideologues able freely to cross international borders in a world that was daily becoming (though no one could call it such) globalized.[63]

Given how closely linked in the United States anarchists had been to the German American diaspora, one might have thought that the diaspora's image would have suffered a long-term blow from which recovery would be difficult if not impossible. Yet this did not happen, and not even at the height of the post-Haymarket xenophobia did the German diaspora find itself being regarded with anything remotely approaching, say, the level of suspicious disdain that would be encountered by the Muslim diaspora in the United States (and Canada) after 9/11, which we will cover in the next chapter. No doubt there were several reasons why the damage to the German American image caused by anarchism, and the reaction thereto, was both minimal and of short duration. Partly, it was a function of political violence having been a more familiar feature of American life in an era when the United States had just emerged from a bloody unification struggle that cost more than six hundred thousand lives, and when the country's army was continuing to do battle out west against Indian tribes. Partly it was a function of the kind of relative indifference toward domestic terrorist cells that we saw in the previous chapter's discussion of the Irish American "Swat Valley" from which acts of violence against targets in the UK were being routinely, and openly, plot-ted with little fear of any governmental crackdown on the cells. Partly it was the sheer size of the German American diaspora, which ran into the millions at a time when authorities could confidently assume the country's anarchists numbered a mere thousand or two at most: ergo, simple arithmetical logic ruled against branding German America a community of subversives, since it was palpably clear that virtually the entire diaspora was anything *but.*

Finally, there was an important strategic aspect associated with the image of German Americans during the early phases of the anarchist era, adumbrated in the previous section's discussion of the diplomatic relationship between the United States and Prussia/Germany during and following the Civil War. Throughout the 1870s and 1880s, and for many years to come, Germany remained to most Americans a friendly state, one with which it was hard to connect any negative experiences of the sort that the United States had known so often in its dealings with the British and the French. Moreover, as we saw in that previous section, the new German state that had emerged in 1871 was to remain, for some years, the apple of the eye of many an American "progressive." If Germany, the reasoning went, could be so good, then it must follow that German Americans, the occasional malcontent like Most excepted, must also be pretty good, for how else could one be in admiration of the cat that was Germany without at the same time appreciating the virtues of the kitty that was German America? Of course, the dynamic could also work in reverse, such that any considerable downturn in the state of relations between the United States and Germany could be expected to redound negatively to the fortunes of the German American image in the United States. This is exactly what was to occur, ever so gradually until the approach of war in 1914, and then very dramatically during the period from August 1914 to April 1917.

Prior to the near-total degradation of the German image in American opinion, however, it was still possible for German Americans to enjoy the esteem of their fellow citizens in the host country. For a period toward the end of the nineteenth century, they were even able, in a way that a century later would not be possible for Muslim North Americans to duplicate, to bathe in an appreciative warm glow from an American public, for reasons related both to the elaboration of new and so-called scientific theories regarding race, as well as to the reconceptualization of American national identity at a moment when the source and complexion of America's immigrant intake was undergoing the radical transformation we have come to remember as the aforementioned new immigration. In respect of the first development, the new "science" of race, there was for a time much reason, in certain quarters, to lavish praise upon the sterling "politico-genetic" qualities of a people being lumped together (temporarily) in the category "Teutons." In respect of the second development, there was a lively debate within the United States as to the proper means of assessing the contributions of the respective claimants to the honor of having done the most to "build" America.

Let us take these two discussions in reverse order, for as we shall see in the next section of this chapter, controversies swirling around identity and the related theme of "ontological security" were to serve as a mighty goad to German American diasporic activism, leading a heretofore largely apolitical community to seek and find organizational representation enabling it for the first time to emerge as a significant factor in the politics of pressure in the United States. The result would be an intensive campaign of ethnic lobbying during the years preceding American entry into the First World War. One of the key laments voiced by German Americans during the first decade of the twentieth century concerned the manner in which America's political traditions had been allowed to be misconstrued, or so they maintained, by those who wanted to believe that everything good and great about the country had to be traced back to the origins of English settlement in New England, sometimes to the 1630 founding of Massachusetts Bay Colony but more often to the event of ten years earlier, the arrival of the Pilgrims in Plymouth.

Things looked decidedly otherwise to a German American intellectual leadership growing ever more anxious about the meaning, for their own identity, of the ominous trends in global politics following the turn of the twentieth century. So they began to insist upon a counter-narrative of America's greatness, in which their group played, not surprisingly, a starring role. From America's very origins as a string of European colonial dependencies in the early seventeenth century, down to the present, this counter-narrative had German Americans doing their part, and much more, in nation building. "On every battle-field of every war that has been fought for the republic," proclaimed Georg von Skal, editor of the *New Yorker Staats-Zeitung*, "German blood has flowed freely. They have done their full share in the upbuilding of this great country. . . . They have made a lasting impression on the character of the American people."[64] Did not the success of the American Revolution owe more to Steuben and de Kalb than it did to that Frenchman, Lafayette?[65] Was not Lincoln's election in 1860 due to the German vote—indeed, was not Lincoln himself a descendant of Germans named Linkhorn? Had not the German Americans championed the cause of abolitionism and saved the Union by their wide-scale enlistment in the Northern army during the Civil War?[66] How different would America have been without these contributions![67]

To these not entirely accurate historical reconstructions could be adjoined some new image-boosters linked to a body of racial theorizing that privileged "Nordics" and "Teutons" above all others on the planet, not even excluding the "Anglo-Saxons," these latter being simply regarded as a branch of the Teutonic family. Taken in conjunction with the argument making the rounds during that prewar decade, namely that

American civilization had been nourished in *equal* parts by three different cultural tributaries—the Anglo-American, the German American, and the German Empire—it was not at all difficult for some to consider the saga of America as representing nothing other than what one writer would aptly term the "latest link in the genetic chain of Teutonic liberty."[68] According to the Teutonic thesis, liberty, and its doctrinal cousin, democracy, both owed their origins not to ancient Greece or any other land around the Mediterranean basin, but rather to the forests of Germany.[69] As expressed by the Cincinnati *Freie Presse* in September 1903, it all started with Hermann, chief of the Cheruscians, who chased the Romans out of Germany in 9 BCE. "Without Hermann, no Hengst, no Hersa, no Alfred the Great, no Magna Charta, no Milton, no Shakespeare"—and was it even necessary to add, no America?[70]

To be sure, the enthusiasts of this thesis never could agree exactly among themselves where to draw the boundary lines separating the Teutons from the non-Teutons, but as to the core constituents—that is, Germany, the UK, Scandinavia, the Netherlands, the United States—there was little disagreement,[71] until such time, that is, as geopolitical antagonism between the three largest states of the Teutonic triangle would make a nonsense of their presumed ethnic affinity, with Germany effectively finding itself booted out of the collective identity altogether, which henceforth would become an "Anglo-Saxon" ideational configuration.[72] To those doing the booting, it became ever more imperative somehow to rid the "Teutonic virtues" of the Teutons, and instead to vest the myth of free Anglo-Saxons in a time and place closer to home, making the great story of liberty's unfolding find its opening chapters in the struggle for religious freedom (of a kind) occurring in England in the sixteenth century, if not a century or so earlier.[73]

While it lasted, however, the Teutonic thesis did contribute to keeping the German Americans' status aloft in the judgment of many Americans. It certainly did the same, but even more so, for the self-image of the German Americans, these latter being comforted by the pleasant expectation that America's very future would be decided by its Germanic element, taken in its broadest sense as embracing all branches of the Stamm—that is, the Scandinavians, the Anglo-Saxons, and the Germans. In the words of Lutheran pastor Adolph Spaeth, uttered in the late 1890s, "[n]ot Latin or Slavic, but Germanic will be and must remain the head and heart of America, if it is to fulfill its world-historical mission."[74]

And even after the souring of relations between the United States and Germany had fully set in, it was still possible for the truest believers in Teutonism to continue making the case for geostrategic unity within the Teutonic triangle. No one was more relentlessly consistent in believing that the winds of progress blew in a Teutonic direction than an American political scientist, Columbia University's John W. Burgess, who as late as a decade prior to the Great War could still cling tightly to his Teutonic faith, and profess that current tensions between, especially, the UK and Germany could and would be smoothed over, as a result of America's playing the role of a linchpin connecting its two kin countries. As Burgess saw things, "[i]n a large and general sense, Germany is the motherland of Great Britain, as Great Britain is the motherland of the United States. Moreover, Germany is not merely the motherland of our motherland; she is in some degree, racially, the *immediate* motherland of the United States."[75] It followed from this, he reasoned, that America had a unique role to play—exactly the kind of role that, as we saw in the previous chapter, some Canadians envisioned their country's playing in bringing about world peace during the interwar era: the role of *linchpin*.

The difference, of course, between Burgess and the interwar Canadians was that what he desired was America's binding together itself, Britain, and *Germany* in strategic embrace, while they wanted a more exclusionary alliance directed against Germany (as well as any other potential disturbers of the world's peace). To explain how he envisioned America's part in fomenting alliance within the Teutonic triangle, Burgess returned to the familiar, if somewhat strained, familial metaphor, in insisting that Anglo-American rapprochement was simply a harbinger of a Teutonic alliance, for

> when the Americans consent to dwell under the same diplomatic roof with the mother who has chastised them, they are not going to allow the grand-mother, who has always taken their part [viz., Germany], to be left out in the cold. Interest, sentiment and duty to the world alike require the three countries to come together before any two of them can do so; and the Britons will do well to heed the views and feeling of a very large part of the American people on this subject. . . . [I]t is the United States upon which the transcendent duty falls of taking the first steps to bring the Teutons of the world together in the great work of world civilization. It is not only a duty, it is a glorious privilege, a magnificent opportunity.[76]

What finally put paid to the Teutonic thesis, of course, was the war, which did so much to sully the image of the hitherto progressive country that Americans had, not all that long ago, known Germany to be.[77] And with the deterioration of the German image came, and *had* to have come, a parallel deterioration in the image of German America. This, in turn, sparked a burst of diasporic activism on behalf of a political agenda without precedent in America's existence, at the time or since—activism that would result in a union between those two strangest of bedfellows, the German American and Irish American diasporas, as reflected in the rhetoric and activities of the organizations claiming to speak on behalf of their respective ethnic communities. Let us see who they were, what they thought, and what they tried to accomplish.

KULTURKAMPF: CULTURE WARS AND ETHNIC LOBBYING PRIOR
TO U.S. ENTRY INTO THE GREAT WAR

Anyone bothering to take the temper of "cultural" (that is, ethnic) politics
in America in the half century following the Civil War would have been
bound to notice two indisputable demographic facts. One was the large
size of the German and Irish American communities. The other was the
tremendous disparity, and typically antagonism, that existed between
members of these two groups during most of this period; for to employ
possibly anachronistic but not inaccurate imagery stemming from a later
time, Irish Americans coming into contact with Germans and German
Americans found the latter to be "an aggravated form of Englishman.
There is wanting the element of personal sympathy. . . . As is often said
here, beer and whisky do not mix well."[78]

At the level of the collectivity, with the relevant gauge being measures
of socioeconomic progress, the German Americans were far outdistanc-
ing their Irish American counterparts, both objectively as revealed by
statistics appertaining to their occupations and incomes, and subjectively,
as discerned through assessments made of each group by the dominant
"Anglo-Americans." And while the Irish Americans, as one writer suggestively put it, eventually managed to become "white" prior to the nineteenth century's end,[79] the German Americans beat them to this particular punch, getting themselves ensconced in the collective imagery of the
country's Anglo majority as a fairly acceptable folk around the time of the
Civil War.

True, Irish America had been closing this image gap, but who was
rash enough to predict, in the new century, a continuation of recent
trends? Nothing, it seemed, was guaranteed in an era when such exponents of the exotic new field of "eugenics" as Charles B. Davenport[80]
were busily ascribing a biological basis to social differentiations. Especially noteworthy to him and some of his colleagues was the contrast between such virtuous social traits of the German Americans as thrift, intelligence, and honesty, on the one hand, and on the other the deleterious
ones he attached to the Irish Americans, including not only the individual's "genetic" predisposition to "alcoholism, considerable mental defec-
tiveness, and a tendency to tuberculosis," but also the collectivity's fond-
ness for, and tolerance of, political corruption.[81]

Even less judgmental and racialist observers could easily provide
many reasons to assume that unity between German America and Irish
America would be highly unlikely ever to develop. These included religious differences, for not only were most German Americans Protestant
and most Irish Americans Catholic, but there was also a considerable
degree of antagonism between German Catholics and their Irish coreligionists, with the former resenting and resisting the latter's growing stran-
glehold upon an institution in America sometimes described, not entirely

tongue-in-cheek, as "One Holy, Apostolic and Irish" church.[82] To these religious differences had to be added linguistic ones, because while the Irish Americans may have had a well-advertised disdain for the English, they expressed it almost exclusively *in* English, and this at a time when German America was zealously attempting to safeguard the maintenance of educational, religious, and media opportunities in *German*. For good measure, the two ethnic communities had been cheering for different foreign countries in Europe's most recent great-power conflict, as we saw in the previous section: France had no more "rabid" backers[83] in the United States during its war with Prussia than the Irish Americans, and it had no more determined foes than the German Americans.

To top it all off, trends in racialist theorizing such as those we discussed above might also have been regarded as wedges between German and Irish Americans. The growing legions of "Anglo-Saxons" in the transatlantic world of the second half of the nineteenth century did not lack for epigones. We have seen, in the case of the Teutonic thesis, how the Germans and German Americans, as well as some ethnic outliers like Burgess, sought to join this particular racial party by expanding the invitation list so as to include, and for many among them to *privilege*, Germany. This latter country, when one thinks about it, could indeed be said to have been the original stomping grounds both of the Saxons and the Angles, one of the reasons why Mr. Dooley could utter his memorable quip about an Anglo-Saxon being "a German that's forgot who was his parents."[84] But Irish nationalists, on both sides of the Atlantic, were themselves hardly slow in exploiting the meaning of genealogical descent for current political debates, in an era of such rampant racialism as was the fin de siècle. And thus there came into being another collective identity to stand in contradistinction to both the Anglo-Saxons *and* the Teutons. This was the Celts.

Ironically, recent archaeological research has cast serious doubt on whether in fact the inhabitants of the British Isles actually did descend from the Celts of continental Europe during the Iron Age, which they were, and are, widely assumed to have done.[85] Nevertheless, there were many cultural nationalists, both in Ireland and in America, who were convinced that the Celts (and as they were known in Ireland, the Gaels) really could trace their ancestry to continental Europe. And not just any ancestors were those mainland Celts; no, they had been a culturally and politically superior folk, so that appealing to this lineage could provide quite a boost to collective self-esteem. And this is why so many cultural nationalists both in Ireland and America made precisely such appeals, in the final decades of the half century following the Civil War.

As Thomas N. Brown explains, the budding "Celtic interpretation of history" had a special value to Irish Americans locked in cultural combat against Anglo-Saxonism. In a manner similar to the German Americans, who themselves naturally sought to locate the roots of modern American civilization in as much German soil as possible, Irish Americans insisted that all that was good and great about America had to be traced back to the Emerald Isle. If they certainly acknowledged that the Teutonists were correct to insist that American identity was not an English cultural concoction, they disagreed about the true source of America's goodness. According to adherents of the Celtic thesis, John Burgess, Herbert Baxter Adams,[86] and their Teutonic ilk were searching for America's geopolitical soul in the wrong place: the "origins of democratic institutions, which [they] traced back to the 'tun' of the dark German forests, the philo-celts found on the sunny slopes of Tara. Representative government, trial by jury, popular education were among the gifts tendered the modern world by the Celts of Ireland."[87]

Yet despite all of these sources of discord between the two ethnic diasporas, including their competing narratives about American identity, there would come into being, commencing in the decade preceding the First World War and continuing until April 1917 and America's entry into the global conflict, an extraordinary marriage of geopolitical convenience between these two cultural groupings, such that to analyze the "lobbying" efforts mounted by either diaspora's leadership group requires our taking them in combination. Moreover, putting these two together has the added merit of demonstrating how potent the new realities of ethnic lobbying in the United States could appear to be, both to analysts in that country as well as to those residing in the UK—analysts such as the editor of the influential British newspaper the *Observer*, who in January 1910 commented worriedly on a recently concluded compact between German and Irish American diasporic organizations, bent on brandishing the threat of the ethnic vote to keep in line any American politicians foolish enough to advocate closer security cooperation with the UK. "The new alliance between the Irish and German vote in the United States," warned James L. Garvin, "is a more important thing than almost anybody here seems to realise. It is one of the greatest dangers that have ever threatened the Empire."[88]

What so upset Garvin was an alliance forged in 1907 between the very old and established Irish American entity, the Ancient Order of Hibernians (AOH), and the very new and promising German American organization, the National German-American Alliance (NGAA, or as it was officially called in German, the Deutsch-Amerikanischer National-Bund der Vereinigten Staaten von Amerika). This latter organization was an outgrowth of a Pennsylvania German American organization founded in 1899 by Charles John Hexamer, the Deutsch-Amerikanischen Zentralbundes von Pennsylvanien. Two years later, the NGAA was created, with Hexamer becoming its first president, a position he would hold until late 1917. Its mission statement was to promote "everything that is good in German character and culture and that might be to the benefit and welfare of the whole American nation."[89] At its peak, the NGAA boasted of a membership of some 2.5 million, and even if that figure may have been inflated as some have argued, it was nevertheless revealing— and to pro-Allied publicists, it was more than merely revealing, it was positively frightening; for after 1914 the NGAA would come to find itself being branded as little more than a puppet of German imperialism in the heart of America.[90]

Nor was the NGAA, largely considered to be a Protestant organiza- tion populated by too many free thinkers, as far as the large German American Catholic community was concerned, the only organizational entity in German America. The Catholics had their own group, the Cath- olic Central Verein (CCV), which by the time war arrived in 1914 would be interacting more cooperatively with the NGAA than hitherto, testa- ment to the ability of a language- and nationality-based collective iden- tity to mitigate the divisiveness of religion, for as Joseph Frey, the presi- dent of the CCV put it, in announcing his group's full sympathy with Germany shortly after the war began, "Blood is thicker than water."[91] It was also, apparently, thicker than communion wine, for Frey made no secret of his detestation of fellow Catholics who happened to prefer the Allied cause to the German one.[92] Backing up the German American political and cultural elite was a vast network of German-language publi- cations, more than 800 in number (most of them weeklies) by the 1890s, and even as late as 1917 still totalling 522 publications, or half of all foreign-language publications in America.[93] Most of these were enthu- siastic in their defense of both the Kaiser's policies and the kin-state— until, that is, April 1917 when America entered the war against Germany, forcing German Americans to confront an agonizing choice, between their host-state and their kin-state. In the vast majority, German Americans would find themselves, if reluctantly, opting for the former, some to the extent even of going off to fight against their kinfolk on the battlefields of Europe.[94] But the German American commitment to the war effort betrayed some interesting variations on a theme, so poignantly (and imaginatively) captured in the admission of Herman Pellinger, pres- ident of the Cleveland, Ohio, branch of the NGAA, to the effect that all German Americans, though "backing America as against Germany, are praying for the defeat of Great Britain and her allies."[95]

Pellinger made this comment in April 1917. Some sixteen years earlier, at the time of its formation, things looked much brighter for the NGAA, as they did for the prospects of ethnic lobbying attaining the will-o'-the- wisp of "influence" over America's foreign policy. That third and final necessary condition for successful ethnic politicking appeared, as the new century began, to be in place at last: a strong organization capable of spearheading a coherent campaign of pressure, and riding shotgun on the myriad other entities within what would shortly develop into an Irish-German diasporic combination, uniting in a shared anti-British (and therefore anti-Canadian) cause the two largest (non-English) ethnic entities in the United States. In addition to the venerable AOH, and in many ways much more important than it, the Irish side of the alliance was buttressed by the Clan na Gael, whose principal leaders in the wartime era were the editor of the *Gaelic American*, John Devoy, and a judge of the New York state supreme court, Daniel Florence Cohalan, both key figures in the group of "professional Irish" who did so much to energize, as well as to stand as surrogates for, the large, and by the nature of things, often inchoate Irish diaspora in the United States.[96]

Also arising from within Irish American ranks was a third group, formed during the second year of the war, the Friends of Irish Freedom, which would serve as an umbrella group for the AOH and the Clan na Gael, and whose own leadership cadre was supplied heavily by figures from the latter, including and especially Devoy and Cohalan. The latter explained to the 2,300 delegates assembled at New York's Hotel Astor on 4 March 1916, for a convention of what was billed the "Irish race," that "[i]f it hadn't been for the men of this race . . . a Treaty of Alliance under the name of an Arbitration Treaty" would have been struck between the United States and the UK, and as a result of that, "we would have been compelled to enter the war upon the side of England."[97] Rounding out the roster of entities either formally or informally linking Irish American and German American diasporic activists were several other enterprises, among them the American Neutrality League, the American Independence League, the Friends of Peace, and Jeremiah O'Leary's interestingly named American Truth Society, decried by one British critic for being "neither American nor truthful."[98]

In the previous chapter, we became more than familiar with what it was that motivated the Irish American diasporic activists: to hurt Britain, and above all to prevent the emergence of an Anglo-American alliance. But what was it that inspired the newly formed NGAA to activism? Perhaps surprisingly, it was initially a *domestic* issue that supplied momentum to the German American organizational efforts. namely the worrisome rise in prohibitionist tendencies in Anglo-American society, which to German America constituted both an assault on traditional civil liberties and a potential menace for German America's own associational practices, especially as prohibitionist zealotry often went hand in hand with a determination to ensure that Sabbath laws be more strictly enforced by municipal and state authorities. With German American cultural mores according a central place to Sunday afternoon family gatherings in beer gardens, it is not difficult to understand how temperance movements could have been regarded as a threat to the diaspora's identity.[99]

Before long, this domestic agenda item took a decidedly backseat to foreign policy as a mobilizing vehicle for German America. The deterioration in the European balance of power and the growing threat of war on the old continent would turn the German Americans more and more toward international affairs, inspired by two overarching considerations. One was to defend the honor of the Fatherland, which German Americans felt was increasingly being victimized by a pro-British (and to a much lesser extent, pro-French) press in the United States; needless to say, anything that besmirched the image of Germany in the United States could be counted upon also to besmirch that of German America. The other was to ensure that should war come to Europe, America would maintain the strictest neutrality, in keeping with what German Americans insisted was good old-fashioned American geopolitical wisdom, handed down from George Washington's "Farewell Address" of 1796, urging his countrymen to eschew any entanglement with the European great powers.[100]

Between August 1914 and April 1917, from the perspective of a German American intellectual elite that had convinced itself of the diaspora's outsized contributions to the building of America, there would sometimes surface a temptation to bend, if only slightly, George Washington's precept, in hopes that perhaps the host country might see its way to backing the kin-country, rather than to support Britain and its allies, Canada among them. But this, as we saw above, was *schnitzel* in the sky, save to all but the most misled German American nationalists. Practically, as few if any sentient individuals in the diaspora really *could* foresee America's going to war alongside Germany and against Britain (and Canada), notwithstanding that it might have made plain sense to them that it do just that, the next best alternative was to prevent the country's formidable economic and political (possibly even military) weight being brought into the struggle on behalf of the Allies. This meant militating in favor of the strictest possible neutrality. To this end, there would be three major intermediate steps. First of these was to prevent the sale of arms and munitions to either side. Such sales were permitted by both international law and America's domestic legislation, but the Allies' control of the seas meant that of the European combatants, only Britain and France could realistically expect to derive benefit from shopping in America's armaments market. The second was to prevent loans being extended to either side (read: the Allies primarily) by American public and private institutions. And the third was to elect in 1916 a president who could be counted on to be, if not pro-German, then at least not anti-German.

In all three instances, the NGAA quarterbacked an ethnic lobbying effort of unprecedented proportions on behalf of the kin-state. Working with its Irish American counterparts, as well as with German American representatives in Congress, it managed to get two similar munitions bills introduced into the House Committee on Foreign Affairs in late 1914. These measures were sponsored by a Republican congressman from Missouri, Richard Bartholdt, who had become the principal voice for the German American diaspora within the foreign policy community,[101] and a Democratic congressman from Iowa, Henry Vollmer. The intent of the two measures was to stanch the flow of munitions to all belligerents, by giving the president discretion to restrict such sales. Neither measure, however, made it out of committee so as to enable a vote to be held on the House floor, to the chagrin of the German and Irish American activists. These latter deplored the fact that while the law might indeed permit munitions sales being made to either side, the spirit of "neutrality" would seem to require that with only one camp (the Allies) able in practice to avail itself of the American marketplace (thanks to the British fleet), allowing a continuance of munitions sales was an ethical, even if not a legal, breach of neutrality. In the bitter words of one leading German-American activist, George Sylvester Viereck, editor of the newspaper *Fatherland,* "[w]e appealed to the spirit of the law, and you give us the letter." [102]

More luck was had, albeit only for a brief time, with the campaign against loans to the Allies, given that pressure from the NGAA and other members of the German-Irish alliance network did dampen enthusiasm for purchasing Allied bonds on the part of some American bankers, particularly in the Midwest, who were worried that they might risk losing their German American depositors. Even the Wilson administration hesitated, though only momentarily, to bestow its blessing upon the policy of permitting belligerents to raise capital in American financial markets, before determining that the same logic that decreed the legitimacy of selling munitions to belligerents must also prevail in the matter of providing credits for those purchases. [103]

Rebuffed in these two attempts to get American policy steered in a direction that they knew to be more congenial to their interpretation of the requirements of "genuine" neutrality, the German Americans, with the more than eager participation of Irish American diasporic leadership, turned their attention to the most important objective of all. This was an objective to which the very logic of ethnic lobbying pointed so unmistakably: brandishing the "ethnic vote" in the forthcoming presidential election, so as to turn out of office the man that both groups' leadership was convinced had made a mockery of the venerated tradition of noninvolvement in European affairs, and had plunged America headlong on a course leading inexorably to war against Germany, at the side of the despised British, with their Canadian subalterns. Thus as 1916 began, the near-exclusive objective of German and Irish American groups was to tap the electoral clout of the two large diasporas in such a way as to guarantee that America would stay out of the war. As we witnessed in the previous chapter's discussion of the McDowell-Bagenal thesis, there were many observers of the American political scene who appeared to think that the Irish Americans *all by themselves* possessed inordinate control over electoral outcomes. Now, added to this was a growing body of opinion that foresaw the German Americans, again all by themselves, wielding an even greater controlling vote in the United States.

In the judgment of one British America-watcher, writing in early 1915 under the pseudonym (appropriately enough) of "Watchman," Britain was well on the way to losing the battle for public opinion in the United States, and worse, there was not very much it could do about it. In effect, the United States had become so "Germanized" as a result of the astounding growth in the numbers of German Americans as to make any prospect of an Anglo-American alliance nothing other than a pipe dream. The underlying cause of this British disadvantage lay nearly exclusively in the realm of electoral politics. British immigrants in America did not naturalize, thus could not vote, whereas German immigrants beat a path to the front door of the nearest naturalization bureau as soon as they set foot on American soil. The conclusion was obvious: the absence of a "British vote in this country" dooms in advance to failure any public diplomacy intended to sway American opinion in a pro-Allied direction, and British officials would do well to disabuse themselves of the "grotesque suggestion" that somehow the United States could be brought around to backing the Allies. "People who imagine this can never have been West of Washington. They have no conception of the Germanisation of the United States . . . [where] a large body of American public opinion is gradually swerving to the German side, a fact of serious concern for all who are anxious for the harmony of the English-speaking world."[104]

If either diasporic group acting alone could have been so potent, imagine what the effect must be of their *combined* attempt to determine, through the ballot box, the course of American foreign policy! One wonders why President Wilson even bothered to think he could be returned to office in November 1916. In addition to evicting the president from the White House, the presumed German-Irish electoral steamroller had the subsidiary aim of seeing to it that enough Irish and German American candidates in the congressional races got elected so as to guarantee "neutrality" even in the event, unlikely, that the pro-Allied chief executive somehow managed to cling to office. But it was the presidency, rather than the Congress, that remained the chief target of the combined diasporas' offensive, with the goal not simply being to turn out Wilson, but also to ensure that the Republicans did not nominate in the summer of 1916 a man the NGAA reckoned to be an even greater Satan, former president Theodore Roosevelt. He had not been regarded as being particularly anti-German—if anything, the reverse—during his years in the White House from 1901 to 1909.[105] But after the sinking of the *Lusitania* in May 1915, Roosevelt showed himself to be a strident advocate of a distinctly pro-Allied campaign of "preparedness" and "Americanization."[106] In contrast to the German Americans, the Irish diaspora's leaders fixated more upon the twenty-eighth president than the twenty-sixth one, even if for the NGAA, no one could possibly be worse than the latter, though Wilson certainly came close. Hence the pithiness of the slogan adopted by the Illinois branch of Hexamer's organization in March 1916: *"Alle gegen Roosevelt und Wilson."* [107]

As we know from chapter three, some scholars are of the view that ethnic minorities can and do exercise an outsized impact upon elections, including and especially national ones. [108] If this is really so, then 1916's presidential contest should have constituted the ultimate test of the potency of ethnic lobbying (broadly construed, as noted earlier, to include voting). Admittedly, presidential elections do not really turn, all that often, on questions of foreign policy. Sometimes, however, they do, and never more so than when war is raging, with the threat of America's becoming involved in the fighting if it has not already joined it, or getting ensnared further in it, if already involved. So 1916 should have been, mutatis mutandis, what Walter Dean Burnham labelled several decades ago a "critical" election in America, save that his use of the adjective was intended to suggest an election that led to a realignment, not of grand strategy, but rather of the fortunes of national political parties. [109]

To begin with, as a Democrat, Wilson was facing an uphill battle in a country that had been nearly always opting for Republican presidential candidates, going back to 1860 with the election of Abraham Lincoln. And while one Democrat prior to Wilson in 1912 had managed to break the string of Republican victories, and to have done so twice (in 1884 and 1892), not even he, Grover Cleveland, could manage to get himself re-elected as incumbent in 1888. Besides, it was known by all that Wilson only owed his 1912 victory to the fact that the Republican vote had been split between the sitting president, William Howard Taft, and the former one, Roosevelt. And now, in 1916, Wilson not only had to battle precedent, but also to confront the formidable prospect of winning an election in which both large diasporas were panting, or so their leadership maintained, for his defeat.

The year prior to the election, a trial run of sorts for the ethnic-vote thesis was conducted, when in a special vote held to fill a seat in the House of Representatives for New York's 23rd district, Jeremiah O'Leary stumped on behalf of the Republican candidate William S. Bennet, out of pique with the Democratic candidate, Ellsworth Healy, who had publicly refused to support the American Truth Society's campaign to ban loans to the Allies, and this even though Healy was the nephew-in-law of Boss Murphy, of Tammany Hall, the cynosure of Irish power in America. Bennet took this district, which normally was won by Democrats with comfortable majorities, and his narrow victory in this 1915 contest gave O'Leary the idea that the vote had been a repudiation of Wilson's foreign policy, and could be replicated elsewhere in the country in the following year's general election. So O'Leary cabled the president, gloating about what had just happened, and what was going to happen again, in 1916, when traditionally Democratic Irish American voters would bolt to the Republicans "as a protest against your administration, which has always placed England first." O'Leary pursued the theme into the 1916 electoral season, once more cabling Wilson, in September, a warning of the retribution about to be visited upon him unless there was a radical and rapid shift in foreign policy. This last cable occasioned a response from the president that has to rank as one of the sharpest, and certainly most interesting, rebukes a candidate for elected office ever delivered to a presumptive power broker. As quoted in the *New York Times* of 30 September 1916, the president acknowledged that he had received O'Leary's latest message, and wanted to let him know that "I would feel deeply mortified to have you or anybody like you vote for me. Since you have access to many disloyal Americans and I have not, I will ask you to convey this message to them."[110]

Not all politicians were as blasé about the prospect of losing the ethnic vote in 1916. Former president Taft wrote to a friend in April that should Roosevelt obtain the Republican nomination at that summer's party convention, it would "drive the Germans to Wilson," such was their hatred for the former president.[111] But as we have already seen, as far as the NGAA was concerned, Wilson was no improvement over Roosevelt.[112] Thus the organization bent its efforts to lobbying on behalf of the man who eventually would secure the Republican nomination in June 1916, an associate justice of the U.S. Supreme Court and former governor of New York, Charles Evans Hughes, somewhat surprisingly given that when Hughes had run for reelection as governor eight years earlier, the German American groups in the state had opposed him because he had been regarded as too zealous in enforcing the blue laws.[113]

Hughes was not a particularly dynamic campaigner, but the race nevertheless turned out to be incredibly tight. The German Americans, along with their Irish American partners, might have been entitled, and they certainly missed no opportunity, to claim that they had been instrumental in Hughes's having secured the Republican nomination, but they were unable to spell the difference between victory and defeat for the despised Wilson. Though often interpreted as one of those rare presidential elections in which foreign policy proved to be the dominant issue,[114] 1916's outcome has, perhaps surprisingly, been regarded by some as largely a function of domestic issues, the claim being that Wilson's progressive legislative record accounted for his ability to take all but four states west of the Mississippi, and therefore narrowly to secure victory, with 277 electoral votes to Hughes's 254. It would not be until California's returns were in that the outcome was known, for had Wilson's Republican challenger garnered that state's 13 electoral votes, the president would have lost the electoral vote, 267 to 264, even though he scored a margin of victory nationwide of 600,000 in the popular vote. Wilson squeaked by in California with a razor-thin edge of 3,773 votes, and in so doing he became the first Democratic incumbent since Andrew Jackson in 1832 to achieve reelection.

Obviously, foreign policy also factored into the campaign, given that a war was raging and American lives were being lost at sea. But because both candidates were running on a "peace" ticket, each promising to keep America out of the European war, it is hard, even today, to gauge the effectiveness of the greatest attempt at ethnic lobbying that would ever be mounted in an American election. It is true that many have interpreted the follow-on presidential election, in 1920, as having been the repudiation, on foreign policy grounds, by an angry pair of diasporic blocs, but here again there is actually little evidence that German American and Irish American voters "deserted" the Democratic party that year in numbers that were disproportionate to the general defection of nearly *all* the country's voting blocs, ethnic or otherwise, from the Democrats.[115] The Republican candidate, Warren G. Harding, might indeed have taken the German, and possibly the Irish, vote, but he took just about everyone else's vote, as well, outside of the solidly Democratic South, in the process racking up an unprecedented, then and now, margin of popular-vote victory of more than 26 percent over his Democratic rival, Ohio's governor, James M. Cox, and garnering 404 of the 531 electoral votes.[116]

THE "TRAGEDY" OF GERMAN AMERICA?

Scholars who have explored the saga of the German Americans' struggle for influence over U.S. foreign policy, especially as it became conjoined with similar efforts mounted by Irish American diasporic leadership — the latter to such an extent that once the war began it was working hand in glove with Berlin to secure a German armed intervention in Ireland itself[117] — have drawn the conclusion that the German American diaspora turned out to be detrimental to the interests of the kin-state, Germany. To some, Germany would have been better off if it, like France, had *no* diaspora at all to speak of in the United States in the early twentieth century.[118] This thesis had been propagated even before the ethnic-lobbying drama had fully played itself out, when a little-known German American theologian named Reinhold Niebuhr published an article in the January 1916 issue of the *Atlantic Monthly*, proclaiming that the relatively retrograde German Americans had sullied the good name of Germany as far as the majority of Americans were concerned. To this twenty-three-year-old pastor in Detroit, and future luminary of international relations (IR) theory in the United States, German America, though well-integrated economically into the host country, had failed to become politically assimilated, unlike, he said, the much more effective Irish Americans. As a result, the "failure of German-Americanism . . . may be a contributory cause not only of the lack of esteem in which German-Americanism is now held in this country but also of the lack of understanding between Germany and this nation."[119]

The same theme would be echoed a generation later, and in the early stages of another world war involving Germany, when John Hawgood published his classic study, *The Tragedy of German-America*.[120] As did Niebuhr before him, so too did Hawgood insist that the relative political and social isolation in which German Americans preferred to live their lives meant that they had no hope of thriving in the manner of more well-adapted diasporas, such as the Irish American one, hence the "tragedy" of their experience. Others have gone even further, suggesting that not only did German America let down the Fatherland, but it also dragged Irish America down with it, in effect causing the activism of this other large diaspora to become tarred by the brush of disloyalty associated with an Irish American leadership's unwise decision to bet upon a German victory in the early stages of the Great War.[121] As stated by one scholar who has studied the impact of ethnic diasporas upon America's foreign policy, there was a fatal flaw in the campaign mounted by Irish American activists in the prewar years as well as during the early stages of the war, and it was something that would "damage the reputation of Irish America in the eyes of the majority of Americans for several decades. This was the alliance forged with German Americans, under the influence of Berlin, in the defense of yet another symbol of American nationhood: resistance to foreign entanglements which Washington had warned against in his Farewell Message."[122]

I have given the subtitle "The Principle of the Opposite Effect, Applied" to this chapter *not* because I happen to believe that the Niebuhr/Hawgood thesis is valid; after all, there is plenty of evidence, as we have already seen, attesting to the rather lofty regard in which German Americans were held by the majority of their fellow Americans, even down to the period just preceding America's entry into the war. Nor do I accept the view that it was the unwise decision of Irish American leaders (the "professional Irish" in Buckley's terminology) to side with Germany in 1914 that condemned their activism to failure, insofar as concerned the core objective of securing the independence of Ireland from British rule. We can surely say, to the extent both diasporas' political agendas had been so firmly fixated upon keeping America from joining the war on the British (and Canadian) side, that they certainly failed to achieve their ends. But this is hardly tantamount to asserting that they lacked "influence" upon American foreign policy.

There is another way to look at things, and it leads to the conclusion that the two diasporas actually *were* quite influential, except that the resultant of their activism was precisely the opposite of what had been intended. Clearly, the concluding paragraphs of a very long chapter are scarcely the place to develop an argument that would require a book of its own to demonstrate adequately. So let me just, in closing, raise an alternative means of assessing the impact of ethnic diasporas upon North American and global security a century ago. This alternative assessment focuses upon what we might term the great puzzle of the wartime experience, at least from the perspective of U.S. foreign policy—the puzzle of America's entry into the war some thirty-two months after it had begun. There are two ways of approaching this puzzle. One is to stress how tardy America was in getting into the fight, certainly when compared with fellow liberal democracies in the North Atlantic triangle, Canada and Great Britain, participants from the very outset. The second is to de-emphasize chronology (and ideology) in favor of ontology, and to concentrate upon what is most in need of being explained regarding April 1917—not that it took so long for the United States to enter the fray but rather that it entered it at all.

The suggestion I make here is that it is on the home front, rather than on the Western Front or the high seas, that one might better look in a bid to uncover the most causally significant events leading to the April 1917 decision. More than this, I suggest that those "causally significant events" inhered in a bitter culture clash between two identity-based factions that had taken shape around issues of ethnicity. In effect, the Irish Americans, with more than a little help from their German American friends, succeeded in "getting America's English up," in the process mobilizing America's large "hidden diaspora," the one consisting of the English-descended Americans who had heretofore been inclined to regard the British themselves as having been Americans' "significant oppositional others," so necessary for establishing the very meaning of the American national identity.

The Germans Americans and Irish Americans, therefore, "constructed" a politically mobilized entity, with strategic interests and consequences that would redound to the benefit of Britain and Canada. It became so constructed because their combined and incessant attacks on all things English from 1914 on brought America's English-descended majority to the belated realization that they had a great deal in common with America's "hereditary foe" and former mother country; it converted this majority from its traditional anti-British political stance into a group not only prepared to tolerate an Anglo-American alliance, but as time went on during the wartime period to insist upon one. Most importantly, the English-descended majority understood fully well that attacks on English identity, being made with great regularity and acerbity by both the German American and Irish American activists, were attacks on *themselves*. Just as for the German Americans, whose defense of the Fatherland became an emotionally charged matter of ontological security, so too for the English-descended Americans was the defense of the "Motherland" all of a sudden fraught with ontological significance.

The surprise is not that the influence attempts of the combined diasporic assault on England should have backfired in this way. Rather, the surprise is that so little attention has been given to this particular implication of the culture wars of a century ago, mostly I suspect due to the scholarly fallacy discussed in chapter three of this book, of refusing to recognize that English-descended Americans also constituted an "ethnic grouping" in their own right, with all that this would imply for U.S. foreign policy as well as for security cooperation with both Canada and the UK in the early decades of the twentieth century.

NOTES

1. Karl Jünger, *Deutsch-Amerika mobil!* (Berlin: B. Behr, 1915).

2. Aaron L. Friedberg, *The Weary Titan: Britain and the Experience of Relative Decline, 1895–1905* (Princeton, N.J.: Princeton University Press, 1988); and Donald Cameron Watt, *Succeeding John Bull: America in Britain's Place, 1900–1975* (Cambridge: Cambridge University Press, 1984).

3. Watt, *Succeeding John Bull*, p. 7. For a survey of the worldwide Deutschtum, see Mathias Schulze, James M. Skidmore, David G. John, Grit Liebscher, and Sebastian Siebel-Achenbach, eds., *German Diasporic Experiences: Identity, Migration, and Loss* (Waterloo, ON: Wilfrid Laurier Press, 2008).

4. Jünger, *Deutsch-Amerika mobil!*, pp. 140–42. At the time the war broke out, the German "element" in Canada numbered around 400,000, roughly 5 percent of the country's total population of approximately 8 million. Additionally, some 120,000 "Austrians" were said to be residing in the country in 1914, but they were mainly Ukrainians who had been living in portions of the Austro-Hungarian Empire. See John Herd Thompson, *Ethnic Minorities during Two World Wars* (Ottawa: Canadian Historical Association, 1991), p. 4.

5. On German government activities involving potential use of American soil to strike at targets in Canada, see Reinhard R. Doerries, *Imperial Challenge: Ambassador Count Bernstorff and German-American Relations, 1908–1917* (Chapel Hill: University of North Carolina Press, 1989), pp. 178–81.

6. Earl R. Beck, *Germany Rediscovers America* (Tallahassee: Florida State University Press, 1968), p. 2.

7. For a summary of the Weber article and a critique of it, see "Do the German-Americans Dictate Our Foreign Policy?" *American Review of Reviews*, no. 41 (March 1910), pp. 349–50.

8. Quoted in the novelist Owen Wister's foreword to Gustavus Ohlinger, *Their True Faith and Allegiance* (New York: Macmillan, 1916), pp. xiv–xv.

9. Quoted in Philipp Blom, *The Vertigo Years: Europe, 1900–1914* (New York: Basic Books, 2008), p. 172.

10. Notes one scholar regarding the Kaiser's oratorical and other communicative quirkiness: "There can be no doubt about the bizarre tone and content of many of the Kaiser's personal communications, interviews and speeches on foreign and domestic political themes. . . . He was an extreme exemplar of that Edwardian social category, the club bore who is forever explaining some pet project to the man in the next chair." Christopher Clark, *The Sleepwalkers: How Europe Went to War in 1914* (New York: HarperCollins, 2013), pp. 178–79, 182.

11. Roosevelt to John St. Loe Strachey, 27 January 1900, in *The Letters of Theodore Roosevelt*, ed. Elting E. Morison, vol. 2: *The Years of Preparation, 1898–1900* (Cambridge, Mass.: Harvard University Press, 1951), pp. 1143–46.

12. J. Lee Thompson, *Never Call Retreat: Theodore Roosevelt and the Great War* (New York: Palgrave Macmillan, 2013); and Serge Ricard, "World War One and the Rooseveltian Gospel of Undiluted Americanism," in *Hyphenated Diplomacy: European Immi-*

gration and U.S. Foreign Policy, 1914–1984, ed. Hélène Christol and Ricard (Aix-en-Provence, France: Publications Université de Provence, 1985), pp. 19–30.

13. Quoted in Henry Blumenthal, "George Bancroft in Berlin, 1867–1874," *New England Quarterly* 37 (June 1964): 224–41, quote at p. 230.

14. For these wartime incidents involving Canada, see Graeme S. Mount, *Canada's Enemies: Spies and Spying in the Peaceable Kingdom* (Toronto: Dundurn, 1993), pp. 29–37. For sabotage directed at American sites, see Chad Millman, *The Detonators: The Secret Plot to Destroy America and an Epic Hunt for Justice* (New York: Little, Brown, 2006), which examines in detail the late July 1916 destruction of New Jersey's Black Tom terminal.

15. James Middleton, "Are Americans More German than English?" *World's Work* 31 (December 1915): 141–47.

16. One leading American enthusiast for strategic condominium was John Randolph Dos Passos, *The Anglo-Saxon Century and the Unification of the English-Speaking Peoples*, 2nd ed. (New York: G. P. Putnam's Sons, 1903). For scholarly assessments of this budding collective identity and its potential strategic implications, see Stuart Anderson, *Race and Rapprochement: Anglo-Saxonism and Anglo-American Relations, 1895–1904* (Rutherford, N.J.: Fairleigh Dickinson University Press, 1981); and Duncan Bell, *The Idea of Greater Britain: Empire and the Future of World Order, 1860–1900* (Princeton, N.J.: Princeton University Press, 2007). The impact of this identity upon the North American security situation is analyzed in Edward P. Kohn, *This Kindred People: Canadian-American Relations and the Anglo-Saxon Idea, 1895–1903* (Montreal and Kingston: McGill-Queen's University Press, 2004).

17. Homer Lea, *The Day of the Saxon* (New York: Harper and Brothers, 1912).

18. Frank Bass, "U.S. Ethnic Mix Boasts German Accent amid Surge of Hispanics," *Bloomberg News*, 6 March 2012, available at http://www.bloomberg.com/news/2012-03-06. Also see U.S. Census Bureau, *Statistical Abstract of the United States: 2012*, available at http://www.census.gov/compendia/statab/2012.

19. So identified in George Bernard Shaw's 1904 comedy of the same name.

20. Samuel P. Huntington, *Who Are We? The Challenges to America's National Identity* (New York: Simon & Schuster, 2004), pp. 45–47.

21. See Alexander Emmerich, *Die Geschichte der Deutschen in Amerika: Von 1680 bis zur Gegenwart* (Köln, Germany: Fackelträger, 2010); and Richard O'Connor, with Henry Marx, *Die Deutsch-Amerikaner: So wurden es 33 Millionen*, trans. Uwe Bahnsen (Hamburg: Hoffmann und Campe, 1970).

22. Cited in Jill Lepore, *The Name of War: King Philip's War and the Origins of American Identity* (New York: Knopf, 1998), p. 111 (emphasis added).

23. Edmund S. Morgan, *Benjamin Franklin* (New Haven, Conn.: Yale University Press, 2002), pp. 72–73. Also see Aaron Spencer Fogleman, *Hopeful Journeys: German Immigration, Settlement, and Political Culture in Colonial America, 1717–1775* (Philadelphia: University of Pennsylvania Press, 1989); and Andreas Dorpalen, "The Political Influence of the German Element in Colonial America," *Pennsylvania History* 6 (October 1939): 221–39.

24. Fredric Klees, *The Pennsylvania Dutch* (New York: Macmillan, 1961).

25. La Vern J. Rippley, *The German-Americans* (Boston: Twayne, 1976), p. 21.

26. Walter T. K. Nugent, *Crossings: The Great Transatlantic Migrations, 1870–1914* (Bloomington: Indiana University Press, 1995).

27. John A. Hawgood, *The Tragedy of German-America: The Germans in the United States of America during the Nineteenth Century—and After* (New York: G. P. Putnam's Sons, 1940), pp. xi–xii; and Wilhelm Mönckmeier, *Die deutsche Überseeauswanderung* (Jena, Germany: Verlag von Gustav Fischer, 1912).

28. Mack Walker, *Germany and the Emigration, 1816–1885* (Cambridge, Mass.: Harvard University Press, 1964).

29. Frederick C. Luebke, *Bonds of Loyalty: German-Americans and World War I* (De Kalb: Northern Illinois University Press, 1974), pp. 29–30, 34.

30. James M. Berquist, "German Communities in American Cities: An Interpretation of the Nineteenth-Century Experience," *Journal of American Ethnic History* 4 (Fall 1984): 9–30, quote at p. 9.

31. Hawgood, *Tragedy of German-America*, pp. 59–60; and Hans W. Gatzke, *Germany and the United States: A 'Special Relationship'?* (Cambridge, Mass.: Harvard University Press, 1980), pp. 28–31.

32. On the causes and implications of German disunity prior to 1871, see Gordon A. Craig, *The Germans* (New York: Meridian, 1983), pp. 16–26.

33. But for the claim that there *was* a sense of nationalism among German immigrants during the period before the 1870s, compare Heinrich H. Maurer, "The Earlier German Nationalism in America," *American Journal of Sociology* 22 (January 1917): 519–43.

34. See Carl F. Wittke, *Refugees of Revolution: The German Forty-Eighters in America* (Philadelphia: University of Pennsylvania Press, 1952); and Adolf E. Zucker, ed., *The Forty-Eighters: Political Refugees of the German Revolution of 1848* (New York: Columbia University Press, 1950).

35. France during the era of the Civil War, of course, was a complicating factor, to put it mildly, elsewhere in North America, in Mexico to be specific, with implications that no American government could or did overlook. See Lynn Marshall Case, ed., *French Opinion on the United States and Mexico, 1860–1867* (Hamden, Conn.: Archon Books, 1969).

36. See, for an elaboration, my "France and the Issue of a 'Usable' Diaspora in (North) America: The Duroselle-Tardieu Thesis Reconsidered," *International History Review* 34 (March 2012): 71–88.

37. Jean-Baptiste Duroselle, *France and the United States: From the Beginnings to the Present*, trans. Derek Coltman (Chicago: University of Chicago Press, 1978), pp. 46–48. Also see this same author's preface in Yves-Henri Nouailhat, *France et États-Unis: Août 1914–Avril 1917* (Paris: Presses de la Sorbonne, 1979), pp. 1–3.

38. André Tardieu, *France and America: Some Experiences in Cooperation* (Boston: Houghton Mifflin, 1927), pp. 302–3.

39. See Guido A. Dobbert, "German-Americans between New and Old Fatherland, 1870–1914," *American Quarterly* 19 (Winter 1967): 663–80; and Louis L. Gerson, *The Hyphenate in Recent American Politics and Diplomacy* (Lawrence: University Press of Kansas, 1964), pp. 48–50.

40. Quoted in John G. Gazley, *American Opinion of German Unification, 1848–1871* (New York: Columbia University Press, 1926), pp. 486–87.

41. Warren Reed West, *Contemporary French Opinion on the American Civil War* (Baltimore: Johns Hopkins Press, 1924); Lynn Marshall Case and Warren F. Spencer, *The United States and France: Civil War Diplomacy* (Philadelphia: University of Pennsylvania Press, 1970); and Belle Becker Sideman and Lillian Friedman, eds., *Europe Looks at the Civil War: An Anthology* (New York: Orion, 1960).

42. Manfred Jonas, *The United States and Germany: A Diplomatic History* (Ithaca, N.Y.: Cornell University Press, 1984), p. 18. Also see Jürgen Herbst, *The German Historical School in American Scholarship: A Study in the Transfer of Culture* (Ithaca, N.Y.: Cornell University Press, 1965); Carl Diehl, *Americans and German Scholarship, 1770–1870* (New Haven, Conn.: Yale University Press, 1978); and Charles F. Thwing, *The American and German University: One Hundred Years of History* (New York: Macmillan, 1928).

43. Quoted in Elizabeth Brett White, *American Opinion of France: From Lafayette to Poincaré* (New York: Alfred A. Knopf, 1927), pp. 178–79.

44. On the rise and decline of the German image in America see Daniel T. Rodgers, *Atlantic Crossings: Social Politics in a Progressive Age* (Cambridge, Mass.: Harvard University Press, 1998); Clara Eve Schieber, *The Transformation of American Sentiment toward Germany, 1870–1914* (New York: Russell and Russell, 1923); and Ido Oren, "The Subjectivity of the 'Democratic' Peace: Changing U.S. Perceptions of Imperial Germany," in *Debating the Democratic Peace*, ed. Michael E. Brown, Sean M. Lynn-Jones, and Steven E. Miller (Cambridge, Mass.: MIT Press, 1997), pp. 263–300.

45. Quoted in Henry Blumenthal, *A Reappraisal of Franco-American Relations, 1830–1871* (Chapel Hill: University of North Carolina Press, 1959), p. 196.

46. Compare the comment of one historian who asserted that given the lopsided disproportion in the respective diasporas' size—German-born Americans accounting in 1870 for 1.7 million out of a total population of slightly more than 38 million (or 4 percent) versus fewer than 100,000 French-born Americans when the war started—"[h]ere was an opportunity to play for the German vote which no politician could fail to see." Gazley, *American Opinion of German Unification*, pp. 336–37.

47. Henry Cord Meyer, *Five Images of Germany: Half a Century of American Views on German History* (Washington, D.C.: Service Center for Teachers of History, 1960), pp. 3–4.

48. See Stanley Nadel, *Little Germany: Ethnicity, Religion, and Class in New York City, 1845–80* (Urbana: University of Illinois Press, 1990), p. 82: "[T]he one political issue that could be counted on to unite the Germans was opposition to Sunday closing laws, which threatened not only German-American culture but particularly the livelihood of the German-American saloonkeepers."

49. Josiah Flynt, "The German and the German-American," *Atlantic Monthly* 78 (November 1896): 655–65, quote at pp. 662–63.

50. John Higham, *Strangers in the Land: Patterns of American Nativism, 1860–1925* (New York: Atheneum, 1971), p. 196; and Frederick A. Bushee, *Ethnic Factors in the Population of Boston* (New York: Macmillan/American Economic Association, 1903).

51. Howard B. Woolston, "Rating the Nations: A Study in the Statistics of Opinion," *American Journal of Sociology* 22 (November 1916): 381–90. Not only did this analyst regard German Americans to be the highest-quality immigrants, but he claimed that as an *ethnicity* they were only outranked by "native white Americans" in esteem accorded to group (p. 383).

52. Catholics made up a significant minority (around 35 percent) of a German immigrant stream into the United States that remained, throughout the nineteenth century, majoritarian Protestant. See Philip Gleason, *The Conservative Reformers: German-American Catholics and the Social Order* (Notre Dame, Ind.: University of Notre Dame Press, 1968).

53. James Joll, *The Anarchists* (New York: Grosset and Dunlap, 1966), p. 96. Also see Paul Avrich, *The Russian Anarchists* (Princeton, N.J.: Princeton University Press, 1971); and George Woodcock, *Anarchism: A History of Libertarian Ideas and Movements* (New York: World, 1962).

54. Quoted in Tom Goyens, *Beer and Revolution: The German Anarchist Movement in New York City, 1880–1914* (Urbana: University of Illinois Press, 2007), p. 21.

55. Nadel, *Little Germany*, p. 41.

56. See Rudolf Rocker, *Johann Most, das Leben eines Rebellen* (Berlin: Verlag Syndikalist, 1924); and Frederic Trautmann, *The Voice of Terror: A Biography of Johann Most* (Westport, Conn.: Greenwood Press, 1980).

57. Niall Whelehan, *The Dynamiters: Irish Nationalism and Political Violence in the Wider World, 1867–1900* (Cambridge: Cambridge University Press, 2012), p. 160.

58. Johann Most, *Revolutionäre Kriegswissenschaft: Eine Handbüchlein zur Anleitung Betreffend Gebrauches und Herstellung von Nitro-Glycerin, Dynamit, Schiessbaumwolle, Knallquecksilber, Bomben, Brandsätzen, Giften usw., usw.* (New York: Internationaler Zeitung-Verein, 1885).

59. Paul H. Avrich, *The Haymarket Tragedy* (Princeton, N.J.: Princeton University Press, 1984), p. 209. Also see Henry David, *The History of the Haymarket Affair: A Study in the American Social-Revolutionary and Labor Movements*, 2nd ed. (New York: Russell and Russell, 1958); and Richard Green, *Death in the Market: A Story of Chicago, the First Labor Movement, and the Bombing that Divided Gilded Age America* (New York: Pantheon Books, 2006).

60. Avrich, *Haymarket Tragedy*, pp. 376–78. Also see, for Haymarket's impact on the German (and German American) image, Jörg Nagler, "From Culture to *Kultur*: Changing American Perceptions of Imperial Germany, 1870–1914," in *Transatlantic Images*

and Perceptions: Germany and America Since 1776, ed. David E. Barclay and Elisabeth Glaser-Schmidt (Cambridge: Cambridge University Press, 1997), pp. 131–54, citing pp. 148–49.

61. See Richard Jensen, "Daggers, Rifles and Dynamite: Anarchist Terrorism in Nineteenth Century Europe," *Terrorism and Political Violence* 16 (Spring 2004): 116–53; and, for a contemporary assessment, F. L. Oswald, "The Assassination Mania: Its Social and Ethical Significance," *North American Review* 171 (September 1900): 314–19.

62. Eric Rauchway, *Murdering McKinley: The Making of Theodore Roosevelt's America* (New York: Hill and Wang, 2003), p. 17. Also see Sidney Fine, "Anarchism and the Assassination of McKinley," *American Historical Review* 60 (July 1955): 777–99.

63. Dov S. Zakheim, "What's in a Name? Ending the 'War' on Terror," *American Interest* 3 (May/June 2008): 17–24, quote on p. 18.

64. Georg von Skal, *History of German Immigration in the United States and Successful German-Americans and Their Descendants* (New York: F. T. and J. Smiley, 1908), p. 41.

65. Von Skal, *History of German Immigration in the United States*, p. 21.

66. In fact, claims such as these have been subject to much critical scrutiny in the past several decades, none more so than the thesis that Lincoln's election was owed to the German American vote in 1860. See Joseph Schafer, "Who Elected Lincoln?" *American Historical Review* 47 (October 1941): 51–63; and Andreas Dorpalen, "The German Element and the Issues of the Civil War," *Mississippi Valley Historical Review* 29 (June 1942): 55–76.

67. Rudolf Cronau, *Drei Jahrhunderte deutschen Lebens in Amerika: Eine Geschichte der Deutschen in den Vereinigten Staaten* (Berlin: Dietrich Reimer, 1909).

68. Dorothy Ross, "Historical Consciousness in Nineteenth-Century America," *American Historical Review* 89 (October 1984): 909–28, quote at p. 919.

69. Price Collier, *Germany and the Germans: From an American Point of View* (London: Duckworth, 1913), p. 15.

70. Quoted in Dobbert, "German-Americans between New and Old Fatherland," p. 676.

71. Edward N. Saveth, *American Historians and European Immigrants, 1875–1925* (New York: Russell and Russell, 1965; orig. pub. 1948), p. 42.

72. One racialist theoretician would go even further during the war, ejecting the Germans from the so-called Teutonic camp altogether, on the basis of their actually being much more an "Alpine" than a "Nordic" people, with Teutons considered a subset of the latter! See Madison Grant, *The Passing of the Great Race, or the Racial Basis of European History* (London: G. Bell and Sons, 1919), pp. 231–32.

73. See Richard T. Vann, "The Free Anglo-Saxons: A Historical Myth," *Journal of the History of Ideas* 19 (April 1958): 259–72; and Reginald Horsman, *Race and Manifest Destiny: The Origins of American Racial Anglo-Saxonism* (Cambridge, Mass.: Harvard University Press, 1981), pp. 10–24.

74. Quoted in Russell A. Kazal, *Becoming Old Stock: The Paradox of German-American Identity* (Princeton, N.J.: Princeton University Press, 2004), p. 119.

75. John W. Burgess, "Germany, Great Britain, and the United States," *Political Science Quarterly* 19 (March 1904): 1–19, quote at p. 2 (emphasis added).

76. Burgess, "Germany, Great Britain, and the United States," pp. 13–14, 18–19. Nor was Burgess the only Ivy League professor enthusiastic about a Teutonic alliance. As late as July 1916 Harvard's Hugo Münsterberg could argue, in an article in the *New York Times Magazine* entitled "The Allies of the Future," in favor of a geostrategic bonding between the "three Teutonic master nations" (the United States, the UK, and Germany). Quoted in Phyllis Keller, *States of Belonging: German-American Intellectuals and the First World War* (Cambridge, Mass.: Harvard University Press, 1979), pp. 100–1.

77. See, for the impact of geopolitical developments upon political cognitive frameworks, Ido Oren, *Our Enemies and US: America's Rivalries and the Making of Political Science* (Ithaca, N.Y.: Cornell University Press, 2003).

78. This comment was made by the British ambassador to the United States, Cecil Spring Rice, to his country's foreign minister, Edward Grey, ironically at a moment, in

mid-June 1916, when the British government itself was very concerned that beer and whisky were mixing rather too well in America; quoted in Stephen Hartley, *The Irish Question as a Problem in British Foreign Policy, 1914–18* (London: Macmillan, 1987), p. 114.

79. Noel Ignatiev, *How the Irish Became White* (New York: Routledge, 1995).

80. Charles B. Davenport, *Heredity in Relation to Eugenics* (New York: H. Holt, 1911). For a critique of this and other contemporary attempts to "scientifically" establish a genetic basis of socioeconomic differentiation, see Stephen Jay Gould, *The Mismeasure of Man* (New York: W. W. Norton, 1981).

81. Quoted in Matthew Frye Jacobson, *Barbarian Virtues: The United States Encounters Foreign Peoples at Home and Abroad, 1876–1917* (New York: Hill and Wang, 2000), pp. 158–59.

82. Kevin Kenny, *The American Irish: A History* (New York: Longman, 2000), p. 169. Also see, on tension between the two ethnic groups, Colman J. Barry, *The Catholic Church and German Americans* (Milwaukee, Wisc.: Bruce, 1953).

83. Gazley, *American Opinion of German Unification*, pp. 367–68.

84. Finley Peter Dunne, *Mr. Dooley in Peace and in War* (Boston: Small, Maynard, 1898), chap. 13: "On the Anglo-Saxon."

85. For a skeptical view of the thesis that Ireland and Britain were ever conquered by Celts from the continent, see Simon James, *The Atlantic Celts: Ancient People or Modern Invention?* (Madison: University of Wisconsin Press, 1999).

86. See Raymond J. Cunningham, "The German Historical World of Herbert Baxter Adams: 1874–1876," *Journal of American History* 68 (September 1981): 261–75.

87. Thomas N. Brown, "The Origins and Character of Irish-American Nationalism," *Review of Politics* 18 (July 1956): 327–58, quote at pp. 342–43.

88. Quoted in Hartley, *Irish Question*, pp. 3–4.

89. Quoted in Don Heinrich Tolzmann, ed., *German Achievements in America: Rudolf Cronau's Survey History* (Bowie, Md.: Heritage Books, 1995), pp. 218–19. This is a reprint, with an editorial preface, of Rudolf Cronau's *German Achievements in America: A Tribute to the Memory of the Men and Women Who Worked, Fought and Died for the Welfare of This Country; and a Recognition of the Living Who with Equal Enterprise, Genius and Patriotism Helped in the Making of the United States* (New York: Rudolf Cronau, 1916).

90. Charles Thomas Johnson, *Culture at Twilight: The National German-American Alliance, 1901–1918* (New York: Peter Lang, 1999). For attempts to portray the NGAA as the Kaiser's minion, see Frederic William Wile, *The German-American Plot* (London: Pearson, 1915); and William H. Skaggs, *German Conspiracies in America* (London: T. Fisher Unwin, 1915).

91. Quoted in Dean R. Esslinger, "American German and Irish Attitudes toward Neutrality, 1914–1917: A Study of Catholic Minorities," *Catholic Historical Review* 53 (July 1967): 194–216, quote at p. 203. This is especially significant given how riven the German American diaspora had earlier been, on religious grounds; apropos of which one scholar has written, "[n]o other European people had been so divided historically between Catholic and Protestants . . . Suspicion, envy, persecution, and hatred of Germans for Germans was standard . . . [N]one was so deeply divided along religious lines as the German." Luebke, *Bonds of Loyalty*, p. 34.

92. See, on this point, Edward Cuddy, "Pro-Germanism and American Catholicism, 1914–1917," *Catholic Historical Review* 54 (October 1968): 427–54, citing from p. 446.

93. Luebke, *Bonds of Loyalty*, pp. 45–47. Also see Carl F. Wittke, *The German Language Press in America* (Lexington: University Press of Kentucky, 1957).

94. Somewhere between 10 and 15 percent of the soldiers in the American Expeditionary Force were said to have been German Americans. See Ronald Fernandez, "Getting Germans to Fight Germans: The Americanizers of World War I," *Journal of Ethnic Studies* 9 (Summer 1981): 53–68.

95. Quoted in Clifton James Child, *The German-Americans in Politics, 1914–1917* (Madison: University of Wisconsin Press, 1939), pp. 163–64.

96. John P. Buckley, *The New York Irish: Their View of American Foreign Policy, 1914–1921* (New York: Arno Press, 1976).

97. Quoted in Michael Doorley, *Irish-American Diaspora Nationalism: The Friends of Irish Freedom, 1916–1935* (Dublin: Four Courts Press, 2005), pp. 37–38.

98. Hartley, *Irish Question*, p. 30, quoting the Washington correspondent of London's *Morning Post*.

99. See Goyens, *Beer and Revolution*.

100. See Felix Gilbert, *To the Farewell Address: Ideas of Early American Foreign Policy* (Princeton, N.J.: Princeton University Press, 1961).

101. Early in the following year Bartholdt would become the first president of the joint German-Irish "American Independence League." See his memoirs, *From Steerage to Congress: Reminiscences and Reflections* (Philadelphia: Dorrance, 1930), pp. 376–79.

102. Quoted in Clifton James Child, "German-American Attempts to Prevent Exportation of Munitions of War, 1914–1915," *Mississippi Valley Historical Review* 25 (December 1938): 351–68, quote at p. 353.

103. Child, *German-Americans in Politics*, pp. 58–65.

104. "The Germanisation of the United States," *National Review* 65 (March 1915): 41–51, quote at pp. 50–51.

105. In fact, one of his biographers reports that Roosevelt, who had as a teenager spent five months in Dresden in 1873, and who was reasonably proficient in German, never could bring himself to feel that Germans "were really foreigners"; quoted in H. W. Brands, *T.R.: The Last Romantic* (New York: Basic Books, 1997), p. 43. Also see, for Roosevelt's "complex relationship" with Germany, Séverine Antigone Marin, "Personalized Competition: Theodore Roosevelt and Kaiser Wilhelm in German-American Relations," in *America's Transatlantic Turn: Theodore Roosevelt and the "Discovery" of Europe*, ed. Hans Krabbendam and John M. Thompson (New York: Palgrave Macmillan, 2012), pp. 121–40.

106. On Roosevelt's changing assessment of Germany, see Russell Buchanan, "Theodore Roosevelt and American Neutrality, 1914–1917," *American Historical Review* 43 (July 1938): 775–90; and Lloyd E. Ambrosius, "The Great War, Americanism Revisited, and the Anti-Wilson Crusade," in *A Companion to Theodore Roosevelt*, ed. Serge Ricard (Chichester, UK: Wiley-Blackwell, 2011), pp. 468–84.

107. "All against Roosevelt and Wilson," quoted in Johnson, *Culture at Twilight*, p. 116.

108. In particular, see Mark R. Levy and Michael S. Kramer, *The Ethnic Factor: How America's Minorities Decide Elections* (New York: Simon & Schuster, 1972).

109. Walter Dean Burnham, *Critical Elections and the Mainsprings of American Politics* (New York: W. W. Norton, 1970).

110. The respective cables are quoted in Buckley, *New York Irish*, pp. 90–91, 95–96.

111. Quoted in S. D. Lovell, *The Presidential Election of 1916* (Carbondale: Southern Illinois University Press, 1980), p. 18.

112. Ironically, the German ambassador in Washington, Johann Heinrich von Bernstorff, actually preferred that Wilson be reelected in 1916, though for obvious reasons he kept this hope to himself; see his *My Three Years in America* (New York: Charles Scribner's Sons, 1920), pp. 3–5.

113. Thomas J. Kerr IV, "German-Americans and Neutrality in the 1916 Election," *Mid-America* 43 (April 1961): 95–105.

114. According to one scholar, 1916 was the first presidential election since 1796 in which votes were "so readily determined by the stand which people had taken toward one side or the other in a foreign crisis in which the United States itself was, after all, not directly concerned." Child, *German-Americans in Politics*, pp. 152–53.

115. See R. A. Burchell, "Did the Irish and German Voters Desert the Democrats in 1920? A Tentative Statistical Answer," *Journal of American Studies* 6 (August 1972): 153–64.

116. Harding's popular-vote margin of victory (26.1 percent), though not his electoral-vote one, exceeded even the lopsided differentials registered by Franklin D. Roose-

velt over Alf Landon in 1936 (24.3 percent), Lyndon B. Johnson over Barry Goldwater in 1964 (22.6 percent), Richard Nixon over George McGovern in 1972 (23.2 percent), and Ronald Reagan over Walter Mondale in 1984 (18.2 percent).

117. Details of the extent of collaboration between Irish diasporic leaders and Berlin can be found in Charles Callan Tansill, *America and the Fight for Irish Freedom, 1866–1922: An Old Story Based upon New Data* (New York: Devin-Adair, 1957), pp. 174–87. Also see Felician Prill, *Ireland, Britain and Germany, 1871–1914: Problems of Nationalism and Religion in Nineteenth-Century Europe* (Dublin: Gill and Macmillan, 1975); Reinhard R. Doerries, *Iren und Deutsche in der Neuen Welt* (Stuttgart: Franz Steiner Verlag Wiesbaden, 1986); Doerries, "Die Mission Sir Roger Casements im Deutschen Reich, 1914–1916," *Historische Zeitschrift* 222 (1976): 578–625; and Giovanni Costigan, "The Treason of Sir Roger Casement," *American Historical Review* 60 (January 1955): 283–302.

118. In fact, there actually was a fairly sizable French diaspora in the United States at this time, it is just that it was not a particularly useful one insofar as French foreign policy objectives were concerned, as it was mainly a "secondhand" diaspora comprised of emigrants from French-speaking Quebec who had little love for the secular France of the Third Republic. See above, n. 36, as well as François Weil, *Les Franco-Américains, 1860–1980* (Paris: Belin, 1989).

119. Reinhold Niebuhr, "The Failure of German-Americanism," *Atlantic Monthly* 118 (January 1916): 13–18; reprinted as a chapter under the same title in *World War I at Home: Readings on American Life, 1914–1920*, ed. David F. Trask (New York: John Wiley and Sons, 1970), pp. 145–49.

120. See n. 27 above.

121. For an unapologetic expression of that logic, as expounded by an Irish American former mayor of Syracuse, N.Y., during the first year of the European fighting, see James K. McGuire, *The King, the Kaiser, and Irish Freedom* (New York: Devin-Adair, 1915).

122. Laurence Halley, *Ancient Affections: Ethnic Groups and Foreign Policy* (New York: Praeger, 1985), pp. 160–61.

SIX

"New Fenians" and "Homegrowns"

Jihadism and the Evolving North American Security Community

ON ANALOGIES AND METAPHORS

Over the past few years, a troubling and ostensibly novel phenomenon has arisen to complicate the regional and global security picture. That phenomenon bears the name of "homegrown" terrorism,[1] about which a great deal is being said and written lately, as a result of the ubiquitous presence of foreign jihadis on battlefields in Syria, Iraq, and elsewhere in the Middle East and northern Africa.[2] The phenomenon relates as fully to my objective in this book—namely, to assess the implications of certain demographic flows upon the origins and evolution of the North American security community—as any of the issues upon which we have concentrated in the two previous chapters. This is so, notwithstanding the number of obvious, sometimes even glaring, differences between the cases. What they have in common is the nexus between demography and continental security, each case in its own way demonstrating how diaspora-based political activists can and sometimes do pursue initiatives fraught with security consequences, both within North America and beyond. This is not to say that, in the case of Muslim North America, diasporic *leadership* entities are in any way supportive of activities linked to homegrown terrorism; quite the reverse, for groups claiming to speak and act on behalf of the diaspora have been nothing if not consistent in condemning the phenomenon, just as they have been consistent in condemning terrorism in general.[3] But simply recall the analogy drawn in chapter three, where diasporas stood as proxies for what Mao Zedong's theory of "agrarian socialism" took the peasantry to represent: they are the lake in which the activists swim, the presumption being that if there were no diaspora, there would be no homegrowns.

Because this chapter, with its focus on Muslim North Americans, is the third and last of the case studies, appeal can be had to some themes and tropes encountered previously. Right off the bat, it is not too difficult to adduce an *Irish* analogy, given that one conspicuous variant of recent and contemporary diasporic-based activity bears resemblance to a pattern of behavior that first began to characterize diasporic activism in the early post-Civil War years, when it was lumped under the rubric of Fenianism. Without running too much risk of semantic contortionism, we might even speak of the "new Fenianism" in reference to an aspect of jihadi activity dating from the latter half of the 1990s. This activity featured some radical Islamists, much like the Fenians of yore, seeking to use territory of one of the North American neighbors to strike at targets in the other; the difference this time, of course, is that Canada was to be the launching pad for attacks on the United States, rather than the reverse. For sure, no jihadis entertained the thought of mounting anything remotely approximating the kind of "invasion" that was the apple of many a Fenian's eye in the first few post-Civil War years; withal, there did occur a few instances of lone-wolf attackers hoping to inflict damage on high-profile American targets, and as we will discover later in this chapter, one of these episodes did have some fairly significant consequences for regional security, especially as concerned the management of the Canada-United States border, a topic we addressed in chapter one.

A second Irish motif is also discernable, this one in connection with the current widespread employment of the horticultural metaphor "homegrowns." As we remember, even though filibustering became a thing of the Fenian past following the last raid on Canada in 1870, physical-force nationalists continued to trouble North American security relations, partly as a result of their intermittent efforts to utilize a continental safe haven (in the event, the American "Waziristan") to mount operations across the Atlantic, especially during the 1880s' "dynamite war" on cities in the United Kingdom, at a time when Canadian and British strategic interests were largely overlapping, due to the imperial connection. Many of those bombing missions were carried out by discontented political activists who had either immigrated as children to the United States or had been born there to immigrant parents, the two biographical attributes so often associated with contemporary discussions of the continent's homegrowns—that they be born, or at least raised, in one or the other of the North American countries. One of the most active of all the Irish homegrowns was Luke Dillon, the dynamite campaign veteran who had arrived in the United States as a child, from his birthplace of Yorkshire in England, to which his parents had emigrated from County Sligo, in Ireland. Interestingly, Dillon is not known ever to have set foot on the soil of his ancestral homeland, Ireland, yet his commitment to the cause of fighting British rule over the Emerald Isle never wavered throughout his adult years.[4]

If at the level of tactics there are some similarities between the Irish American case and certain aspects of the contemporary Muslim North American one, there are also a great many differences worthy of note, which will be explored in detail below. For the moment, though, let us see how and why North American Muslims should have been finding themselves increasingly caught up in debates about the continent's regional security arrangements. The reason, of course, is not too difficult to comprehend, and is to be encountered in a widespread association, over the past two decades, between terrorism and Islamism throughout the transatlantic world and beyond—an association that comes into crispest focus when analysis turns to the jihadis.[5]

Terrorism, we know, is a far older and much more comprehensive political phenomenon than contemporary jihadism, which constitutes but an appendix in the lengthy record of what in the introduction was categorized as political activity mounted by "non-state armed actors," or "clandestine transnational actors." But it is a very important appendix, and it represents, to many, *the* face of contemporary terrorism, doing so since around the middle of the 1990s. This near-total identification of terrorism with jihadism accelerated in the years following 9/11. The result, not surprisingly, is that a diaspora that hitherto had been regarded as virtually irrelevant to North American security began to look like a latter-day equivalent of Irish America, or possibly even German America (though in a different sense, to be discussed in the concluding chapter). At least it so looked to a growing number of security analysts in the United States, and Canada, too, who saw in the political activism of some diaspora-related jihadis a host of looming problems with the potential of driving a wedge between the two North American neighbors, with worrisome implications for their security community.

For one student of North American regional security, jihadism a half-dozen years ago was said to be posing an irresolvable policy challenge for Canadian and U.S. security officials—a challenge to which he affixed the label the "homeland security dilemma." This scholar, Frank Harvey, summed up the dilemma epigrammatically, commenting that "the more security you have, the more security you will need."[6] The implication, for Canada as much as for the United States, was that government efforts to resolve the problem of terrorism striking North America would ultimately fall short of what the public demanded, for the public demands perfection and no matter how successful counterterrorism campaigns show themselves to be, if they do not achieve the impossible—perfection in preventing terrorist attacks—they will be deemed to have failed. Hence Harvey's pessimistic conclusion: the homeland security dilemma is permanent. Regardless of the energy and resources Canada might expend combatting terrorism, including (at the time he was writing) in far-off places such as Afghanistan, the crucial question would always remain not whether Canadian efforts had enhanced North American security, rather it would be "whether it really matters *even if they have.*" By this he suggests that nothing Canada does, or can do, will count for much in Washington "after the next failure."[7]

Harvey has not been alone in dwelling upon the somber implications for Canada that must inevitably stem from jihadist initiatives. In some respects, he can even be made to seem like a bit of an optimist. For during the alarming aftermath of 9/11, other analysts were beginning to wonder just how stable the North American security community could be, in face of the new and radically enhanced threat environment on the continent. In the context of that crisis atmosphere, the problem was often being conceptualized in terms of a *Canada-based* terrorist attack against *American* targets, of which there were a staggering number. One security expert in this emotionally intense period toted up the numbers of potential sites subject to terrorist assault in the United States, and found that the country possessed "almost 600,000 bridges, 170,000 water systems, more than 2,800 power plants (104 of them nuclear), 190,000 miles of interstate pipelines for natural gas, 463 skyscrapers, . . . nearly 20,000 miles of border, airports, stadiums, train tracks."[8]

While no one believed that there were enough terrorists in North America, or even the world, to threaten most, or even many, of these sites, it was imagined that some of these could and would be hit, what with the demonstration effect of the attacks on the World Trade Center and the Pentagon so fresh in people's minds. And should any attack be traceable back to a Canadian address, the consequences could be ominous, the assumption being that any likely U.S. response to such an attack would be bound to be so robust as effectively to put paid to Canada's claim to possess sovereign jurisdiction over its own territory. Nor was it only political scientists and other nongovernmental policy analysts who harbored doubts about the durability of what has been the world's most long-standing *uninterrupted* security community.[9] Some policy makers, as well, occasionally expressed similar forebodings. For instance, Jean Lapierre, while serving as Canada's minister of transport, disclosed to Harvard University's Graham Allison what he termed his "worst nightmare," namely that of a devastating terrorist attack mounted against American soil emanating from Canada.[10]

Lapierre left to the imagination what he thought the U.S. response to such an attack might be. Scholars who have pondered the same question have been less reticent to spell out that which politicians prefer either to avoid discussing altogether or only to skirt through generalities, should discussion prove unavoidable. One such academic observer is Patrick Lennox, who has studied Canada's own tougher response to terrorism in the period since 9/11 and has reached the conclusion that it was prompted more by anxiety about *the United States* than about the jihadis. As Lennox saw things, Canada "was compelled to take on the new security state form as defined and specified by its superordinate partner, the United States. Not mimicking the American response to the new transnational security threat in this way jeopardized Canada's economic *and sovereign* survival."[11] Although their manner of wording differed from his, both Joel Sokolsky and Philippe Lagassé concluded similarly, in asserting that "if the United States is harmed or perceives any imminent [terrorist] threat from the Canadian approach, the American government will do whatever is necessary to protect the homeland—be it closing the Canada-US border *or unilateral deployment of American forces into Canadian waters, airspace, or territory.*"[12]

Needless to say, the continued existence of the North American security community would certainly seem to be less than a safe bet, in the event that presentiments like these become realities. Still, it bears asking whether it really is, or ever was, the case that Canada *only* acted as it did on the homeland security front in order to forestall an otherwise unfortunate (for it) American response. In fact, there is reason to suspect that the scholars have drastically understated the degree to which Canadian policy makers themselves understood the jihadist threat as being one aimed not only at the United States, but at Canada as well, even if at first only indirectly so. What I mean is that prior to the emergence of clear evidence that Canadian homegrowns had been involved in plotting terrorist mayhem at home and actually carrying out attacks abroad (both to be addressed in subsequent sections of this chapter), it was not quite accurate to interpret Canada's response to 9/11, as so many have done, as representing either a preemptive bid to keep the United States from violating Canadian sovereignty, or a necessary means of keeping the border open to trade—and nothing else.

It is obvious that Canadian officials have been very concerned about keeping the border as open to peaceful exchange as it was possible to make it, just as it goes without saying that they cherish the goal of preserving inviolate the country's territorial sovereignty. But there was also an aspect of what Samuel Huntington once called "civilizational rallying"[13] associated with the Canadian response to the terrorist attacks on New York and Washington, if only for a very short time, and this sometimes gets overlooked by those who insist upon construing Ottawa's policy on counterterrorism as constituting solely a grudgingly obedient reaction to Washington's policies and dictates. This emotional overtone to Canadian policy can be glimpsed in the initial reaction of Canadian public and elite opinion in the days and weeks following 9/11, when massive pro-American rallies were held in Ottawa and elsewhere. The mood was captured best by the country's minister of foreign affairs, soon to become deputy prime minister, John Manley, who hinted that Ottawa was likely to adopt a fairly robust response to terrorism, and to do so side by side with its American ally. Speaking impromptu outside the House of Commons less than a week after the 9/11 attacks, Manley remarked that, despite what some in the country appeared (or wanted) to believe, "Canada does not have a history as a pacifist or neutralist country. Canada has soldiers that are buried all over Europe because we fought in defense of liberty. And we're not about to back away from a challenge now because we think somebody might get hurt."[14]

Admittedly, this spirit of solidarity would soon come under great strain, initially as a result of a particularly unfortunate incident in April 2002 in which an American F-16 pilot dropped a bomb on a Canadian night-training exercise in southern Afghanistan, killing four soldiers.[15] Then, a year later, occurred the divisive decision of the George W. Bush administration to invade Iraq, even though it was not apparent to most Canadians what Saddam Hussein had had to do with the 9/11 attacks. As the decade progressed, it looked as if Canada-United States relations had begun the same kind of downward trajectory evident in America's relations with some of its key European allies, France and Germany in particular. Often, though not always, it was divergent approaches to the "global war on terror" (the GWOT, as it was sometimes styled) that were at the root of bilateral tensions. But the rise of the homegrowns, as we will see later in this chapter, has had a paradoxical impact upon Canada-United States security cooperation, not unlike the one we discussed in the previous chapter, in which the "principle of the opposite effect" became triggered by German American (and Irish American) diasporic activism during the period immediately preceding America's entry into the First World War. I explain in fuller detail below what I mean in making this perhaps counterintuitive comment.

First, though, we need to attend to a few background matters, beginning with a discussion of the contemporary nature of the jihadi challenge. Following this comes an analysis of the Muslim diasporas in the two North American countries, after which we shall proceed to trace some of the more prominent instances of jihadi activity within North America, from the initial filibustering phase to the contemporary anxiety about the homegrowns.

ORIGINS AND EVOLUTION OF JIHADISM

In the early summer of 2014, the Obama administration announced that it would be reinserting some American military forces into Iraq.[16] More than half of the five hundred or so soldiers initially earmarked for this mission were intended to serve not as combatants but as advisers to the beleaguered government of Nuri Kamal al Maliki, at the time confronting a surprisingly virile challenge from Sunni extremists orchestrated under the banner of the Islamic State in Iraq and Syria (ISIS), the same group that has been so active in the Syrian civil war.[17] The reemergence of Islamic terrorism as the cynosure of Western security preoccupations — until, that is, the crisis in Ukraine and the sharp downturn in the West's relations with Russia resulting from the July 2014 downing of Malaysian Airlines Flight 17 by Russian-backed Ukrainian separatists[18] — is not something that would have been expected just a few years earlier, when it began to look as if the corner in the struggle against jihadis had definitively been turned. Indeed, during the first year of the Obama administration, the omens were reasonably propitious on the terrorism front, and to many security officials in and out of power in Washington, Ottawa, and other capitals, it seemed as if the worst was behind them, with al Qaeda in particular held to be gravely, and quite likely mortally, wounded.

Even prior to the November 2008 election of Barack Obama it was becoming possible to descry the impending collapse of the jihadi challenge to Western security interests, with many analysts starting to argue not only that the terrorist threat was inflated, but that it had *always* been inflated, in keeping with a persistent pattern, or so they said, of threat exaggeration in the United States that stretched back for many, many years.[19] John Mueller, a professor of international relations at Ohio State University, could lament in mid-2008 his country's "false sense of insecurity."[20] Six months later, another American, this time a journalist not a professor, could add the comforting reassurance that the "likelihood of a terrorist attack on the United States in its early stages by [a]l Qaeda is close to zero."[21] Others, elsewhere, agreed, and not just in respect of jihadis' ability to strike at America, but also at its allies. By the late summer of 2009 the respected Paris daily *Le Monde* would publish a special supplement on al Qaeda that came close to pronouncing the terrorist group defunct.[22] Frequent were the allusions to different, more serious, hazards facing citizens of the United States and other Western countries, where it was routinely (and not necessarily inaccurately) being remarked that they ran a far, far greater risk of being done in by lightning bolts, bathtub drownings, or even falling coconuts, than they did of being killed by terrorists.[23]

Today, we realize how premature tidings of counterterrorism progress really were, even if for the moment the *direct* threat to North American security is much less than it was at the start of this century, and that lightning and bathtubs (though not coconuts) are indeed claiming more lives on North American soil each year than are terrorists. While it is probably true that al Qaeda itself is in less than robust condition when contrasted with its salad days of a decade and a half ago, other groups, some related to it, some not, have sprouted to join it on the list of sworn enemies of Western countries, in a dizzying profusion of new guises. These groups are increasingly spreading chaos and destruction to broader regions, including in parts of sub-Saharan and eastern Africa.[24] So diffuse has been the nature of the current stable of entities involved, one way or the other, in Islamist terrorism that to ascribe to jihadis any *particular* agenda, or set of agreed objectives to be secured through political violence, is a Herculean task. But let us try nonetheless to establish whether there exists some overarching desideratum that might provide clues as to whether the contemporary challenge, especially as it can be and has been associated with diasporic groups in North America and elsewhere, is likely to be resolved any time soon. In this respect, it should be kept in mind that the Irish Question about which so much was said in chapter four remained for *several decades* both a leading problem in transatlantic security and a visible reminder of the impact diasporic activism could have upon the North American regional security order, and beyond. By contrast, German American diasporic activism—almost all of it of a nonviolent nature—had a relatively short existence, lasting only fifteen or so years, with important consequences, even if not the ones intended by the activists, for North American and transatlantic security.

To determine whether there may be, as some prematurely assumed a few years ago, light at the end of the proverbial tunnel when it comes to Islamist terrorism, let us try to make some analytical sense of the current struggle being prosecuted by the jihadis.[25] The first comment that requires being made is that the ongoing chaos we are daily witnessing cannot realistically be said to represent the mooted Huntingtonian "clash of civilizations" that was making the rounds, in some quarters, twenty years ago. Back then, it did look to Samuel Huntington and some others as if the principal fault lines in international security were henceforth to be "civilizational" ones, the most salient of which would be that separating a presumably coherent Islamic entity from its mooted religious-civilizational adversaries, comparably coherent, elsewhere (take your pick: Christians, Jews, Hindus, Buddhists, animists, etc.). While it is obvious that some jihadi violence, for instance in parts of Africa, does indeed betray signs of a clash between Islamic elements and their "civilizational" foes, the most significant violence associated with jihadis these days actually involves their combat against fellow Muslims. The ongoing civil conflicts in Syria and now Iraq show some signs of developing into evernastier sectarian struggles, pitting many Sunni Muslims (followers of the traditions, or *sunnah*) against their coreligionists, the Shia Muslims (partisans of Ali).

This internecine religious cleavage, with roots going back to the seventh century, is *the* "fault line" of most importance in the contemporary Middle East,[26] and it is this civil war within Islam that is doing so much to fuel the growing concern with the horticultural metaphor of homegrowns. Specifically, the worry in the West is that radicalized elements of the Muslim diasporas in the United States, Canada, and other Western countries will heed the call of jihad, as interpreted according to their own lights (or at least the lights of their radicalizing mentors), and go off to combat sectarian (i.e., "infidel") foes abroad, often though not exclusively to be found in parts of the Muslim world where non-Sunnis either hold or attempt to hold on to power. The risk is twofold: that these homegrowns will jeopardize Western interests indirectly by spreading chaos in regions of strategic significance to the West, and more worrisomely, *directly* by returning home to carry on the struggle against whatever they take to be their enemy within their respective host countries.[27] As expressed by one Canadian journalist, the latter prospect is even more of a problem: "Hundreds of ISIL fighters are young men from North America and Europe. If they survive, many will eventually make their way home, creating unknown but surely scary possibilities."[28]

So, what *do* the jihadis assume to be their enemy within that part of the world (i.e., the West, including North America) in which their sectarian foes of the moment, not just the Shias but also many fellow Sunnis, do not happen either to be in power or even to be particularly thick on the ground? To answer this, let us take a look at what some scholars have referred to as terrorism's "fourth wave,"[29] one in which political activism is primarily motivated by a religious orientation toward reality, with that orientation largely though not entirely stemming from within Sunni Islam. In finer detail, the agenda of contemporary jihadism is fuelled by a *Salafist* interpretation of God and reality.[30]

We can take Salafi terrorism as referring to a cause with two principal objectives. First, it seeks the imposition of the Sharia (Islamic law) as the fundamental law in every land where Muslims live in preponderant numbers. Second, it looks forward to the eventual creation of a single government over the *ummah* (or world Islamic community) stretching from Morocco to the Philippines and Indonesia.[31] *Salafiyah* means tradition (from the Arabic *salaf*, or "ancient one"), as distilled through a very literal reading of the Koran. Salafis are not at all enthusiasts of figurative interpretations of Koranic precepts, but instead evince a puritanism dedicated to restoring Islam to its original, presumably unadulterated, form. Not all Salafis support the use of violence, though; in fact, historically, the best known Salafi movement was a nonviolent one, the Tablighi Jamaat (Society for the Propagation of Islam), created in India in 1927.[32]

Salafis who embrace violence do so in the name of jihad (striving). Islamic scholars disagree about the proper sense of the concept of jihad, with many holding that what they sometimes refer to as "greater jihad" is meant to be a spiritual not a physical struggle waged by individual Muslims, warding off the constant and many temptations of sin against the faith. Others, however, take jihad in a more literal, and kinetic, sense, one that presupposes an ongoing war against real-world "enemies" of Islam, wherever they may be encountered. Reflective of this interpretation of the meaning of jihad are the words of Abdallah Azzam, who had been a key figure in rallying foreign mujahedeen against the Soviet Union in Afghanistan: "a Muslim who is not performing jihad today is just like one who breaks the fast in Ramadan without permission, or a rich person who withholds legal alms. Indeed, failing to carry out jihad is more serious still."[33]

Kinetic jihad, like any other kind of combat, can be waged either offensively or defensively, the difference between the two revolving primarily around the agency of that, or those, spearheading the struggle — that is, whether it is the government of an Islamic state, or individual Muslims no matter where they may happen to reside. When we speak of the homegrowns, it is obviously defensive jihadism that springs first to mind, with its primary manifestation being a general call to arms in defense of the land of Islam under threat from infidels, or even of lands that once were under Islamic rule, but ceased to be. Again, to quote Azzam apropos the anti-Soviet campaign in Afghanistan a generation ago, the duty of jihad "shall not lapse with victory in Afghanistan, and the jihad will remain an individual obligation until all lands which formerly were Muslim come back to us and Islam reigns within them once again. Before us lie Palestine, Bukhara, Lebanon, Chad, Eritrea, Somalia, the Philippines, Burma, South Yemen, Tashkent, Andalusia."[34] This was quite a shopping list, and certainly was one that inspired Azzam's quondam subaltern, Osama bin Laden, who had an even more capacious sense of the battlefield.[35]

For bin Laden, attacking the West, *anywhere*, was part of a defensive jihad waged to protect the Muslim community as a whole against foreign intrusion. Hence his obsession with what he took to be the most egregious such incursion, the one set in motion by the deployment of U.S. troops to Saudi Arabia and elsewhere in the Middle East to counteract Saddam Hussein's forcible annexation of Kuwait in the summer of 1990. Responses to the infidel would not be limited to the region of the Persian Gulf, but could also be conducted in such other places as Palestine, Chechnya, Bosnia, Tajikistan, Burma, the Philippines, Kashmir, Somalia, Lebanon — and even North America and Western Europe. As bin Laden interpreted matters, "every Muslim who is capable of doing so has the personal duty to kill Americans and their allies, whether civilians or military personnel, in every country where this is possible."[36]

Nor was the target list merely to be restricted to Americans and their allies; just about everyone else could be fair game, as bin Laden's lieutenant Ayman al Zawahiri explained in his manifesto, "Knights under the Prophet's Banner." To the enemy list of Western crusaders had to be added Russian ones as well, and for good measure could be tossed in the United Nations, multinational corporations, Middle Eastern regimes allied with any or all of the above, and international broadcasting outlets, as well as a wide variety of nongovernmental organizations involved in providing humanitarian assistance.[37] After defensive jihad had secured the immediate goal of expelling the crusaders from the land of Islam, the offensive stage of kinetic jihad could begin, for once Muslim unity became enshrined through the establishment of the caliphate, the latter could be energized to take the struggle far and wide, with the ultimate aim being, as Sayyd Qutb, one of the inspirations of contemporary Salafists, put it some half century ago, nothing less than to "establish the Divine system on earth." [38]

Interpreted thusly, Salafi jihadism can easily translate into a never-ending struggle to bring about, in the delusional manner of so many millenarian movements that have preceded it, heaven on earth. Interpreted thusly, therefore, one can take two things for granted: 1) the dream of the Salafi militants cannot, and never will, be capable of realization, not in this world at least; and 2) Salafist jihadis will, like the poor, always be with us. Does this mean therefore that diasporic activism, because of the connection between it, Salafist jihadis, and the homegrowns, must be a constant security problem, in North America as elsewhere? After all, when contrasted with the Salafists' agenda, the Irish American nationalists' struggle for a republic, and a fortiori the German Americans' quest to defend both their identity and the interests of the Fatherland, can appear to be consummate flashes in the pan, as well as the very embodiment of modesty in geopolitical imaginings. The Irish American physical force enthusiasts had, be it recalled, a very selective target list, one that dwindled virtually to nothing once the Free State came into being. As for German American diasporic activism that ran in the direction of violent endeavors (not very much of it actually did, since the bulk of that diaspora's energies was dedicated to lobbying, broadly construed), this was even more restrictive in its focus, with saboteurs attempting a few strikes at infrastructural targets in Canada and the United States (bridges, railway lines, munitions factories, and port facilities) during the years 1914–1917. By contrast, as far as the Salafist jihadis are concerned, the sky seems to be the limit: no one, and nowhere, is deemed safe from their violent ministrations, such that even should the vanquishing of the "near enemy" occur (it won't), this would simply set the stage for pouncing ever more robustly upon the "far enemy." [39]

Before we are tempted to leap to the conclusion that, of our three cases of diasporic activism surveyed in this book, this recent one is by far the most worrisome one due to its expansive objectives, we need to take a closer look at the North American Muslim diaspora. This might enable us to arrive at a kind of "situational awareness" of what, to say again, is not a new problem in North American security affairs, but rather just a variation on an old theme. Situational awareness is not an invitation to complacency, merely a reminder that there may be value, not only for scholars but also for policy makers, in assessing matters in a comparative historical context. Before moving on, in the concluding chapter seven, to such an assessment, let us wrap up this particular case study by concentrating, in this chapter's next two sections, on analyzing the North American Muslim diaspora, examining the experience of the "filibustering" incidents of the second half of the 1990s, and discussing the implications of the more recent homegrown phenomenon for Canada-United States security cooperation.

NORTH AMERICA'S MUSLIM DIASPORA

The mention made, in this book's preface, to Peter T. King's committee hearings on radicalization and the Muslim diaspora, was apposite, for more than one reason. The hearings provided an ironical, if unintentional, entrée into this book's broad thematic emphasis upon diasporic-related activism and the North American security community, by drawing in the two diasporas that serve to bracket, chronologically, the three case study chapters, the Irish Americans (King's own group) and the Muslim North Americans. As well, by raising the specter of "disloyalty" on the part of Muslim diasporic leadership, the King committee also served as a handy conceptual bridge to the German American case study, for it was above all suspicion about their "dual" loyalties that rendered the position of German Americans so difficult once the United States entered the First World War in April 1917. Thus the Muslim North Americans have something in common with both the Irish Americans (the shared experience of the homegrowns) and the German Americans (the suspicion that they might not be as diligent as they should be in combatting the threat from within diasporic ranks—that is, that they are not to be trusted as loyal Americans or Canadians).

For a while, it was not unusual to find the threat being framed in terms that were deliberatively evocative of the era of great-power warfare, albeit with the reference being more to the Second than to the First World War. This evocative analogy was clearly intended by those who chose to construe the phenomenon of Salafist jihadism as representing nothing other than "Islamofascism,"[40] though some scholars of fascism could and did find the comparison between what is essentially a modern political movement with one so rooted in pre-modernity to be more than a little jarring, and certainly anachronistic.[41] Nested inside this suggestive label was a second image, of "fifth columnists" who were prepared to wreak their havoc from *within* (the numerical allusion in this case paying tribute to the boast made by one of Francisco Franco's generals, Emilio Mola, that the Spanish capital would fall not because of the four armed nationalist columns descending upon Madrid during the country's civil war, but because of a fifth one, inside the city itself). To be sure, none of the congressmen who were taking testimony regarding the activities of the Council on American-Islamic Relations made explicit reference to fifth columnists, but it was obvious from the thrust of the Republican majority's criticism of the Council on American-Islamic Relations (CAIR) that they held the organization, and presumably other diasporic activists in leadership roles, to be responsible for encouraging, or at least not preventing, the spread of radicalism among Muslim youth, with the implication being fairly clear as to the security threat this spread constituted for the United States. To the extent that similar radicalization was occurring north of the border, so too was Canadian security said to be at risk. In the event the two North American countries should adopt different responses to the threat, there was then a further danger, namely of their security community being called into question.

So to cut to the contemporary chase, we can say that the Muslim North American diaspora attracts attention because of the worry that it constitutes a security challenge of serious proportions. But is it really this kind of challenge? To answer this, a bit of contextualization is in order. At the outset, two important differences between Muslim North America and both Irish America and German America need highlighting. The first concerns that aspect of identity that presumably serves to orient group allegiance, and in so doing provides the necessary element of "collective identity" that stimulates and gives purpose to group activism. The second concerns size.

As to the first of these issues, it is clear that whatever might be said to represent the core of a Muslim collective identity, it is not, and cannot be, a sentimental attachment to an "ancestral homeland," unless such attachment is rooted in the notion of the *ummah* as construed more in a territorial and juridical sense than in a spiritual one. As we realize from chapter three, some students of diasporas will even tell us that absent the homeland—real or imagined—there can be no affective linkage sufficient to justify anyone's labelling *any* community as a diaspora. To these analysts, diasporas must have as their referent object some spot of land with which their membership develops strong emotional bonds fortified by nationalism. But as we also discovered in that same chapter, there are those who do insist upon expanding the list of "objective correlatives" of diasporic emotionalism beyond those politico-juridical entities we call states, or even those sociological ones we call nations. And for these analysts, religion can also serve as the rallying point for such emotionalism. Needless to say, my purposes in this book have required me to adopt a more expansive understanding of "ethnicity," and therefore of ethnic diasporas, one that has the ideational cement of collective identity being supplied by many ingredients, including (along with territory) language, physical resemblance, and *religion*.[42] In any event, the expansive application of the concept has already become such a commonplace as to render any attempt to restrict the diaspora category only to those groups whose affective attentions are focused upon territorial-based entities an exercise in futility. Thus it is hardly unusual to encounter references to the "Muslim diaspora," in North America and elsewhere.[43]

Still, it does matter whether the referent object of a group's collective striving is a territorial homeland or something less rooted in real estate. It matters because religions are more subject to sectarianism, by their very nature, than are collective identities expressed in and through nationalism. This does not, of course, in any way exempt nationalism from the taint of factionalism, for if it did the history of Irish, and especially Irish American, nationalist strivings would have been very different, to take just one example among many. But it does lead to the supposition that, all things being equal, collective identities shaped around religion tend to be more prone to fracturing than do those "constructed" with the goal of responding to the exigencies of homeland interest, however this latter may be conceived by diasporic activists. Moreover, as we saw with the German Americans' experience in the previous chapter, concern for those exigencies had a way of trumping collective identities that had been initially anchored in religion (in this case, those of a majority Protestant German community versus a large minority of German Catholics). The thrust, then, of these observations would appear apparent: diasporas whose identity is mainly predicated upon religious sentiments will not be as effective in promoting a coherent agenda as are those that have the lure of an established or imagined homeland to give shape and energy to their strivings.

Thus while in a certain superficial sense it must be obvious that North America's Muslim populations would have a common ideational core of their collective political yearnings, especially as these latter are quite legal and consistent with the broad definition of "lobbying" offered in chapter three, it is not surprising to find serious obstacles placed by sectarianism in the path of sustained and coherent action. Contrary to widespread perceptions of Islam as somehow being monolithic, a considerable degree of internal diversity and even rivalry exists within the religion, which has unavoidable spillover effects upon the Muslim diaspora, in North America no less than elsewhere. Nor is it simply a matter of the abovementioned cleavage between the Sunnis and the Shias, so reminiscent of an earlier armed split within Christianity, separating Roman Catholics from Protestants. Sunnis are in the majority among Muslims globally, and while they are often in disagreement—religiously and politically—with Shia coreligionists, they are also themselves divided doctrinally. As we have seen, Salafis conceive of a "pure" Islam, while other Sunni groups can be found who accord greater scope to Koranic interpretation. In like manner, the Shia are divided, with some (the Nizari Ismailis) being followers of the Aga Khan. Then there are those Muslims such as the Druze and Ahmadis, whose status within the Islamic family is a matter of contention, to say nothing of the Sufis, adherents of a more mystical and even theosophical version of Islam.

In the United States, close to half of all Muslims are Sunni, with Shia embracing less than a fifth, and "others" or those with no clear affiliation making up the remainder.[44] Added to the internal religious diversity are cultural divisions reflecting mores and customs of the divers ethnic groups subscribing to Islam. For in America, many Muslims are converts to the faith, bringing as do other U.S.-born Muslims a large dose of the domestic culture to their religious practices. Among the non-converts, cultural diversity is the rule, with Pakistani American Muslims, for instance, practicing an Islam quite similar to that of Indian Muslims but very distinct from that of African (and African American) Muslims or Turkish Muslims. So while these various groups may share the core beliefs of Islam along with many of its rituals, they have differing histories, mother tongues, national narratives, and standing within the American cultural fabric. Not all is diversity, however, for these subgroups all share some commonalities, among which is a notional connection to Mecca, a reverence for the Koran, a strong belief in Allah and the Prophet Muhammad (as well as in Abraham, Moses, and Jesus), and most importantly, a self-understanding as Muslims within the *ummah,* or "community."

The second contextual matter warranting discussion here is size. When Lawrence Fuchs commented, back in 1959, upon America's two "king-sized minority groups," the German and Irish diasporas, he certainly knew whereof he wrote.[45] As we discovered in the two previous chapters, estimates as to the size of these groups a century ago could, and did, vary, but if we construe their numbers in terms of the category, "element," which comprises but is much larger than the related category of "stock," it would not be too far off to regard the combined diasporic pairing as constituting around 35 percent of the total American population in the years shortly before the First World War. In contrast, the Muslim diaspora in North America is a far, far smaller entity than was either of the large diasporas during their heyday. The difference is crucial.

It is true that, in both the United States and Canada, Islam has been a growing demographic presence, even after the trauma of 9/11.[46] As was the case with both the Irish and German diasporas, so too is it the case with the Muslim diaspora in the United States: its exact size is difficult to assess, in part because the American census form does not include questions of religious affiliation, deemed ever since 1976 to be constitutionally out-of-bounds for the government to be posing.[47] There have, however, been a number of independent studies seeking to gauge the size of the Muslim presence in the country. Although it is a ballpark estimate, it would not be unreasonable to assume that at least 4.5 million Muslims live today in the United States, a figure arrived at by averaging some of the more widely cited estimates published in the past decade or so. Two demographic studies are of particular relevance in this matter of assessing the size of the diaspora. One, released by the U.S. Institute of Peace in February 2006, claimed that between 6 and 7.5 million Muslims resided in America.[48] The other, issued by the Pew Research Center nearly five years later, reported a lower figure, of around 2.6 million.[49] The discrepancy here is possibly owing to a conflation of two different "ethnic" communities in America, the Arab Americans and the Muslim Americans. The former community numbers around 3.5 million, but significantly, only a quarter of this group is made up of Muslims, with the majority of Arab Americans actually being Christian.[50]

Needless to say, and quite in contrast with the North America-based share of either the global Irish or German diasporas, the percentage of all Muslims living on the continent today is miniscule. Worldwide, the Muslim population is estimated to be nearly 1.7 billion, and on the assumption that fewer than 6 million are to be found in the United States and Canada combined, it is apparent that the North American share of the entire diaspora comes not even to half a percentage point, much less than, say, Europe's share (more than 2 percent) of the same diaspora—and decidedly less than the U.S. (or North American) shares of either the Irish or German diasporas a century ago, respectively 70 and 90 percent. The majority of global Muslims (at least 60 percent) are concentrated in the Asia-Pacific region, wherein are found the diaspora's three largest cohorts, respectively in Indonesia (204 million), Pakistan (178 million), and India (177 million). In comparison, the Middle East and North Africa, generally regarded as heartland regions of Islamic settlement, and certainly among the major geographical foci of U.S. foreign policy during the past few decades, are home to only a fifth of the global Muslim population. The geographic origin of Muslims in the United States is an approximate reflection of this global distribution pattern, with about a quarter of the country's Islamic population hailing from the Asian subcontinent, followed by around 13 percent from the Arab Middle Eastern countries, with a further 6 percent from contemporary Africa, nearly 4 percent from Iran, and not quite 3 percent from Turkey.[51] As well, a substantial proportion, possibly as much as a third, of America's Muslims are African Americans, whose roots in North America extend back to the era of slavery.[52]

The relationship between Islam and America predates the country's founding as an independent republic, for if we include slaves, it is clear that even prior to the Declaration of Independence Muslims were already numerous in what would become the United States.[53] With independence came an injection of Islam into debates over the new country's religious mores, Pennsylvania for a time becoming a constitutional battleground pitting factions stressing tolerance against those seeking to keep the new state firmly Protestant.[54] Though the tolerance faction won this particular skirmish and managed to have a religious liberty clause inserted into Pennsylvania's first constitution, early American views of Islam often (though not always) featured negative assessments of the religion.[55] Withal, it was a ruler from the Muslim world who would be the first to recognize the United States as a sovereign state: Morocco's Sultan Muhammad III did this in December 1777, nearly six years before the Treaty of Paris brought to a formal end America's independence struggle.[56] Morocco is also noteworthy because it was with this country that the newly independent United States signed a "treaty of friendship" in 1786, a pact that was ratified the following year and remains in effect to this day, making it America's longest-standing such treaty with any country.

These diplomatic footnotes aside, it has really only been in more recent times that Muslims have figured importantly in American foreign and domestic policy, doing so in part as a result of having woven themselves more into the country's demographic fabric than had previously been the case. Starting in the late nineteenth century, there have been five waves of Muslim migration to the United States, the first of which lasted roughly from 1875 until 1912, years that witnessed an influx of families from Palestine, Lebanon, Jordan, and Syria. The second and third waves of Muslim migration unfolded from 1918 to 1922 and throughout the 1930s, years, respectively, when hardship impelled out-migration from the economically depressed Middle East and North Africa, regions thrown into turmoil in the wake of the unravelling of the Ottoman Empire that followed the First World War. The fourth and fifth migratory waves, unlike the first three, tended to consist in more educated and generally wealthier Muslims, this time from South Asia and the Balkans. The fourth wave occurred subsequent to the Second World War, which saw significant numbers of arrivals hailing primarily from urban centers in Pakistan and India. The fifth and final wave was triggered by the implementation of the Immigration and Nationality Act in 1965, during the administration of Lyndon B. Johnson.[57] As we discovered in chapter three, this legislation threw open America's doors once more to widespread immigration, reversing the restrictionist pattern in place ever since the 1920s.[58] The 1965 legislation relaxed the former quota policy and streamlined the process for family reunification, especially as it applied to professionals, scientists, and artists of "exceptional ability," along with political refugees, immediate kin of American citizens, and workers in occupations with shortages.[59]

Canada, albeit under differing circumstances and with different mechanisms, also experienced a rapid surge in immigration, including from the Muslim world, over the past several decades.[60] By 2001, census figures revealed the presence in Canada of 580,000 Muslims, a total that would come close to doubling over the next decade, standing at nearly a million by 2010. Currently Muslims make up around 3 percent of the country's overall population of 33 million, with some analysts expecting this percentage share to triple during the coming two decades.[61] The history of Muslims in Canada (and British North America) predates Confederation in 1867, though the numbers were microscopic, the 1871 census revealing only 13 Muslims in the entire country.[62] Numbers were kept low by the existence of restrictive quotas, with the few Muslims who did make it to Canada typically having Arab or Turkish backgrounds. As with their counterparts in the United States, early Muslim immigrants to Canada possessed little education or wealth, working mainly as laborers. But beginning in the 1960s and continuing thereafter, Muslim immigration increased rapidly, with intakes spiking during years featuring a major crisis in the Islamic world, which is to say, a great number of years in recent decades.

As we saw in previous chapters of this book, an additional consideration to keep in mind is the efficacy of this practice we have been calling "lobbying" (broadly construed), so as to include ethnic voting as well as institutionalized application of the politics of pressure, primarily in national legislatures. In the previous case studies, I have hinted that while their lobbying did indeed have purpose and effect in the American political system, as well as upon the broader canvas of North American security, the influence attempts made by Irish Americans and German Americans did not universally yield the desired outcomes, and in the case of the emotional debate over U.S. entry into the First World War, they were likely even counterproductive, paradoxically making more probable that which the lobbying efforts sought to prevent. What, in this light, can we say about the lobbying efforts of Muslim North America? Basically, we can say two things.

First, the Muslim North American diaspora, like the Irish American and German American diasporas in earlier times, has sought and managed to develop institutional means of promoting group interests, as these latter are assessed and promoted by diasporic leadership. Groups include the American Muslim Council, Canadian Islamic Congress, International Institute of Islamic Thought, and both the Council on American-Islamic Relations (CAIR) and the Council on American-Islamic Relations Canada (CAIR-CAN).[63] No doubt such groups have become increasingly mobilized following 9/11, faced as they have been by the need to defend the image of Islam in North America in the wake of the global challenge of Salafist jihadism, and the reaction thereto. But it would be a very large conceptual stretch for anyone to imagine that such lobbying is steering either American or Canadian foreign policy along paths deemed congruent with a continental Muslim "interest," assuming such could even be identified, given what has been said above about the diversity within the diaspora, as well as its size. We know from earlier chapters that a controversy continues to rage in the United States about the postulated impact of an "Israel lobby" on U.S. foreign policy, and while analysts might differ radically as to the impact of such a lobby, no one can credibly demonstrate (though a few have tried) that there exists a counterpart "Muslim lobby" in either the United States or Canada, capable of somehow influencing the overall shaping of foreign policy, especially toward the Middle East.[64]

Second, a very important reason for Muslim North American lobbying's failure to register much if any influence over foreign policy concerns that *other* aspect of lobbying, the one associated with the ballot box. The small size of the diaspora in both North American countries means that little influence is to be expected to emanate from the polling booths, and this notwithstanding claims regularly made about politicians "pandering" to the ethnic vote, in Canada perhaps even more so than in the United States. It is not that the "Muslim vote" is an uninteresting phenomenon in either North American country. To the contrary, there is, in the United States, a fascinatingly ironic tale unfolding in respect of this slice of the electorate, for prior to 9/11 America's Muslims tended overwhelmingly to stump for the *Republican* party in national elections, supporting it en masse just as Irish Americans had almost always given their allegiance to the Democratic party. The reasons for the Muslims' pro-Republicanism were not hard to detect, relating to the category of "family values," as well as to the GOP's generally "business-friendly" image. Both Presidents Bush managed to reap an abundant harvest from this component of the electorate, the elder (George H. W. Bush) enjoying a two-to-one lead among Muslims in his successful campaign in 1988, and his son (George W. Bush) polling equally strongly in 2000's election, when he took 70 percent of the Muslim vote while his Democratic rival, Al Gore, was scoring even more heavily among the Jewish electorate. Not for nothing did one wag suggest that by doing so well among this tranche of the electorate in what was said to be the country's most important "swing state," Florida, George W. Bush became president on the strength of the Muslim vote![65]

The foreign policy of the Bush administration would soon render the earlier Muslim support for the GOP a fading memory, triggering as it did a widespread exodus of Muslim voters from the ranks of the Republicans. Much more importantly than whether George W. Bush owed his election to the Muslim vote (it could equally be said that he owed it to the candidacy of the Arab American *Christian*, Ralph Nader, who it is claimed took enough votes away from Al Gore in Florida to tip the state and its twenty-five electoral votes into the Republican column), the reality is that there is not much "electoral clout" to be associated with the Muslim diaspora, both in the United States and Canada — certainly nothing remotely comparable to the assumed ballot heft possessed by either Irish Americans or German Americans in bygone years. This means that to the extent the Muslim North American diaspora can be argued to figure in discussions related to the current state and future prospects of the North American security community, it has almost entirely been because of the kinds of activities that, in the case of the Irish American diaspora, were grouped under the rubric of "physical force." So let us take a look at the most important such activities, and their implications.

NSAAS AND CTAS: THE GIFT THAT KEEPS ON GIVING?

In the initial chapters of this book, and again at the start of this chapter, we came across a pair of terms some political scientists employ to identify what they have taken to be new and significant "agents" in regional security affairs, in North America as elsewhere. These agents have been given the name of "non-state armed actors" (NSAAs) or "clandestine transnational actors" (CTAs).[66] To this nominal mix has been added, as we also saw above, yet another descriptive expression, differing hardly at all in its broadest signification from either the NSAAs or the CTAs but injecting, in a way neither of this pairing does or can do, some ethnic specificity into the contemporary discussion. It is the concept of "homegrowns," with the clear implication being that radicalized young members (usually male, but not always) of the North American Muslim diaspora possess the ability greatly to disturb the tranquility of continental security arrangements. Hence the allusion in the subtitle of this section, to the German word for poison (*gift*), raising as it does the question as to what Salafist jihadis have been up to in North America, and whether the implications of these activities can be said to be hazardous to the continued existence of the security community, as has been hinted by some of the analysts we canvassed earlier in this chapter.

There have been two phases in the continent's recent jihadist saga. The initial phase featured worries, dimly articulated during the latter half of the 1990s before exploding with great intensity after 9/11, that the principal problem was one of Canada-based terrorists exploiting the advantages of contiguity and interdependence in North America to attack targets in the United States. The more recent phase is rather different, in that the concern today seems more to focus on the ability of jihadis based in either North American country to stage attacks *within* their respective countries, or outside of North America altogether, with the latter becoming more likely to occur. This is not to suggest that the earlier, transborder, worries have dissipated completely, for they have not; despite the numerous and costly policy measures adopted by Ottawa in a bid to demonstrate that it does take homeland security every bit as seriously as its neighbor, skeptical voices can still be heard in the United States, with some American observers continuing to regard Canada as the harbor for terrorists that it looked to have been in the 1990s.[67] But it *is* to suggest that the second phase of jihadism in North America has yielded policy responses that call into question some of the direst suppositions of scholars and others of a decade or so ago, when they pondered the dilemma(s) of homeland security on the continent. In short, the second phase, as we will see, contains an optimistic message for those who ponder the ongoing robustness of the North American security community.

If one name can be invoked as representative of the initial phase of the jihadi problem in North America, it is that of Ahmed Ressam, an Algerian who imagined that his contribution to the cause was going to be the detonation of a powerful explosive at LAX, the Los Angeles international airport, on 31 December 1999—the New Year's Eve marking the turn both of the century and of the millennium, hence his nickname, the "Millennium bomber." This was not the first time a Canada-related plot had been concocted to attack an important transportation site in the United States: close to three years before, Gazi Ibrahim Abu Mezer had crossed into the United States bent upon bombing the Atlantic Avenue subway station, in Brooklyn, doing so with the collaboration of a New York accomplice who like himself had also been born and raised in Palestine, Lafi Khalil. The targeted station was not only a busy one, with ten subway lines as well as the Long Island Rail Road using it, but it was also located in the part of town in which the "Blind Sheikh," the Salafist Omar Abdel Rahman, had been a regular fixture, preaching his fire-and-brimstone denunciations of the United States and the West at a mosque on Atlantic Avenue. Mezer and Khalil were arrested in late July 1997, before they could put their scheme into operation. Though Mezer had been granted a visa to study in Canada in 1993, and had subsequently filed for asylum in the country, his role in the failed plot did not attract the kind of criticism of "lax" Canadian refugee-vetting processes that would soon come loudly to be heard in respect of the Ressam case, partly because Canada eventually refused to let Mezer back into the country after one of his apprehensions for having illegally entered the United States, thereby making his continued presence on American soil come to appear more a failing of America's than of Canada's border authorities.[68]

With Ressam the situation was different, and for a while this Algerian-born would-be saboteur came single-handedly to personify jihadism on the North American continent. Growing up in a town west of Algiers, Ressam had not been particularly religious, or politically engaged. But along the way, the steps of his life's journey took him from Algeria to Salafist militancy and ultimately to lengthy imprisonment in the United States, where he will likely remain for at least three more decades. In between then and now, he spent time in France, Canada, and Afghanistan. He left Algeria in 1992 in quest of economic opportunity in France, but two years later was bound for Canada, which he entered illegally in February 1994, travelling on a falsified French passport bearing the name of Tahar Medjadi. Immigration agents at Montreal's Mirabel airport (still in use in those days for regular commercial flights) expressed doubts about the authenticity of the document, which led Ressam to admit that it was indeed bogus, and that he was claiming asylum status in Canada, explaining that he had been wrongly imprisoned in Algeria "for arms trafficking and association with terrorists." One chronicler of the case notes that while this admission "should have set off alarm bells in the immigration department, it didn't, and he was soon released. It would be the first of the government's many mistakes in handling his case."[69]

For the next four years, Ressam lived in a Montreal apartment later deemed to have lodged a cell linked to al Qaeda and to Ressam's new group of associates in the Algerian Armed Islamic Group (GIA, in the French acronym, for Groupe islamique armé). Thanks to welfare benefits of some $500 a month provided by the Canadian taxpayer, supplemented by criminal moonlighting efforts (stealing credit cards from tourists being one of his specialties) that were only rarely interrupted by arrests, Ressam had been able to keep body and soul together during his first year in his new host-country. Because he missed his asylum hearing in June 1995, his application for refugee status was rejected, and he was ordered to leave Canada. Leave he did, albeit three years later, and this time under a new name (Benni Antoine Noris), and with a genuine passport — a Canadian one that he had been able to "trade up" to thanks to a forged baptismal record purloined from a church in Québec, supported by a Université de Montréal student identity card. (Canadian passport-application procedures, needless to say, have subsequently been tightened up considerably, with one of the changes being the inadmissibility of baptismal records as proof of birth in Canada.) He employed his new passport to travel to Afghanistan, where he matriculated at Osama bin Laden's camps. It was there that he came up with his plan to bomb LAX, and acquired the technical expertise to do the job.

Ressam never did get to touch off his fireworks display, for he was apprehended by American border guards on 14 December 1999, trying to enter the state of Washington from the province of British Columbia, by ferry from Vancouver Island, with bomb-making gear stashed in the trunk of his rented Chrysler.[70] The Ressam affair is generally recollected as not only having been a very close call, but also as something even more troubling, betraying to many Americans (and quite a few Canadians) a level of ineptitude on Ottawa's part that could, unless corrected, have dangerous implications for North American security. Attesting to these implications were some rather sharp words penned by one American diplomat with experience in Canada, who expressed his concern about Canadian lack of diligence in an article published some three years after the Ressam affair. According to that official, David T. Jones, "the reality continues that terrorists and their supporters have operated out of Canada. It would strain credulity to believe that Ahmed Ressam, the prospective millennium bomber for Los Angeles International Airport, was a solitary clot of manure in a field of flowers." Particularly annoying to Jones was what he took to be a patronizing attitude on the part of Canadian officials who persisted in refusing to understand the gravity of the threat—an attitude that he said led them constantly to mollify a Washington they regarded as a "a batty uncle who otherwise would change his inheritance provisions" unless some accommodative gestures were made. Jones concluded with the minatory and certainly undiplomatic reminder that it was "a brutish political reality that systematic open disrespect by a small weak state for a large and powerful state rarely ends to the benefit of the former."[71]

Ironically, a few observers closer to the center of counterterrorism initiatives took a less dim view of the quality of Canada-United States cooperation, even and especially in respect of the Ressam affair. For instance, none other than the U.S. attorney general, John Ashcroft, made a point of telling a group of (surprised) Canadian reporters on 3 December 2001, nearly two years after the failed LAX plot, that Canada had not bungled the Ressam affair, but had instead provided the United States with invaluable information that enabled it to make the arrest. Ashcroft, in Ottawa to sign a border agreement with Canada, lauded the "outstanding co-operation of Canadian authorities" on the Ressam case. It is not obvious (at least to me) whether the comment was made as a gesture of support for Ashcroft's Canadian counterpart, or because it reflected the truth; those who know the details of this case can be presumed not to be saying all they know, for reasons related to ongoing operational security.[72]

What we can observe, and indeed already have observed, is the tendency of many analysts in Canada and the United States to buy into the notion that the *only* reason Ottawa has shown itself so willing to buttress its own homeland security resources, which it assuredly *has* done over the past dozen years, has been to assuage Washington. Earlier in this chapter, I criticized that assumption, albeit in noting that as compared with that of the United States, Canada's own sense of being threatened by Salafist jihadis had indeed tended to be minimal. This differentiated perception of threat owed a great deal to structural considerations derivative of the two countries' relative capabilities. Whatever might be said about the "advantages" (if that is what they are) of being the international system's strongest power,[73] there is one major drawback to "unipolarity": everyone discontented with the international status quo, including but not only Salafist jihadis, will be able to nourish, and if they get the chance, act upon grievances against the one state that they see to be standing between them and the attainment of their goals; hence America will come to be regarded by revisionists of any persuasion as both a necessary and a legitimate target.

Added to and related to this structural feature has been an empirical reality, namely that during the initial phase of Salafist jihadi activism in North America, Canada was simply not considered to be much of a target worth attacking. Figures linked to al Qaeda did not often, and certainly never with any consistency, refer to Canada as such a target prior to 2002. It was only after Canada's deployment to Afghanistan that the country began to loom larger in jihadist rhetoric. By September 2006, al Qaeda's deputy leader, Ayman al Zawahiri, was denouncing Canada's role in Afghanistan as that of a "second-rate crusader," a statement that was followed a month later by threats of retaliation should Canada fail to withdraw its forces from that country.[74] This bluster was a far cry from what had been heard prior to 9/11 or even during the first few years after 9/11, when terrorist organizations located on Canada's soil much preferred to regard it as a base area from which to plan and mount attacks, rather than as a potential target in its own right.[75]

That same year, 2006, would signal the transit from the first to the second phase of jihadism on the North American continent, one that would see the emphasis shift from near-exclusive concern about transborder attacks to a more diffuse worry about terrorist violence directed against targets in either North American country, on the part of jihadists located within each, with no crossing of international frontiers being required to perpetrate the misdeeds. The most notorious incident of such homegrown activity in Canada occurred in early June 2006, when a group of youthful but deadly serious jihadists (dubbed by the media the "Toronto 18") sought to kill and maim as many fellow Canadians as they could, primarily by detonating a truck bomb in downtown Toronto, but also through acts of violence further east in Ontario, both at Canadian Forces Base Trenton and on Parliament Hill, in Ottawa, where it was envisioned that the prime minister and other government officials could be slain and, in some cases (including that of Prime Minister Stephen Harper) beheaded, for good measure.[76] The youthful plotters were in the process of amassing their makeshift arsenal when they were arrested by Canadian authorities, who had for some time been closely monitoring the group's activities and had even penetrated their membership, such that the likelihood of an attack actually taking place was close to zero. By late 2009, some of those implicated in the plot, including its putative ringleader Zakaria Amara, had pleaded guilty in a widely publicized case that led many Canadians (though not all, for some continued to insist the plot was all a figment of overzealous imaginations)[77] to realize that Salafist violence was not something that only occurred elsewhere than in Canada. In short, these events, along with subsequent details of plotting involving other suspects and other targets over the next few years, constituted a bit of a wake-up call for Canadians, suddenly apprised from all quarters about the new and troubling homegrown phenomenon, which some professed to believe simply could not have arisen in a country so respectful of "multiculturalism" as Canada was routinely touted as being.[78]

America's comparable awakening to homegrown challenges occurred a month after the Toronto 18 trial, only in this case there was not just a desire for blood but the actual spilling of the same. The episode took place at the U.S. army base at Fort Hood, Texas, where in November 2009 a radicalized army major distressed at the prospect of possibly being deployed to theaters of operation pitting his comrades against his fellow Muslims went on a shooting spree that led to thirteen dead on the base, and a further twenty-nine wounded. The gunman, a Virginia-born Muslim of Palestinian descent named Nidal Malik Hasan, was apparently radicalized by Internet discussions he had had with Salafist jihadis, including with fellow American Anwar al Awlaki, who four days after the attack hailed Hasan as a "hero."[79] Although this was the bloodiest single instance of Salafist homegrown violence in the United States, it was not the most infamous one. That dubious title was accorded the bombing of the Boston Marathon in April 2013, the work of twenty-six-year-old Tamerlan Tsarnaev and his nineteen-year-old brother, Dzhokhar, ethnic Chechens who, though born in the former Soviet Union, resettled in the United States during the decade prior to the bombing. The youngest even became an American citizen on 11 September 2012, while his older brother's citizenship application was in process at the time he died following a shoot-out with police in the early hours of Friday, 19 April 2013.[80]

The Boston events had no connection with Canada other than that of constituting the kind of problem both North American countries face in common (if in unequal proportions, with the United States being more often the target of such attacks than Canada). Even so, there was in the immediate aftermath of the April 2013 carnage a sense of anxiety palpable among security officials in Canada as to whether the attackers might somehow be traced back to north of the border. Paul Koring captured this anxiety accurately enough when he wrote, the day after the attack, that "[f]or Canada, the nightmare scenario would be a determination that the Boston attack was linked to or involved extremists north of the border or those who transited through Canada."[81]

By this time, and notwithstanding the residual worries such as that expressed immediately above, the focus of counterterrorism initiatives in North America had shifted decidedly away from the near-obsession with the border, of just a few years earlier.[82] Moreover, the North American dimension of the homegrown challenge was getting increasingly wrapped up in an extracontinental concern with similar challenges elsewhere, especially in Europe, which had been grappling with the problem earlier than either the United States or Canada.[83] Not only were the homegrowns hardly unique to North America; they were not even most prevalent on this continent, for reasons that may, as some are prepared to argue, be related to both North American societies' greater willingness and ability to assimilate their Muslim diasporas,[84] but that may in fact simply be a function of the smaller relative sizes of those diasporas, when contrasted with similar communities elsewhere. Whatever the relative success (or lack thereof) experienced by North American attempts to grapple with the homegrown phenomenon, countries elsewhere in the West have also been encountering it, with the assumption being fairly widely held that Europe is more at risk than anywhere else in the Western world.

All of this is simply to note that anxiety about homegrowns continues to mount throughout the West, stoked by developments in Syria, Iraq, and elsewhere. Illustratively, the lead story in the *New York Times* that arrived on my doorstep the morning I was completing the original draft of this chapter concerned the suicide-bombing death of a young American, Moner Mohammad Abusalha, who blew himself up in an attack upon a restaurant in northern Syria two months previously.[85] This was but the latest in a series of similar incidents involving American homegrowns. Comparable events have involved Canadian homegrowns,[86] perhaps the most notorious of which took place in an early 2013 hostage-taking incident in southern Algeria, where Salafist jihadis attacked the natural gas facility of In Amenas, located in Tiguentourine. Two of the jihadis, Ali Medlej and Xristos Katsiroubas, were from London, Ontario. They met their deaths, along with three dozen hostages and nearly as many of their fellow terrorists, when Algerian forces counterattacked the facility.[87]

To say again, no one who follows these developments seriously pretends that diasporic leadership is supporting Salafist jihadism in any Western country. Nor is it considered that the numbers involved in Salafist jihadism are anything but tiny, in the broad scheme of things, with estimates of North American jihadis currently fighting abroad ranging from the several dozens to the few hundreds, compared with Europe-sourced jihadis, numbering close to a thousand. To take the case of the United States alone, in the entire decade that followed the 9/11 attacks, fewer than two hundred Muslim Americans were picked up on terrorism-related charges—and this, out of a total population of Muslims in the United States that approaches, as we have seen, five (some say six) million people. In Canada, the absolute numbers of homegrowns apprehended over the past decade have been much fewer, even though the Muslim population, of around a million, is a relatively larger share of the total population (3 percent) than is the Muslim population of the United States (around 2 percent).[88]

Their numbers aside, it is widely accepted that the radicalized homegrowns constitute a problem. Disagreements exist, to be sure, as to how to remedy the problem, but on one matter of great relevance to the topic of this book, there should be little disagreement. It is the perhaps surprising consequence for Canada-United States security cooperation that stems from the recent transformation of the North American jihadi challenge as it has been outlined in this section of the chapter. Simply put, the homegrown phenomenon has played a part in changing the frame of reference, in two ways. First, the Canadian-based homegrowns have elevated a sense of threat perception from terrorism in Ottawa that, if it does not equal the perception of threat felt in Washington, comes closer to it than heretofore. This in turn signals to Americans that Canadians, now that they themselves have known the feeling of being targets, can be counted on to take even more seriously the requirements of homeland security—and not simply to appease the "batty uncle" (to advert to David Jones's imagery, cited earlier). The second "contribution" made by the homegrowns to bettering the bilateral relationship on the homeland security file can be attributed to the American-based plotters of mayhem. What they have done, by drawing attention to the prospect of the United States harboring an "enemy within," is to lessen the relative significance of the Canada-United States border as *the* primary danger to American physical security, which it seemed to be for many, a decade ago. The reason here is obvious: if the terrorist challenge emanates from within America itself, that is to say, if America *itself* has become a "safe haven" for terrorists, then how much solace could possibly be derived even were the Canada-United States border to be hermetically sealed?

This is not to make light of the homegrown phenomenon, or to deny the ongoing challenge of assuring transborder security. Homegrowns continue to present problems for North American security, even if not so grave as those presented by European homegrowns to European security. But the homegrowns' effect upon North American security cooperation also suggests something else. Rather than driving the two neighbors apart, as looked to be happening a decade or so ago, it brings them closer together. Not for the first time in history, and certainly not for the last, we see in operation the "principle of the opposite effect." The point is important as we now turn to the concluding chapter, which attempts to frame some generalizations based on the three case studies.

NOTES

1. See James Kirchick, "The Homegrown-Terrorist Threat," *Commentary* 129 (February 2010): 16–20; as well as Thomas Hegghammer, "Should I Stay or Should I Go? Explaining Variation in Western Jihadists' Choice between Domestic and Foreign Fighting," *American Political Science Review* 107 (February 2013):1–15; Barry Cooper, "Homegrown Jihadists and the Evolution of al-Qaeda," *CDFAI Policy Paper* (Calgary, AB: Canadian Defence and Foreign Affairs Institute, February 2013); and Matt Kwong, "Ahmad Waseem Case Illustrates Canada's Foreign Fighter Problem," *CBC News Canada*, 5 August 2014 ; available at http://www.cbc.ca/news/canada/ahmad-waseem-case-illustrates-canada-s-foreign-fighter-problem-1.2727328.

2. See, for instance, Mark Mazzetti, Eric Schmitt, and Michael S. Schmidt, "U.S. Identifies Florida Man as Suicide Bomber," *New York Times*, 31 May 2014 , pp. A1, A7; Alissa J. Rubin, "France Targets Flow of Jihadis to Syrian War," *New York Times*, 3 June 2014, pp. A1, A5; Kimiko de Freytas-Tamura, "Foreign Jihadis Fighting in Syria Pose Risk in West," *New York Times*, 30 May 2014, pp. A1, A12; Michael Zekulin, "Homeward Bound: Made-in-Canada Terror," *Globe and Mail* (Toronto), 11 June 2014, p. A15; and Michel Coulombe, "Canadians in Terrorist Armies Threaten Us All," *Globe and Mail* (Toronto), 23 August 2014, p. F2.

3. For a particularly trenchant condemnation of homegrowns from within the Muslim community in Canada, see Sheema Khan, "Two Stark Visions for Canadian Muslims," *Globe and Mail*, 4 July 2008, p. A15. Khan writes of such perpetrators of mayhem that "theirs is not a path of *jihad*—it is a path of *hirabah* (barbarism). We should refrain from calling them *jihadis*." Also see Kim Mackrael, "Muslim Groups, Police Struggle to Counter Militant Recruitment," *Globe and Mail*, 29 August 2014, pp. A1, A8. Similarly cautioning against conflating the Muslim diaspora (in this case, in

the United States) with the homegrowns is the report coauthored by David Schanzer, Charles Kurzman, and Ebrahim Moosa, *Anti-Terror Lessons of Muslim-Americans* (Washington, D.C.: National Institute of Justice, October 2012).

4. Colm J. Brannigan, "The Luke Dillon Case and the Welland Canal Explosion of 1900: Non-Events in the History of the Niagara Frontier Region," *Niagara Frontier* 24 (Summer 1977): 36–44, especially p. 42, where Brannigan notes that Dillon "remained bitter and an extreme Republican until his death in 1929. Even on his deathbed, he stated that he would bomb the British again if he could."

5. Gary J. Schmitt, ed., *Safety, Liberty, and Islamist Terrorism: American and European Approaches to Domestic Counterterrorism* (Washington, D.C.: AEI Press, 2010). Also see Jocelyne Cesari Botman, *When Islam and Democracy Meet: Muslims in Europe and in the United States* (New York: Palgrave MacMillan, 2014).

6. Frank P. Harvey, "The Homeland Security Dilemma: Imagination, Failure and the Escalating Costs of Perfecting Security," *Canadian Journal of Political Science* 40 (June 2007): 283–316, quote at pp. 283–84. Also see this same author's *The Homeland Security Dilemma: Fear, Failure and the Future of American Insecurity* (New York: Routledge, 2008).

7. Harvey, "Homeland Security Dilemma," pp. 309–10 (emphasis in the original).

8. Quoted in Richard K. Betts, "The Soft Underbelly of American Primacy: Tactical Advantages of Terror," *Political Science Quarterly* 117 (Spring 2002): 19–36, quote at p. 30. Also see Stephen Flynn, "America the Vulnerable," *Foreign Affairs* 81 (January 2002): 60–74.

9. As noted in chapter two, while the first pluralistic security community in the Western world may well have been the one embracing Norway and Sweden, it went into abeyance during the Second World War years, when Germany was occupying Norway.

10. Quoted in Graham Allison, "Is Nuclear Terrorism a Threat to Canada's National Security?" *International Journal* 60 (Summer 2005): 713–22, quote at p. 717. But for more restrained assessments of the problem of nuclear terrorism, compare Francis J. Gavin, "Same As It Ever Was: Nuclear Alarmism, Proliferation, and the Cold War," *International Security* 34 (Winter 2009/10): 7–37; and Robin M. Frost, "Nuclear Terrorism after 9/11," *Adelphi Papers* 45/378 (2005).

11. Patrick Lennox, "From Golden Straitjacket to Kevlar Vest: Canada's Transformation to a Security State," *Canadian Journal of Political Science* 40 (December 2007): 1017–38, quote at p. 119 (emphasis added). Also see this same author's *At Home and Abroad: The Canada-US Relationship and Canada's Place in the World* (Vancouver: UBC Press, 2009), esp. pp. 115–30.

12. Joel J. Sokolsky and Philippe Lagassé, "Suspenders and a Belt: Perimeter and Border Security in Canada-US Relations," *Canadian Foreign Policy Journal* 12 (January 2006): 15–29, quote at p. 20 (emphasis added).

13. The term is Samuel P. Huntington's, though the idea is much older, and certainly was discernible during the vogue of "Anglo-Saxonist" ideology we encountered in the previous chapter. See Samuel P. Huntington, *The Clash of Civilizations and the Remaking of World Order* (New York: Simon & Schuster, 1996), pp. 156, 217. For a thoughtful critique of the term's utility, see Kim Richard Nossal, "Throwing the Baby Out with the Bathwater? Huntington's 'Kin-Country' Thesis and Australian-Canadian Relations," in *Shaping Nations: Constitutionalism and Society in Australia and Canada*, ed. Linda Cardinal and David Headon (Ottawa: University of Ottawa Press, 2002), pp. 167–81.

14. Quoted in Randy Boswell, "A Life's Journey," *Ottawa Citizen*, 2 February 2002, p. B1.

15. Murray Campbell, "Nation's Grief Turns to Anger," *Globe and Mail*, 19 April 2002, pp. A1, A7; Margaret Wente, "A PR Nightmare on the Home Front," *Globe and Mail*, 19 April 2002, pp. A1, A7; and Clifford Krauss, "Canada's Link to U.S. Tested by the Deaths of 4 Soldiers," *International Herald Tribune*, 10 February 2003, p. 5. Also see

Mark Yaniszewski, "Reporting on Fratricide: Canadian Newspapers and the Incident at Tarnak Farm, Afghanistan," *International Journal* 62 (Spring 2007): 362–80.

16. Mark Landler and Michael R. Gordon, "Obama Sending Advisers to Iraq," *New York Times*, 20 June 2014, pp. A1, A8.

17. Tim Arango, "Uneasy Alliance Gives Insurgents an Edge in Iraq," *New York Times*, 19 June 2014, pp. A1, A11. Sometimes, ISIS has also been known under a slightly different acronym, ISIL (standing for the Islamic State in Iraq and the Levant), as well, increasingly, simply as IS, subsequent to the declaration in July 2014 by the group's leader, Abu Bakr al Baghdadi, of the Islamic State, or caliphate; see Patrick J. Lyons and Mona el-Naggar, "What to Call Iraq Fighters? Experts Vary on S's and L's," *New York Times*, p. A11; "Terror's New Headquarters," *Economist*, 14 June 2014, p. 11; and Helene Cooper and Mark Landler, "U.S. Mobilizes Allies to Widen Assault on ISIS," *New York Times*, 27 August 2014, pp. A1, A8.

18. "Eyes of the World Are on Putin," *Globe and Mail*, 21 July 2014, pp. A6–A7; "U.S. Points to Rebels in Downing of Jet," *International New York Times*, 19–20 July 2014, pp. 1, 4–5; and Peter Baker, "Obama Urges Calm in Face of Two Crises," *New York Times*, 29 August 2014, pp. A1, A12.

19. Generally, on the phenomenon of "threat inflating," see Christopher J. Fettweis, "Threat and Anxiety in US Foreign Policy," *Survival* 52 (April–May 2010): 59–82; A. Trevor Thrall, "A Bear in the Woods? Threat Framing and the Marketplace of Values," *Security Studies* 16 (July–September 2007): 452–88; and John A. Thompson, "The Exaggeration of American Vulnerability: The Anatomy of a Tradition," *Diplomatic History* 16 (January 1992): 23–43.

20. John E. Mueller, "Terrorphobia: Our False Sense of Insecurity," *American Interest* 3 (May/June 2008): 6–13; also see Mueller, *Overblown: How Politicians and the Terrorism Industry Inflate National Security Threats, and Why We Believe Them* (New York: Free Press 2006).

21. Peter L. Bergen, "How Worried Should We Be?" *International Herald Tribune*, 15 December 2008, p. 8.

22. For this assessment, see the supplement published under the title "Spécial Al-Qaida," *Le Monde*, 9 September 2009.

23. As one author phrased it, "[i]n almost any given year, Americans are far more likely to drown accidentally in a bathtub than to be killed by a terrorist." See Peter L. Bergen, *Manhunt: The Ten-Year Search for Bin Laden from 9/11 to Abbottabad* (New York: Random House, 2012), p. 254.

24. Adam Nossiter, "A Jihadist's Face Taunts Nigeria from Shadows," *New York Times*, 19 May 2014, pp. A1, A3; Eliza Griswold, "The Next Front," *New York Times Magazine*, 15 June 2014, pp. 24–31ff; and David D. Kirkpatrick, "As Moderate Islamists Retreat, Extremists Surge Unchecked," *New York Times*, 19 June 2014, pp. A1, A11.

25. See Mary Habeck, *Knowing the Enemy: Jihadist Ideology and the War on Terror* (New Haven, Conn.: Yale University Press, 2006); and Farhad Khosrokhavar, *Inside Jihadism: Understanding Jihadi Movements Worldwide* (New York: Paradigm, 2009).

26. An indispensable source for this cleavage is Vali Nasr, *The Shia Revival: How Conflicts within Islam Will Shape the Future* (New York: W. W. Norton, 2006). Also see Emmanuel Sivan, "The Clash within Islam," *Survival* 45 (Spring 2003): 25–44.

27. Doug Saunders, "Homegrown Terror: Be Afraid, Sort of Afraid," *Globe and Mail*, 6 September 2014, pp. F1–F2.

28. Konrad Yakabuski, "Obama Learns It Can Be Stupider To Do Nothing," *Globe and Mail*, 14 August 2014, p. A11.

29. The waves, in this case, extending from the first (the anarchists of the late nineteenth century and early twentieth century), through the second (national liberation fighters in the era of decolonization following the Second World War), third (leftist ideologues, often inspired by the Soviet Union, during the Cold War), to the fourth, and contemporary, one (religiously motivated violence); see David C. Rapoport, "The Four Waves of Modern Terrorism" in *Attacking Terrorism: Elements of a Grand Strategy,*

ed. Audrey Kurth Cronin and James Ludes (Washington, D.C.: Georgetown University Press, 2004), pp. 46–73.

30. See Frazer Egerton, *Jihad in the West: The Rise of Militant Salafism* (Cambridge: Cambridge University Press, 2011); Gilles Kepel, *The War for Muslim Minds: Islam and the West*, trans. Pascale Ghazaleh (Cambridge, Mass.: Belknap Press, 2004); and Jarret M. Brachman, *Global Jihadism: Theory and Practice* (New York: Routledge, 2008).

31. Peter G. Mandaville, *Transnational Muslim Politics: Reimagining the Umma* (New York: Routledge, 2001).

32. Marc Sageman, *Understanding Terror Networks* (Philadelphia: University of Pennsylvania Press, 2004), pp. 1–9.

33. Abdallah Azam, "Join the Caravan," in *Al Qaeda in Its Own Words*, comp. Gilles Kepel and Jean-Pierre Milelli, (Cambridge, Mass.: Belknap Press, 2008), pp. 110–25, quote at p. 117.

34. Azam, "Join the Caravan," pp. 146–47.

35. See Lawrence Wright, *The Looming Tower: Al Qaeda and the Road to 9/11* (New York: Vintage, 2006).

36. See his August 1996 "Declaration of War against the Americans Occupying the Land of the Two Holy Places," quoted in *Al Qaeda in Its Own Words*, pp. 47–50.

37. "Knights under the Prophet's Banner," in *Al Qaeda in Its Own Words*, pp. 193–205.

38. Quoted in Marc Sageman, "Understanding Terror Networks," *E-notes*, 1 November 2004 (Washington, D.C.: Foreign Policy Research Institute, 1 November 2004), p. 13; available at http://www.fpri.org/enotes/20041101.middleeast.sageman.understandingterrornetworks.html.

39. See Fawaz A. Gerges, *The Far Enemy: Why Jihad Went Global* (Cambridge: Cambridge University Press 2005).

40. Norman Podhoretz, *World War IV: The Long Struggle against Islamofascism* (New York: Doubleday, 2007).

41. An indispensable critique of the misapplication of "fascism" in the generic sense, predating the more recent invocations of "Islamofascism," remains Gilbert Allardyce, "What Fascism Is Not: Thoughts on the Deflation of a Concept," *American Historical Review* 84 (April 1979): 367–88.

42. Henry E. Hale, *The Foundations of Ethnic Politics: Separatism of States and Nations in Eurasia and the World* (New York: Cambridge University Press, 2008), p. 47. Also see the similarly capacious understanding of ethnicity as representing "a combination of language, custom and ritual, inculcated in the home, the school and the temple," in Niall Ferguson, *The War of the World: Twentieth-Century Conflict and the Descent of the West* (New York: Penguin, 2006), p. xlvii.

43. See, for instance, Haideh Moghissi, Saeed Rahnema, and Mark J. Goodman, eds., *Diaspora by Design: Muslims in Canada and Beyond* (Toronto: University of Toronto Press, 2009); Behrooz Ghamari-Tabrizi, "Loving America and Longing for Home: Isma'il al-Faruqi and the Emergence of the Muslim Diaspora in North America," *International Migration* 42 (June 2004): 61–86; Christoph Schumann, "A Muslim 'Diaspora' in the United States?" *Muslim World* 97 (2007): 12–13; and Darcy A. Zabel, ed., *Arabs in the Americas: Interdisciplinary Essays on the Arab Diaspora* (New York: Peter Lang, 2006).

44. "Muslim Americans: Middle East and Mostly Mainstream," *Pew Research Center,* 22 May 2007; available at http://pewresearch.org/assets/pdf/muslim-americans.pdf.

45. Lawrence H. Fuchs, "Minority Groups and Foreign Policy," *Political Science Quarterly* 74 (June 1959): 161–75, quote at p. 162.

46. Sadia R. Chaudhury and Lisa Miller, "Religious Identity Formation among Bangladeshi American Muslim Adolescents," *Journal of Adolescent Research* 23 (July 2008): 383–410, citing from pp. 383–84.

47. Carl Bialek, "Elusive Numbers: U.S. Population by Religion," *Wall Street Journal*, 23 August 2010, online ed.

48. Qumar al-Huda, "The Diversity of Muslims in the United States," *United States Institute of Peace Special Report*, no. 59 (February 2006) p. 1; available at http://www. usip.org/files/resources/sr159.pdf.

49. "The Future of the Global Muslim Population," *Pew Forum on Religion and Public Life*, 27 January 2011; available at http://www.pewforum.org/The-Future-of-the-Global-Muslim-Population.aspx.

50. Nader Ayish, "Stereotypes, Popular Culture, and School Curricula: How Arab-American Muslim High School Students Perceive and Cope with Being the 'Other'," in Zabel, ed., *Arabs in the Americas*, pp. 79–116, citing from p. 103.

51. Ayish, "Stereotypes, Popular Culture, and School Curricula," pp. 79–116, citing from p. 103.

52. Ali A. Mazrui, "Between the Crescent and the Star-Spangled Banner: American Muslims and US Foreign Policy," *International Affairs* 72 (July 1996): 493–506, citing from p. 495.

53. James H. Hutson, "The Founding Fathers and Islam," *Library of Congress Information Bulletin* 61 (May 2002); available at http://www.loc.gov/loc/lcib/0205/tolerance.html. It is estimated that up to 30 percent of all slaves brought to America were from Muslim-majority parts of West Africa.

54. Charles D. Russell, "Islam as a Danger to Republican Virtue: Broadening Religious Liberty in Revolutionary Pennsylvania," *Pennsylvania History* 76 (Summer 2009): 250–75.

55. Since becoming a state, Pennsylvania has had five constitutions.

56. "A Guide to the United States' History of Recognition, Diplomatic, and Consular Relations," *U.S. Department of State, Office of Historian*; available at http://history.state.gov/countries/morocco.

57. For details, see Jocelyne Cesari, "Islam in the West from Immigration to Global Islam," *Harvard Middle Eastern and Islamic Review* 8 (2009): 148–75.

58. See Leonard Dinnerstein and David M. Reimers, *Ethnic Americans: A History of Immigration*, 4th ed. (New York: Columbia University Press, 1999); Roger Daniels, *Coming to America: A History of Immigration and Ethnicity in American Life* (New York: HarperCollins, 1990); and Edward Prince Hutchinson, *Legislative History of American Immigration Policy, 1798–1965* (Philadelphia: University of Pennsylvania Press, 1981).

59. "The Immigration Act," *Asian Nation: Asian-American History, Demographics, and Issues*; available at http://www.asian-nation.org/1965-immigration-act.shtml.

60. For an insightful analysis of Canada's Muslim diaspora, see Abolmohammad Kazemipur, *The Muslim Question in Canada: A Story of Segmented Integration* (Vancouver: UBC Press, 2014).

61. Charles Lewis, "Number of Muslims in Canada Predicted to Triple Over Next 20 Years," *National Post* (Toronto), 31 January 2011, online ed.

62. Karim H. Karim, "Crescent Dawn in the Great White North: Muslim Participation in the Canadian Public Sphere," in *Muslims in the West: From Sojourners to Citizens*, ed. Yvonne Yazbeck Haddad (New York: Oxford University Press, 2002), p. 263.

63. See Anny Bakalian and Mehdi Bozorgmehr, "Muslim American Mobilization," *Diaspora: A Journal of Transnational Studies* 14 (Spring 2005): 7–43; and Sami Aoun, "Muslim Communities: The Pitfalls of Decision-Making in Canadian Foreign Policy," in *Canada and the Middle East: In Theory and Practice*, ed. Paul Heinbecker and Bessma Momani (Waterloo, ON: Wilfrid Laurier Press, 2007), pp. 109–22.

64. One analyst who has sought to invest domestic ethnic groups with such influence is Mitchell Bard, *The Arab Lobby: The Invisible Alliance That Undermines America's Interests in the Middle East* (New York: HarperCollins, 2010). Also see Nabeel A. Khoury, "The Arab Lobby: Problems and Prospects," *Middle East Journal* 41 (Summer 1987): 379–96; and Steven J. Rosen, "The Arab Lobby: The European Component," *Middle East Quarterly* (Fall 2010): 17–32. More typically, the argument is made that to the extent any "ethnicity" can be associated with the influencing of foreign policy toward the Middle East, it is Jews not Muslims or Arabs who are well-endowed with "agency." Illustrative of this thesis are John J. Mearsheimer and Stephen M. Walt, *The*

Israel Lobby and US Foreign Policy (New York: Farrar, Straus and Giroux, 2007); Janice J. Terry, *US Foreign Policy in the Middle East: The Role of Lobbies and Special Interest Groups* (London: Pluto, 2005); and Edward Tivnan, *The Lobby: Jewish Political Power and American Foreign Policy* (New York: Simon & Schuster, 1987). For discussions of the Canadian case, see Brent E. Sasley and Tami Amanda Jacoby, "Canada's Jewish and Arab Communities and Canadian Foreign Policy," in Heinbecker and Momani, eds., *Canada and the Middle East*, pp. 185–204; and Elizabeth Riddell-Dixon, "Assessing the Impact of Recent Immigration Trends on Canadian Foreign Policy," in *The World in Canada: Diaspora, Demography and Domestic Politics*, ed. David Bercuson and David Carment (Montreal and Kingston: McGill-Queen's University Press, 2008), pp. 31–49.

65. Cited in Suhail A. Khan, "America's First Muslim President," *Foreign Policy*, 23 August 2010; available at http://www.foreignpolicy.com/articles/2010/08/23/americas_first_muslim_president.

66. See, respectively, Diane E. Davis, "Non-State Armed Actors, New Imagined Communities, and Shifting Patterns of Sovereignty and Insecurity in the Modern World," *Contemporary Security Policy* 30 (August 2009): 221–45; and Peter Andreas, "Redrawing the Line: Borders and Security in the Twenty-First Century," *International Security* 28 (Autumn 2003): 78–111.

67. For instance, see David T. Jones, "Open Borders and Closing Threats," *International Journal* 67 (Spring 2012): 527–40, as well as the reply thereto of Frank Harvey, "Closing Borders and Opening Debate," *International Journal* 67 (Spring 2012): 541–50. For earlier charges that Canada had functioned as such a harbor, see *Country Reports on Terrorism 2005* (Washington, D.C.: Department of State, Office of the Coordinator for Counterterrorism, April 2006), 1:567.

68. See the special report, "Bombs in Brooklyn: How the Two Illegal Aliens Arrested for Plotting to Bomb the New York Subway Entered and Remained in the United States" (Washington, D.C.: Department of Justice, Office of the Inspector General, March 1998), available at www.http://fas.org/irp/agency/doj/oig/brookb/brbrtoc.htm.

69. Stewart Bell, *Cold Terror: How Canada Nurtures and Exports Terrorism around the World*, rev. ed. (Toronto: John Wiley and Sons, 2007), p. 161.

70. For details, see Joseph T. McCann, *Terrorism on American Soil: A Concise History of Plots and Perpetrators from the Famous to the Forgotten* (Boulder, Colo.: Sentient Publications, 2006), pp. 268–69.

71. David T. Jones, "Yo, Canada! A Wake-Up Call for Y'All Up There," *Policy Options* 24 (February 2003): 45–48, quote at pp. 47–48.

72. Quoted in Daniel Leblanc, "Canada Praised for Tip to U.S. on Ressam," *Globe and Mail*, 4 December 2001, pp. A1, A13.

73. For interesting perspectives regarding the merits (or lack thereof) of being no. 1 in the international system, see Daniel W. Drezner, "Military Primacy Doesn't Pay (Nearly As Much As You Think)," *International Security* 38 (Summer 2013): 52–79; Stephen G. Brooks and William C. Wohlforth, "International Relations Theory and the Case against Unilateralism," *Perspectives on Politics* 3 (September 2005): 509–24; and Martha Finnemore, "Legitimacy, Hypocrisy, and the Social Structure of Unipolarity: Why Being a Unipole Isn't All It's Cracked Up to Be," *World Politics* 61 (January 2009): 58–85.

74. Quoted in Stewart Bell, "Al-Qaeda Warns Canada," *National Post*, 28 October 2006, p. 1.

75. A 1998 report of the Canadian Security Intelligence Service noted that more than fifty terrorist organizations were active in the country during that decade, but that it was considered to be a "primary venue of opportunity to support, plan or mount" terrorist attacks, rather than as a target; Justin Massie, "Canada's (In)dependence in the North American Security Community: The Asymmetrical Norm of Common Fate," *American Review of Canadian Studies* 37 (Winter 2007): 493–516, quote at p. 506.

76. See Alex S. Wilner, "Enemies Within: Confronting Homegrown Terrorism in Canada" (Halifax: Atlantic Institute for Market Studies, September 2008). Also see

Wilner, "Terrorism in Canada: Victims and Perpetrators," *Journal of Military and Strategic Studies* 12 (Spring 2010): 72–99.

77. One defense attorney, Faisal Mirza, even tried to convince a Canadian judge, John Sproat of the Ontario Superior Court, that since jihad constituted lawful armed resistance, it should be *protected* under the country's Charter of Rights and Freedoms! See Christie Blatchford, "There's No Charter Right to Jihad . . . at Least Not Yet," *Globe and Mail*, 26 April 2008, p. A2.

78. See Colin Freeze, "Terror Plot Finds Its End—Not with a Bang but with a Whimper," *Globe and Mail*, 8 October 2009, online ed.

79. See Robert D. McFadden, "Army Doctor Held in Fort Hood Rampage," *New York Times*, 5 November 2009, online ed.; and Scott Shane, "Homegrown Terror Gets New Assessment," *International Herald Tribune*, 14 December 2009, p. 4. Al Awlaki would be killed a few years later in a drone strike in Yemen; see Mark Mazzetti, Charlie Savage, and Scott Shane, "A U.S. Citizen, in America's Cross Hairs," *New York Times*, 10 March 2013, pp. 1, 12–13.

80. John Schwartz, "Bomb Investigation Pivots to a New Mystery: Motive," *New York Times*, 21 April 2013, pp. 1, 12.

81. Paul Koring, "Cities across U.S. Increase Security Moments after the Explosion," *Globe and Mail*, 16 April 2013, p. A7.

82. See Samuel Musa and Samuel Bendett, *Islamic Radicalization in the United States: New Trends and a Proposed Methodology for Disruption* (Washington, D.C.: National Defense University, Center for Technology and National Security Policy, September 2010).

83. See Fidel Sendagorta, "Jihad in Europe: The Wider Context," *Survival* 47 (Autumn 2005): 63–72.

84. See, for an example of this upbeat perspective, Rima Berns-McGown, *The Perception and Reality of "Imported Conflict" in Canada* (Toronto: Mosaic Institute, March 2014).

85. Michael S. Schmidt and Mark Mazzetti, "Suicide Bomber from U.S. Came Home before Attack," *New York Times*, 31 July 2014, pp. A1, A10.

86. As detailed in Joe Friesen, Colin Freeze, and Omar El Akkad, "Jihad Rising," *Globe and Mail*, 6 September 2014, pp. F6–F7.

87. See Ian Austen, "2 Canadians Who Joined Algeria Attack Are Identified," *New York Times*, 3 April 2013, p. A4; Colin Freeze, Tu Thanh Ha, and Ann Hui, "From a High School in Ontario to Terror in the Algerian Desert," *Globe and Mail*, 3 April 2013, pp. A1–4; and Christie Blatchford, "Alarm Bells Ringing on Deaf Ears," *National Post*, 3 April 2013, p. A5. Two other Canadians from the same high school are also thought to be implicated in homegrown terrorist activities, Mujahid Enderi and Aaron Yoon. See Murray Brewster, Stephanie Levits, and Allison Jones, "Fourth London, Ont., Man Sought for Terror Ties," *Globe and Mail*, 13 April 2013, p. A3.

88. Charles Kurzman, David Schanzer, and Ebrahim Moosa, "Muslim American Terrorism Since 9/11: Why So Rare?" *Muslim World* 101 (July 2011): 464–83.

Conclusion

Three sets of concluding remarks suggest themselves, based on the theoretical and empirical results presented in this book. The first set contains a pair of epistemological issues arising from the attempt, such as has been made in these pages, to "contextualize" the relationship between demographic flux and security relations within North America. How has the phenomenon of "people in motion" been implicated in the story of the rise and evolution of the Canada-United States security community, as well as more generally in the process of institutionalized collective-defense arrangements that bind the two states in pursuit of objectives that often (though not always) overlap? The second set of remarks goes to the manner in which normative considerations get inserted into the discussion of contemporary security linkages between Canada and the United States. And the third set addresses some of the developments that we might be expected to see arising in future, based on what we think we know about what happened in the past. In this concluding chapter, I take these in turn.

In the introduction, I made reference to an argument advanced by Paul Pierson, stating the social-science bona fides of analysts' seeking to "put politics in time." Also in that same chapter, I listed (perhaps somewhat rashly) as being among my objectives in this book the generation of something called "generic knowledge," in this case knowledge pertaining to the impact that those demographic entities known as ethnic diasporas might have for international security writ broadly, and North American security in particular. In this section, I want to pursue this quest, doing so in part by introducing an approach that some international relations (IR) scholars, myself among them, have been finding of utility in recent years, "strategic culture." Specifically, I want to ask how introducing this approach might cast some light on the quest for contextualization. For among devotees of strategic culture, there has been in recent years a lively if inconclusive debate over the meaning of "context," a debate that highlights some important considerations regarding just how politics *is* to be put in time. Now, Pierson himself is neither a scholar of IR nor, as far as I can tell, does he take any inspiration from the category of strategic culture. This is hardly a criticism, for that category is nothing if not a bundle of confusing and often contradictory claims and counterclaims.[1] In fact, it is otherwise irrelevant to the story I have sought to tell in these pages—at the very least, that story can be recounted with no

appeal whatsoever to strategic culture—but there is, nevertheless, a reason to bring it into the discussion, even at such a late stage in a book as its
concluding chapter.

The reason is precisely because of that debate within the ranks of
strategic culturalists over what "context" is to mean, and how it should
be employed. Context, it turns out, has been the object of many a strategic
culturalist's conceptual fancy, and often when it is up for discussion
among this breed of IR analyst, it is employed as a surrogate for another
item of disputation, one touching the very core of the epistemological
enterprise in the human sciences. This other item is the familiar intellectual struggle between the "positivists" and their ostensive philosophical
adversaries, the anti-positivists or "interpretivists."[2] This struggle within
strategic cultural ranks can be regarded, therefore, as simply a continuation of a long-standing controversy within the human sciences in general
as to what their basal purpose should or can be, with the former (the
positivists) espousing the quest for "explanation" of social reality, and
the latter claiming to content themselves with "understanding" the
same—as if the two undertakings are so fundamentally at odds with each
other as to admit of no possibility of synergy.[3]

And this is why Pierson's approach is so helpful, for his insistence
upon the positivist credentials of contextualization can tell us something
valuable about the way in which ethnic diasporas might be theorized as
important elements in the regional security setting of North America. As
we recall from the introduction, Pierson believes that "path dependence"
can be the mechanism for alerting analysts to the situational awareness
bequeathed by history. For sure, path dependence is itself hardly a
straightforward, much less an uncontested, epistemological approach.[4]
To the extent it means anything at all, it must, again as Pierson writes,
stand in contradistinction to certain assumptions of rational choice theory
that claim "large" causes should result in "large" outcomes.[5] I take him
here to be advancing more than the simple claim, commonsensical as that
claim may otherwise be, that policy choices made long in the past can go
on limiting policy options into the present and the future.[6] Something
else must be invoked if path dependence is to be able to play a part in our
"process-tracing" enterprise.[7] Indeed, path dependence implies that the
process itself through which history unfolds takes on causal importance,
in what some scholars have been referring to as "narrative positivism."[8]

Thus, for path dependence to connote anything, it cannot simply be
sensitive dependence upon "initial conditions"; rather, it must suggest a
break point after which the ability of those initial conditions to shape the
future can be shown to have altered substantially.[9] Some will label that
break point "contingency"; others will term it a "critical juncture," by
which they will mean those moments when choices get made that prove
to have lasting impact, because they foreclose alternative future possibilities, through the generation of "self-reinforcing path-dependent process-

es,"[10] referred to varyingly as "positive feedback," or "lock-in," or "increasing returns" (this third formulation often being favored by economists). Although there is no *necessary* reason for the logic of positive feedback to yield positive outcomes for interstate cooperation, usually the tendency of those who are enamored of path-dependent approaches is to dwell upon "efficient cooperation" as that which is being "locked in," and hence to forget that sometimes path dependency can consist in "reactive sequences" capable of generating negative outcomes for cooperation.[11]

How can this perhaps esoteric bit of reflection be applied specifically to this book's focus upon ethnic diasporas and the Canada-United States security community? To begin with, let us recollect Mabel Walker's assessment of the meaning of Irish America for bilateral security relations in North America, something touched upon in chapter four. At that time I noted that she seemed to be somewhat euphemistically taking the measure of Irish American diasporic activism by referring to it as having "occasionally complicated" U.S. foreign policy. Indeed. Compared with the other two diasporic cases examined in this book, it can easily be said that Irish America stands out in the manner in which it served as a wedge, at least for a time, inhibiting closer security and defense cooperation between the two North American neighbors, and because of this it can certainly be implicated in the somewhat tardy arrival upon the continental scene of their security community, as was discussed in chapter two. The reason for this early "success" of the diaspora had partly to do with the fact that some activists were trying to invade Canada, and partly the belief (possibly mistaken) that the Irish possessed a very powerful electoral shillelagh, with which to bludgeon into line any American politician unwise enough to go against their preferences at election time. Mainly, however—and here is where path dependence enters the picture—it had a great deal to do with the temporary correspondence of interest between a large anti-English diaspora pulsating with nationalist sentimentality and an even larger body of domestic public opinion steeped in anti-British political ideology. Until such time as diplomatic amity could be effected as between the United States and the United Kingdom, which as we saw in chapter two did not occur until the end of the nineteenth century, what Irish America "wanted" in foreign policy was essentially congruent with the interests of the country itself, or at least was not so out of step with those interests as to occasion a backlash against diasporic activism on the part of the majority.

Thus, following path-dependent logic, we can say that after the turn of the last century, the nature of ethnic-diasporic "influence" upon U.S. foreign policy—and especially upon Canadian-American relations—was going to change, sometimes in surprising ways. Whether we date it from 1895, 1898, or even 1896, it is obvious that at some moment in the nineteenth century's final quinquennium, there emerged a critical juncture in the development of security relations within both the North Atlantic triangle and the North American continent. The point cannot be overstressed, for if we accept that contingency at that time resulted in the setting of Anglo-American relations upon a new and more cooperative footing, then there would be profound implications for how we assess this quality so energetically sought by ethnic-diasporic activists a century or so ago—namely, the quality we call influence. What this contingent moment means, therefore, for North American security arrangements is that henceforth it can be safely assumed that the negative consequences of diasporic activism could never loom as large as they once did, at a time when, at the very least, it could be said that a correspondence of geopolitical interest existed between an Irish American diaspora intent somehow to punish Britain, and an American government rather inclined to think that its doing so might not be such a bad idea.

The rapprochement, of course, spawned neither a security community in North America nor the Canada-United States alliance, despite what has sometimes been claimed, erroneously, about the era of close security and defense relations between the members of the North Atlantic triangle having begun at the dawn of the twentieth century. Both the security community and the alliance were, at that time, several years in the future. Still, we can take the rapprochement as representing a necessary condition of improved security relations. This, in turn, leads us to a second important contextual issue relating to epistemology, the issue of how we are to understand the meaning of influence when it comes to attempts made by ethnic diasporas to achieve a voice in foreign policy decision making. Once again, contextualizing things can help us grasp some important dynamics associated with ethnic-diasporic activism. As we realize from chapter three's lengthy inquiry into the topic, the scholars are much divided on this topic. Some appear to believe that ethnic interests have too much impact upon policy, and that it is a bad thing. Others feel those interests should have even more voice, for it is good that they can exercise sway over decisions affecting relations between (usually) the United States and their kin-states, because by doing so they improve the quality of American foreign policy. Still others wonder whether the entire matter has been blown out of proportion, convinced as they are that on decisions concerning the "national" interest, it remains that central state entities continue to call the shots. Despite their disagreements, all would agree that influence per se should be assessed in terms of what it is that the ethnic pressure groups in question are seeking to accomplish. The corollary assumption is that if they fail in their attempt at gaining influence—and as we saw in chapter five, the combined Irish-German influence quests aimed at keeping America neutral during the First World War did not achieve their sought-after objective—then they can be adjudged to be bereft of influence.

This strikes me as a perverse way to grasp the significance of influence. There is, as I tried to argue in chapter five, another way of looking at the matter—a way that might also be added to the generic-knowledge side of the ledger, under the column reserved for matters of epistemology. That chapter's subtitle, evoking the "principle of the opposite effect," alerts us to the need to take influence to embrace not merely policy responses that were *intended* as well as elicited, but also those that were neither intended nor much desired. Seen in this perspective, then, the impact of ethnic-diasporic activism a century ago upon Canada-United States security relations looks different from the traditional version, which holds that Irish and German American lobbying was bad for regional security cooperation in North America, because it prevented America from entering the First World War sooner, with all that this delay must have entailed for Canadian (and British) interests. According to the traditional version, not much really *had* changed for the better in respect of ethnic lobbying in the United States over the half century following the Civil War: the phenomenon continued to redound negatively for Canada, perhaps not as dramatically as had the earlier experience with radical Irish nationalism, but still it was a phenomenon that yielded adverse results. To so argue, however, would be wrong.

The two large diasporas of a century ago surely did aspire to achieve influence over American foreign policy. Ironically, they obtained it. But it did not bring the desired fruits. Instead, the ethnic lobbying of the years 1914 to 1917 generated a backlash that rendered, or so it can be hypothesized here, American involvement in the war alongside Britain (and Canada) more rather than less likely. It would take a separate book to flesh out this argument, which I introduce here merely to signal the importance of "emotion" to assessments of decision making, a field of inquiry that has been attracting growing scholarly interest in the past few years.[12] For it was the emotional response of the majority (English-descended) population in America that led to a short-lived, but critically important, process of "civilizational rallying" on behalf of the British (and Canadian) war effort, by providing not just the permissive conditions for America's entering the conflict, but also compelling popular pressure to transform those permissive conditions into sufficient ones.

The insertion of emotion into discussions of foreign policy enables us to suggest a second sense, this time a normative one, of the contribution that contextualization might make to policy debates regarding ethnicity and security, especially contemporary debates. From chapter one's analysis, we remember that a decade or so ago there occurred an upsurge in acrimonious discussion among policy elites on either side of the Canada-United States border. The dialogue, if that is what it was during those years, took on an ever-more acerbic tone, for reasons related to, though not entirely caused by, the divergent approaches the two countries took toward the Iraq war in 2003. In the words of two policy analysts cited in chapter one, who were writing a few years after the overthrow of Saddam Hussein, each side appeared to be hard at work on the task of perfecting its own role as an "injustice collector,"[13] to the detriment of harmonious bilateral relations. On each side, there was an appalling lack of contextual understanding of the generic issue around which this book has been structured, and in the face of prevailing ignorance it was easy for intemperate observers to think the worst of their policy counterparts across the border. In this fraught atmosphere, a little historical context might have gone a long way to lower the shrillness and harshness of this particular policy dispute whose roots were to be found in the conjunction of demography with security. For what was so setting minds at unease was the conviction that North America was suddenly facing a problem the likes of which had *never* been encountered before, and for which there existed no inventory of prior policy debates and adaptations. In short, there was no analytical or normative context to provide guidance to policy makers—or so it appeared, to many.

But of course, the problem—to the extent that it was getting increasingly focused upon "NSAAs" and "CTAs"[14] (aka terrorists) linked in no undisguised manner to ethnic diasporas in North America—was hardly novel. It was, in fact, rather a familiar problem, or would have so seemed had anyone taken the trouble to think about it in historical context. Had they done so, it is possible that clarity might have more readily been brought to bear on the post-9/11 challenge, or at the very least that the urge to score points at the expense of the other country might have been somewhat sublimated. Illustratively, Canada in the early 2000s was being said by some American officials to be developing into a threat to U.S. security, because of a fear that recent refugee claimants in Canada happened to be infused with Salafist ideology that, in their minds, staked out America as a legitimate target. Some American officials were beginning to wonder whether their Canadian counterparts had simply forgotten all about that norm from 1938 (the "Kingston dispensation") obliging each North American country to take *very* seriously the legitimate physical security interests of the other; such was their worry that through inadvertence Ottawa was continuing to permit the entry into continental confines of any number of terrorists bent on harming America, and who could do so as a result of the ease of transit over the Canada-United States border. For sure, this did appear for a time as a troubling prospect, but if it was such, it certainly paled into virtual insignificance when contrasted with earlier, and similar, episodes of diaspora-linked security challenges, such as those related to the generic problem of Fenianism we encountered in earlier chapters.

For their part, many Canadians, equally indifferent to the historical record, were convincing themselves that America was becoming dangerously inattentive to the safeguarding of civil liberties, such was the zeal of officials to ensure homeland security, with all that it implied, not just for border management procedures, but for the integrity of the country's own constitutional guarantees of rights. Symbolically, the deteriorating tenor of Canada-United States policy discourse came for a time to focus upon one individual, Omar Khadr, who as a youth had been recruited into Salafist jihadism by his parents, and had left Canada for combat in Afghanistan, where he was implicated in the killing of an American soldier in October 2002. For this, he was later tried by a U.S. military court, leading to his entering a plea of guilty, and being kept in Guantánamo Bay prison in Cuba, before being turned over to Canadian authorities for the completion of his sentence in Canada.

In the United States, Khadr represented the human face of the threat that would come to be known as homegrown terrorism, just as Ahmed Ressam represented the filibustering face of the "new Fenianism." In Canada, Khadr was sometimes seen as an innocent victim of others,[15] in the first instance of his parents, and in the second of an oppressive security establishment whose failings are epitomized by Guantánamo, the offshore facility so frequently in use over the last decade to incarcerate Islamists and others deemed a threat to homeland security in the United States. In chapter four, I suggested that Khadr had an Irish American counterpart from the nineteenth century, and although the parallels between the two cases are hardly perfect, the analogy here is meant to convey a simple point: just about everything that some Canadians had been alleging was going wrong with American justice had, at one time, also been said about Canadian justice by Irish Americans, for whom Luke Dillon served as the cause célèbre of a generation of activists who held Kingston Penitentiary in the same contempt as today's civil libertarians regard Guantánamo.

In the Canada of recent years, there has been a growing chorus of critics of what was taken to be both an American overreaction to the new security challenges as well as a worrisome degradation of domestic civil liberties. I invoke the analogy of the Irish challenge of yore, although I am well aware that this mode of reasoning has flaws, which is why some scholars will warn against policy makers' *anywhere* being urged to put too much stock in analogies.[16] Analogical reasoning, it is said, can sometimes exacerbate the emotional tone of policy discussions about international security, in the West as well as elsewhere in the world—and in this respect, attention has often been drawn to the manner in which challenges during the era of the Cold War were routinely, and unwisely, held to betray affinities with "Munich 1938," that is, with the perils of "appeasement," and as a result, analogies contributed to major errors of policy judgment.[17] Sometimes, however, the failing is elsewhere, not in asserting but in denying that there could be value in consulting the historical legacy. In sum, there can be an upside to analogical reasoning. Not only does it provide a template for addressing contemporary policy problems analytically; it can also serve as a means of turning down the emotional heat associated with policy disputes.

In this respect, what the Irish analogy, along with the German analogy (though in a different sense), suggests quite strongly for the normative assessment of North American regional security politics is this: neither Canada nor the United States holds any particular bragging rights when it comes either to respecting the norms and practices of good continental "neighborliness," or (more to the point) to upholding civil liberties at moments of international crisis. Both countries have been deficient on each score. Canadians resented, and rightly so, having been seen for a while as the weak link in America's chain of homeland defenses—and if there was some merit, as we saw in chapter one that there was, in the criticism of Canadian security lapses in the 1990s and subsequent years, those lapses certainly paled in comparison with how America once constituted not just a "weak link" in, but *the* principal threat to, Canada's own homeland security at certain moments following the American Civil War—and this, for reasons rooted in diasporic activism. Those were years, ironically, during which both countries appeared well-embarked on their respective voyages on the good ship "liberal democracy," so it might have been anticipated, following the logic of "democratic peace theory," that their erstwhile pattern of bad-neighborly interaction had well and truly become a relic of the past by 1867, the year of the founding of present-day Canada. But this did not transpire, at least not immediately, and in the American case it was often argued that the Constitution and its protection for freedoms of speech and assembly actually was one reason why cells planning violent action against either Canada or Britain, or both (viz., the American Waziristan), were allowed to carry on their plotting unmolested by state authorities, even though Canadian and British authorities wanted and demanded a more energetic crackdown from the authorities, along the lines of those that had been triggered in both Canada and the UK during the height of "Fenian fever." Nor did either Canada or the United States cover itself in glory in the manner with which their respective German diasporas were treated during the First World War—for the entirety of the conflict in Canada's case, and for its final year and a half, in America's. In both countries, it became a very unwise practice for German North Americans to militate on behalf of the kin-state, or even to utter favorable words about it in public.

And though during the Second World War both Canada and the United States were relatively less inclined to trammel upon the civil liberties of their respective German communities, the shockingly harsh manner in which both countries treated their citizens and residents of Japanese descent brought more than an ample heaping of shame to each, albeit if only in retrospect. This record of manifold blemishes on both sides of the border is one reason why some Americans have been known to take poorly to Canadian criticism of the U.S. record on civil liberties—criticism they take to reek of hypocrisy. Apropos this criticism, one American foreign policy analyst, Walter Russell Mead, has somewhat tartly, if not necessarily inaccurately, discerned a "tone of whiny self-righteousness today among some Canadians who, accepting the undoubted superiority of American military power, feel that their distinctive contributions to the alliance can and should be a quality in which Americans are poor, while Canada is specially, even uniquely rich—morality." He goes on, wryly, to note that "[o]ne of the most annoying things for foreigners about Americans is that we sometimes sound to them the way Canadians sound to us."[18]

As we saw in chapter six, the emotionalism of the contemporary challenge posed to North America by Salafist jihadism has in recent years become muted, at least insofar as that emotionalism could be said to hinder bilateral security cooperation. To no small degree, this has been as a result of changing circumstances linked to the rise of the "homegrown" phenomenon. Far from continuing to be a wedge issue serving to divide policy elites on either side of the border, as it looked a decade or so ago that it might become, jihadism has presented an occasion for the deepening of security and defense cooperation between the North American neighbors, especially in the area of homeland security. For today, both countries share a reasonably similar perception of the threat, and each is grappling with policy measures, including domestic measures aimed at "de-radicalizing" current as well as wannabe jihadists. Martin Luther's apothegm pertaining to threat assessing—namely that "it makes a difference whose ox is gored"—speaks volumes in this regard. For gone are the days when it could be imagined by some in Canada that, to the extent Salafist jihadism posed a problem in North America, its most worrisome feature from the Canadian perspective was its impact upon American border-management practices; today, officials in Ottawa understand the threat to be more comprehensive than that, even if no one would deny the crucial impact of border policy on Canadian economic prospects.[19]

This observation gets us to our final set of concluding comments, concerning whether generic knowledge might be gleaned from this book, with applicability to that zone of temporal inquiry about which no one possesses good information, the future. Can anything usefully be said, based on the first two case studies, in chapters four and five, with relevance to today's challenge as discussed in chapter six? I suggest the answer is in the affirmative. First, it seems apparent that if ethnic-diasporic activism has, as I have tried in this book to argue, possessed bearing upon the manner in which the Canada-United States security community has arisen and evolved (this latter to include its relationship to the two countries' alliance), then it seems incontrovertible that the divisive potential of such activism in North America has been on a downward trajectory for a lengthy period of time. The impact of diasporic activism upon Canada-United States relations has become less worrisome as the years have gone by, and this notwithstanding the widespread assumption that in an era characterized, such as the present is routinely said to be, by "globalization," the security implications of people in motion might be thought to be compounding. It may well be that elsewhere on earth, they are doing precisely this, but not in North America, at least not if our field of geographic focus is that large part of the continent shared by Canada and the United States.

If this is so, what if anything does the record of diasporic activism in North America suggest about the future? First, it tells us that size is important, for reasons related both to the more kinetic kinds of security activism in which Irish America, in particular, once specialized, but also to the more important cluster of influence attempts associated with, and subsumed under, the rubric of ethnic lobbying. There can be no question regarding the presumed "clout" of the Muslim North American diaspora in respect of lobbying activity, whether narrowly or broadly conceived: there is not much clout to speak of. Any comparison, on this grounds alone, with either of the other two cases in this book is simply unwarranted—and as we saw, even the ability of the *combined* lobbying efforts of Irish and German America a century ago to attain the desired impact has been grossly overstated, if not completely misconstrued.

What, though, of the illegal aspects of activism as evinced by some whose roots can be said to lie within diasporic soil in North America? Here again, the comparisons are revealing more for the contrasts than the similarities. Apart from size, there are two major differences setting the Muslim North American diaspora apart from the predecessor Irish and German American ones. First, the leadership of both Irish America and German America, at the height of the period during which influence was sought over U.S. foreign policy, was committed to a policy agenda that had to be seen as detrimental, at the outset, to Canadian interests—an agenda that, by and large, received widespread support from the "rank and file" of diasporic membership. In stark contrast, today's leadership cadres in the Muslim diasporas of both Canada and the United States are as committed to the struggle against Salafist jihadism as anyone else— perhaps even more so, given their understandable (and not illogical) concerns about the dangers of an anti-Muslim backlash being stoked should homegrown-terrorist violence become more pronounced than it has been to date.

A second major contrast concerns the nonexistence, for that selfsame diasporic leadership, of any extant or imagined kin-state around which to rally (we can take it as a given that diaspora leaders are hardly inclined to rally around the self-proclaimed "Islamic State" of Abu Bakr al Baghdadi, which as of this writing looks to have a rather short lease on life). In the case of the Irish Americans, the core objective all along had been to revise the political status quo of the Emerald Isle, thus it is hardly surprising that once this goal had been chiefly accomplished with the Anglo-Irish treaty of late 1921, there set in a rapid and dramatic decline of diasporic activism possessed of security-policy implications, in North America as elsewhere. And even with the slight uptick in such activism later in the twentieth century, of the sort that once inspired Peter T. King to militate on behalf of the IRA in Northern Ireland, the renewed militancy could hardly be said to possess any serious (or even minor) implications for Canada-U.S. security relations. Similarly with the German Americans, their policy activism, which was genuine and almost exclusively of a legal, constitutional, nature during the run-up to the American entry into the First World War, dissolved following that entry, virtually overnight. The point here is that for each of the two most important cases of diaspora-related security challenges North America had ever known, the "problem" basically disappeared as a result of developments outside the continent.

Might something similar be said of our third case? Is there some external solution to the domestic problem of homegrown terrorism in North America? On the positive side, we do know that "de-radicalization" (of a sort) became the order of the day for both Irish America and German America, so much so that at present it would be exceedingly difficult to the point of being impossible to argue that the "interests" of members of either diaspora, insofar as concerns foreign policy, are in any way different from the preferences expressed by mainstream American opinion. Might something similar take place in respect of that extremely tiny portion of the North American Muslim diaspora today inclined toward Salafist jihadism, that somehow it will find itself reentering something approximating a North American consensus on what constitutes politically acceptable behavior, and what does not? Here the case for optimism must be a bit more subdued, partly because no one really understands what drives Western homegrowns toward Salafist jihadism in the first place.[20] Moreover, even if they did know the answer, it is not at all clear what the solution to the problem may be, notwithstanding that the fighting against the Islamic State (IS, aka ISIS, sometimes ISIL) represents one of those very rare moments in recent international security politics where unanimity on the UN Security Council has been reached regarding an identified threat, along with a sweeping array of programs intended to combat it, some of the latter involving military measures, and some aimed at inhibiting the ability of Western homegrowns either to travel to the Middle Eastern killing fields or, once there, to return home from them.[21]

Perhaps it is fitting, therefore, to give the last word on the contemporary challenge posed by certain "people in motion" to an obscure Chilean political figure of a century ago, who was more remembered (if remembered he even is) for *lack* of motion than for its opposite. Nevertheless, what this former president of Chile (1910–1915) is said, perhaps apocryphally, to have remarked about political challenges is suggestive for the challenges to North American regional security that have, from time to time, been associated with the phenomenon of diasporic activism. Asked by a reporter whether he was finding his job of trying to run Chile difficult, Ramón Barros Luco replied in the negative. This was because, in his experience in politics, there were really only two kinds of problems, "those that solve themselves, and those that have no solution.[22]

We know that, in respect of the Irish and German American diasporic challenge to regional security in North America, it turned out to be the former. What no one can say is whether that pattern will hold with the current challenge.

NOTES

1. For a conceptual analysis that emphasizes the varying manner in which the category is employed, see my "What Good Is Strategic Culture?" in *Strategic Culture and Weapons of Mass Destruction: Culturally Based Insights into Comparative National Security Policymaking*, ed. Jeannie L. Johnson, Kerry M. Kartchner, and Jeffrey A. Larsen (New York: Palgrave Macmillan, 2009), pp. 15–31.

2. For this scholarly tussle, see Alastair Iain Johnston, "Thinking about Strategic Culture," *International Security* 19 (Spring 1995): 32–64; Colin S. Gray, "Strategic Culture as Context: The First Generation of Theory Strikes Back," *Review of International Studies* 25 (January 1999): 49–69; and Stuart Poore, "What Is the Context? A Reply to the Gray-Johnston Debate on Strategic Culture," *Review of International Studies* 29 (April 2003): 279–84.

3. For a strong statement that the difference is real, and significant, see Martin Hollis and Steve Smith, *Explaining and Understanding International Relations* (Oxford: Clarendon Press, 1990). But for the argument that the epistemological distinction might just be overdrawn, see Georg Henrik von Wright, *Explanation and Understanding* (Ithaca, N.Y.: Cornell University Press, 1971).

4. See, for instance, the thoughtful critique by Andrew R. Rutten, "Review Essay: Politics in Time," *Independent Review* 11 (Fall 2006): 299–305.

5. Paul Pierson, "Increasing Returns, Path Dependence, and the Study of Politics," *American Political Science Review* 94 (June 2000): 251–68, quote at p. 252. Also see Margaret R. Somers, "'We're No Angels': Realism, Rational Choice, and Relationality in Social Science," *American Journal of Sociology* 104 (November 1998): 722–84.

6. See Theda Skocpol, "Sociology's Historical Imagination," in *Vision and Method in Historical Sociology*, ed. Skocpol (Cambridge: Cambridge University Press, 1984), pp. 1–21.

7. For explications of this currently voguish qualitative methodology among some IR specialists, see Alexander L. George and Andrew Bennett, *Case Studies and Theory Development in the Social Sciences* (Cambridge, Mass.: MIT Press, 2005), as well as David Collier, "Understanding Process Tracing," *PS: Political Science and Politics* 44 (October 2011): 823–30.

8. Andrew Abbott, "From Causes to Events: Notes on Narrative Positivism," *Sociological Methods and Research* 20 (May 1992): 428–55. Also relevant here are Kevin Fox Gotham and William G. Staples, "Narrative Analysis and the New Historical Sociology," *Sociological Quarterly* 37 (Summer 1996): 481–501; John Gerard Ruggie, "Peace in Our Time? Causality, Social Facts, and Narrative Knowing," *American Society of International Law: Proceedings 89th Annual Meeting* (1995): 93–100; and Lawrence Stone, "The Revival of the Narrative: Reflections on a New Old History," *Past and Present* 85 (November 1979): 3–24.

9. See Jack A. Goldstone, "Initial Conditions, General Laws, Path Dependence, and Explanation in Historical Sociology," *American Journal of Sociology* 104 (November 1998): 829–45.

10. Giovanni Capoccia and R. Daniel Kelemen, "The Study of Critical Junctures: Theory, Narrative, and Counterfactuals in Historical Institutionalism," *World Politics* 59 (April 2007): 341–69, quote at p. 341.

11. James Mahoney, "Path Dependence in Historical Sociology," *Theory and Society* 29 (August 2000): 507–48.

12. For examples of this renewed interest in what had been a core concept of an earlier generation of classical realists (emotion), see Simon Koschut, "Emotional (Security) Communities: The Significance of Emotion Norms in Inter-Allied Conflict Management," *Review of International Studies* 40 (July 2014): 533–58; Jonathan Mercer, "Human Nature and the First Image: Emotion in International Politics," *Journal of International Relations and Development* 9 (September 2006): 288–303; and Brent E. Sasley, "Theorizing States' Emotions," *International Studies Review* 13 (September 2011): 452–76.

13. David T. Jones and David Kilgour, *Uneasy Neighbo(u)rs: Canada, the USA and the Dynamics of State, Industry and Culture* (Mississauga, ON: John Wiley and Sons, 2007), pp. xiii–xiv.

14. Respectively, for two categories introduced in the first chapters of this book: non-state armed actors, and clandestine transnational actors.

15. Although it has to be said that not all Canadians have jumped aboard this particular bandwagon; for one extreme critic of Khadr's, see Ezra Levant, *The Enemy Within: Terror, Lies and the Whitewashing of Omar Khadr* (Toronto: McClelland and Stewart, 2011). But for a decidedly different perspective, see Konrad Yakabuski, "Omar Khadr Is a 'Good Kid'—Not a Bogeyman," *Globe and Mail* (Toronto), 31 July 2014, p. A11.

16. For this cautionary note, see Robert Jervis, "International History and International Politics: Why Are They Studied Differently?" in *Bridges and Boundaries: Historians, Political Scientists, and the Study of International Relations*, ed. Colin Elman and Miriam Fendius Elman (Cambridge, Mass.: MIT Press, 2001), pp. 385–402.

17. See, for this claim, Neta C. Crawford, "The Passion of World Politics: Propositions on Emotion and Emotional Relationships," *International Security* 24 (Spring 2000): 116–56, citing from p. 145: "Analogies may . . . be emotionally persuasive. . . . Those who wish to drive home a point may thus purposely bring emotions into play by using emotionally charged analogies." Also see Yuen Foong Khong, *Analogies at War: Korea, Munich, Dien Bien Phu, and the Vietnam Decisions of 1965* (Princeton, N.J.: Princeton University Press, 1992); and Yaacov Y. I. Vertzberger, *The World in Their Minds: Information Processing, Cognition, and Perception in Foreign Policy Decisionmaking* (Stanford, Calif.: Stanford University Press, 1990).

18. Walter Russell Mead, *God and Gold: Britain, America, and the Making of the Modern World* (New York: Alfred A. Knopf, 2008), pp. 47–48.

19. As an example of current levels of anxiety regarding homegrown Salafist radicalism, see Kim Mackrael, "Foiled Australian Plot Stokes Fear in Canada," *Globe and Mail*, 19 September 2014, p. A3.

20. For instance, the ringleader of the "Toronto 18" plot discussed in the previous chapter, Fahim Ahmad, explained in late September 2014 at a parole hearing that what led him to jihad was less religious conviction than a desire to escape a disappointing marriage. Extremist religious messages he consumed on the Internet, he said, provided him a sense of the "glamorous" direction in which he could steer his life by embracing jihadism. Quoted in Colin Freeze, "Extremism Offered 'Glamorous' Escape," *Globe and Mail*, 25 September 2014, p. A3.

21. Mark Landler, "President, at U.N., Vows to Counter Extremist Threat," *New York Times*, 25 September 2014, pp. A1, A11; Kim Mackrael and Paul Koring, "Security Council Backs Obama's IS Fight," *Globe and Mail*, 25 September 2014, pp. A1, A11; and Helene Cooper and Michael R. Gordon, "U.S. Is Carrying Out Vast Majority of Strikes on ISIS, Military Officials Say," *New York Times*, 24 September 2014, p. A14.

22. Quoted in Simon Collier and William F. Sater, *A History of Chile, 1808–1994* (New York: Cambridge University Press, 1996), p. 197.

Index

Abusalha, Moner Mohammad, 226
Adams, Charles Francis, 140
Adams, Herbert Baxter, 181
Afghanistan, 209–210
Air India disaster (1985), 17
Akenson, Donald, 129
Alaska boundary dispute (1903), 51–56
Alcott, Louis May, 169
Alexander II (Czar), 174
Allen, Harry Cranbrook, 120
alliances: Anglo-American, 60, 77, 116,
    158; Canadian-American, 66, 77,
    148; and implications for security
    communities, 61, 66–67; and "theory
    of democratic alliance", 63
Allison, Graham, 204
al Qaeda, viii, 207, 222
Altgeld, John Peter, 173
Alverstone (Lord). *See* Webster,
    Richard
Amara, Zakaria, 224
Ambrose, Joe, 133
American Independence League, 183
American Muslim Council, 218
American Neutrality League, 183
The American Review of Reviews, 159
American Truth Society, 183, 187
anarchism, 171. *See also* terrorism
Ancient Order of Hibernians, 181
Andreas, Peter, 25
Anglo-American rapprochement, 35,
    48, 52, 55, 56; and constructivism,
    59; implications for North American
    zone of peace, 56–61, 142, 237–238;
    and structural realism, 59. *See also*
    alliances
Anglo-Saxonism, 59, 60, 162, 176–177,
    180
Anglosphere, 48. *See also* Anglo-
    Saxonism

Arbatov, Georgi, 86
Argall, Samuel, 30
Armenian diaspora, 85
Ashcroft, John, 223
The Atlantic Monthly, 189
Awad, Nihad, vii
Aylesworth, Allen Bristol, 55
Azzam, Abdallah, 209–210

Bacevich, Andrew, 76
Bagenal, Philip, 145
al Baghdadi, Abu Bakr, 244
Bancroft, George, 168, 169
Barros Luco, Ramón, 246
Bartholdt, Richard, 184
Baumgartner, Frank, 104
Bennet, William, 187
Berquist, James, 165
Binational Planning Group (BPG), 66
bin Laden, Osama, 210
Bismarck, Otto von, 125, 161
Bissett, James, 17
Boer War (1899-1902), 60
Borchers, Hans, 27
Borden, Robert, 117, 118, 143, 146, 148
Boston Marathon bombing (2013), 225
Brebner, John Bartlet, 6
Brimelow, Peter, 92
Brinton, Crane, 29
British Guiana. *See* Venezuela crisis
    (1895)
Brooks, Sydney, 129
Brown, Thomas, 127, 180
Brubaker, Rogers, 79–80
Bruce, James, 136
Bryan, William Jennings, 57
Buchanan, Patrick, 92
Burgess, John, 177–178, 180, 181
Burnham, Walter Dean, 187
Burns, Arthur, 119

About the Author

David Haglund is professor of political studies at Queen's University (Kingston, Ontario). After receiving his PhD in international relations in 1978 from the Johns Hopkins School of Advanced International Studies, in Washington, DC, he assumed teaching and research positions at the University of British Columbia. In 1983 he came to Queen's. From 1985 to 1995, and again from 1996 to 2002, he served as director of the Queen's Centre for International Relations. From 1992 to 1996 he also served as head of Queen's Department of Political Studies. He has held visiting professorships in France and Germany, and was the Visiting Seagram Chair at the McGill Institute for the Study of Canada in the 2004–2005 academic year. In 2009–2010 he held the Chaire d'études canadiennes at l'Université Paris 3/La Sorbonne Nouvelle. In the winter of 2014 he was a visiting scholar at the Dickey Center for International Understanding of Dartmouth College.

His research focuses on transatlantic security, and on Canadian and American international security policy. Among his books are *Latin America and the Transformation of U.S. Strategic Thought, 1936–1940* (1984); *Alliance within the Alliance? Franco-German Military Cooperation and the European Pillar of Defense* (1991); *Will NATO Go East? The Debate over Enlarging the Atlantic Alliance* (1996); and *The North Atlantic Triangle Revisited: Canadian Grand Strategy at Century's End* (2000).